D1608913

THE EARLY ARCHITECTURE
OF WESTERN PENNSYLVANIA

1828

Entrance Doorway of the Feast Hall in Economy

The Early Architecture of Western Pennsylvania

A RECORD OF BUILDING BEFORE 1860 · BASED UPON THE WESTERN PENN-SYLVANIA ARCHITECTURAL SURVEY · A PROJECT OF THE PITTSBURGH CHAPTER OF THE AMERICAN INSTITUTE OF ARCHITECTS · WITH AN INTRODUCTION BY FISKE KIMBALL

Text by
CHARLES MORSE STOTZ, A.I.A.
Chairman of the Survey

With a New Introduction by
DELL UPTON

UNIVERSITY OF PITTSBURGH PRESS
PITTSBURGH AND LONDON

Copyright © 1936
The Buhl Foundation
Pittsburgh, Pa.

"Introduction" by Charles Morse Stotz
Copyright © 1966
University of Pittsburgh Press

"The Story of the Book" by Dell Upton
Copyright © 1995
University of Pittsburgh Press

All rights reserved

Manufactured in the United States of America
Printed on acid-free paper

LIBRARY OF CONGRESS CATALOGING-IN-PUBLICATION DATA

Stotz, Charles Morse.
    The early architecture of western Pennsylvania / Charles Morse Stotz
       p.   cm.
    Originally published: 1936.
    This edition based on 1966 ed.
  Includes bibliographical references and index.
  ISBN 0-8229-3787-5
      1. Architecture, Modern—17th–18th centuries—Pennsylvania.
    2. Architecture, Modern—19th century—Pennsylvania.
    3. Architecture—Pennsylvania. I. Title.
  NA730.P4S75 1994
  720'.9748—dc20   94-20793
                                             CIP

A CIP catalogue record for this book is available from the British Library.

Eurospan, London

Grateful appreciation is due to Jim Burke, of the University of Pittsburgh Center for Instructional Resources,
for his skilled and painstaking attention to developing the original negatives for this volume.
Thanks also to Marilyn Holt and Gilbert Pietrzak of the Pennsylvania Department, Carnegie Library of Pittsburgh.

The Western Pennsylvania Architectural Survey

A PROJECT OF THE PITTSBURGH CHAPTER
OF THE AMERICAN INSTITUTE OF ARCHITECTS
AND THE BUHL FOUNDATION

CHARLES M. STOTZ, *Chairman*

RODY PATTERSON, *Secretary*

Executive Committee

CHARLES M. STOTZ

ROBERT W. SCHMERTZ

SIDNEY H. BROWN

RODY PATTERSON

RALPH E. GRISWOLD

Advisory Committee

CHARLES T. INGHAM

FREDERICK BIGGER

LOUIS STEVENS

JAMES M. MACQUEEN

SOLON J. BUCK

Photographic Adviser

LUKE SWANK

TO THE EARLY BUILDERS

of

WESTERN PENNSYLVANIA

TO THE MEMBERS

of

THE PITTSBURGH CHAPTER OF
THE AMERICAN INSTITUTE OF ARCHITECTS
WHO MADE THIS CONTRIBUTION
TO THEIR COMMUNITY
AS A LABOR OF LOVE

CONTENTS

The Story of the Book   xi
Note on the 1995 Edition   xli
Introduction   xliii
Foreword   liii
Map Showing Location of Structures   10

PART ONE

Chapter   I   The Background of the Early Architecture   11
Chapter   II   The Origin and Development of Styles   15
Chapter   III   The Early Builders—Materials and Methods   19
Chapter   IV   The Preservation of Our Early Buildings   31

PART TWO

Introduction to Drawings and Photographs   33
Section One   Domestic Architecture
  A. Log Houses   34
  B. The Post-Colonial Period   43
  C. The Greek Revival   108
Section Two   Accessory Buildings and Details   144
Section Three   The Architecture of Transportation   173
Section Four   The Harmony Society   193
Section Five   Institutional Architecture   214
Section Six   Governmental and Military Architecture   252
Section Seven   Commercial and Industrial Architecture   267

PART THREE

The Story of the Survey   280
List of Structures   284
Historic American Buildings Survey   287
General Index   289
Bibliography   293
Bibliography for the 1995 Edition   295

THE STORY OF THE BOOK

All over the eastern United States, architects and historians took to the roads in the 1920s and 1930s to document the regional architecture of early America. Energized by the excitement of discovery and goaded on by a sense of impending loss, they produced thousands of photographs, sketches, and measured drawings and published hundreds of books and articles. *The Early Architecture of Western Pennsylvania* was one of 154 books on American architectural history to appear in 1936 alone.[1]

These researchers were convinced that in the remains of preindustrial America lay clues to the country's character—"the spirit which is implicit in all the characteristic transactions of the time, and which may almost be defined as the sum of its manners, customs, and mode of living," as the Connecticut architect J. Frederick Kelly put it.[2] If old buildings were monuments to a cultural moment, so—it appears from a vantage point sixty years on—were the books themselves. To appreciate the magnitude of their achievements and to assess their value for modern readers, we need to understand the methods, the motives, and the personalities who created them.

Nowhere is this more true than for *The Early Architecture of Western Pennsylvania,* a product of the Western Pennsylvania Architectural Survey (WPAS). The survey was created by an energetic Pittsburgh architect, Charles Morse Stotz (1898–1985), who took advantage of the Depression-era stagnation in building to transform a leisure-time avocation into a large-scale, systematic research project. In introducing the national architectural passion into Western Pennsylvania, Stotz brought with it characteristic assumptions about American history. At the same time, the distinctive social and physical setting of 1930s Pittsburgh and its environs gave the survey a local cast that was at once idiosyncratic and innovative when compared with similar projects elsewhere. Consequently, *The Early Architecture of Western Pennsylvania* stands as a characteristic document of a critical period in the formation of an American self-image; yet, in its thoroughness and accuracy, it also remains the most important record of Western Pennsylvania's earliest buildings, many of which have disappeared since the WPAS recorded them.

I

Charles M. Stotz was born at Ingram, Pennsylvania, the third child of Edward and Arminda Stotz (fig. 1). Edward was the son of a wholesale grain and flour merchant who was also an active Republican member of the Select Council. The latter may have had something to do with the twenty-six-year-old architect's first major commission, for the Fifth Avenue High School, awarded after only five minutes' discussion by the school board. The building, the first fireproof school in the city, launched Edward Stotz's long career as an architect primarily of institutional buildings. His closest brush with fame was the publication of his enormous Schenley High School in the *American Architect* in 1917, but he enjoyed a prosperous local practice as the designer of 903 buildings, a founder of the Pittsburgh chapter of the American Institute of Architects, member of the city Building Code Commission, and a lifelong Republican, Presbyterian, Mason, and Knight Templar.[3]

Figure 1. Charles Morse Stotz in his studio at the time of the Western Pennsylvania Architectural Survey (courtesy Virginia Stotz).

Edward Stotz's son Charles attended Carnegie Institute of Technology in 1916–1917; then, after a year in the army, went off to Cornell's architecture school, where he earned a bachelor's degree in 1921 and a Master of Architecture degree in 1922. At Cornell, Charles Stotz achieved his own moment of national fame through a prank concocted in collaboration with the university president's wife. Disguised in a false beard, he billed himself as Dr. Herman Vosberg, a pupil of Freud's, and gave two psychobabble lectures entitled "Dreams and the Calculus." Accounts of the prank in the Ithaca paper were picked up by the Associated Press and ran in newspapers nationally and internationally. Stotz claimed that Freud himself, on hearing of it, remarked that "'like every inquiry into observations of the human mind, it carries with it an element of danger for gullibles, who are the ready victims of amateur exponents.'"[4]

The episode became, in Stotz's mind and those of his friends and acquaintances thereafter, the characterizing incident of his life. It required considerable erudition and a familiarity with the advanced theories of the day. At the same time, it revealed a mind that was energetically good-humored yet skeptical of contemporary ideas.

In later years, Stotz recalled a boyhood interest in drawing and sketching and, not unnaturally, in architecture. It was at Cornell, however, that he was put in the way of ideas and attitudes that blossomed into the WPAS. On a holiday at Canandaigua Lake in central New York in 1917, he was introduced to the "charm of the simple farmhouses in that region," while Cornell provided him with a framework within which to understand them and a method for studying them. He wrote a master's thesis on Greek Revival farmhouses in the Finger Lakes district of New York, and some of his measured drawings were published in Architecture in 1923 and 1924 (fig. 2). Charles M. Stotz had become one of the many men and women combing the American countryside in search of old buildings.[5]

II

The qualities that give The Early Architecture of Western Pennsylvania its distinctive character—the loyalty to the old and the local in the context of a more general fascination with early American architecture, the romanticization of early rural life coupled with a discomfort with modern urban civilization, the fieldwork ethos that drove the WPAS architects to comb the countryside for old buildings, and the technique of studying and presenting architecture through precise measured (scaled) drawings—were deeply rooted in longstanding Euro-American cultural values and professional architectural practices. A look at some of the most important of these roots will go a long way toward helping us understand Stotz's accomplishment.

A keen interest in the oldest relics of one's own community, one of the central motives behind The Early Architecture of Western Pennsylvania, is a venerable English tradition. Since the sixteenth century, monuments ranging from Stonehenge down to obscure local antiquities had been studied, sketched, and interpreted for clues to the English national character. This patriotic antiquarianism made an early and easy transition to America, gaining momentum from the late eighteenth century. In 1793 the Salem, Massachusetts, diarist William Bentley purchased a seventeenth-century chair once owned by victims of the witchcraft trials. Another antique chair was given to the newly formed Massachusetts Historical Society in the same year. Around 1820, Philadelphia antiquarian John Fanning Watson began work on his "Manuscript Annals," two large volumes recording the city's early history through oral testimony, anecdote, newspaper clippings, and colonial documents, as well as views of old buildings and snippets of material culture such as textile swaths and paper money. At about the time Watson began his research, the city of Philadelphia acquired the former state house as a city hall, refurbishing its "Hall of Independence" for Lafayette's visit in 1824, thus commencing a history of nearly continuous restorations of Independence Hall that continues to the present.[6]

The interest in American antiquities evident among these and many like-minded pioneer collectors grew throughout the nineteenth century, but after the Civil War it took a distinctive turn, expanding far beyond the audience of curmudgeons and scholarly eccentrics who had traditionally carried the antiquarian flame. Antiquarianism became a vehicle not simply for reverence for ancestors and patriotic nostalgia, but for local, national, and ethnic pride, aesthetic theory, scholarly curiosity, and the pleasure of the exotic. It served as well as an expression of a grow-

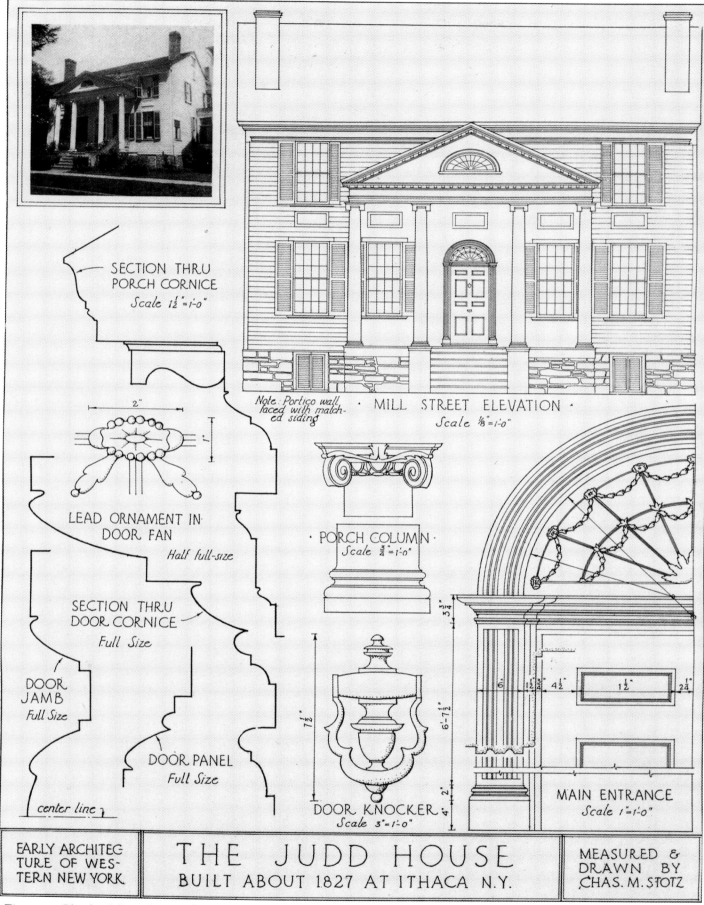

Figure 2. Charles Morse Stotz, the Judd house, Ithaca, N.Y., from "Early Architecture of Western New York," a series of plates derived from his M.Arch. thesis and published in *Architecture* in 1923.

ing, though vague, popular desire for a simpler life, as a reaction against the increased pace, complexity, and corruption of Gilded Age America. The centennial celebrations of 1876 helped to focus this yearning on prerevolutionary America, an apparently purer, more upright time. Historians have called this new variant of patriotic antiquarianism the Colonial Revival.[7]

Colonial Revivalist designers, scholars, and members of the general public shared a fascination with early American life, particularly material life. Colonial Revivalists practiced architectural history, historic preservation and restoration, the design of architecture, furniture, and other decorative arts, painting, antique collecting, tourism, museum building, and even civic instruction and cultural evangelism directed toward recent immigrants. As the nineteenth century turned into the twentieth, the era of Colonial Revival interests expanded from the years before 1776 to encompass all the years before the onset of industrialization, which most placed sometime between 1820 and 1840.[8]

It is evident that this long-lasting cultural phenomenon was complex and diffuse. Depending upon whom one consulted, the colonial style testified to the good breeding or the simple determination of earlier Americans, or it certified the civilized origins of remote or provincial neighborhoods. Colonial artifacts, particularly buildings, proved that Americans had matched European standards, or that they had struck out on their own path. They demonstrated the superiority of prerevolutionary design when compared with the "degenerate" state of contemporary work, or they simply provided welcome relief from the clichés of nineteenth-century design. They represented roots or they offered escape. In short, the Colonial Revival had a "remarkable ability to shift its ground and to absorb whatever happened to be the current fashion, whether visual or ideological," as David Gebhard notes. This flexibility has allowed it to survive in American culture into the present.[9]

Whatever else it may have been, the Colonial Revival was an exercise in American self-definition, an exploration of identity through the manipulation of familiar symbols. The association of the colonial with the country's founders, for example, made it an appropriate totem of peculiarly American values. According to R. T. H. Halsey and Elizabeth Tower, the new American

Wing of the Metropolitan Museum of Art, a collection of furniture, paintings, decorative arts and architectural fragments that opened in 1924, "for the first time made a convincing demonstration to our own people, and particularly to the world in general, that our American arts unconsciously developed a style of their own" and furnished a "setting for the traditions so dear to us." Colonial design "belonged peculiarly to the nation and had been wrought by long years of experience and effort; of struggle and of trial." For Joseph Hergesheimer, in fact, the American character sprang from the buildings themselves: "The America they formed was created by their honesty of construction and correct proportion." Thus the colonial was an appropriate foundation for a national cultural consensus.[10]

The colonial style was equally available as an index of regional distinctiveness and an emblem of local pride. Twentieth-century scholars were particularly likely to credit local loyalties as stimuli to their work. In 1922 George Fletcher Bennett wrote a book on the early architecture of Delaware "out of [his] interest in the architecture of his native state," while Charles Stotz himself was prodded to publish partly by his feeling that "books that treat of the subject, even those of a comprehensive nature, completely ignore our district." He was particularly annoyed by Boston architect Eleanor Raymond's *Early Domestic Architecture of Pennsylvania* (1931), which "included little beyond the western borders of Germantown."[11]

In short, as the Colonial Revival matured, Revivalists came to recognize the complexity of their subject. Thus, while nineteenth-century Colonial Revivalists tended to treat all early American architecture as a unity, most scholars agreed by the 1930s, when the WPAS was undertaken, that the national scene was a pastiche of many local ones that required individual investigation. In that spirit, Thomas T. Waterman and John A. Barrows saw their 1932 study of tidewater Virginia mansions as contributing to a synthesis. The history of American colonial architecture, they wrote, "has countless local phases and mannerisms. Until regional architecture of the United States is examined and catalogued, a comprehensive survey of our early building will be impossible."[12]

If the colonial encompassed both national values and regional traits, it was obviously locked in the past as well, the product of a society whose qualities contrasted dramatically with those of contemporary America. In this respect, it appealed to the intense nineteenth-century preoccupation with "otherness," with playing one's sense of self off societies that were radically different from one's own by virtue of their location in a remote time or place. For example, an important strain of Anglo-American thought held up the Middle Ages as a standard against which to judge the present. In *Contrasts or, A Parallel Between the Noble Edifices of the Fourteenth and Fifteenth Centuries and Similar Buildings of the Present Day* (1836), the English architect Augustus Welby Northmore Pugin presented a series of paired images of imaginary scenes of 1440 and 1840 that showed industrial England to disadvantage. Pugin's work inaugurated a long Anglo-American tradition of social commentary on design. His successors, who included the religious Ecclesiologists, the mid-century High Victorians, and the late nineteenth-century Queen Anne and Arts and Crafts movements, disagreed politically and aesthetically, but all followed Pugin's lead in using some version of the Gothic as a club to beat the nineteenth century with. Following their lead, American architects of the 1870 and 1880s were initially attracted to "American Colonial" because of its perceived similarity with the forms and ideals of English Queen Anne architecture, a romantic pastiche of vernacular and classical elements. The attachment was later strengthened under the influence of the Arts and Crafts Movement, which celebrated handwork over machine production. All three—colonial, Queen Anne, and Arts and Crafts—were understood to preserve the spirit of the medieval and thus to hold promise for the reform of contemporary design.[13]

The medieval past, its differences from modern times emphasized and romanticized, was a powerful tool for defining and criticizing the present. Another was the distant present. Euro-American imperial expansion into Asia, Africa, the Pacific, and the North American West brought indigenous people from all those regions into the public eye. In attempting to expand and systematize knowledge of these populations, the new profession of anthropology helped to whet the public appetite for strange new worlds outside one's own experience.

The desire to know about others from the past

and from faraway fused with the quest for self-definition in the enormously popular world's fairs that flourished from 1851 until the First World War. The industrial products of Western nations, arrayed according to elaborate classification schemes, were the centerpiece of world's fairs, but these were complemented by historical and ethnographic exhibits. At American world's fairs, for instance, visitors could dine in "colonial" kitchens and visit historical displays mounted in pavilions that were replicas of famous landmarks or even authentic old buildings brought to the site. Nearby, they could see native Asian, African, Australian, Pacific Island, and South American peoples in both "serious" and sideshow-type settings. Both the colonial and the "primitive" exhibits, in other words, served as a context for viewing the manufactured goods of the West. They emphasized difference from modern urban life and offered not simply amusement and escape but lessons in the advantages and disadvantages of Western civilization.[14]

A third mirror for urbanites appeared in the half century after the Philadelphia Centennial, as Europeans and Americans discovered that "primitive" populations lived in their own midst. These were people who clung to seemingly preindustrial lifeways. Although they were removed by cultural, rather than temporal or geographical, distance from contemporary life, they were the moral equivalents of medieval peasants or African tribespeople and deserved equal attention. Horace Kephart, writing in 1913, lamented the unknown state of this "mysterious realm" when compared with the attention given "the Filipinos, . . . the Chinese and the Syrians."[15]

Consequently, a curious synthesis formed in the United States as the century turned. Geographical, cultural, and historical distance were conflated. On the one hand, living American "primitives" (such as mountaineers, traditional farmers, and even American Indians) were understood as equivalents of the historical. In this spirit, Henry Chapman Mercer of Doylestown, Pennsylvania, collected old tools, stove plates, and ceramics, but he also collected people— "fellow citizens of a past generation"—whom he thought lived essentially as the makers of his antiques had. At the same time, the living and historical past were imagined to survive in a remote country vaguely equated with rural America, which was still not easily accessible to urban

Americans before World War I. Kephart recalled, "I had a passion for early American history; and, in Far Appalachia, it seemed that I might realize the past in the present, seeing with my own eyes what life must have been to my pioneer ancestors of a century ago." It was possible to do so because "the mountain folk still live in the eighteenth century." They were, in William Goodell Frost's memorable phrase, "our contemporary ancestors."[16]

This fusion of remote space, time, and culture created an idealized Other America, a kind of Shangri-La that had its bad points as well as good ones. If urban America was characterized by change and the Other America by stability, for example, the advantage was not one-sided and the present was not to be dismissed lightly. Even the most passionate devotee of old houses was forced to admit, "We must change the kitchen services and add plumbing." In ways small and large, to remain entirely in the past was to be "decivilized," in Kephart's words, to have "no heritage" in "human progress."[17]

Nevertheless, the idealized Other America served primarily as a beacon of safety in a storm of changes of several sorts. Among the most conspicuous was the visual transformation of the material world under industrial capitalism. Manufacturing made more goods available more cheaply to more people, and it did so with an ingenuity that seemed marvelous at first. Expensive natural materials could be replaced by cheap artificial ones; inexpensive mechanical decoration could surpass in intricacy the most expensive handwork. Yet as early as the 1830s voices were raised in opposition to these developments. The argument quickly took on moral tones: imitations were "dishonest," a sign of cultural degeneration. By the turn of the century, growing numbers of middle-class Americans increasingly sought renewed contact with the "authentic." One place to find it was in the mores and the material remains of past and contemporary ancestors. Southern highlanders "have retained some of the country traits and graces, some of the amenities which seem to disappear with the coming of extensive machinery and other forms of sophistication associated with material progress," wrote Allen Eaton in 1937. By the same token, their "handicrafts have given character and fascination [to their homes] far beyond what would have been possible had their furnishings been 'store-bought.'" The mountaineer's house—in-

evitably "the log cabin of the American pioneer"—was built of "honest logs. . . . It is what it seems, a genuine thing, a jewel in the rough."[18]

The homes of historic ancestors were equally significant touchstones of authenticity. Alfred Easton Poor praised the "simplicity and straightforward plan" of the Cape Cod house, while Joseph Hergesheimer contrasted early houses' "honesty and correctness" with modern houses that "are neither honest in material nor correct in design." To J. Frederick Kelly, "The early domestic architecture of the American colonies . . . was unmistakably pure and virile. The most superficial examination of the period is enough to prove that it was productive of a 'true' style in architecture. Its building is honest, straightforward, devoid of affectation and sham."[19]

Authenticity was threatened not only by industrial products, but also by the waves of new workers industry required. The passion for an Other America contained large doses of the nativist, or antiforeign, sentiment, that has infected the United States since the late eighteenth century. In contrast to an urban America whose population was comprised largely of immigrants and their children, the Other America was thought to have been relatively homogeneous. Kephart noted, "The mountains proper are free not only from foreigners but from negroes as well." In the Colonial Revival landscape blacks were little more than comic minstrel-show figures or enslaved accessories of planter elegance while all non-English-speaking people were northern Europeans, fellow members of a superior "Teutonic" (later "Nordic") race.[20]

The new industrial workers had little appreciation for authentic American values. Halsey and Tower lamented the widespread ignorance of American "traditions" and "principles" and the "tremendous change in the character of our nation, and the influx of foreign ideas utterly at variance with those held by the men who gave us the Republic." During his survey of Ohio architecture, Ihna Thayer Frary was similarly dismayed to find that "great numbers of the old houses have long since been deserted by the original families, and are now occupied by strangers, often of foreign birth, to whom the old names and the old traditions mean nothing. Occupants of my own grandfather's farm were unfamiliar with the family name when I asked permission to photograph the house."[21]

Most dangerous of all the changes was the

sheer scale of urban physical and economic growth, which threatened to engulf the Other America as it pushed into the countryside. Kephart writes, "Suddenly the mountaineer is awakened from his eighteenth-century bed by the blare of steam whistles and the boom of dynamite," just as for Kimball "the ruthless march of urban 'improvement'" suddenly replaced the "remote and pastoral places." Hergesheimer also laments these changes:

> Month by month, almost day by day, better roads, laid in concrete, were taking the place of the old country lanes with, in spring, their banks dark with violets. Day by day, it seemed, the cities were reaching out into the country with their hideous and inappropriate houses, suburbs of bungalows and villas. . . . Lovely serene buildings were torn down, to make way for the villas and bungalows, without any faint realization of the fatality that ignoble destruction was bringing about.[22]

Yet there was room for optimism, for the Other America contained the seeds of its own defense. A centuries-old Euro-American faith in the power of the physical environment to affect behavior encouraged Colonial Revivalists to believe that contact with the remains of the Other America could teach desirable values. Protecting what survived could preserve the values of the past for modern Americans.

Protection took several forms. One might save individual relics, such as Mount Vernon, as reminders of prominent people. One might collect more widely to save buildings and artifacts redolent more of past lifeways than of specific individuals. Or one might encourage people not to abandon the old ways. Both the latter aims were evident as mountain crafts collectives were set up to encourage the continuation of handicraft traditions, museums collected crafts, and folk festivals performed a parallel function for oral culture. Exurbanites were encouraged to purchase and live in old houses rather than constructing new ones: Stotz noted hopefully, "Many log houses have recently been converted with great success for use as summer homes or as quaint accessory buildings on estates."[23]

The values of the past could also be protected by imitating old forms in new work. On this assumption, schools were established throughout Appalachia to teach "traditional" crafts (some newly invented) as a way of instilling self-

confidence, creativity, and an aesthetic sense in mountaineers who were thought to be demoralized by their isolation. Urban settlement houses were furnished with Colonial Revival furniture to inspire immigrant clients with middle-class ideals of housekeeping, while other immigrants were "Americanized" in special schools located in colonial-style buildings. Most of all, the use of colonial features in contemporary architecture and decorative arts could counteract "the extravagance and crudity of the current building," in the words of architectural critic Montgomery Schuyler in 1894. After the late 1870s, Colonial Revival buildings, gardens, and town plans formed an ever-expanding component of the American landscape. Turn-of-the-century antiquarians like Henry Chapman Mercer and Wallace Nutting manufactured reproduction furniture as well as new objects designed in the spirit of the old to furnish these reproduced, or revived, colonial settings.[24]

A last-ditch preservation tactic, but also a precondition for the other defenses, was the intensive study and careful recording of the remains of the Other America before it disappeared. Beginning in the last quarter of the nineteenth century, fieldworkers swarmed over the nation to capture old buildings, Native American ceremonies, folk songs, antique furniture, traditional lore, outmoded technologies, and even the natural landscape itself, in anticipation of the onslaught of urban industrial civilization.[25]

III

The Early Architecture of Western Pennsylvania was thus one product of an ambitious, energetic, romantic project devoted to saving the Other America for posterity. These fieldworkers saw themselves as members of a vast disaster-relief army working feverishly in advance of a flood. Architectural publications in particular emphasized the emergency. Fiske Kimball wrote of John Mead Howells's *Lost Examples of Colonial Architecture* (1931), "To turn these pages is to realize the depth of our artistic and historic loss through the destruction of old buildings by war, by fire, by revolutions of taste, and by the ruthless march of urban 'improvement.' . . . Thanks to Mr. Howells' pious researches, at least the forms and the flavor of these buildings survive for us." In 1932 Alfred Easton Poor was working "to make a record of these [Cape Cod] houses of our ancestors before time and 'modernization' take their toll," as was Rexford New-comb, who recorded the California missions in 1916 "before the last vestige of the buildings themselves had disappeared from the earth." Charles Stotz, too, hoped to furnish future gen-erations with a "graphic record of our civiliza-tion" that they would otherwise lack "due to its complete obliteration."[26]

Yet the architects differed from anthropolo-gists, folklorists, and historians in one important respect. While all shared the larger cultural out-look represented by the quest for the Other America, architects inherited an additional pro-fessional obligation. Architectural history had long been indentured to architectural design. Centuries before anyone was interested in archi-tectural history for itself, architects had turned to the past for inspiration and instruction. In Stotz's day, architectural historical research was still expected to have practical value for working architects, a duty that most architect-historians acknowledged. They expressed a desire to be "an inspiration to those who are now building our small houses," to "be of value as architectural material for other American homes," to "assist, in a practical way, the cause of architecture." Stotz was a little more ambivalent, denying that *The Early Architecture of Western Pennsylvania* was "intended to encourage a revival of building in the old manner." He conceded, however, that "for those interested in perpetuating local build-ing traditions, this book will for the first time furnish authentic source material," adding his hope that the work might also lead to the preser-vation of the finest structures depicted in it.[27]

Along with their professional obligation to advance design, architect-historians inherited a long-established method for conducting and pre-senting their research: through precise measured drawings based on careful field study of surviv-ing structures. An unbroken fieldwork tradition stretched from Stotz's day back at least to the Renaissance, when the artist Donatello and the architect Filippo Brunelleschi traveled to Rome in 1405 to measure and draw antique build-ings. For Renaissance architects, ancient Roman building as described in the only surviving an-tique treatise, Marcus Vitruvius Pollio's *The Ten Books on Architecture,* was the authoritative his-toric precedent. However, Vitruvius's book had been passed down without illustrations, and much of his text was ambiguous. Thus, architects

turned to the field study of ancient ruins to fill the gap. The sixteenth-century architect Andrea Palladio is the best known of these Renaissance architects who became historians by default. His *Four Books of Architecture* (1570) featured reconstruction drawings of Roman temples based on his study of their ruins. Palladio noted, "Vitruvius has been a very great help to me; be-cause, what I saw, agreeing with what he teach-eth us, it was not difficult for me to come at the knowledge of their aspect, and of their form." At the same time, he wrote, "I make no doubt, but that they who shall read this book, and shall consider the designs in it carefully, may be able to understand many places, which in Vitruvius are reputed very difficult."[28]

From the Renaissance to Stotz's time, the prin-ciples Palladio set forth, calling for the accurate recording of that which survived leading to in-formed conjectural reconstruction of that which did not, all presented in measured drawings, remained unchanged. Architectural fieldwork boomed after the mid-eighteenth century, as northern European architects—their pockets (or their patrons' pockets) filled by the prosperity of their region and their curiosities piqued by reve-lations of previously unknown sites such as Pompeii and Herculaneum—swarmed south to examine ancient ruins for themselves. In com-pany with local architects such as Giambattista Piranesi, they made careful measured drawings as well as impressionistic sketches, recording sur-viving classical architecture both in its romantic ruined state and in technically precise recon-struction drawings.[29]

If their field techniques were derived from the Renaissance, the purview of eighteenth- and early nineteenth-century architect-historians eventually expanded beyond the classical monu-ments Palladio and his contemporaries studied. Napoleon's engineers made elaborate drawings of Egyptian antiquities. At the same time, stay-at-homes in England and France began to draw their own medieval monuments, so that by the early nineteenth century the architects' profes-sional curiosity had intersected with the older tradition of patriotic antiquarianism.[30]

These meticulously recorded images of historic buildings were offered to the public in large-format volumes containing elegantly drawn copperplate engravings accompanied by brief commentaries. In addition, some of this archaeological information was recycled after the mid-eighteenth century in another kind of architectural publication that made more directly practical use of architectural history. This was the architectural handbook or pattern book, a book of technical advice for architects and carpenters that commonly taught the classical orders using examples taken from archaeological works such as James Stuart's and Nicholas Revett's *The Antiquities of Athens* (1762–1814). Many handbooks also included brief surveys of architectural history. Formally these handbooks often resembled the archaeological volumes. They were usually a little less sumptuous than the books of antiquities, but they were illustrated with similar engraved line drawings, with a page or two of text added to explain each plate.[31]

A second model for the architectural study of old buildings, in addition to the scholarly measured-drawing expedition, was the informal sketching tour that architects often used to complete their educations. A year or two spent touring the cities of Europe provided the fledgling designer with a sketchbook chock full of images that could be referred to over the course of a long career. By no means invented in the nineteenth century, the sketching tradition may have been given renewed vigor by the work of John Ruskin, whose influential architectural commentaries, particularly *The Stones of Venice* (1851–1853), were illustrated with his own evocative sketches of architectural details.

The first Colonial Revival scholars of old buildings took these two architectural traditions as their models, with patriotic antiquarianism as a constant subtext of their aesthetic investigations. The public debate over the fate of the Hancock house in Boston, residence of the famous signer of the Declaration of Independence, is a case in point. Just before its demolition in 1863, patriotic sentiments prompted architect John Hubbard Sturgis to make the first known measured drawings of an American house. These drawings were used as source materials for a number of Colonial Revival designs by Sturgis and other late nineteenth-century architects. Peabody and Stearns's Massachusetts State Building at the World's Columbian Exposition of 1893 is the best known of the Hancock house's progeny.[32]

When architects set out in earnest to study early American architecture, their first efforts followed the pattern of the sketching tour. The architectural partners-to-be Charles Follen McKim, William Rutherford Mead, Stanford White, and William Bigelow undertook a "celebrated" tour, as they called it, through coastal New England in the summer of 1877. Mead recalled, "We made sketches and measured drawings of many of the important colonial houses, which still remain in our scrap-book."[33]

Although the first students of early American architecture measured as well as sketched, the earliest published works favored sketches as illustrations: they aimed to evoke a mood rather than to provide reproducible details. Even Norman Morrison Isham, whose *Early Rhode Island Houses* (1895) was one of the first books to use measured plans and details as its principal illustrations, included many sketch views and indeed employed a sketchy drafting style for his measured drawings.[34]

Under the influence of architectural educational practice, however, measured drawings eventually became the standard. It had long been customary to teach architectural history by requiring students to draw great buildings by copying from books. The introduction of French ideas into architectural training in the late nineteenth century reinforced this tradition. After the 1850s, many American architects were trained at the famous École des Beaux-Arts in Paris or by teachers who had attended it and then set up similar programs in American universities. For example, Stotz's Cornell became "one of the strongest adherents of the Beaux-Arts in America" after the arrival of École graduate John V. Van Pelt in 1896, and three years later it added a prolific architectural historian, Arthur C. Phelps, who remained on the faculty until 1937.[35]

The École had institutionalized eighteenth-century archaeological research. During their five years' stay in Rome, winners of the École's Prix de Rome were expected to produce measured and restoration drawings of a classical monument. Similar projects became possible in American architectural schools in the late nineteenth century, as American Georgian architecture came to be accepted as a subcategory of the Renaissance style and therefore worthy of study. Some architectural instructors then began to assign archaeological drawings of American monuments. William Robert Ware had his students draw Georgian church towers as early as 1874, while measured drawings of Louisiana architecture were part of the Tulane University School of Architecture's curriculum from its founding in 1907.[36]

Stimuli outside the architectural profession encouraged this turn to measured drawing. At the turn of the century, the rage for "science" as a mode of understanding many aspects of everyday life permeated American popular culture. Consequently, some architect-historians like Isham, who never went to architecture school, were attracted to "accurate measured drawings" as a technique for "the collection of scientific data" superior to the antiquarian's "vague descriptions."[37]

Whatever the reason, measured drawings of early American architecture began to appear in professional journals in the 1880s. By the second and third decades of the twentieth century, plates of measured drawings like Stotz's "Early Architecture of Western New York" series (1923–1924) were regular features of most journals, inserted almost incidentally and often (like his) without accompanying text.

Some of the earliest of these journal drawings were brought together at the end of the century in a major serial publication, The Georgian Period, edited by William Rotch Ware and issued in twelve parts between 1898 and 1902. Through The Georgian Period, architects like Charles Stotz (who considered it the first work of the type and an important precedent of his own work) awoke to the variety of early American architecture. The Georgian Period also inspired a host of similar publications, notably the White Pine Series of Architectural Monographs, another of Stotz's acknowledged sources, which commenced in 1915 and was published every two months until 1940. Publications like these not only taught American architectural history but also codified the pattern-book type of plate as the standard mode of illustration.[38]

Stotz complained, however, that only one of the hundreds of plates of The Georgian Period illustrated a Western Pennsylvania building. The issue was not simply seaboard chauvinism. The first American architectural historians worked at sites in or near the large coastal cities and resort towns that were easily accessible by public transportation. Many of the riches of early American building remained hidden in the Other America beyond the reach of any but the hardiest of travelers.[39]

All that changed around World War I, as the historians knew. For those working in the 1920s and the 1930s, the automobile epitomized the ambivalent relationship between modern America and the Other America, the double orientation to past and present that characterized the Colonial Revival. As Charles Stotz commented, "The excellent modern roads which made the Survey trips possible likewise spelled the speedy end of many of these structures, in opening sections of the country which had laid dormant since early times."[40]

On the one hand, that is, the automobile was the single most frequently cited agent of change in the countryside. In 1931 Fiske Kimball blamed the car for killing the riverboats that had given life to the colonial houses that Waterman and Barrows studied, while for Joseph Hergesheimer the spread of the city was heralded by "better roads, laid in concrete." Stotz offered the most detailed description of the process in his introduction to the reissue of The Early Architecture of Western Pennsylvania in 1966:

> The unprecedented road building programs of the past thirty years have brought the widening and realignment of almost all country roads. Turnpikes and throughways have cut ruthlessly through farmland tracts and rural communities. The streets of once unspoiled villages and towns have been widened and lined with the commercial buildings of a modern age; trees have been removed and existing buildings altered or demolished. Stores and service stations occupy prominent corner sites once graced by stately homes. Shopping centers and used-car lots have cut great swathes through a once tranquil scene.[41]

On the other hand, Stotz and his colleagues recognized that the automobile that was destroying the Other America also gave them new access to it. I. T. Frary began his 1936 study of early Ohio houses "as a byproduct of outings in the family automobile," while Eleanor Raymond's survey of eastern Pennsylvania (1931) depended on "a trusty Ford." As Kimball was forced to admit, "The automobile has made its own amends, bringing roads and a new accessibility by land, a new opportunity for patient and prolonged study."[42]

It was thus with a sense of the urgency of witnesses to a evanescent scene that the automobile historians ventured into the countryside.

But it was also with a taste for high adventure, informed by a feeling for the exoticism of the Other America. They saw themselves, as much as any eighteenth-century European in Tahiti or twentieth-century urbanite in the North Carolina mountains, as explorers of a romantic territory and agents of civilization. All emphasized the arduousness of their task, the miles they had driven, the remoteness and inaccessibility of their quarry, the excitement of discovery. George Fletcher Bennett made "innumerable journeys" to "penetrate to out-of-the-way villages and country by-ways often closed to the stranger," while Eleanor Raymond left the task to her "field scout" Ruth Crook. Raymond explains:

> [Ruth Crook performed the] arduous task of hunting down most of the material I have used, and of photographing and measuring much of it. It has taken over five months of constant searching to find these buildings, which lie scattered over the eastern part of Pennsylvania from Harrisburg to Philadelphia. While the material is prolific, much of it is hidden away where a less zealous hunter than Miss Crook would have failed to find it.

Waterman and Barrows's Virginia quarry had likewise "remained inaccessible to the hurried architect of the industrial world." As researchers seek them out, "a whole province of great mansions . . . is rediscovered. The background of a vanished civilization is exactly set forth." Even John Mead Howells, whose 1931 book was simply a collection of photographs of demolished buildings had, said Kimball, devoted "seven years of loving labor . . . to track[ing] down the buildings shown."[43]

At the same time, these expeditions were obviously less arduous than a trip up the Congo River, and some of the language of discovery was offered in a spirit of fun. In the 1930s Samuel Gaillard Stoney and his colleagues explored the [South] Carolina Low Country in the company of rambunctious parties of men, women, and children:

> Everyone worked; the men with grandiloquent gestures of machetes clearing underbrush grown second story high, the women with soon toughened thumbs pressing the ends of tapes to crumbling walls, the children clearing trash and rubbish so that buried corners could be found and lost partitions located. Thus we uncovered houses and churches in fair order,

and buildings only piles of earthquake rubble, gardens in full glory, and gardens hidden under scrub pine and snaky briar patches; all were measured and their plans delineated. Probably the workers enjoyed the ruins most, because each could speculate gloriously on the details that were hopelessly lost.[44]

Field trips on the WPAS, on the other hand, had more of the quality of a boys' night out than a family picnic. The surveyors loved to tell the story of Stotz, cigar in teeth and head concealed under the canopy of a view camera, besieged by an enraged bull. "The chairman became entangled in the equipment, setting fire to the cloth with the cigar, and only obtained a successful picture when the sympathetic farmer took the situation in hand." When the brothers Mario and Raymond Celli measured the second story of the Isaac Meason house (pp. 60–67, 162), they were forced to wade through the waist-high loose wool that filled the rooms. After long days of such high jinks, Stotz felt obliged to tip his hat to "the long sufferance of the 'survey widows.' "[45]

However lighthearted the effort, the intention was a serious one, and the payoff was a direct encounter with authenticity. These labors brought the scholar a pleasing sense of the immediacy of history. For Waterman and Barrows, the Virginia byways they traveled had "a feeling of remoteness that brings the past very near."[46]

The quest for authenticity mixed romantic imagery with the language of science, and, in the spirit of Isham, the interwar historians assured their readers that these fragments of vanishing early America had been brought back alive. J. Frederick Kelly acknowledged that his book's "chief value" lay in "the accuracy with which it was done. It has been [my] sincere endeavor throughout, therefore, to avoid speculation and to make no generalizations which were not backed either by personal observations in existing work or by authentic documentary evidence." Careful measured drawings were one way to assure precision. So were photographs, and after World War I photography replaced sketching among those who wished to be thought serious scholars. As Thomas T. Waterman wrote of Frances Benjamin Johnston's work, which he used in his 1941 publication *Early Architecture of North Carolina*, Johnston's photographs were "absolutely literal."[47]

The books produced by scholars between the wars were of several types, all relying to some extent on the traditions of eighteenth-century archaeological publications and nineteenth-century pattern books (in which the interwar historians were intensely interested). One strain was represented by J. Frederick Kelly's *Early Domestic Architecture of Connecticut* (1924). Kelly was a protegé of Norman Isham, and like Isham he chose to rely on drawings to convey his message. His photographs were incidental to his argument. Kelly's text broke the house down into its components, including plans, structure, decorative details such as doorways, window frames, moldings, paneling and mantels, and materials. He was uninterested in historical background, preferring to stress visual qualities instead. In 1937 Antoinette Forrester Downing, another Isham protegé, produced a less technical, more art historical book on early Rhode Island, also weighted toward text, as did I. T. Frary for Ohio houses. Frary's 1936 book, illustrated entirely with photographs, combined Kelly-type architectural commentary with notes on the family histories of individual houses.[48]

The majority of interwar books, however, followed the eighteenth- and nineteenth-century folios much more closely. They included little narrative other than a brief preface, often written by reigning colonialists Fiske Kimball or John Mead Howells, that established the rationale for the work and served something of the purpose of blurbs now printed on dust jackets. An equally brief introduction described the scope of the work, while a paragraph or two of historical or architectural observation on each building completed the text. Sometimes even this minimal commentary was omitted, for to architects trained in the classical mode the images themselves were the "documents" to be studied. As Albert Simons and Samuel Lapham, Jr., observed in their 1927 study of Charleston, their "vista of the evolution of taste" could be "visually enjoyed without the distractions of literary comment." Thus, the books relied for their impact on plates containing photographs and detailed measured drawings large enough to be examined closely and even copied.[49]

John Mead Howells's own *Architectural heritage of the Piscataqua* (1937) is a good example of the genre. A brief Howells preface and a few pages of rambling, nearly random comments contributed by the Colonial Revivalist and society architect William Lawrence Bottomley, entitled "Memoranda on an Early Portsmouth Builder and of Possible Architects and Design Sources," introduce the book. A series of photographs of New Hampshire and Maine buildings, each captioned with a sentence identifying the original owner, comprise the body of the work. Interspersed among the photographs are plates of measured drawings, mostly illustrating interior details but also depicting exterior elevations and floor and site plans.

Howells in turn contributed a preface to Stoney's *Plantations of the Carolina Low Country,* which combined prefatory essays on "The Country and the People" and "Architectural Trends," with a remarkably large proportion of measured drawings among the plates. Each major building was discussed in a historical and architectural summary accompanied by a floor plan, which was by no means standard in works of this sort. The measured drawings in these large books were visually busy but carefully conceived productions; Stoney's were exceptionally elegant. A single plate might show sample balusters, moulding profiles, and even whole stairs or walls of panels in an array that recalled the pattern books but was equally strongly influenced by the disciplined, artful sheet layout stressed in École-type architectural education, where presentation was a major criterion for the judgment of student work.[50]

Publications such as Howells's and Stoney's were the products of centuries of architectural practice, colored by the cultural values of the American Colonial Revival and the quest for the Other America. Such works in turn offered models from which Charles Stotz could work when he turned to study Western Pennsylvania.

IV

After Cornell, Stotz moved to New York to serve his architectural apprenticeship in the offices of Welles Bosworth, Cass Gilbert, and Delano and Aldrich. All three firms designed large buildings in historic styles for wealthy public and private clients, and their work showed an intimate familiarity with architectural history. After World War I, Bosworth had helped restore the war-damaged Reims Cathedral and the palaces at Versailles and Fontainebleau. Cass Gilbert was the architect of such monuments as the classical Detroit Public Library and New York's Gothic Woolworth Building, while Delano and Aldrich were well-known builders of country houses and of urban houses in a Georgian Revival style. Armed with this experience, Stotz left New York after two years to join his father's office.[51]

The Pittsburgh to which Stotz returned in 1923 was very different from the Ithaca of his college days or even the New York of the elite architectural offices in which he had worked. The city had grown from a relatively small place, with a population under 100,000 in 1870, to one of nearly half a million people, eighth largest in the nation, by the eve of World War I. Most of this growth was the result of immigration. Italians, Hungarians, and other eastern Europeans formed over half the foreign-born population in Pittsburgh in 1910 and the foreign-born in turn accounted for over 40 percent of the working-class population.[52]

The dire condition of Pittsburgh's immigrants and native working class during the years immediately preceding World War I prompted a group of social scientists led by Paul U. Kellogg to undertake a pioneering "social survey" of the city in 1907–1908, and their efforts were issued in six volumes over the next few years. The Pittsburgh Survey complemented the study of the Other America. Like the architectural historians and folklorists, its researchers wished to understand the effect of industrialism on America's environment and social values. For example, Margaret Byington focused on the lifeways of industrial workers in her classic Pittsburgh Survey study *Homestead: The Households of a Mill Town*. Byington distinguished "the sturdy Scotch and Welsh and German of the early immigration, the sons of Yankee 'buckwheats,' and the daughters of Pennsylvania Dutch farmers," the descendants of the builders of the Other America, from the "Slavs" and African-Americans. Concentrating in particular on the house, its furnishings, and its household organization, Byington chronicled the deleterious effects of wage cuts, industrial strife, dangerous working conditions, and corporate irresponsibility on the workers' domestic life. She also noted the baleful influence of popular culture, and she recorded as well hopeful signs that genteel cultural institutions such as the Carnegie Library might convert these workers to the middle-class ideals she cherished. In short,

while the sociologists' subject matter was less overtly romantic than the Colonial Revivalists', the two groups shared a vision of a true America undermined by modern changes. The work of the Pittsburgh Survey revolved around the paradox of the wonderful feats of human ingenuity that had created Pittsburgh's enormous industrial enterprises but had also destroyed the environment and immiserated many of its residents. Conditions had reached such a crisis point that one critic described the city during the years of the Western Pennsylvania Architectural Survey as a "scene so dreadfully hideous, so intolerably bleak and forlorn that it reduced the whole aspirations of man to a macabre and depressing joke."[53]

As architects who specialized in institutional buildings, constructing the hospitals, orphanages, schools, and factories required by the industrial city, the Stotzes, father and son, were familiar with the Pittsburgh depicted in the survey. Edward Stotz's Fifth Avenue High School, for example, had been built in a ward populated entirely by immigrants. Undoubtedly they were also acutely aware of the changes that had shaped Pittsburgh in the two decades after 1910. Immigrants' children helped raise the proportion of native-born population as the city's growth slowed. This did not signal an amelioration of social conditions, however. After 1920, nearly a decade before the onset of the national Depression, Pittsburgh's economy began to decline, owing to the city's overcommitment to a few large, relatively inflexible industries. Unemployment soared to nearly 10 percent of the work force during the 1920s.[54]

It was not an auspicious climate in which to launch an architectural career, so it is probably not surprising that throughout the 1920s Stotz's energies were directed toward social and educational pursuits. "Robust and handsome," reports Tally McKee, with "a kind of bumpkin, hayseed quality about him that, while charming, belies his Cornell master's degree," Stotz worked in the late 1920s on the *Spectator, Pittsburgh's Smart Magazine*, where he wrote a feature that imitated the *New Yorker's* "Talk of the Town" column. "Unquestionably the most literate of Pittsburgh architects," according to a contemporary, he was one of the leading lights behind the Pittsburgh Architectural Club's *Charette*, a magazine that between the wars devoted rather more space to chummy gossip and amateur liter-

ary efforts than to professional issues. Most important, while the firm was building such works
as the Coraopolis Junior High School (1925), the
National Tube Company's research lab (1927),
the Monongahela National Bank (1928), and the
Ellwood City Hospital (1929), Charles Stotz
undertook a study tour of Europe and, after his
return, devoted much of his leisure time to a
search for the Other America.[55]

Stotz published romantic sketches of Pittsburgh reminiscent of those nineteenth- and early
twentieth-century architects drew on their
sketching tours. These made broken-down corners of the industrial metropolis appear to be picturesque remnants of a medieval European town
such as Mont Saint-Michel, the subject of a Stotz
article in the *Architectural Forum* (fig. 3). At the
same time, he began to explore the region around
Pittsburgh in the company of fellow architects
Robert W. Schmertz and Rody Patterson.
He organized an architects' tour to Plantation
Plenty, the Isaac Manchester house that was
later featured prominently in *The Early Architecture of Western Pennsylvania*. He provided an
itinerary, with accompanying sketches, for a self-
guided automobile tour of Washington and
Fayette counties, again featuring buildings that
would reappear in the book. And he became en-
amored of the architecture of the Harmony society's villages at Harmony and Old Economy.[56]

In the mid-1920s, the Stotz circle began to
make measured drawings, including several of
Harmony, in the name of the Committee on Preservation of Historic Monuments and Sites, of the
Pittsburgh chapter of the American Institute of
Architects. This committee, charged with the
oversight of local landmarks, was founded in
1906 but had been moribund for twenty years. It
seems to have interpreted its task as providing
unspecified support for officially owned landmarks. Since the Pittsburgh region contained
nothing except Old Economy (state property
after 1919), "The field of activity is very small,
unless a good private residence or a good type
of log cabin could be considered an Historical
Monument." Year after year, the chair reported
to the chapter that the committee had "held no
meetings and done nothing." In 1920 the committee did sponsor measured drawings of Old Economy, but these were soon lost. A year later, it
stirred itself to suggest that Carnegie Tech might
place "more emphasis upon this character of

Figure 3. Charles Morse Stotz, drawing of downtown
Pittsburgh from an article in the *Pittsburgh Record,* April-
May 1932 (copy in Charles Morse Stotz Papers, Historical
Society of Western Pennsylvania).

work" than the one measured drawing problem
per year then assigned. The arrival of Stotz and
his friends on the scene signaled the beginning of
the committee's active life. They joined it formally in 1930, with Stotz as chair. It was to be
the platform from which the Western Pennsylvania Architectural Survey was launched.[57]

V

The Depression was an economic disaster, but
to those who were interested in the Other America it also provided an opportunity. In Stotz's
words, "An unprecedented economic depression
was made to yield dividends which are not measured in material worth but by their spiritual
value." Armies of highly skilled men and women
were available to work in the cause of preservation, which no longer need be the "hobby," as
Stotz called it, of a few people. In the 1930s,
these underemployed professionals contributed
to a massive reinvigoration of the quest to document the Other America. They took photographs

of urban and rural life, inventoried historic documents, made watercolors of examples of American design, collected folk songs, and interviewed
ex-slaves, creating archival resources that are still
widely used. Among the first such projects were
those mounted by architects, and among the
architects' projects the Western Pennsylvania
Architectural Survey was the largest nongovern-
mental undertaking.[58]

Stotz claimed both priority and originality for
the WPAS, but the situation was more complicated than that. Other efforts preceded and coin-
cided with his, although none was quite like it.
At about the time Stotz began his formal survey,
a committee of New York architects led by
William Lawrence Bottomley and John Mead
Howells formed the Architects' Emergency Committee to purchase drawings of important colonial
monuments from jobless draftsmen. Between
1932 and 1937, they employed 110 different men
and published the results in the two volumes of
Great Georgian Houses of America. A year after
Stotz began, National Park Service architect
Charles E. Peterson proposed a similar, national
project to be conducted as a joint venture of the
Park Service, the Library of Congress, and the
American Institute of Architects. Regional directors for the new Historic American Buildings
Survey (HABS), organized in December 1933,
were recruited by the American Institute of Architects from among practitioners already interested in the field, such as Louisiana restorationist
Richard Koch, Boston architect Frank Chouteau
Brown, and Stotz. HABS drawing projects were
to emphasize structures in danger of demolition,
but otherwise the selection was left to the local
directors' discretion.[59]

In his own view, Stotz's work differed from
these. He was adamant that the Western Pennsylvania Architectural Survey was "in no sense a
relief [or] welfare" project. It was strictly a scholarly work with no ulterior motives, for which
draftsmen were chosen "purely on the basis of
producing the highest quality of results." In fact,
he claimed that had HABS existed before he began work, it would not have been possible to
accomplish the WPAS. Stotz's lifelong insistence
on this point is curious and probably says more
about his political views than his architectural
views.[60]

More important, neither the Architects' Emergency Committee project nor HABS was a sur-

vey in the sense of a comprehensive inventory of
the architecture of a specific locality. *Great Georgian Houses* presented a relatively small number
of famous buildings drawn from the entire east
coast, while HABS recorded endangered gems.
However, at least one survey did precede Western Pennsylvania's. The Kentucky chapter of the
American Institute of Architects decided in 1925
to make "a survey record of Old Kentucky Architecture" and arranged for University of Illinois
architecture professor Rexford Newcomb, in
conjunction with another architect and a photographer, to undertake the project. Although
the work was completed in 1925–1927, the results appeared only in 1940, in a large-format,
minimum-text book of the familiar type. It is not
clear how systematic the Kentucky survey was,
however, or even whether it was originally conceived as a comprehensive inventory. At any
rate, Stotz never cited it as an antecedent. In his
account the WPAS was organized simply because "it was obviously a waste of time and
money to grope about in search of early buildings
without some reasonably complete knowledge of
their numbers and locations," but there was "no
precedent which was known to the Survey Committee for the exhaustive survey of a territory as
large as that of Western Pennsylvania." It is
tempting to think that, in the home of the Pittsburgh Survey, the idea if not the methodology of
a survey may have come to Stotz from that
quarter. At any rate, a comprehensive survey is
certainly consonant with the concern for "science" and authenticity that both shared.[61]

Stotz and Schmertz made a number of recon-
naissance trips through Western Pennsylvania
"which encouraged the desire to make a general
survey and record" of its architecture. An application to the Buhl Foundation in early 1932
produced a grant of $6,500 for the survey and
writing. Stotz formed a small survey committee
drawn from his fieldwork companions of the
1920s, and work began.[62]

The first step was to solicit information about
potential candidates for the inventory. In addition to radio and newspaper announcements, a
four-page brochure was prepared and 2,500 copies mailed throughout the region. The brochure
argued the need for such a project—the pride in
local buildings and the threat to them—as well
as the architects' right to undertake it as a matter
of professional interest. It called for help from

anyone knowing of standing buldings erected before 1860, a date that marked "practically the
disappearance of those building characteristics
peculiar to the so-called 'Colonial' and 'Greek
Revival' styles and their more or less local variations." Anything of later date would "not receive
any consideration in this project." A form was
sent to likely informants requesting basic information about the building's location, material,
owner, and type. These elicited 600 replies.
Throughout the course of the survey, the initial
collection was supplemented with other forms
and follow-up letters designed to fill in missing
data.[63]

Among other information, the follow-up letter
asked for "Origin of design, stories, traditions
etc," which might include the popular name of
the building, stories about how it came to be
built, or rumors of other structures that may
have inspired the builder. Although the survey
committee emphasized their desire for historical
accuracy based on rigorous documentation, they
were willing to take leads of any sort. In fact, it is
evident that in some cases the informant's word
was deemed adequate without verification. Alice
Manchester, owner of the Manchester house
(pp. 78–83, 158, 163) was asked the birthplace of
Isaac Manchester and the original covering of the
flat roof deck, not information that most lay
people would know. Similarly, the account of
early Pittsburgh architect John Chislett was
based on both local documents and conversations
with a descendant.[64]

Mailed-in tips were compiled in fifteen loose-
leaf binders that the committee used when selecting buildings to visit. However, most of the sites
surveyed were discovered through road tra-
verses, that is, by driving across each county on
its principal roads in search of old buildings,
rather than through informants' advice. The second phase of the survey consisted of a series of
twenty-nine car trips of one to four days' dura-
tion during 1932 and 1933. Stotz and Patterson,
occasionally accompanied by other members of
the committee, visited 3,000 sites, sometimes as
many as twenty a day. They recorded 542 sites
in photographs and mapped every structure on
USGS topographical maps.[65]

The travelers' "thrilling adventure of discovery" was tempered by their mixed reactions to
local residents shaped by the architects' social
class bias, their views of country people, and

their visions of the Other America. On the one
hand, much of their correspondence was directed
to local notables and the descendants of the early
Western Pennsylvania elite, whose information
and interpretation of local history they treated
with deference. For example, Stotz assured one
correspondent that they sought information on
Dr. William A. Irvine "with a sincere interest to
record for posterity the remarkable work of this
citizen who did so much to advance the culture
of our early days."[66]

On the other hand, the surveyors' stance toward the ordinary people was more ambivalent.
As a part of the Other America, Western Pennsylvania was a treasure trove of early architecture and a place where some of its more engaging
qualities survived. A Butler County farmer with
fourteen children invited Stotz and Patterson to
dinner, since "two more would make little difference," and urged them to spend the night and
take part in the local Fourth of July festivities the
next day. Yet while the region formed the upper
end of the much romanticized Appalachia, complete with the requisite log houses, it also had
long been industrialized. Thus it combined some
of the evil effects of both rural isolation and
industrial disruption: benighted rustics, disad-
vantaged immigrants, and demoralized industrial
workers, many of whom failed to treat the old
buildings as anything special and made alterations of which the surveyors disapproved. Typical was one old house occupied by "three Polish
families and eight coal miners" who had cut a
stovepipe hole in a fine mantel.[67]

The locals were equally ambivalent about the
surveyors. Some were simply amused, remarking
that they would rather have a coal mine or a load
of manure than an old house. A few would have
nothing to do with people they did not know.
The Butler County farmer's neighbor turned
away the fieldworkers as "'city fellers,'" and indeed wherever they went, the surveyors were
recognized as familiar representatives of urbanization. The fieldworkers carried "an impressive
large yellow official survey questionnaire" with
which to overawe their informants, but few were
mystified by it. Instead, to their frustration, the
country people classed them with the Fuller brush
men, real estate agents, and "antique fiends" who
had infested the countryside for years.[68]

Lacking patience for those unable to see the
survey as the altruistic contribution to the public

good that the architects intended, committee members were often short with recalcitrant farmers. In a shakily written letter, the owner of a log house near Sewickley (pp. 36, 38) told the surveyors, "You are taking up quite a bet [sic] of my time. If there is anything in this for me I would be very glad to give you some information about the old log cabin." Stotz snapped back, "This is not a money-making or commercial survey. I give my time and so do the other members of the Committee. . . . We have interviewed or written to over 1200 persons in Western Pennsylvania . . . and so far you are one of the very few who has demanded anything for the little we ask."[69]

The third phase of the survey, after the collection of data and the initial fieldwork, was to select sites for further study and to inaugurate a program of measured drawings. Ostensibly these sites were chosen after evaluation of the 3,000 structures surveyed, but a large proportion of the buildings drawn had already been singled out in Stotz's *Charette* pieces of the 1920s. Twenty-eight draftsmen and architects were hired, mostly from among the committee's circle of friends and employees. For example, Raymond Celli, one of Stotz's employees, in turn hired his brother Mario to assist him. Stotz assigned buildings according to his assessment of individual capabilities, and Mario Celli believes that the brothers' assignment to three of the high points of the survey—the Meason house, the Manchester house, and the Dorsey house at Brownsville (pp. 52–56, 171)—was a tribute to his brother's drawing skill. However complex their assignments, the draftsmen were paid a flat rate of $80 per finished sheet.[70]

After the committee made an initial appointment, the workers were on their own to record the buildings as they saw fit, although they were required to work on 8½ × 11-inch paper for ease of filing. The draftsmen's field drawings were personal, utilitarian things that ranged from careful scaled sketches on graph paper such as the Celli brothers produced to rougher work like Raymond McGrew's or Stotz's own (figs. 4, 5). After a day or two in the field, it was back to the drafting room, where the situation was much different. There, control was much more centralized, so that "the finished work would constitute a true and authentic document" and the drawings as a group would form "a uniform collection"

after a careful final drawing was produced on 23 × 30-inch paper supplied by the survey office. Each drawing was submitted in pencil for approval of the sheet layout before being inked: in the Beaux-Arts tradition, presentation was paramount. For reasons of consistency of style again, one draftsman was appointed to do all the lettering.[71]

Ultimately 106 drawings were produced, of which 81 were used in the finished volume (fig. 6). In style and format, these drawings closely resembled those of western New York State that Stotz had published a decade and a half earlier. They are somewhat simpler and less packed with details than similar plates in contemporary works, but stand with any in their elegance and visual appeal. While the draftsmen were instructed to record evidence of alteration to the structures, the finished drawings show the buildings as the WPAS thought they had appeared when first constructed. In silently restoring the works, they chose an older approach to measured drawings, one stretching back to the time of Palladio, over the method favored since the establishment of HABS, of showing struc-

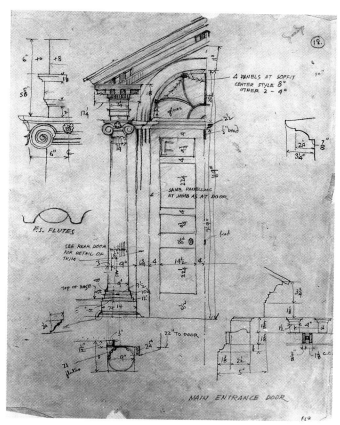

Figure 4. Mario C. Celli, field notes of Meason house doorway, ca. 1933 (Carnegie Library, Western Pennsylvania Architectural Survey files).

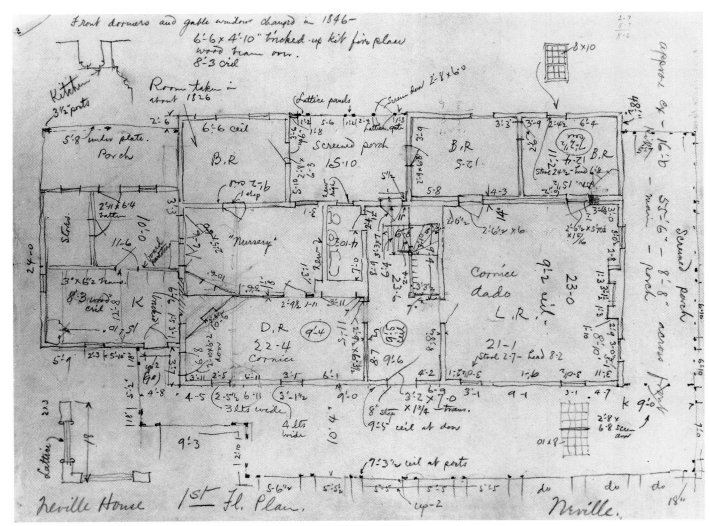

Figure 5. Raymond McGrew, field notes of Neville house plan, ca. 1933 (Carnegie Library, Western Pennsylvania Architectural Survey files).

tures exactly as they existed at the time of recording. To Stotz, the latter practice undermined a drawing's historical value. The two approaches reflected varying interpretations of the concept of scientific accuracy. The HABS policy stressed strict, non-judgmental empiricism, while the WPAS practice emphasized informed expert interpretation.[72]

VI

The final phase of the project was Stotz's task alone—the writing of *The Early Architecture of Western Pennsylvania*. In doing so, he created a distinctive format that integrated the text-oriented study of the sort produced by J. Frederick Kelly or Antoinette Downing with the picture book, such as those of Eleanor Raymond or John Mead Howells. The text is divided into three general chapters treating background, architectural style, craftsmanship, and historic

preservation, followed by a second part containing the plates. This was subdivided into chronological chapters on houses and on specific buildings types, and one on the Harmonists, Stotz's particular love.

It is worth considering the structure and the argument of the book in some detail, because it helps us to understand the ways in which *The Early Architecture of Western Pennsylvania* was shaped by its Colonial Revival roots, how Stotz related his interpretation of Western Pennsylvania to the existing landscape, and how this interpretation differed from those of Stotz's contemporaries and from how the region might be studied today.

On the surface, it is curious that a work written to reveal the distinctive architectural contributions of Western Pennsylvania should stress the region's conformity with the rest of the nation. This is less surprising if we consider Stotz's

background in architectural history. His fundamental historical assumptions derived from his
Cornell education. In commencing the work
with a freestanding "background" chapter inserted as a prelude to a subsequent, essentially
visual architectural discussion and in assuming
the importance of style as a way of understanding the architecture of Western Pennsylvania,
Stotz revealed his debt to Banister Fletcher's *History of Architecture on the Comparative Method,*
first published in 1896 and the standard architectural history text for forty years. Each of Banister
Fletcher's chapters was preceded by a section of
"influences" that contained the same sorts of information that Stotz's first chapter does. One of
the most striking illustrations in later editions of
Banister Fletcher was a plate entitled "The Tree
of Architecture," whose roots were labeled *geography, climate, religion, social, history.* Greek, Roman, and Romanesque architecture formed the

trunk, while the branches blossomed forth with
national styles. In 1920s editions, the uppermost
tip of the tree, at the center, represented *American architecture.* Stotz was clearly thinking of
this plate when he described architectural history as "tree of which the roots are represented
by Greece, the trunk by Rome, . . . and a terminating offshoot by America."[73]

This conception of history as, in Alan
Gowans's phrase, a "line of progress" of stylistic
development shaped an influential work on
American architectural history that appeared in
1922. Fiske Kimball's *Domestic Architecture of
the American Colonies and of the Early Republic*
told the story of the advance of architectural sophistication in America. Kimball's analysis drew
on earlier work on U.S. architectural history, but
it was recast with such force and consistency
that the book remains the standard interpretation of early American architecture. According
to Kimball, the first English architecture in
North America was crude, improvised building
that gave way to the "medieval" holdovers of the
seventeenth century and ultimately to the increasingly sophisticated classical architecture of
the eighteenth and early nineteenth centuries. In
his eyes, architecture improved to the extent that
it came to conform to contemporary European
practice. Aesthetic growth was promoted by the
importation of European craftsmen and most of
all by the dissemination of European architectural handbooks. As a book-derived architecture,
"the ideal of the Colonial style remained always
conformity to English usage." With the appearance on the postrevolutionary scene of men like
Thomas Jefferson and Benjamin Henry Latrobe,
men who understood and could use the new
ideas in an original rather than an imitative way,
came a "truly American contribution to architectural style."[74]

To most of his contemporaries, Kimball's account was authoritative, and, more than any
other source, it shaped *The Early Architecture of
Western Pennsylvania.* Whereas Kimball's New
England began with pioneer huts and wigwams,
the story of Stotz's Pennsylvania commenced
with a brief look at log building, "the architecture of the forest." The next, postcolonial section
is the longest in the book because that period
represented, on the one hand, "the Indian Summer of Colonial architecture" (p. 16), and on the
other, the triumph of civilization, the introduc-

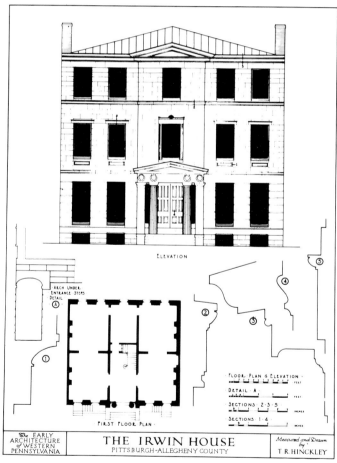

Figure 6. T. R. Hinckley, measured drawing of the Irwin
house, "Burke's Building," Pittsburgh, ca. 1933, a Western
Pennsylvania Architectural Survey plate not used in *The
Early Architecture of Western Pennsylvania* (Carnegie Library, WPAS portfolio 1, qo 720.9748 W56d).

tion of European styles into the wilderness, and the era of "America's really characteristic achievement in architecture," as Kimball put it. This was the time when Western Pennsylvania's architecture was most distinctive; but even then, owing to the constant influx of immigrants from many parts of the country, there was little chance for the region to develop "a distinctive local style such as occurred in Annapolis, Germantown, and the James River district" (p. 43). This opportunity was completely closed off by the arrival of the Greek Revival, "our first distinctly national style." It was national because it was a book-based phenomenon, a "gigantic exhibition of architectural archaeology," as Stotz says, quoting Harold Eberlein (p. 108). The rise of the handbook and of the professional architect became an important subtheme of the works of the post-Kimball era, and Stotz devoted an entire chapter to the subject. The notion that aesthetic progress depended on the expertise and the writings of architects obviously appealed to architect-historians and to those, like Kimball and Stotz, inclined to understand progress as the work of the elite.[75]

Stotz's third chapter discusses craftsmen, engineers, building technologies, laws, costs, and materials as well as architects. In this respect, *The Early Architecture of Western Pennsylvania* was informed by professional interests and by a respect for preindustrial building technology that was a legacy of the late nineteenth-century Arts and Crafts Movement. In broaching these and other topics, Stotz departed from the routine line-of-stylistic-progress account, crosscutting and even undercutting it. These parallel inquiries made the book conceptually lumpy but also more interesting and more prescient than most of its sort.[76]

Some of Stotz's alternate agendas arose simply from his powers of observation. For example, standard style histories were based mostly on houses and a few public buildings. Although these formed a large portion of *The Early Architecture of Western Pennsylvania,* Stotz knew that there were also houses that did not fit the style sequence. He called them "buildings without traditional style" (p. 17); now we call them vernacular buildings. Working buildings of various sorts were also difficult to fit into the march of styles, but Stotz was determined from the first to include them, as the initial flyer reveals:

Of fully equal interest are public buildings such as churches, court houses and schools, also taverns, barns, mills, manufactories, furnaces, bridges, canal structures, toll houses and fortifications. Some attention will also be paid to examples of early craftsmanship such as hardware accessories. The survey further hopes to present some drawings, rubbings, or photographs of tomb stones, memorial plaques and the like, while landscape treatment will likely also be given some consideration.

Stotz's interest in such disparate buildings and artifacts was a legacy of nineteenth-century antiquarianism, which was similarly catholic in its purview, but paradoxically it also looked forward to more recent material culture studies, which stress understanding objects in their total contexts. The broad net cast by the survey is one of the reasons *The Early Architecture of Western Pennsylvania* remains such a valuable resource.[77]

Other innovative aspects of Stotz's interpretation arose out of his sensitivity to his location. Despite the influence of the Other America myth on Stotz, he knew that early Western Pennsylvania was not a colonial Arcadia but a trading and manufacturing hub. Stotz recognized that its location at the nexus of major transportation networks—"one of the pivots of [America's] great system of internal improvements," as the nineteenth-century visitor Michael Chevalier put it—had shaped its architectural and economic history. This reinforced his view of the region as one engulfed in national architectural currents, and it stimulated his interest, as well, in kinds of buildings that did not usually attract the attention of Colonial Revivalists—the bridges, furnaces, tollhouses, and other relics of early American economic growth. The decision to include them did not please all his readers. In a review in the *Art Bulletin,* Columbia University architectural historian Everard M. Upjohn wrote,

The tendency today appears to be that the house and the church do not alone present the architectural ensemble of any region—which is true. In order to get "total recall," commercial and industrial architecture must be included. To question the desirability of this inclusion is impossible. At least one sees what is there. Nevertheless some danger may lurk in stressing such material. A few quite exceptional stores or arcades make a real contribution, but let us realize that the bulk of industrial or even commercial building is architecturally negligible; . . . to admit that a woodshed, a foundry chimney, or an outhouse is architecture is absurd.[78]

Stotz's catholicity of interest has left us, in The Early Architecture of Western Pennsylvania and especially in the Western Pennsylvania Architectural Survey on which it is based, a remarkably wide-ranging record of Western Pennsylvania's surviving architectural legacy. Nevertheless, his interpretation of this legacy differs somewhat from the ways in which contemporary scholars might approach the topic. We need to examine these differences briefly, not from any sense that Stotz ought to have done things that no one thought of until decades after he wrote, but to highlight how his intellectual milieu helped shape the book and to suggest, as well, how modern scholarship might build on and refine Stotz's ground-breaking research.

Stotz's assumptions about the primacy of style left him uncertain how to treat log houses: "It may seem questionable to speak of log architecture as a style, or, in fact, to consider it as architecture at all" (p. 12). Log buildings were "symbolic of the pioneer's primitive mode of life" (p. 34), but there was little else to say about them. Because the section on log buildings is consequently the shortest in the book, an important, ubiquitous tradition in Western Pennsylvania building is relatively underrepresented in The Early Architecture of Western Pennsylvania. Current scholars treat log architecture as a problem in building technology and spatial form rather than style. In that spirit, the folklorist Henry Glassie made an (unpublished) survey of log building in Washington and Greene counties in the 1970s. His studies of log building looked closely at their structural systems—how the corners were notched, or joined, in particular—and their plans—how the spaces inside them were arranged and used.[79]

This type of study casts light on the routes over which log building made its way across America and on how people lived their lives in log houses. From these materials, in addition, scholars have had success in elucidating an issue that Stotz grappled with less conclusively. Not surprisingly in a region whose population was so disparate, Stotz was obsessed with ethnic origins during the original survey. Although much of this material was omitted from the published book, Stotz's worksheets included space for recording the birthplace and "extraction" of the original owners, which he assumed affected architectural appearance. Thus, since the builder of the Alexander Johnston house at Greensburg was born in Ireland, Stotz categorized the building as "Irish Georgian," although there is little to distinguish it visually from other houses in the survey. Building on the work of 1930s Swedish ethnohistorian Sigurd Erixon, however, contemporary historians have shown building technologies and plans to be more sensitive clues to the ethnic origins of builders and owners than a building's appearance.[80]

A more significant difference between contemporary and 1930s architectural history relates to the issue of inclusiveness: what is interesting? Although Stotz acknowledged more freely than many of his contemporaries the need to "see what is there," his vision, like any historian's, was limited by his preconceptions. His net was cast wide, but the buildings he ultimately chose to include in his book were more limited. As a consequence of the omission of most log buildings and of the preponderance of large stone and brick buildings in The Early Architecture of Western Pennsylvania, Stotz's portrait of the region is skewed toward the top of the socioeconomic hierarchy. The size and elaboration of masonry building and its tendency to survive the passage of time makes it conspicuous in the modern landscape, but throughout antebellum America, masonry buildings always comprised a minority of the total architectural scene.

Stotz's sharp distinction between the architectures of pre- and postindustrial America is perhaps the clearest mark of the era in which he wrote. In pushing the "fatal decline" of industrialism forward to 1860 (and indeed by including a Gothic Revival church in the book), Stotz was more liberal than others in his assessment of American building, but once the border had been passed, there was no turning back. The surveyors were more than once disgusted to chase down a lead only to discover "a horrible example" of Victorian architecture.[81]

Stotz's hard line between pre- and post–Civil War buildings, when combined with his understanding of Western Pennsylvania's early economic history, lend a certain ambivalence to his treatment of the industrial landscape before 1860. Even as he acknowledged early industrialism, Stotz shared his contemporaries' and his predecessors' scorn for its consequences: "We, who have substituted the craft of the machine for the craft of the hand, live in a new world of totally different architectural problems, and what we have gained in sophistication we have lost in directness." The engineer's role was discussed, but no specimens of advanced engineering were illustrated. There were stone bridges but none of iron, for example. Overall, the industrial relics included in *The Early Architecture of Western Pennsylvania* were seen through very rosy lenses that create a strange disjunction between the landscape depicted in the book and that from which it was distilled.[82]

Urban historians have noted that the city of Pittsburgh succeeded very early in its history in subjugating its hinterland as an adjunct of its economy. Coal was being taken from the region before the end of the eighteenth century. By the 1830s, when many of the buildings in the book were constructed, the city was engulfed "with a dense, black smoke which, bursting forth in volumes from the foundries, forges, glass-houses, and the chimneys of all the factories and houses, falls in flakes of soot upon the dwellings and persons of the inhabitants. It is, therefore, the dirtiest town in the United States." Coal mining was soon followed by the production of iron and coke, carrying into the countryside with them the same cloud of foul air, so that by the time Stotz began traveling in southwestern Pennsylvania, it had become a landscape "ugly by day with banks of coke ovens, tipples, sidings, and fields gnawed to the rock with strip-coal operations; luridly beautiful by night when the glare of the ovens paints the sky and works magic with headframes and sooty buildings." Casting his eye over this landscape, Stotz nevertheless decided that "originally the civilization of Western Pennsylvania was chiefly rural." He omitted most urban buildings from the book and at the same time represented rural civilization through structures like the Meason house, singled out in Fiske Kimball's introduction as the jewel of the region but built by one of the men who began the industrialization of the countryside. The power of the Other America was such that while Stotz in-

cluded pieces of industrial Pennsylvania, he saw the landscape as a whole in a very different light from the "glare of the ovens."[83]

Nevertheless, *The Early Architecture of Western Pennsylvania* remains the standard work on the subject, and for very good reasons beyond its singularity. It is a thorough and accurate overview of a critical region that still has not, any more than in his own day, received the study it deserves. Stotz's book brought early Western Pennsylvania architecture into the regional and national consciousness and provided the Western Pennsylvania material for Talbot Hamlin's *Greek Revival Architecture in America* (1944), still the standard survey of the period. Subsequent chronicles of the region's architecture, notably Walter Kidney's *Landmark Architecture: Pittsburgh and Allegheny County* (1985), are no longer squeamish about post–Civil War architecture, but for the most part Stotz's history of the earliest architecture of Western Pennsylvania stands unchallenged as the authoritative account. In addition, *The Early Architecture of Western Pennsylvania* is the only record of many important structures lost to development or neglect during the past sixty years.

And a fine record it is. It says much about the quality of the WPAS that it is possible to ask questions of *The Early Architecture of Western Pennsylvania* that did not occur to the surveyors. The book's plates provide more information than the text takes into account, thus allowing us to infer more than Stotz says. For example, there are manuscript charts in Stotz's papers showing that he attempted to arrive at a systematic understanding of house plans, but never could. Yet because Stotz presciently insisted that plans of all buildings be drawn—a policy rare in the 1930s and one of which he was justly proud—it is possible to see that most of the houses are versions of the central-hall, two-room-deep kind of dwelling that historians now call the Georgian-plan house. Its ubiquity confirms Stotz's assessment that early Western Pennsylvania was governed more by national popular culture than by regional peculiarities.[84]

VII

The Early Architecture of Western Pennsylvania appeared in December 1936 to uniformly good notices. Even Everard Upjohn's cranky review grudgingly admitted that the work was good of its kind. However, Stotz was proudest of Fiske Kimball's introduction endorsing it, as well as a follow-up letter calling it the "finest and most complete book on the architecture in any region in America."[85]

It had been a prodigious effort, one that required the efforts of many people. The informants, the members of the survey committee, and particularly the draftsmen helped to create a much more comprehensive regional overview in a much shorter time than one or two people working on their own in the traditional manner could have done, as a comparison of the number, variety, and geographical distribution of the buildings illustrated in *The Early Architecture of Western Pennsylvania* with any similar work of the period makes plain. Rody Patterson, the committee secretary, was involved particularly closely, and the texts of his annual reports to the Pittsburgh chapter during the years that the Western Pennsylvania Architectural Survey was under way contain early versions of many of the central theses and characteristic anecdotes of the book. Reading these makes it possible to see the book coming together, as the committee refined their conception of early and present Western Pennsylvania. Even some of the language of the book comes directly from Patterson's reports and from committee letters to informants and supporters.

Nevertheless, it is clear in retrospect (as it was to his contemporaries) that Stotz's was the central intelligence and the driving energy behind the project. Consequently, when the Historic American Buildings Survey was founded in December 1933, Stotz was the obvious choice for district officer, even though the WPAS was still under way. Between January and April 1934, he supervised four teams totaling eighteen men who made ninety-seven sheets of drawings of eight structures, including the Pittsburgh Arsenal, the Croghan house in Pittsburgh, and the Washington and Jefferson College administration building. After a lapse, the project was revived in the winter months of 1935. Stotz abruptly resigned in January 1935 or 1936, owing to an "unexpected turn in personal circumstances," but it is clear that he was never happy with HABS. He was contemptuous of its status as "a government relief project" and he objected to the division

chief's suggestion that sites previously drawn for the WPAS be redrawn in HABS format. It was always his position that the survey had already dealt with the important buildings of Western Pennsylvania, although he acknowledged condescendingly that HABS had been useful in recording the second-rate sites that the WPAS had been too busy to cover. On some level Stotz seems to have viewed HABS, even under his own direction, as an intruder into his territory, an impasse that the Washington office had tried to avoid through its diplomatic policy of seeking out those already working in the "historic field" as local directors.[86]

The publication of *The Early Architecture of Western Pennsylvania* marked an important turning point in Stotz's career. It appeared in the same year that Edward Stotz retired from the family firm, leaving it to Charles and his brother Edward, Jr. Stotz's sense of having passed a significant milestone is apparent in his decision to use all three of his names on the title page. When Cleveland publisher J. H. Jansen wrote to thank Stotz for the gift of a copy of the book, he added, "For a long time I wondered what the middle initial represented in your name. It was not until I saw a copy of *The Early Architecture of Western Pennsylvania* that you blossomed forth with the flossy middle name. The book can carry it very well."[87]

Indeed 1936 was a milestone, for the visibility the book brought Charles Morse Stotz led to his emergence as the reigning preservation architect and local architectural historian in Western Pennsylvania. He restored many of the buildings included in *The Early Architecture of Western Pennsylvania,* among them George Washington's grist mill at Perryopolis, the Erie customs house, and most important of all, Old Economy at Ambridge, the work of over twenty years beginning in 1939. The interest in military architecture evident in the book grew throughout his later life. As one of the designers of Point State Park in Pittsburgh, Stotz undertook the restoration of the Fort Pitt blockhouse there as well as the reconstruction of two bastions. He was also the architect of the ambitious reconstruction of Fort Ligonier, begun in 1946.

In addition to his restoration practice, Stotz continued to write. A 1973 article reported on the Harmonists and the restoration of their village and another one of about the same time recorded the Fort Ligonier work. There was also a second book, *Outposts of the War for Empire,* that summarized his decades-long study of early military building.[88]

In these activities, the course of Stotz's career after 1936 followed a pattern common among other fieldworkers of the interwar era. As a result of their work for HABS or as authors, most enjoyed a reputation as the primary historic architectural experts in their regions and built up lifelong practices of restoration and new design in historic styles as a result. Men like Norman Isham in Connecticut and Rhode Island, J. Frederick Kelly in Connecticut, George Fletcher Bennett in Delaware, Thomas T. Waterman in Virginia, and Richard Koch and Samuel Wilson, Jr., in Louisiana enjoyed a preeminence sometimes approaching monopoly of this work.

Yet restoration and research remained, for the most part, a sideline for Charles Stotz. He estimated in 1965 that only one-tenth of his practice lay in restoration; the field was simply too small to support an entire firm. Even as *The Early Architecture of Western Pennsylvania* was taking shape, Stotz won an Allegheny County Better Housing Competition with a project derived, significantly enough, from buildings included in the survey. The firm went on to produce nearly 150 houses during his career. Other work included the design of buildings in Colonial Revival styles that did not make use of Western Pennsylvania sources. The Fox Chapel Presbyterian Church (1962), for example, was based on colonial New England; its steeple was modeled directly on Boston's Old South Church (1729).[89]

Most of the firm's work, however, remained in the area of institutional building, as it had during the days of Edward Stotz, Sr. Such structures as the Mellon Institute laboratories at Bushy Run, the U.S. Steel Corporation research center at Monroeville, and Weirton Steel's quality control laboratory at Weirton, West Virginia, paid the bills. Although his historical work was firmly rooted in an antimodern tradition, Stotz the architect of hospitals and laboratories had more complex views of his position as a twentieth-century architect. "Having been born in the past century and trained in the last days of the Beaux Arts system," he wrote in a 1965 letter to former WPAS draftsman Lawrence Wolfe, "I have participated in the gamut from the 'twisted column' to the 'Mexican hairless' styles. It is a very dull architect who has not understood and participated in the emergence of new styles but a still duller one who turns his back on those styles in which the historic forms are rooted." He took on restoration work only "as a matter of course and having tolerant partners." Yet he admitted that "it is in many ways the most interesting and rewarding because these buildings, curiously enough, will be cherished and preserved after many of the later modern buildings have been discarded."[90]

The historian's most difficult task is to study a topic no one has ever tackled. When starting fresh, the work seems impossibly vast, and any predecessor, however inadequate, is a godsend, for at least it offers something to play off. Otherwise, the scholar must solve every problem anew. Where does one begin? What are the important issues, the key landmarks? What is the appropriate research strategy? Like many of his contemporaries in American architectural history, Charles Morse Stotz faced this daunting blank slate. Like them, he filled it, and he did so with a breadth of interest and a systematic approach that none of the others quite matched. If today we have new questions to ask of the early architecture of Western Pennsylvania, we can ask them in large part because he answered so many fundamental ones so well.

DELL UPTON
Berkeley, 1995

Notes

I am grateful to Fred Hetzel, Mario C. Celli, the architectural firm of MacLachlan, Cornelius and Filoni, and the
staffs of the Carnegie Library of Pittsburgh, the Historical
Society of Western Pennsylvania, and the Pittsburgh History and Landmarks Foundation for valuable assistance
with this project. I am particularly indebted to the gener-
osity of Virginia Stotz in supplying copies of her father's
papers and of Karen Koegler and Ken Pavelchak in showing me Charles Stotz's Western Pennsylvania. Finally, I
wish to thank Zeynep Kezer for help in compiling the
updated bibliography.

1. Frank J. Roos, Jr., *Bibliography of Early American
Architecture: Writings on Architecture Constructed before
1860 in Eastern and Central United States* (Urbana: University of Illinois Press, 1968), p. 4.

2. J. Frederick Kelly, *Early Domestic Architecture of
Connecticut* (New Haven: Yale University Press, 1924;
rpt. New York: Dover, 1963), p. 1.

3. The story of Edward Stotz's career has been compiled
from an anonymous publication, *Pittsburgh of Today*,
published ca. 1931, and other ephemera contained in the
Charles Morse Stotz Papers, Historical Society of Western
Pennsylvania [CMSPW]; Tally McKee, "Charles Morse
Stotz," *Charette: Pittsburgh's Journal of Architecture*, November 1948, p. 11; a history of Edward Stotz's firm and its
successors, *In Detail: The Celebration of a Century of Architecture* (Pittsburgh: MacLachlan, Cornelius and Filoni,
1989); "Schenley High School, Pittsburgh, Pa., Mr. Ed-
ward Stotz, architect," *American Architect* 111, no. 2146
(February 7, 1917): 93–94 and plates; Walter C. Kidney,
Landmark Architecture: Pittsburgh and Allegheny County
(Pittsburgh: Pittsburgh History and Landmarks Foundation, 1985); and Franklin Toker, *Pittsburgh: An Urban
Portrait* (University Park: Pennsylvania State University
Press, 1986).

4. Charles Morse Stotz, "The Lighter Side of History,"
MS, May 2, 1973, in Charles Morse Stotz papers in posses-
sion of Virginia Stotz [CMSPS], p. 18. Except as noted, the
biographical details in this and subsequent paragraphs
were compiled from McKee, "Charles Morse Stotz,"
pp. 11–13; Stotz, "The Early Architecture of Western
Pennsylvania: An Exhibition of Drawings and Photo-
graphs Assembled by a Local Survey," *Carnegie Magazine*,
January 1936, 239–43; Stotz, "Lighter Side of History";
Stotz, "The Beginnings of an Architectural Hobby and the
Western Pennsylvania Architectural Survey," MS., n.d.,
CMSPS; and miscellaneous clippings and obituaries in
CMSPW and CMSPS.

5. Stotz, "Beginnings of an Architectural Hobby," p. 1;
Stotz, "Early Architecture of Western New York," *Architecture* 47, no. 5 (1923): pl. 125, 48, no. 5 (November 1923):
pls. 167–69, 50, no. 2 (1924): pl. 123.

6. Stuart Piggott, *Ruins in a Landscape: Essays in Anti-
quarianism* (Edinburgh: Edinburgh University Press,
1976), pp. 1–24, 101–32; Robert F. Trent, ed., *Pilgrim
Century Furniture, An Historical Survey* (New York: Main
Street/Universe books, 1976), pp. 12, 14; Edward M. Riley,
"The Independence Hall Group," in *Historic Philadelphia*,

*from the Founding until the Early Nineteenth Century: Pa-
pers Dealing with its People and Buildings* (Philadelphia:
American Philosophical Society, 1953), pp. 33–34. The
manuscript annals were deposited in the Historical Society
of Pennsylvania, where they remain.

7. William B. Rhoads, *The Colonial Revival* (New
York: Garland, 1977) is the basic work on the Colonial
Revival in American architecture. See also Vincent J.
Scully, Jr., *The Shingle Style and the Stick Style: Architec-
tural Theory and Design from Downing to the Origins of
Wright* (rev. ed.; New Haven: Yale University Press,
1971), esp. pp. 28–31.

8. Alan Axelrod, ed., *The Colonial Revival in America*
(New York: Norton for the Henry Francis du Pont Winterthur Museum, 1985) contains essays on all these aspects
of the Colonial Revival.

9. David Gebhard, "The American Colonial Revival in
the 1930s," *Winterthur Portfolio* 22, nos. 2–3 (1987): 109;
Karal Ann Marling, *George Washington Slept Here: Colonial Revivals and American Culture, 1876–1986* (Cambridge: Harvard University Press, 1988).

10. R. T. H. Halsey and Elizabeth Tower, *The Homes of
Our Ancestors, as Shown in the American Wing of the
Metropolitan Museum of Art of New York, from the Begin-
nings of New England Through the Early Days of the Re-
public* (Garden City, N.Y.: Doubleday, Doran and Co.,
1925, 1935), p. xxiii, xxii; foreword to Edith Tunis
Sale, *Colonial Interiors*, 2d ser.: *Southern Colonial and
Early Federal* (New York: William Helburn, 1930); Joseph
Hergesheimer, introduction to Philip B. Wallace, *Colonial
Houses, Philadelphia: Pre-revolutionary Period* (New York:
Architectural Book Publishing Co., 1931); William B.
Rhoads, "The Colonial Revival and American National-
ism," *Journal of the Society of Architectural Historians*
[*JSAH*] 35, no. 4 (1976): 239–54. The best analysis of the
complex meanings of the Colonial Revival is Kenneth L.
Ames's introduction to *Colonial Revival in America*,
ed. Axelrod, pp. 1–14. Ames sums up the Colonial Revival
as a response to modernization (p. 11).

11. Joseph L. Copeland, introduction to George
Fletcher Bennett, *Early Architecture of Delaware* (n.p.:
Historical Press, 1932; rpt. New York: Bonanza books,
n.d.); Charles Morse Stotz, "Obsolete Text and Data"
notebook, ca. 1935, CMSPW, ser. V, box 19; Gebhard,
"American Colonial Revival," p. 134; Charles B. Hosmer,
Jr., *Preservation Comes of Age: From Williamsburg to the
National Trust, 1926–1949* (Charlottesville: University
Press of Virginia for the Preservation Press, 1981), p. 439.
In fact, Raymond's book concentrated on the traditional
Pennsylvania German heartland from Philadelphia west to
the Susquehanna River.

12. Thomas Tileston Waterman and John A. Barrows,
Domestic Colonial Architecture of Tidewater Virginia
(New York: Scribner's, 1932; rpt. New York: Dover, 1969),
p. xii.

13. Scully, *Shingle Style*, pp. 19–33.

14. Rodris Roth, "The New England, or 'Old Tyme'
Kitchen Exhibit at Nineteenth-century Fairs," in *Colonial
Revival in America*, ed. Axelrod, pp. 159–83; Marling,

George Washington Slept Here, pp. 89–91; Susan Prendergast Schoelwer, "Curious Relics and Quaint Scenes: The Colonial Revival at Chicago's Great Fair," in *Colonial Revival in America*, ed. Axelrod, pp. 184–216; Robert W. Rydell, *All the World's a Fair: Visions of Empire at American International Expositions, 1876–1916* (Chicago: University of Chicago Press, 1984), esp. pp. 235–36; Timothy Mitchell, "Orientalism and the Exhibitionary Order," in *Colonialism and Culture*, ed. Nicholas B. Dirks (Ann Arbor: University of Michigan Press, 1992).

15. Horace Kephart, *Our Southern Highlanders: A Narrative of Adventure in the Southern Appalachians and a Study of Life among the Mountaineers*, rev. ed. (New York: Macmillan, 1922; rpt. Knoxville: University of Tennessee Press, 1976), pp. 13, 16.

16. Peter B. Hales, *William Henry Jackson and the Transformation of the American Landscape* (Philadelphia: Temple University Press, 1988), pp. 145–46; Bucks County Historical Society Publications Committee, *The Mercer Mile: The Story of Dr. Henry Chapman Mercer and His Concrete Buildings* (Doylestown, Pa.: Bucks County Historical Society, 1972), p. 5; Kephart, *Our Southern Highlanders*, pp. 29–30, 18; Henry D. Shapiro, *Appalachia on Our Mind: The Southern Mountains and Mountaineers in the American Consciousness, 1870–1920* (Chapel Hill: University of North Carolina Press, 1978), pp. 261–63, xiii–xiv, 119.

17. John Mead Howells, introduction to Samuel Gaillard Stoney, *Plantations of the Carolina Low Country* (Charleston: Carolina Art Association, 1938; 7th ed. [1977], rpt. New York: Dover, 1989), p. 6; Kephart, *Our Southern Highlanders*, p. 18; Shapiro, *Appalachia on Our Mind*, p. 118.

18. Miles Orvell, *The Real Thing: Imitation and Authenticity in American Culture, 1880–1940* (Chapel Hill: University of North Carolina Press, 1989), p. xv and passim; Allen H. Eaton, *Handicrafts of the Southern Highlands* (New York: Russell Sage Foundation, 1937; rpt. New York: Dover, 1973), p. 38; Shapiro, *Appalachia on Our Mind*, p. 261; Kephart, *Our Southern Highlanders*, pp. 314, 316. Although only a few chroniclers of the Other America attacked capitalism directly, most criticized industrialism or "commercialism" in some way.

19. Foreword to Alfred Easton Poor, *Colonial Achitecture of Cape Cod, Nantucket and Martha's Vineyard* (New York: William Helburn, 1932; rpt. New York: Dover, 1970); Hergesheimer, introduction to Wallace, *Colonial Houses*; Kelly, *Early Domestic Architecture*, p. 1.

20. Kephart, *Our Southern Highlanders*, p. 453; John Higham, *Strangers in the Land: Patterns of American Nativism 1860–1925*, 2d ed. (New York: Athenaeum, 1969), pp. 154–56.

21. Halsey and Tower, *Homes of Our Ancestors*, p. xxii; I. T. Frary, *Early Homes of Ohio* (Richmond: Garret and Massie, 1936; rpt. New York: Dover, 1970), pp. xiii–xiv.

22. Kephart, *Our Southern Highlanders*, p. 454; Fiske Kimball, introduction to John Mead Howells, *Lost Examples of Colonial Architecture: Buildings That Have Disappeared or Been So Altered As to Be Denatured* (New York: William Helburn, 1931; rpt. New York: Dover, 1963); Hergesheimer, introduction to Wallace, *Colonial Houses*.

23. Eaton, *Handicrafts*, pp. 237–44, 255–61; David E. Whisnant, *All That Is Native and Fine: The Politics of Culture in an American Region* (Chapel Hill: University of North Carolina Press, 1983), esp. pp. 181–252; Stotz, *Early Architecture of Western Pennsylvania* [*EAWP*], p. 32.

24. Eaton, *Handicrafts*, pp. 34–38; Whisnant, *All That Is Native and Fine*, pp. 17–101; Lizabeth A. Cohen, "Embellishing a Life of Labor: An Interpretation of the Material Culture of American Working-class Homes, 1885–1915," in *Common Places: Readings in American Vernacular Architecture*, ed. Dell Upton and John Michael Vlach (Athens: University of Georgia Press, 1986), pp. 263–66; William B. Rhoads, "The Colonial Revival and the Americanization of Immigrants," in *Colonial Revival in America*, ed. Axelrod, pp. 341–61; Montgomery Schuyler, "Modern Architecture" (1894), in *American Architecture and Other Writings*, ed. William H. Jordy and Ralph Coe (New York: Athenaeum, 1964), p. 64; William L. Dulaney, "Wallace Nutting, Collector and Entrepreneur," *Winterthur Portfolio* 13 (1979): 47–60.

25. As examples: Paula Richardson Fleming and Judith Luskey, eds., *The North American Indians in Early Photographs* (New York: Harper and Row, 1986); Arthur Kyle Davis, Jr., ed., *Traditional Ballads of Virginia, Collected under the Auspices of the Virginia Folk-Lore Society* (Cambridge: Harvard University Press, 1929); Irving Whitall Lyon, *The Colonial Furniture of New England: A Study of the Domestic Furniture in Use in the Seventeenth and Eighteenth Centuries* (Boston: Houghton, Mifflin, 1891); Samuel Adams Drake, *A Book of New England Legends and Folk Lore, in Prose and Poetry*, rev. ed. (Boston: Little, Brown, 1906; rpt. Rutland, Vt.: Charles E. Tuttle, 1971); Henry Chapman Mercer, *Ancient Carpenters' Tools, Together with Lumbermen's, Joiners' and Cabinet Makers' Tools in Use in the Eighteenth Century*, 5th ed. (1929; rpt. New York: Horizon Press for the Bucks County Historical Society, 1975); Hales, *William Henry Jackson*.

26. Kimball, introduction to Howells, *Lost Examples*; foreword to Poor, *Colonial Architecture*; Rexford Newcomb, *The Franciscan Mission Architecture of Alta California* (New York: Architectural Book Publishing Co., 1916; rpt. New York: Dover, 1973), p. v; Stotz, draft introduction to *EAWP*, CMSPW, ser. V, box 19, folder 1, p. 30.

27. Dell Upton, "Architectural History or Landscape History?" *Journal of Architectural Education* 44 no. 4 (1991): 195–96; Dell Upton, "Outside the Academy: a Century of Vernacular Architecture Studies, 1890–1990," in *The Architectural Historian in America: A Symposium in Celebration of the Fiftieth Anniversary of the Founding of the Society of Architectural Historians*, ed. Elisabeth Blair MacDougall (Washington, D.C.: National Gallery of Art, 1990), pp. 199–213; foreword to Poor, *Colonial Architecture*; Howells, introduction to Stoney, *Plantations*, p. 6; Newcomb, *Franciscan Mission Architecture*, p. v; Stotz, *EAWP*, p. 9. For a discussion of this central aspect of the architect-historian's agenda, see Keith N. Morgan and Richard Cheek, "History in the Service of Design: American Architect-Historians, 1870–1940," in *Architectural Historian in America*, ed. MacDougall, pp. 61–75.

28. Joseph Rykwert, *The First Moderns: The Architects of the Eighteenth Century* (Cambridge: MIT Press, 1980), p. 272; Andrea Palladio, *The Four Books of Architecture* (London: Isaac Ware, 1738; rpt. New York: Dover, 1965), pp. 79–80.

29. A good, brief account of eighteenth-century architectural recording can be found in Peter Collins, *Changing Ideals in Modern Architecture 1750–1950* (Montreal: McGill–Queen's University Press, 1965), pp. 70–95.

30. Ibid., pp. 100–05.

31. On the function and format of these handbooks in early nineteenth-century America, see Dell Upton, "Pattern Books and Professionalism: Aspects of the Transformation of Domestic Architecture in America, 1800–1860," *Winterthur Portfolio* 19 (1984): 114–20.

32. Upton, "Outside the Academy," p. 200; Margaret Henderson Floyd, "Measured Drawings of the Hancock house by John Hubbard Sturgis: A Legacy to the Colonial Revival," in *Architecture in Colonial Massachusetts*, ed. Abbott Lowell Cummings (Boston: Colonial Society of Massachusetts, 1979), pp. 87–111.

33. Scully, *Shingle Style*, pp. 29–30; Marling, *George Washington Slept Here*, p. 88.

34. Floyd, "Measured Drawings," p. 100; Norman Morrison Isham and Albert F. Brown, *Early Rhode Island Houses: An Historical and Architectural Study* (Providence: Preston and Rounds, 1895).

35. Morgan and Cheek, "History in the Service of Design," pp. 62–63; Rhoads, "The Discovery of America's Architectural Past, 1874–1914," in *Architectural Historian in America*, ed. MacDougall, pp. 23, 27; Arthur Clason Weatherhead, "The History of Collegiate Education in Architecture in the United States," Ph.D. diss., Columbia University, 1941, pp. 34–35, 92–94.

36. Weatherhead, "The History of Collegiate Education," pp. 161–63; Richard Guy Wilson, "The Great Civilization," in Wilson, Dianne H. Pilgrim, and Richard N. Murray, *The American Renaissance 1876–1917* (Brooklyn: Brooklyn Museum, 1979), pp. 45–46; Rhoads, "Discovery of America's Architectural Past," p. 23; Samuel Wilson, Jr., "The Survey in Louisiana in the 1930s," in *Historic America: Buildings, Structures, and Sites*, ed. C. Ford Peatross (Washington: Library of Congress, 1983), p. 24.

37. Wilson, "Great Civilization," pp. 57–60; Isham and Brown, *Early Rhode Island Houses*, pp. 5–6. On science in architectural history, see Upton, "Outside the Academy," pp. 202–4.

38. Rhoads, "Discovery of America's Architectural Past," p. 29; Gebhard, "American Colonial Revival," pp. 110–11; Stotz, "Obsolete text and data" notebook; Charles Magruder, "The White Pine Monograph Series," *JSAH* 22 no. 1 (March 1963): 39–41.

39. Stotz, "Obsolete text and data" notebook.

40. Stotz, draft introduction, p. 8.

41. Kimball, introduction to Waterman and Barrows, *Domestic Colonial Architecture*, p. xi; Hergesheimer, introduction to Wallace, *Colonial Houses*; Charles Morse Stotz, *The Architectural Heritage of Western Pennsylvania: A Record of Building before 1860* (Pittsburgh: University of Pittsburgh Press, 1966), p. xii.

42. Frary, *Early Homes of Ohio*, p. xiii; foreword to Eleanor Raymond, *Early Domestic Architecture of Pennsylvania* (New York: William Helburn, 1931; rpt. Exton, Pa.: Schiffer Ltd., 1977); Kimball, introduction to Waterman and Barrows, *Domestic Colonial Architecture*, p. xi.

43. Copeland, introduction to Bennett, *Early Architecture*; foreword to Raymond, *Early Domestic Architecture of Pennsylvania*; Kimball, introduction to Waterman and Barrows, *Domestic Colonial Architecture*, p. xi; Kimball, introduction to Howells, *Lost Examples*.

44. Stoney, *Plantations of the Carolina Low Country*, p. 7.

45. Stotz, draft introduction, p. 15; interview with Mario C. Celli, Pittsburgh, January 8, 1992; *EAWP*, p. 282.

46. Waterman and Barrows, *Domestic Colonial Architecture*, p. xii.

47. Kelly, *Early Domestic Architecture*, p. ix; Waterman, quoted in Fay Campbell Kaynor, "Thomas Tileston Waterman, Student of American Colonial Architecture," *Winterthur Portfolio* 20 (1985): 143.

48. Antoinette Forrester Downing, *Early Homes of Rhode Island* (Richmond: Garrett and Massie, 1937); Frary, *Early Homes of Ohio*.

49. Joan Draper, "The Ecole des Beaux-Arts and the Architectural Profession in the United States: The Case of John Galen Howard," in *The Architect: Chapters in the History of the Profession*, ed. Spiro Kostof (New York: Oxford University Press, 1977), p. 211; Albert Simons and Samuel Lapham, Jr., eds., *The Early Architecture of Charleston* (New York: American Institute of Architects, 1927; 2d ed., Columbia: University of South Carolina Press, 1970), p. 5.

50. Draper, "Ecole des Beaux-Arts," p. 232; Weatherhead, *History of Collegiate Education*, p. 163.

51. Biographical information from the sketches in Mark Alan Hewitt, *The Architect and the American Country House 1890–1940* (New Haven: Yale University Press, 1990), pp. 267–68, 271–72.

52. David Ward, *Cities and Immigrants: A Geography of Change in Nineteenth Century America* (New York: Oxford University Press, 1971), p. 41; Blake McKelvey, *American Urbanization: A Comparative History* (Glenview, Ill.: Scott, Foresman, 1973), p. 77.

53. Sam Bass Warner, Jr., *The Urban Wilderness: A History of the American City* (New York: Harper and Row, 1972), pp. 98–99; Margaret Byington, *Homestead: The Households of a Mill Town* (New York: Russell Sage Foundation, 1910; rpt. Pittsburgh: University Center for International Studies, University of Pittsburgh, 1974), p. 3; Zane L. Miller and Patricia M. Melvin, *The Urbanization of Modern America: A Brief History* (2d ed. San Diego: Harcourt Brace Jovanovich, 1987), p. 189.

54. Toker, *Pittsburgh*, p. 236; McKelvey, *American Urbanization*, p. 77; Miller and Melvin, *Urbanization of Modern America*, p. 189.

55. McKee, "Charles Morse Stotz," p. 11; Kidney, *Landmark Architecture*, pp. 82–83. Comments here and elsewhere on the Edward Stotz firm's commissions are

based on a job list kindly supplied by MacLachlan, Cornelius and Filoni, the successor firm.

56. Charles M. Stotz, "Old Houses and Odd Corners," *Pittsburgh Record,* April/May 1932; Stotz, "Mont-Saint-Michel," *Architectural Forum* 53 no. 1 (1930): 91–94; "Plantation Plenty: the Pittsburgh Architects' Pilgrimage to the Manchester House, West Middletown, Pa.," *Charette* 8, no. 7 (1928): 3–4; Stotz, "What Price Brownsville?" *Charette* 9, no. 8 (1929): 1–5; Stotz, "The Harmonites," *Charette* 10, no. 6 (1930): 7–9.

57. "Report of Committee on Preservation of Historic Monuments and Sites, 1906–1937," folder, CMSPW, ser. V, box 20, folder 11, reports of October 30, 1914; October 27, 1915; January 18, 1921; 1927 (no specific date); Stotz, draft introduction, p. 3.

58. Stotz, draft introduction, p. 2. In the published version, Stotz changed the text to read "dividends that may be measured in both material and spiritual values" (p. 280).

59. Architects' Emergency Committee, *Great Georgian Houses of America* (New York: Editorial Committee of the Great Georgian Houses of America for the benefit of the Architects' Emergency Committee, 1933, 1937; rpt. New York: Dover, 1970), 2:8; Hosmer, *Preservation Comes of Age,* p. 1053; Charles E. Peterson, "The Historic American Buildings Survey: Its Beginnings," in *Historic America,* ed. Peatross, pp. 7–21; Wilson, "Survey in Louisiana," pp. 23–24; "Historic American Buildings Survey" folder, CMSPW, ser. V, box 20, folder 13.

60. Rody Patterson, "First Annual Draft Report," January 16, 1934, "Report of Committee on Preservation of Historic Monuments and Sites" folder, CMSPW. The organizers of the Architects' Emergency Committee hired any willing architectural draftsmen and trained those with no experience in making measured drawings.

61. Foreword to Rexford Newcomb, *Old Kentucky Architecture: Colonial, Federal, Greek Revival, Gothic, and Other Types Erected Prior to the War Between the States,* 3d ser. (New York: William Helburn, 1940; rpt. New York: Bonanza books, n.d.); Stotz, draft introduction, pp. 7–8.

62. A second Buhl Foundation grant of $10,000 provided for preparation of the manuscript and an initial print run of *The Early Architecture of Western Pennsylvania.*

63. Charles M. Stotz, announcement of the Western Pennsylvania Architectural Survey [WPAS], a project of the Pittsburgh chapter—American Institute of Architects, 1932, CMSPS, p. 1; Stotz, draft introduction, p. 8; "Information Blank," CMSPW; WPAS follow-up letter form, CMSPW.

64. WPAS follow-up letter form, CMSPW; Stotz to Alice Manchester, Avella, Pa., April 8, 1935; Stotz to John R. Chislett, Pittsburgh, June 28, 1935, both in CMSPW, ser. II, box 1, folder 2.

65. Survey compilation form, CMSPW; Stotz, draft introduction, pp. 10–11.

66. Stotz to Miss E. L. Newbold, Irvine, Pa., January 8, 1935, CMSPW, ser. II, box 1, folder 2.

67. Stotz, draft introduction, p. 14.

68. Ibid., pp. 12, 14–15; Patterson, "First Annual Draft Report," p. 5.

69. Karl George, Baden, Pa., to WPAS, February 4,

1935, WPAS manuscript file and supplement, Carnegie Library of Pittsburgh [CLP]; Stotz to George, February 6, 1935, CMSPW, ser. II, box 1, folder 2.

70. Stotz, draft introduction, p. 20; Celli interview. Stotz said there were thirty draftsmen, but only twenty-eight signed the existing drawings. In addition to those whose work appears in *EAWP,* there are unpublished drawings by Lamont H. Button, T. R. Hinckley, J. F. McWilliams, Jr., Elmer B. Milligan, and J. Vernon Wilson.

71. Celli interview; "Instructions for Draughtsmen Working on Measured Drawings for the Western Pennsylvania Architectural Survey," CMSPW; Stotz, draft introduction, pp. 20–22.

72. The plates not included in *EAWP* depicted Burke's building and the Church house, both in Pittsburgh; the Muse house, Versailles; the Ferry house, near Sharpsburg; the Armstrong County courthouse and the McCartney house, both in Kittanning; the Barclay office and the Bedford County courthouse, both in Bedford; the Baker house, Altoona; the Passavant house, Zelienople; and a church doorway and headstone at Harmony. There was also an additional drawing of the Way house, Sewickley. All the original drawings are contained in two large volumes in CLP, which also holds the rest of the WPAS materials except for drafts of the manuscript and ephemera contained in CMSPW.

73. Banister Fletcher and Banister F. Fletcher, *A History of Architecture on the Comparative Method for the Student, Craftsman and Amateur,* 6th ed. (London: B. T. Batsford, 1921), p. iii; *EAWP,* p. 15. Banister Fletcher's tree is also illustrated and discussed by Alan Gowans in *Styles and Types of North American Architecture: Social Function and Cultural Expression* (New York: Harper Collins, 1992), p. x.

74. Fiske Kimball, *Domestic Architecture of the American Colonies and of the Early Republic* (New York: Charles Scribner's Sons, 1922; rpt. New York: Dover, 1966), p. 141. On Kimball's importance to early American architectural history, see Upton, "Outside the Academy," pp. 205–06; Lauren Weiss Bricker, "The Writings of Fiske Kimball: A Synthesis of Architectural History and Practice," in *The Architectural Historian in America,* ed. Elisabeth Blair MacDougall (Washington: National Gallery of Art, 1990), pp. 216–18, 222–23.

75. Kimball, *Domestic Architecture,* p. 141.

76. Upton, "Outside the Academy," pp. 200–01.

77. Stotz, announcement of the Western Pennsylvania Architectural Survey; Upton, "Outside the Academy," p. 201.

78. Michel Chevalier, *Society, Manners, and Politics in America: Letters on North America* [1836], ed. John William Ward (New York: Doubleday Anchor, 1961), p. 168; Everard M. Upjohn, review, *Art Bulletin* 22 (1940): 107–08.

79. Fred B. Kniffen and Henry Glassie, "Building in Wood in the Eastern United States: A Time-Place Perspective," in *Common Places: Readings in American Vernacular Architecture,* ed. Dell Upton and John Michael Vlach (Athens: University of Georgia Press, 1986), pp. 159–81; Glassie, "The Types of the Southern Mountain Cabin," in Jan H. Brunvand, *The Study of American*

Folklore: An Introduction, 3d ed. (New York: Norton, 1986), pp. 529–62.

80. CMSPW, ser. V, box 19, folder 1; Sigurd Erixon, "The North-European Technique of Corner Timbering," *Folkliv* 1 (1937): 13–60.

81. Patterson, "First Draft Annual Report," p. 7.

82. Charles Morse Stotz, draft preface, *EAWP*, CMSPW, ser. V, box 19, folder 1.

83. Chevalier, *Society, Manners, and Politics*, p. 166; Muriel Earley Sheppard, *Cloud by Day: The Story of Coal and Coke and People* (Chapel Hill: University of North Carolina Press, 1947; rpt. Pittsburgh: University of Pittsburgh Press, 1991), pp. 1, 30–32; Stotz, draft introduction, p. 8; *EAWP*, p. 270.

84. Henry Glassie, *Pattern in the Material Folk Culture of the Eastern United States* (Philadelphia: University of Pennsylvania Press, 1968), pp. 49, 54–55.

85. Fiske Kimball to Stotz, January 4, 1936[1937], CMSPS.

86. HABS annual report, January 1935; Stotz to John P. O'Neill, National Park Service, January 17, 1935[6?]; Stotz to O'Neill, April 11, 1936, all in CMSPW, ser. V, box 20, folder 13; Peterson, "Historic American Buildings Survey,"

p. 8. Stotz's resignation letter to O'Neill is dated January 1935 but internal evidence suggest that this might be a typo.

87. MacLachlan, Cornelius, and Filoni, *In Detail*, p. 13; J. H. Jansen, Cleveland, to Stotz, February 27, 1937, CMSPS.

88. Charles Morse Stotz, "Threshold of the Golden Kingdom: the Village of Economy and Its Restoration," *Winterthur Portfolio* 8 (1973): 133–69; Stotz, "The Reconstruction of Fort Ligonier: The Anatomy of a Frontier Fort," *Bulletin of the Association for Preservation Technology* 6, no. 4 (1974); Stotz, *Outposts of the War for Empire: The French and the English in Western Pennsylvania: Their Armies, Their Forts, Their People, 1749–1764* (Pittsburgh: University of Pittsburgh Press/Historical Society of Western Pennsylvania, 1985).

89. Stotz, "Early Architecture of Western Pennsylvania," p. 239; John Golightly, "Charles Morse Stotz, Renowned Architect," *Pittsburgh Post-Gazette* obituary [1985], CLP artist files.

90. Stotz to Lawrence Wolfe, Pittsburgh, September 22, 1965, CMSPS.

NOTE ON THE 1995 EDITION

A guiding principle for this reprint of the 1936 edition of *The Early Architecture of Western Pennsylvania* by Charles Morse Stotz has been to supplement the original edition but not to alter the existing book. The most difficult and important task was to reclaim and preserve the book's handsome photographs. In addition to being remarkable records of structures and architectural details of irreplaceable value (many of them now gone), the photographic illustrations are often works of high technical skill and superb artistry in their own right.

This volume is a tribute to the efforts of Charles Morse Stotz as photographer and also to Luke Swank, photographic coordinator of the survey. In a two-year endeavor that required "over 5,000 miles of travel in almost every township of the 27 counties [of western Pennsylvania]," Stotz was amazed by the abundance of old buildings to be registered, most never before recorded. He and his colleagues plotted each structure that interested them on a geodetic survey map, photographed the more important buildings with a field camera, and collected facts about its owner, his origin, the builder, and other details.

In Stotz's words (responding to questions by Charles Hosmer in 1975), "Since there were many buildings in this vast area and we could not return later to photograph, it was vitally important to make acceptable pictures in the field. I received invaluable aid in the use of the field camera from Luke Swank, a remarkable local photographer who later became known nationally for his work in this field, especially in *Life* magazine. After the survey was well along, I commissioned Luke to photograph the best of the buildings. His many negatives and the some 1,500 or so that I made in the field, are included in the archives of the Western Pennsylvania Architectural Survey in the Carnegie Library of Pittsburgh."

To provide prints that were as faithful as possible to the first edition of Stotz's book, it was essential to return to the original negatives, housed for many years in the Carnegie Library's Western Pennsylvania Architectural Survey archives. The University of Pittsburgh's Center for Instructional Resources accepted the project

with enthusiasm—enthusiasm tempered by awe at the size of the project and an awareness of the difficulty of working with negatives that were almost sixty years old and made on very unstable, potentially dangerous nitrate film stock.

According to Jim Burke, of the Center for Instructional Resources, a prime incentive for reprinting *The Early Architecture of Western Pennsylvania* was to generate new high-quality prints for reproduction.* It took 280 hours, over a six-month period, to make the almost four hundred prints. Approximately 1,500 sheets of photographic paper were used to tease the maximum amount of detail and clarity from the negatives. Some printed easily on the first or second try. Others required considerable effort and many attempts before a satisfactory print emerged.

Complicating somewhat the task of printing was the variety of film sizes used to compile the architectural inventory. The most popular size was $2\frac{1}{5} \times 3\frac{1}{5}$ inches, with a total of 161 negatives. An almost equal number, 160, were of the 5×7 format. Also represented were the $3\frac{1}{2} \times 5$ format (41), 4×5 format (2), $2\frac{3}{4} \times 1\frac{3}{4}$ format (1) and—remarkably, one negative of 35 millimeters. The 35 millimeter negative dates from the earliest days of small-camera photography, when the format was held in low regard, particularly by photographers trying to resolve fine detail.

Of all the negatives, those in the 5×7 format were of the highest technical quality. (Possibly Luke Swank took all of these photographs.) The exposures of the negatives were consistently good, as was the composition and framing. They were certainly the easiest to print. That Luke Swank exposed these large-format negatives is evident in the quality of the work. The 5×7 negatives were contact-printed in order to obtain the highest degree of sharpness and resolution.

All of the smaller-format negatives were enlarged and cropped to match the size and composition of the images published in the 1936 edition. Sometimes the negatives were cropmarked with

---

*The following paragraphs are based on a report from Jim Burke of the University of Pittsburgh Center for Instructional Resources, who worked with the original negatives.

xli

grease pencil by the original editor, but in all cases the first edition was consulted to assure correct cropping.

An intriguing kind of detective work showed that some of the photographs in the 1936 edition were altered from their original state. Comparing the published photos with their negatives often revealed extensive masking and retouching to hide unwanted later additions to a structure or a landscape, or a marred architectural detail. For example, the negative for "House on Canal Street, Sharpsburg" (A1 150a) includes large industrial or commercial structures erected behind the house in more recent times. These buildings had been masked out of the photo, giving the illusion of empty sky behind the house. Negative no. C5-37g, "Living Room Mantel of the White House," shows extensive masking to hide changes in the fireplace and decorative additions that do not conform to the classic design of the mantel. In a less dramatic attempt to eliminate modern intrusions, "The Johnson Tavern near Mercer" (M2-24e) shows a small hand-lettered sign nailed to a tree in the foreground directing travelers to a swimming hole. In the reproduction this sign had vanished. The statue of George Washington at the Washington County Courthouse, photographed with anachronistic telephone poles in the background, was retouched for publication. Offending house numbers, utility connections, and commercial advertisements had also been removed. These represent only a few of the attempts to roll back the effects of time and lapses of taste on architectural purity.

A major concern in this undertaking was to protect these delicate negatives and to forestall possible problems in the attempt to print them afresh. All of the negatives were made on a cellulose nitrate-based film stock. Material of this type goes through predictable stages of deterioration. This process, which inevitably ends in the destruction of the negative, can be retarded by proper handling. The inventory negatives were kept at a cool temperature, segregated from other photographic materials, to prevent possible contamination from gases produced by the decaying nitrate. But these were unnecessary precautions, because only a few negatives showed more than a slight discoloration. A few more showed stains and "envelope marks" from improper storage in the early years of their existence, but there was no significant nitrate deterioration.

Major problems, however, were testimony to the inexperience of the photographers who produced most of the medium-format negatives, some of which were in deplorable condition. Almost any photographic error that can be imagined was inflicted on these important negatives. Most were caused by simple carelessness in handling—fingerprints were found on most. Some negatives were water-marked, others marred by stray hairs or dust particles that were not removed from the film before exposure, and some exhibited all of these defects.

Problems were not limited to the effects of carelessness in the darkroom; others were created by bad camera handling in the field. Many negatives were badly exposed, resulting in prints without enough contrast and missing significant detail in shadows or highlights. Some suffered simply from having been taken at the wrong time of day—so that areas of no architectural significance were brightly illuminated, while important details were muted or lost in deep shadow. The effects of these problems were minimized in the original volume by diligent retouching and less than perfect reproduction quality.

All involved in this project were conscious of the high quality of the original materials they were striving to preserve. It is testimony to the skill and hard work of its original creators that others have labored long and hard to bring *The Early Architecture of Western Pennsylvania* to life again.

INTRODUCTION

IT is just thirty years since the publication of *The Early Architecture of Western Pennsylvania*. Shortly after the sale of the original edition of 1,000 numbered copies, 500 additional copies were made available. The last of these was sold some years ago, and there has been a continuing demand for the work; the few copies that have appeared on the rare book market have brought a high price. Since this book remains the only work on the subject, it constitutes an invaluable handbook for the increasing number of persons interested in their architectural heritage.

The University of Pittsburgh Press has therefore reissued *The Early Architecture of Western Pennsylvania* essentially unchanged except for a new title—*The Architectural Heritage of Early Western Pennsylvania*. The original introduction by the late Fiske Kimball, a leading authority on early American architecture and the former Director of the Philadelphia Museum of Art, has been retained as the foreword. The author's original foreword, now called an introduction, has been rewritten and expanded to bring the story up to date. A list of buildings taken from the Historic American Buildings Survey has been added.

Before the start of the Western Pennsylvania Architectural Survey in 1932 the early architecture of the region was so little known, even in the architectural profession, that there was thought to be insufficient material to warrant an extended search or to justify publication. The few worthy buildings that were known had been given but cursory attention and the district had been almost totally ignored in general studies of early American architecture. As a result of the Survey, which involved approximately 6,000 miles of travel into almost every township of the twenty-seven counties (comprising some 22,000 square miles), a regional study was produced which, according to Fiske Kimball, was unsurpassed in "comprehensiveness, scholarly thoroughness and wealth of new material." The book thus supplied a chapter long missing in the story of early American architecture.

In choosing the terminal date of 1860 for the work of the Western Pennsylvania Architectural Survey it was felt that the mid-century marked the end of an era of early American architectural tradition. About the time of the Civil War the advent of the machine in the production of wood trim and the rapid development of mechanical facilities and scientific devices heralded the beginning of Victorian architecture and the ever-increasing cycle of "revivals." With the greater scarcity of pre-Civil War antiques on the market and the rapid disappearance of buildings of the Post-Colonial and Greek Revival styles, new virtues have been discovered in the Victorian architecture of the last half of the nineteenth century, its furniture and accessories. The earlier period has remained relatively neglected.

The Survey was supplemented by research in the military, economic and social history of the district. The effect of the development of transportation, the sources of immigration, the peculiar conditions of our early rural civilization, the influences of the varied local geographical features, and the distribution of building materials—these and other vital factors determining the origin and character of our early architecture were presented as an essential part of the story.

Almost no significant structures have come to light in the past thirty years that were not recorded in the Survey upon which this book was based. It is generally recognized that the work remains the definitive record of pre-1860 architecture in western Pennsylvania. Much supplemental material pertaining to the buildings discussed in the book, as well as numerous examples which could not be included in the limited space available, comprise the archives of the Western Pennsylvania Architectural Survey in the Pennsylvania Room of the Carnegie Library of Pittsburgh. Here any interested person may have access to the photographs, research material, and location of each recorded building as shown on government topographic maps. The reader is referred to "The Story of the Survey" on page 280 for a fuller description of the archives.

Stimulation of Local Interest

During the past thirty years *The Early Architecture of Western Pennsylvania* has helped to awaken in the public a lively interest in the early buildings of our district. The book has been widely cited in historical and architectural works, often with reproductions of illustrations and excerpts from the text, and photographs and drawings from the records have been included in national exhibitions of early American architecture.

The impact of the book was strengthened because, in the years immediately following publication, the writer gave numerous illustrated talks in various parts of western Pennsylvania. At that time it was apparent from the audience reaction that the extent and quality of our early architecture was little known to the general public, although in each community there were usually a few persons familiar with the lore of early buildings and historic sites in their local area. Through these talks many copies of the book were disseminated. People continually asked why their houses were not included or, if they were, why the buildings were not identified with the present owners. It was explained that only representative buildings in an unaltered condition could be incorporated into the limited space of the book. In all cases only the name of the original owner was used. But the most difficult question to answer was how the outstanding buildings of the district could be restored and preserved. Over the years, with increasing general interest in the few remaining major structures, problems of conservation have become critical, as will be discussed later.

Many persons and groups have availed themselves of the location map in the book and the detailed topographic maps in the archives of the Survey to visit buildings previously ignored because of their remote locations. Tours by various groups have spotlighted monuments of both historical and architectural significance. Among these organizations are the Historical Society of Western Pennsylvania and the recently organized Pittsburgh History and Landmarks Foundation. The latter organization has already done much to foster a concern for the architecture of the latter half of the nineteenth and the early twentieth centuries, as well as our pre-1860 architecture.

The Toll of the Years

Had the Western Pennsylvania Architectural Survey of 1932-35 been delayed but a few years the number of surviving structures to be recorded would have been drastically reduced, largely through the effects of the greatly increased use of the automobile. New mobility brought a flood of newcomers to once remote towns and farmlands; family dwellings that had seen little change through two or three generations no longer met new standards of comfort and arrangement. Buildings that had deteriorated through absentee landlordism were altered or replaced by the new owners who were often commuters from the city.

The unprecedented road building programs of the past thirty years have brought the widening and realignment of almost all country roads. Turnpikes and throughways have cut ruthlessly through farmland tracts and rural communities. The streets of once unspoiled villages and towns have been widened and lined with the commercial buildings of a modern age; trees have been removed and existing buildings altered or demolished. Stores and service stations occupy prominent corner sites once graced by stately homes. Shopping centers and used-car lots have cut great swathes through a once tranquil scene. It would be folly to attempt to deny the satisfaction of modern needs, but this inexorable process of expansion and change has all but eliminated the buildings, the communities, and even the landscape that many of us can well remember. Controlled planning and zoning have come too late; redevelopment projects of recent times have been responsible for eliminating many more worthy buildings than they have saved. In 1932 the originators of the Survey bowed to the inevitable in recognizing that since it was both visionary and impracticable to stem the tide of the future, the only effective means of preserving architecture lay between the covers of a book.

The publication schedule of the reissue did not provide time for a systematic survey to determine the present condition of all buildings in this book. Although most of the important examples remain today, the casualty list is high. The remarkable wooden bridges at Juniata Crossings and Everett (p. 192) were carried away in the 1936 flood. Ten Mile Creek Bridge in Waynesburg (p. 191) has been replaced. The stately Great Crossings Bridge at Somerfield (p. 188) now lies under the waters of a Federal flood-control reservoir. Most of the covered bridges have been demolished; rarely have modern highways been designed to bypass and save them. However, in recent years groups of citizens such as the Theodore Burr Covered Bridge Society have been formed to keep some of these picturesque structures.

The Shoenberger and Church Houses (p. 125) were lost in redevelopment projects. The fate of the Croghan House (p. 126) is mentioned below. Burke's Building (p. 273) still stands on Fourth Avenue but efforts to assure the preservation of this fine facade have been unavailing. The many buildings of the United States Allegheny Arsenal in Lawrenceville have been razed, with the exception of the Powder House and one or two other buildings in poor condition. The earlier loss of the first grist mill in the district, erected by order of George Washington on his property near the present Perryopolis (p. 274), was lamented in the original book. Of equal regret was the complete destruction of Hay's Mill in Somerset County (p. 276) which, at the time of the Survey, was intact with all its wooden machinery in good condition. This building was notable as the largest log structure in this and probably any other district.

Our Architectural Heritage

On the other side of the ledger we may be grateful for the survival of most of the important buildings depicted in *The Early Architecture of Western Pennsylvania*, although the future of many of these is uncertain. Almost all are in need of restoration, and only a handful have been assured of permanent preservation. Most of the important houses are occupied by descendants of the original family or by owners who recognize the intrinsic merit of the architecture and the importance of maintaining it without change.

Although the notable Croghan House (p. 126) no longer exists, the ballroom survives. In the late 1930's an architectural exhibition held by the Metropolitan Museum of Art included photographs and drawings of the house, then about to be demolished to make way for a housing development. Learning of this, the Museum sought to secure the ballroom interior for inclusion in its American Wing. In the meantime this distinguished interior had been acquired by the University of Pittsburgh and subsequently installed in the first floor of the Cathedral of Learning, where it may now be viewed.

The Administration Building at Washington and Jefferson College and Bentley Hall at Allegheny College are in active use and serve as mementos of the beginnings of these institutions. In both instances projects for restoration are under consideration.

Historical societies occupy the Le Moyne House in Washington, Pennsylvania, and the Baker House in Altoona. The Cashier's House, a part of the Old Customs House in Erie, is used by the local historical society and both buildings are currently being restored by the Pennsylvania Historical and Museum Commission. The courthouses and churches shown in the book remain in use. The Skew Arch and the Lemon Tavern, which served the railroad section of the Pennsylvania Canal, are still standing. The National Park Service has acquired a portion of the Portage Railroad in a program to preserve such remnants as the Skew Arch, the famous Staple Bend Tunnel and possibly one or more of the planes.

Conservation

All labors of love have their compensations. The field trips made in the conduct of the Survey were a rich experience. It was a frequent delight to come unexpectedly upon an unspoiled building in some remote location. Usually placed with an unerringly pleasant relation to the landscape, its material of local brick, stone or timber, softened by the patina of time and weather, the simple well-proportioned forms with tasteful fenestration—such buildings, however dilapidated, produced an effect that was often breathtakingly beautiful. This charm, imparted by the marks of use and weathering, is lost with the first efforts to repair or renovate and, indeed, can never be regained in a restoration. It seems impossible to reanimate or create a sense of occupancy to the empty shells of our early buildings, however beautiful. The restored building is apt to remain a souvenir or museum piece, and to comprehend the full breathing quality of the original requires the imagination of the viewer.

The skill of the museum worker can help counteract the static character of restorations. Furnishings and interpretive exhibits can do much to supplement the story, to make the past more meaningful. Also, much attention has been given to the creation of "living museums," occupied by persons dressed in the clothes of the past and performing the functions originally conducted in the rooms. Thus in the restoration of Old Economy in Ambridge, Beaver County, it is planned to recreate the old community by such devices as having a shoemaker at work, a full stock of merchandise in the store and a clerk in attendance, a printer using the old press and guides wearing authentic clothing of the Society.

However difficult they may be to execute successfully, conservation projects provide a sound understanding of our cultural heritage. The preservation of a few representative buildings conveys an understanding of the past unsurpassed by any other means. In addition to its historical associations, a fine piece of period design is in itself the consummate museum piece and, in the fullest sense, a work of art. This alone justifies conservation.

The Challenge of Restoration

The problems of conserving our early architecture raise many questions that are difficult to answer. If a building requires restoration alone and evidence can be found for the determination of moulding profiles, cornice details and the like, the development of adequate drawings to guide the workmen is relatively simple. However, if the building is only partially extant or is considerably altered from its original condition, reconstruction is called for. Under such circumstances there is no substitute for a sound knowledge of traditional style forms as well as training in the design of Georgian or Greek Revival architecture. This background is essential to make a competent set of drawings and specifications for conjectural restoration. It cannot be emphasized too strongly that a poor or unauthentic restoration is worse than none at all.

There is far too little activity in architectural restoration to justify a full practice. But there are few architects who would not cheerfully take time from their normal practice to engage in this fascinating work as a professional avocation, even though the usual program budget cannot provide adequate compensation for the demanding nature of design and research required. Architectural restoration is expensive and unpredictable. To begin with the structure must be minutely examined and measured, early drawings and photographs consulted, early building methods studied, and constant attendance on the work is necessary during construction. Modern heating, plumbing and electrical facilities must be introduced unobtrusively. During the removal of later work unanticipated information about the structure is often uncovered, which may entail extensive revision of completed drawings, and, for the owner, additional construction costs.

The uncertain nature of restoration design and construction makes it ill-suited to public bidding and yet this is the only procedure legally available to governmental institutions and authorities through which most restoration work is done. The work must be let to the lowest bidder regardless of competence in this highly specialized field. Since the work is done at a fixed cost, extra charges that are inevitably brought about during progress of the work are a serious problem. The careful architect may eliminate a large part of this hazard but, however painstaking his research before preparing drawings, he cannot anticipate the structural conditions that will be revealed during the demolition of modern elements of the structure.

Ideally, restoration work is done as at Williamsburg with a resident staff, fortified by the most meticulous preliminary site investigation, provided with thorough research studies and a construction schedule geared to continuous review of work in progress. This same method is now largely in effect in the reconstruction of Fort Ligonier. With the use of endowment funds work may be entrusted to those workmen most skilled not only in modern crafts but in the use of early tools and methods. Alas, this arrangement is rarely possible.

In any restoration or reconstruction project provision should be made for archaeological investigation of the site. Such a survey frequently establishes the true location of buildings through remnants of the foundation, and the artifacts recovered by archaeologists can provide incontrovertible evidence of building materials used as well as items desirable for museum display. The foundations of the ramparts of Fort Pitt were found intact in many areas, where they had not been destroyed by the foundations of modern buildings. The uncovering of the foundations of the Fort's Music Bastion led to a permanent display in Point State Park. The traces of the inner walls of Fort Ligonier were revealed by digging, and the underground powder magazine in the East Bastion, with stairs leading to it, was similarly discovered and made a striking feature of the reconstructed fort.

The factors of cost and time work against the inclusion of archaeological investigation in a restoration project, but it is essential to success. Indeed, faithful restoration involves a cost that invariably exceeds the most liberal estimate. And the continuing expense of maintenance for public visitation is so high that private sponsoring individuals or organizations are soon disillusioned, and the project is abandoned as impractical or the quality of the work is compromised by efforts to reduce cost. This kind of conservation is properly the function of a well-established private foundation or governmental agency, such as the Pennsylvania Historical and Museum Commission in Harrisburg. The current statewide Project 70 provides an opportunity for the Historical and Museum Commission to acquire historic sites and buildings in cooperation with the Department of Forests and Waters. (The latter department sponsored the restoration of McConnell's Mill on Slippery Rock Creek.) However, the initiative in seeking out and promoting such projects must come chiefly from private sources. Lacking evidence of public interest and promotion, legislators cannot be expected to vote for the appropriation of funds. It was precisely because of the lack of enthusiasm on the part of the taxpayers that Old Economy and Drake Park, two of the outstanding historic preservation projects in western Pennsylvania, progressed haltingly for some twenty-five years with sporadic and insufficient allocations from the legislature.

The initiative of an interested group of citizens in Washington, Pennsylvania, was solely responsible for the establishment of the project by which the Bradford House was restored. After purchase of the building and grounds by the Commonwealth, the necessary legislation was enacted to provide restoration funds. The work was done under the General State Authority, and the Historical and Museum Commission was designated as the restoration and using agency. Similarly, the Western Pennsylvania Conservancy acquired the ruins of the Old Stone House in Butler and the land about it, a group of citizens in the Butler area raised funds for the reconstruction, and, upon completion, the Commission accepted the responsibility of permanent maintenance and operation. It is increasingly evident that future acquisition and restoration of historic sites by the Commission will be based on similar matching of private and state funds.

Historical and Museum Commission Projects

In the past thirty years, the Commission has made significant contributions to the conservation of early architecture in western Pennsylvania. The architectural direction of this work has been entrusted to the firm of Charles M. and Edward Stotz, Jr., and the succeeding firm of Stotz, Hess and MacLachlan. The most extensive of these projects was the restoration of Old Economy in Ambridge, Beaver County.

Photographs and drawings of some of the buildings constructed by the Harmony Society between 1824 and 1830, together with a brief description of this unique organization, are accorded a separate chapter in the book (pp. 193-213). At the time the measured drawings were prepared for publication little research had been done in the extensive records of the Society or with its architecture. As a result numerous small errors in the drawings were discovered in the course of the restoration, which extended almost continuously from 1937 to 1965, involving twenty-five separate construction projects and the expenditure of nearly $700,000 by the Commonwealth. The state-owned property contains approximately seventeen buildings and an extensive garden, the pride of George Rapp, the Harmonist leader and founder of the Society.

Extensive alterations of both the interior and exterior architecture, made in the late nineteenth century, necessitated two years of pre-construction research in the details of the structures. Early photographs and travelers' accounts were examined, and the then-surviving residents, Mr. John S. Duss and Miss Mary Fruth, were interviewed. Shortly after completion of the drawings and specifications, Lawrence Thurman was appointed curator. He offered valuable assistance during the period of construction. Three of the structures were completely rebuilt, all cornices and roofs restored to their original condition, and countless changes made inside and out. Many modern restorations are by their nature conjectural in character, but Old Economy, because of the available wealth of early records and photos, may confidently be declared one of the most authentic. It is also one of the most complete surviving groups of homogeneous buildings of any early American community.

Drake Well Memorial Park, on Oil Creek some two miles below Titusville in Venango County, is the site of the first drilled oil well in the world and the birthplace of the oil industry. The crude derrick built hastily of scrap lumber from an adjacent saw mill by "Colonel" Edwin L. Drake in 1859, was reconstructed for the Commission in 1947 from photographs made in the early 1860's. This picturesque structure scarcely qualifies as an architectural monument, but it is recognized as the world-wide symbol of the beginning of the petroleum industry. True elevation drawings of the derrick were obtained by reversing the perspectives of the photographs. Each oddly shaped board was reproduced in its correct position. The total project, finished in 1965, includes a revision of the landscape and road system, an entrance control building and a modern museum building housing a notable collection of early tools, photographs and machines. The highlights of the museum exhibits are restorations of Drake's room and a typical cooper shop of the time. As at Economy, Ralph E. Griswold, landscape architect and an original member of the Survey Committee, served as consultant to the writer.

The Bradford House in Washington, Pennsylvania, did not appear in the book because at the time of the Survey the building had been so changed and disfigured by alterations of the nineteenth century as to be virtually unrecognizable as one of the distinguished houses of early western Pennsylvania. Built in 1787, this was the home of David Bradford, a citizen of means and good education who achieved notoriety through his leadership in the Whiskey Insurrection of 1794. A group of citizens of Washington, headed by General Edward Martin and James S. Lyon, successfully promoted the project to purchase and restore this building. Their architect was faced with a reconstruction project of major proportions. The north wall had to be completely replaced and new front and rear walls constructed where the building had been gutted for conversion to use as a furniture and, later, a grocery store. Conjectural period designs of ornate character were prepared for the fireplace walls of the living and dining room walls, which had been the subject of much praise before their removal and subsequent destruction. Most of the wood trim and elaborate stairway were rebuilt. In the additional space provided by the purchase and razing of the building north of the house, the landscape architects, Griswold, Winters and Swain, designed a garden of the period, restored the original well discovered during the work, and provided a generous parking area for visitors.

Point State Park in Pittsburgh includes a partial reconstruction of Fort Pitt, the largest fortification built by the British in America. The foundations of the Music Bastion are exposed to view and the Flag and Monongahela Bastions have been completely rebuilt. The latter bastion contains the Fort Pitt Museum in which may be seen a scale model of the complete fort in its original condition. Exhibits now in the course of design by the writer include full-size interior restorations of an early trader's cabin, a section of the casemate with an artillery laboratory, a typical barracks room, and the living room of an early Pittsburgh townhouse.

Additional restoration projects in progress for the Historical and Museum Commission and the Western Pennsylvania Conservancy include the Old Customs House or United States Bank of Pennsylvania together with its Cashier's House in Erie (p. 271), the Johnson Tavern near Mercer (p. 182), and Fort Franklin in Franklin, Pennsylvania. Other projects are under consideration in the current surge to save the remnants of our architectural heritage.

Preservation by Private Groups and Individuals

The Fort Ligonier Memorial Foundation, Inc., composed of citizens of Ligonier valley, has given generously of time in the creation and administra-

tion of a project to restore Fort Ligonier, built in 1758 during General John Forbes's campaign to take Fort Duquesne. Funds for this work have been provided by public subscription and gifts from the Richard King Mellon Foundation.

Fort Ligonier, like most eighteenth-century forts, was a special kind of architecture, containing log buildings similar in construction and appearance to those built by the early settlers. It included storehouses, barracks, and officers' quarters. Since all vestiges of the fort had disappeared by 1770, research was conducted by the writer in the military archives of this country and Europe. Contemporary drawings by military engineers provided information on the plan layout but no elevations beyond a section through the front of the fort. Much pertinent information was found in the Bouquet Papers, the principal body of military correspondence pertaining to Fort Ligonier; travelers' accounts; and a crude contemporary sketch by one of the commandants. Collections of military drawings of other eighteenth-century fortifications revealed general information from which details could be conjectured. Handbooks prepared for the use of army engineers in the field supplied information on various construction details.

Begun in 1947, construction on the inner fort, with its vertical palisade and horizontal log walls, has been completed and work on the storehouses, barracks, commandant's house and a portion of the outer retrenchment is under way. A noteworthy archaeological project, directed by Jacob L. Grimm of Ligonier, disclosed the accurate location of the fort walls, uncovered an underground powder magazine mentioned in the military records, and resulted in the recovery of thousands of artifacts, the most complete collection of the French and Indian War in existence. Selections from these artifacts are exhibited in a museum building, designed in eighteenth-century character. A special room in the building, re created in the manner of Sir John Ligonier's London townhouse, contains an original portrait of Ligonier by Sir Joshua Reynolds.

Another wing of the museum building was made of the extraordinary living room, once a part of the late eighteenth-century house built by General Arthur St. Clair several miles north of Ligonier. The room is a log structure faced with clapboards, contains an elaborate fireplace wall and ornate cornice, and is tastefully furnished in the period.

The Old Stone House reconstruction (near Butler on Route 8 at the junction with Route 173) preserves a record of this early tavern and its appurtenances. The picturesque ruins of the Old Stone House had stood for many years, the subject of numerous legends. In the heyday of the tavern, the Marquis de Lafayette stopped here on his triumphal tour of 1828 enroute from Pittsburgh to Erie. Portions of the handsome ashlar walls of dressed sandstone remained standing on the site, the stones of the other walls having fallen in confused piles. In the reconstruction each stone that remained in place was marked and replaced after disassembly and the construction of new foundations. Several early photographs provided guidance in the reconstruction plans. The original two-story porch, which had been filled-in with makeshift board walls to provide additional guest space in later days, was restored in the manner of the typical taverns of the time. This was a project of the Western Pennsylvania Conservancy. The Historical and Museum Commission will furnish and maintain the building.

Plans now in progress will expand this historic site into a group of early buildings to be known as the Stone House Center. The Center will include a typical bank barn, a country store, a replica of the octagonal frame school which once stood in the neighborhood, a farm house with such outlying buildings as a smokehouse, carriage house, and blacksmith shop. It will be operated as a demonstration of early life in the rural areas of Butler County.

It is proposed to reconstruct the Neal Cabin in Schenley Park, Pittsburgh (p. 38), the best preserved one-room log house in the district, a project sponsored by the Pittsburgh History and Landmarks Foundation.

It should be emphasized again that the most desirable way of conserving a building, its contents, and its functions is through continued use, provided the original architecture is maintained by intelligent repair and restoration. There is no substitute for occupancy by persons or organizations who fully appreciate the importance of preserving our architectural heirlooms. To name one example, the Manchester House is occupied by direct descendants of Isaac Manchester. The residence and the remarkable group of farm buildings about it remain intact with their original equipment, furnishings, implements and tools, thanks to the loving care of the late Manchester sisters. Necessary modern installations of heating, plumbing and electricity, as well as replacement of deteriorated

exterior woodwork, have been made with due consideration for this superb monument to gracious living in early western Pennsylvania. It is to be hoped that such an example will serve as an inspiration for others to join in the cause of preserving the few remaining early buildings of distinguished character.

The Archives of the Survey

As explained in "The Story of the Survey" (pp. 280-283), the archives of the Western Pennsylvania Architectural Survey, on which this book is based, are arranged for public use. It is important to note that this material includes not only the buildings shown in the book, with related data too extensive for inclusion, but also several hundred additional examples. The archives are located in the Pennsylvania Room of the Carnegie Library of Pittsburgh. Prints may be obtained at cost from the photographic negatives made in the course of the Survey and copies of any of the research data may also be obtained. The precise locations of all buildings recorded in the Survey are indicated on government topographic maps of Pennsylvania. It is gratifying to know that during the past thirty years these archives have been consulted with increasing frequency by the public. In response to a request in the original edition, the public has made some contributions of building records, early photographs and other data pertaining to district buildings erected before 1860. A renewed plea is made here for additional contributions. Early photographs, whether faded or torn, that show buildings before modern alterations were made are invaluable aids for restoration and may be worthy of publication.

The Pittsburgh History and Landmarks Foundation is currently engaged in a comprehensive survey of early buildings extant in Allegheny County with a view to preserving the most noteworthy. There is likewise a new survey of historic sites and buildings being undertaken by the Historical and Museum Commission with the Pennsylvania State Planning Board.

The Historic American Buildings Survey

Soon after the local Survey was completed, the Historic American Buildings Survey was begun as a government relief project. It was based on a triangular agreement between the Department of the Interior, the American Institute of Architects, and the Library of Congress, where the records are maintained and made available to the public. The

Historic American Buildings Survey had aims that were similar to those of the Western Pennsylvania Architectural Survey, but its methods of operation were different and it was not limited to buildings erected before 1860. The draftsman was required to show the building in its existing condition and the original condition was shown by supplemental drawings. The local survey had assembled all essential available information for each building; the Historic American Buildings Survey by its nature could not engage in such detailed research. Nevertheless, this nationwide project produced an important body of source material on our early architecture. The government survey was the means of providing drawings of buildings of secondary importance which had been recorded in the Western Pennsylvania Architectural Survey but had not been measured at the time of the Survey because of limitations of time and budget.

The Historic American Buildings Survey was in active operation locally from 1934 to 1937. In 1960 the project was revived by the Department of Architecture of the Carnegie Institute of Technology, in cooperation with the American Institute of Architects and the Library of Congress, as a required part of the curriculum. In this later program the emphasis is laid on buildings from the mid-nineteenth century to 1910.

Conclusion and Acknowledgments

The Western Pennsylvania Architectural Survey and subsequent publication of *The Early Architecture of Western Pennsylvania* was the work of many hands. First of all, acknowledgment is made of the suggestion by the late Mrs. E. N. (Penelope Redd) Jones that the writer petition the Buhl Foundation for a grant to defray the cost of the Survey and publication. The sympathetic reception by Dr. Charles F. Lewis, then Director of the Buhl Foundation, led to favorable action on the petition. Dr. Lewis followed the work with keen interest and, in recent years, as Director of the Western Pennsylvania Conservancy he has promoted not only the conservation of our historic buildings but also vast areas of countryside, the streams and forests which formed the setting of this architecture. Belated recognition must also be given for the contribution of Dr. C. V. Starrett during his tenure as Associate Director of the Buhl Foundation for reviewing the text of the original edition for stylistic revision.

Few pleasures of personal association could equal the experience of working with the members of the Pittsburgh Chapter of the American Institute of Architects in this labor of love. Small honoraria were paid the architects who measured and prepared drawings of selected examples for publication, and no one else except the secretary received compensation beyond minimum expenses. The enforced leisure of the great depression of the 1930's made available the expert assistance of our leading architects, who with devotion and wholehearted enthusiasm produced a group of measured drawings unsurpassed in any work on regional architecture. At no other period in modern architectural practice could such a contribution in time and talent have been possible.

Of the members of the Executive and Advisory Committees listed in "The Story of the Survey" there remain today only Robert W. Schmertz and Ralph E. Griswold, the two men most intimately associated with the writer from the inception of the project. It was largely through the many hikes and expeditions into the local countryside with Schmertz to sketch and explore unknown areas that the notion of making a permanent record was germinated. Griswold, known for his restoration of the Agora planting in Athens and other such projects in the United States and Europe, shared in this hobby of exploring our backyard. During the past thirty years he has served as landscape consultant to the writer in his role as architect for historical restoration in western Pennsylvania. The delicate spirit of the late Sidney H. Brown, an architect unusually sensitive to the subtleties of the Georgian and Greek Revival styles, was a continual refreshment during the exciting days of the Survey.

By an unanticipated and most fortunate circumstance news of the Survey came to the attention of the late Luke Swank, then living in Johnstown. Destined later to achieve national eminence in architectural photography, Swank came to Pittsburgh determined to participate in an activity so close to his heart. In addition to his appreciation for the fine pictures Swank made for the survey, the writer acknowledges gratitude for the training he received from Swank. This instruction proved invaluable as, by force of circumstances, most of the photographs for the survey and later publication had to be made during many field trips in which Swank could not engage.

The writer's constant companion and right arm throughout the entire project was the late Rody Patterson who served as secretary, maintaining all records and public contacts by correspondence and interviews in the field. He shared in the thrilling but wearing travel through thousands of miles in the varied countryside of western Pennsylvania, the tedious organization of accumulated research data, the notation of travel routes and building locations on topographic maps, the arrangement of drawings and photographs and the endless hours of page composition.

And, finally, a salute to the University of Pittsburgh Press for again making available this contribution by members of the architectural profession to their community.

CHARLES MORSE STOTZ
Pittsburgh, 1966

FOREWORD

LESS than a score of years ago it was still generally believed that no early architecture of merit was to be found west of the Alleghenies. Claude Bragdon, before 1900, had indeed drawn and written about the buildings of the Genesee Valley, but these were regarded rather as isolated exceptions which proved the rule, or as owing their interest less to their own merit than to his beautiful draughtsmanship. I well remember my own astonishment and delight in finding, just before the war, the endlessly varied adaptations of Greek types in the houses of Michigan, and even of southern Wisconsin. Meanwhile, Frary has done his wonderful work of photographing the wealth of old buildings in Ohio, going far back of the Greek influence. Others have ransacked Missouri and Indiana, Tennessee and Alabama, with striking results.

Many gaps have remained to be filled further east, in states where all interest has been concentrated on the older buildings of the seaboard. That has been largely true hitherto of Pennsylvania. The Western Pennsylvania Architectural Survey has now filled this gap, and filled it in an exemplary manner.

This is no mere book of photographs and drawings, as have been too many, with dates and names filled in by guesswork. Solid historical investigation has accompanied the recording of the form of surviving monuments. Geographic and economic factors have not been neglected. Local materials and their sources have been studied. The personalities concerned as craftsmen, builders, engineers, and architects have been sought out and distinguished.

Every phase of building is included, from the earliest surviving log houses to the eve of the Civil War; every type of building, from houses and churches, through banks, mills and arsenals, to barns and out-buildings, bridges, and even iron-furnaces.

Many of the houses illustrated are of extraordinary interest: the Meason House near Uniontown, with its remarkable forecourt and balanced accessories, the Manchester House near West Middletown, superb as a Post-Colonial survival, the magnificent Greek houses such as the Wilkins and Croghan houses in Pittsburgh or the Baker House in Altoona. Nor is there any lack of charming vernacular buildings such as the Neville House near Woodville, to cite one among many. Notable treasures, little appreciated hitherto, are the buildings of the Harmony Society at Harmony and Economy, which justify a special chapter.

In the United States no publication of official inventories of historic monuments, such as those of European countries—of the German states above all—has yet been attempted. Only just now is the Federal government beginning the compilation of a list of outstanding monuments and sites, which cannot include many of a local rather than a national significance. Private initiative has partly supplied the lack, by books dealing with the houses or churches of single states. None of these, however, has undertaken systematically, like this volume, to cover all the surviving buildings of a region. The Buhl Foundation, which supported the enterprise, and the men who have carried it to successful completion, are alike to be congratulated. In all the flood of recent books on the architecture of different states none surpasses this one in comprehensiveness, scholarly thoroughness, and wealth of new material.

FISKE KIMBALL
Philadelphia, 1936

THE EARLY ARCHITECTURE
OF WESTERN PENNSYLVANIA

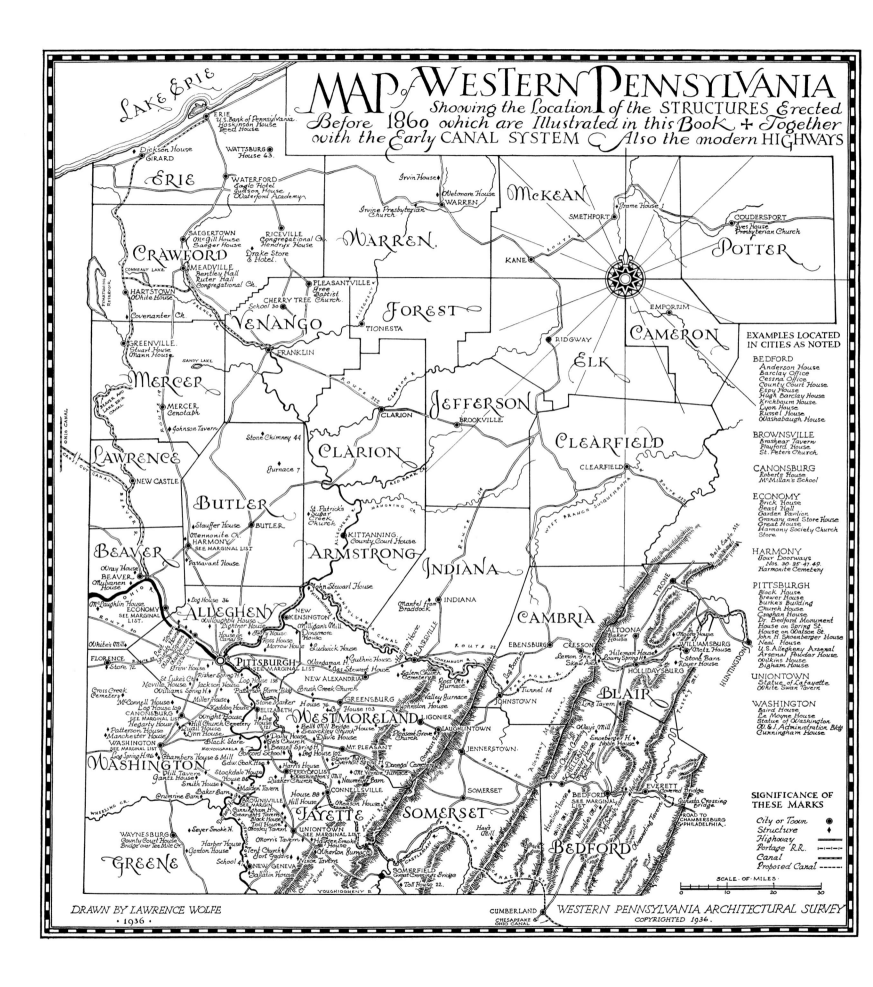

MAP of WESTERN PENNSYLVANIA

Showing the Location of the STRUCTURES Erected Before 1860 which are Illustrated in this Book, Together with the Early CANAL SYSTEM Also the modern HIGHWAYS

EXAMPLES LOCATED IN CITIES AS NOTED

BEDFORD
Anderson House
Barclay Office
Cessna Office
County Court House
Espy House
High Barclay House
Krichbaum House
Lyon House
Russel House
Washabaugh House

BROWNSVILLE
Brashear Tavern
Playford House
St. Peters Church

CANONSBURG
Roberts House
McMillan's School

ECONOMY
Brick House
Feast Hall
Garden Pavilion
Granary and Store House
Great House
Harmony Society Church
Store

HARMONY
Four Doorways
Nos. 30. 35. 47. 49.
Harmonite Cemetery

PITTSBURGH
Block House
Brewer House
Burke's Building
Church House
Croghan House
Dr. Bedford Monument
House on Spring St.
House on Watson St.
John H. Shoenberger House
Neal House
U.S. Allegheny Arsenal
Arsenal Powder House
Oulkins House
Bigham House

UNIONTOWN
Statue of Lafayette
White Swan Tavern

WASHINGTON
Baird House
Le Moyne House
Statue of Washington
Oil & J. Administration Bldg.
Cunningham House

SIGNIFICANCE OF THESE MARKS

City or Town
Structure
Highway
Portage R.R.
Canal
Proposed Canal

SCALE OF MILES

DRAWN BY LAWRENCE WOLFE
• 1936 •

WESTERN PENNSYLVANIA ARCHITECTURAL SURVEY
COPYRIGHTED 1936.

PART ONE

—

Chapter I

THE BACKGROUND OF THE EARLY ARCHITECTURE

SOME years before the middle of the eighteenth century the first white trader drove his pack horses through the forests about the headwaters of the Ohio and built the first rude cabin in western Pennsylvania. From this simple beginning architectural progress was slow and halting. The key position that this region held between the Appalachian frontier and the great central river basin of North America made it the highly prized objective in a series of wars that filled the latter half of the century with turmoil and confusion. The territory was successively claimed by France and England before it became a part of the newly created United States. The native Indian tribes, whose right to the lands involved was largely ignored, did not give up their hunting grounds until they had brought to the border long years of indecisive and harrowing conflict. The story of this period is filled with state disputes, internal dissension, and controversy over claims and grants. These wars and controversies, however dramatic and significant in the history of the young nation, retarded settlement and economic growth in the district and prevented any serious development in its architecture until almost the end of the eighteenth century.

Within this protracted pioneer period extending from 1750 to 1795, most of the buildings were of logs—even the fortresses built by the armies. Log construction was eminently adapted to the precarious life and limited resources of the settlers, whose background, character, and manner of settlement necessarily influenced the style of this primitive architecture.

Throughout the whole turbulent period, in spite of wars and governmental decrees against settlement, the settler was stubbornly taking personal and permanent possession of the land, blazing his property without authority, and establishing a "tomahawk claim" when he could get no better title. The Indians, who viewed the trader with suspicion

and frequently regarded the soldier and government agent with distrust, heard with consternation the sound of the frontiersman's axe and rifle echoing through their forests. Here were the actual destroyers and usurpers of the Indian's shelter and game. Here were men, and women, too, schooled to hardship and suffering, who knew the ways of the forest and forest warfare and who, in their deep-rooted desire for permanent home sites, could not understand the Indian's right to land that he did nothing to develop. In successive waves they advanced the frontier and entrenched themselves upon the land. Making fortresses of their homes and putting little faith in poorly trained frontier armies, they relied on their own vigilance and marksmanship for protection. As Theodore Roosevelt graphically described them, they were "a grim, stern people . . . swayed by gusts of stormy passion, the love of freedom rooted in their very hearts' core."

These settlers were preponderantly of English, Scotch, Irish, Scotch-Irish, and German origin. For the greater part refugees or children of refugees from poverty and persecution in the old country, they had first found homes in Virginia, Maryland, and Pennsylvania on the eastern slopes of the Appalachians. There they were schooled in a manner of wilderness living that stood them in good stead when, answering the call of their restless, adventurous spirits, they crossed the mountains to seek new homes in the western country. Travel was difficult and perilous. The two chief routes were the Nemacolin Trail, leading from the Potomac Valley across the southwestern corner of the district, and the Raystown Path, extending directly westward from Bedford over the Allegheny Plateau to the Forks of the Ohio. The first route was, in part, the course of Braddock's army; the latter, of the Forbes expedition. These roads, even where improved by military forces, were nothing more than narrow paths cut through the forest; yet over them passed the constantly increasing stream of immigrants by whom southwestern Pennsylvania was largely settled between 1769 and 1774. This settlement was confined to the area south of the Ohio and Kiskiminetas rivers, where the greatest number of the old buildings are to be found today. Settlement in the northwestern area of the district was not possible until after the Indian wars, toward the close of the century.

To many adventurous settlers, however, this district was merely the jumping-off place for Ohio, Kentucky, and the receding frontier of the Middle West. In this movement the Ohio River was the great highway to the interior, carrying eighteen thousand pioneers from Pittsburgh in a single year (1788). Travel by river, though more comfortable, was little safer than by road; in fact, as late as 1793 the Pittsburgh-Cincinnati packets were protected by high wooden bulwarks and carried cannon and small arms.

The Architecture of the Forest

Forsaking the main traveled routes of transportation by which they had entered the district, the first settlers chose locations in the wilderness that, however remote, provided the few necessities of their simple life. Desirable building sites provided good spring water, protection against prevailing winds, and land suitable for cultivation and pasturage. After selection of a site, the first act of the settlers was to fell trees. In destroying the forest they deprived their Indian enemies of cover and obtained the timbers with which to build not only their log houses and barns but also, as time went on, various structures of log in which to grind their flour, hold their courts, teach their children, and conduct their simple church services. Such buildings were rapidly constructed and as quickly replaced after their frequent destruction by Indians or by fire. The development of villages, in the true sense of the word, did not begin until late in the period. The first communities consisted of adjoining farm sites about a centrally located blockhouse surrounded by a stockade—a common refuge in time of Indian raids. The few towns that did exist in the district by reason of trade or military necessity were small; in 1790 Pittsburgh had only 376 inhabitants, and by 1796 it contained but 150 houses, most of them of log.

Log architecture made its first appearance in America on the Delaware Valley frontier. According to Fiske Kimball, houses of horizontal logs were

not used by the first colonists; they were, in fact, unknown in Europe except among the Finns and Swedes, who probably brought the form to America, where it appeared in the Delaware Valley settlements. From there the use of this type of construction spread to the eastern Appalachian frontier, where it became common; the settler in western Pennsylvania, therefore, had acquired a previous training in the technique of forest architecture. There was remarkably little variation in log buildings throughout the long period of time and the variety of districts in which they were used. Masonry construction was such a rarity in western Pennsylvania in the early frontier days that journeys to the East held new and thrilling sights for the eyes of the western-born pioneer. As a child, the historian, Doddridge, saw his first stone house—an inn at Bedford—and later wrote, "It was plastered in the inside, both as to the walls and ceiling. . . . I was struck with astonishment . . . I had no idea that there was any house in the world which was not built of logs; but here I looked round the house and could see no logs, and above I could see no joists; whether such a thing had been made by the hands of man, or had grown so of itself, I could not conjecture. I had not the courage to inquire anything about it."

The erection of log buildings continued long after the close of the pioneer period and even well into the middle of the nineteenth century; they remained the simple, direct, and economical answer to living needs in isolated districts abounding in timber. Since many of the most interesting of these log structures still exist, we can with but little imagination reconstruct the architectural background of the pioneer.

Although it may be questionable to speak of log architecture as a style or, in fact, to consider it as architecture at all, its significance as the shelter of the frontiersmen who conquered the wilderness must, nevertheless, be recognized. In this picturesque log architecture is told the story of a people who bequeathed a tradition of restraint and simplicity in the craft of building to their descendants, upon whom fell the task of creating a permanent civilization in a district that but fifty years before had been a hunting ground for the Indians.

The Western Gateway

During the period of expansion between 1795 and 1860 commerce and industry in western Pennsylvania advanced far beyond the dreams of its pioneer founders. Ceaseless change and movement characterized the young nation's expansion into western Pennsylvania and beyond that region into the vast western country finally made desirable by the establishment of peace and the possibility of stable conditions of life. These newcomers from the eastern states were joined by great numbers of Europeans, among whom were increasing proportions of Germans, Scotch, Welsh, and South Irish. James Truslow Adams states that "by 1800 there were a million Americans settled in the territory which the British government had tried to close to pioneers by the Proclamation of 1763. . . . By 1820 there were two and a half million . . . By 1830 one third of the American people were 'men of the Western Waters,' as they liked to call themselves, numbering three and a half million."

The Rivers

Throughout this period activity centered more and more in the southwestern district about the head of the Ohio, that great natural highway system whose providential existence made western Pennsylvania the Gateway to the West. The river was not only a logical route for settlers seeking homes in the rich country that bordered its thousand miles between Pittsburgh and the Mississippi, but likewise provided the commerce that furnished industry in western Pennsylvania with a large and steadily growing market in the vast inland basin. Through New Orleans exports from western Pennsylvania reached American and European seaports, frequently by seagoing vessels built and launched in Pittsburgh, where boat-building was an important industry from the first. Because of the time and labor required to work the boats upstream, river traffic was largely "one-way" until steam navigation became general on inland waters after 1817. Then there commenced a flourishing interchange of commerce between East and West, which gave occupation to thousands, built up industries, and created private fortunes that contributed to the more pretentious architectural development in the district during the period.

The Ohio's main tributaries, the Allegheny and the Monongahela, extended north and south beyond the borders of western Pennsylvania, but no navigable branch extended to the east. The establishment of adequate routes of transportation between these rivers and the eastern sources of immigration and commerce beyond the wide mountain system was the chief problem that remained to challenge the ingenuity and resources of the people in the first half of the nineteenth century.

The stories of transportation and architecture are inextricably interwoven. The significance of transportation to architecture was not merely that it stimulated the acquisition of wealth with which to build but that it brought into the district the people who required the buildings, the artisans to build them, and some of the materials required in their construction. Most important of all, improved travel facilities established an increasingly closer contact with the cultural sources east of the Alleghenies. These routes of transportation, like veins and arteries stretching throughout the district, largely determined the distribution of the buildings.

Turnpikes and Canals

The first dirt roads, constructed between 1790 and 1805, were rough and dusty when dry and almost impassable when wet; wagon travel was slow and costly. With the introduction of the hard-surfaced pike an era of road-building occurred, between 1818 and 1827, during which the principal land routes followed today were established. These routes became the arteries for a traffic of enormous volume; the National Pike, according to Thomas B. Searight, "looked more like the leading avenue of a great city than a road through rural districts." It is said that in the year 1817 twelve thousand wagons passed over the mountains from Philadelphia and Baltimore. With the settlement of Ohio, Indiana, Illinois, and Kentucky, great droves of cattle, mules, sheep, horses, hogs, and turkeys raised clouds of dust as they slowly made their way to the eastern markets. The Conestoga wagons, with their broad-rimmed wheels and graceful canvas arches, traveled in such numbers that they defined the rise and fall of the pike as far as the eye could see. Intermingling with this traffic was that early marvel of rapid transportation, the four-horse stagecoach, sometimes in strings of twenty at a time.

The pikes and their many branches brought prosperity to remote sections; along their courses sprang up stage houses, wagon stands, and drovers' taverns. Many immigrants were diverted from their original western destinations to establish themselves on the farmlands made accessible by these roads or to engage in the business created by them. The story of the building of these roads, with their handsomely arched bridges of stone and picturesque covered bridges of wood, their taverns and tollhouses, some of which are presented in this book, is a fascinating subject in itself. On the map in the back of this book are shown the principal modern highways, whose routes closely approximate the earlier paths and roads. The locations of the buildings illustrating this book are also indicated. The importance of these roads in accounting for the distribution of buildings is obvious; for, even were their routes not shown on the map, the clustering of the examples recorded would define the course of the roads. Most of the towns nourished by the highways, such as Washington, Uniontown, Greensburg, Bedford, Butler, and Erie, remain today the most important centers in their respective regions. The influence of the rivers is apparent in such towns as Brownsville, where great numbers of settlers transferred from wagon to boat. This map also shows the canals constructed in the region between 1826 and 1850 as a part of the thousand-mile canal system that once existed in Pennsylvania. The projected extension of the Chesapeake and Ohio Canal is also indicated.

The roads suffered comparatively little from the competition of the canals, for so steadily did traffic increase that all available means of transportation became taxed to their limit. Though the canals could not be extended so flexibly as the roads, they effected great reductions in freight rates and made passenger travel comparatively rapid and comfortable. The Pennsylvania Canal, with its remarkable Portage Railway over the Allegheny Ridge, connected Philadelphia and Pittsburgh. Its primary object was to compete with the earlier Erie Canal by which New York was threatening Philadelphia's supremacy in trade with the West. To complete communication with the Great Lakes and the Western Reserve, the Beaver and Lake Erie Canal was built from Beaver to Erie, with a branch known as the "Cross-Cut Canal" extending from Mahoningtown westward to Akron, where it joined the Ohio Canal. George Washington was chief promoter and first president of the Potomac Company, which planned a canal from the Chesapeake to Pittsburgh. Many years later, as the Chesapeake and Ohio Canal, it was completed to Cumberland, but plans to extend it to Pittsburgh were abandoned because of railway competition. On early maps of Pittsburgh, however, its projected course down the

Monongahela to the terminus of the Pennsylvania Canal on that river is shown in dotted line.

Railroads and Maturity

These canals opened up great areas of virgin country and, like the roads, brought prosperity to many towns. Along these tiny ribbons of water sprang up warehouses, taverns, and homes. Hollidaysburg changed overnight from a hamlet to an active inland port; Sharon, a sleepy crossroads in a neglected district, became in a few years a bustling town with a thriving iron industry. But the canals were not permitted to achieve their full destiny; for during the 1850's came the most revolutionary method of transportation that had yet been devised—the railroad. The costly canal system of the state became a dead loss to the taxpayer, and most of the canals were soon abandoned. The pikes, too, lost the bulk of their heavy traffic. On the new roads of steel, rapidly laid in all directions, passengers and goods could be moved in quantities and at speeds that overwhelmed all competition.

Throughout this half century, progress was measured by these increasingly mobile means of transport, which stimulated growth in cities at the expense of rural districts. Population steadily mounted in Pittsburgh and Allegheny County. Many of the smaller rural communities suffered an economic setback from which they have never recovered. Some of these, with their early buildings, are preserved today, little changed from the time when the pike and canal were in their heyday; whereas in the larger towns and cities continued growth has largely obliterated the early architecture.

As methods and routes of transportation were developed, industry and commerce in western Pennsylvania were continually accelerated. Iron furnaces, forges, and mills sent manufactured goods north, west, south, and, with the coming of canals and railroads, east. At the close of the period treated in this discussion, with the discovery of the undreamed-of potentialities of its natural resources in oil and gas, and with the fuller utilization of its coal deposits, western Pennsylvania stood on the threshold of the still greater industrial era that made it famous as the Workshop of the World.

Chapter II
THE ORIGIN AND DEVELOPMENT OF STYLES

THE history of architecture, like that of costume or language, is a story of successive transitions from one style into the next—an unbroken chain between ages and peoples. Even though the forms are modified to suit new conditions of life and environment, the architecture of each civilization betrays its origin. Just as Rome received its first architectural impetus from Greece, and as the Italians in the Renaissance received theirs from the ancient Romans, so did England in the eighteenth century receive its greatest stimulus from Italy. In turn, the art of building spread from England to America, where it was dominated by the English influence during the period before the Revolution and for many years thereafter in a lesser degree. This train of influence through the centuries may be compared to a tree of which the roots are represented by Greece, the trunk by Rome, a main branch by the Italian Renaissance, a lesser limb of that branch by England, and a terminating offshoot by America. A consideration of style development in England is, therefore, essential to an appreciation of the architecture of early America and of the phase of it that occurred in western Pennsylvania before 1860.

The Ancestry of American Styles

When North America was first settled, domestic architecture in England was still dominated by medieval influences, but toward the close of the seventeenth century the beginnings of the Renaissance style appeared. This style, which had its birth in Italy, had been introduced into France before its appearance in England. Many of the principal structures of France had been designed by imported Italian architects familiar with the forms of ancient Rome and with their adaptation in the then modern manner.

In England the principles set forth by the Italian, Palladio, later became the rules for building and the basis for the Georgian style, named for the reigning Georges. Abstract design expressed in academic forms acquired equal importance with functional use. So great was the popularity of this new style that Englishmen who aspired to prominence in archi-

tectural practice often supplemented their studies by visits to Italy, where they made original studies of their own based not only upon the buildings of the Renaissance but also upon antique remains. The brothers Adam investigated the ruins of the Roman colony of Spalatro on the Adriatic before they developed the particular phase of the late English Renaissance, or Georgian, style that bears their name. Toward the end of the eighteenth century appeared that expression of the Classic Revival style which sought to return to a more faithful rendition of the monumental plans and forms of ancient Rome.

In the Classic Revival this first, or Roman, phase was followed by a new mode, which sought to achieve a literal adaptation of Greek architecture. Though slow to catch the public fancy in England, the Greek Revival was destined to have far-reaching significance in America. The seed of this style was planted in England in 1762, many years before it was generally accepted, when James Stuart and Nicholas Revett published the results of their archeological studies in *The Antiquities of Athens*.

The same Romanticism that had explored the family tree of architecture all the way back to its roots in Greece turned next to the Gothic style. The height of the Gothic Revival came just before the middle of the nineteenth century in the works of the Englishman, Pugin, and other able champions of the Gothic manner. It was the concluding episode of the traditional revivals and the forerunner of the dark age of confusion that descended upon architecture throughout the western world after the middle of the nineteenth century.

Styles in America

The development of styles in England was reflected in the architecture of her colonies in America, altered only to suit differences in climate, materials, and methods of working. The half-timbered houses of seventeenth-century England had their counterparts in the weatherboarded frame houses of the New England colonies. A late example of these, and the best known, is the House of Seven Gables (1669) at Salem, Massachusetts. In the eighteenth century, under the Georges, the prevailing English modes of building were introduced into the various colonies, where they developed more or less local characteristics. Kimball says, "As in the primitive shelters, there was little in the later buildings of the colonies which did not find its origin or its counterpart in provincial England or other parts of Europe of the same day... the ideal of the Colonial style remained always conformity to current English usage."

The Georgian style was flourishing in the established colonies on the eastern coast of America while western Pennsylvania was yet a wilderness. By the time this district was released from war and was in the process of final settlement, America's outstanding structures of the Georgian style had already been built in the East. Among these were Westover in Virginia (1727–35), the Chase House in Annapolis (1769–71), and Mt. Pleasant in Philadelphia (1761). At the turn of the century, Georgian architecture entered its final, or Adam, phase in America —represented by Homewood in Baltimore and The Octagon in Washington, D.C. The Roman phase of the Classic Revival developed under the enthusiastic leadership of Thomas Jefferson, among whose important works were his home, Monticello (1775 —remodeled 1796–1808), and the original University of Virginia buildings.

The Post-Colonial Period

These styles were slow in reaching western Pennsylvania and found expression only in the isolated instances of the few owners who then had the means and desire to build in the prevailing modes of the flourishing seaboard states. From about 1785, when the first buildings that might be said to possess stylistic tendencies appeared in western Pennsylvania, until the beginning of the Greek Revival about 1830, there appeared in various parts of the district reflections not only of every phase of late Georgian and Classic Revival styles from the eastern states, but also many examples of direct importation from Europe. The architecture created in this "Indian Summer of Colonial architecture," as Howard Major terms it, makes western Pennsylvania a veritable museum of architectural styles.

This complexity of styles resulting from the varied origins of the early builders and from their manner of settlement makes any orderly treatment of this Post-Colonial period from 1785 to 1830 very difficult. In general, the architecture in any part of western Pennsylvania reflects the character of the district from which the majority of the people had emigrated. Virginia exerted the first and strongest influence in southwestern Pennsylvania, notably in Washington, Allegheny, and Fayette counties. This region also received many settlers from Maryland, as did the eastern portion of western Pennsylvania including Bedford, Blair, and Somerset counties. The proximity of eastern Pennsylvania to these latter counties brought many settlers from that district. On the other hand, northwestern Pennsylvania, settled late in the Post-Colonial period, reveals more influence from the wave of migration from New York State and New England than it does from those builders who pushed up from southern and eastern Pennsylvania. Within the text accompanying the illustrations the interesting study of origins in architecture is presented by specific examples, and the illustrations are segregated according to district. The effect of the diversity of origins was to bring into western Pennsylvania a constant and refreshing flow of new ideas. The architecture of this region produced before 1830, though lacking the consistency and perfected development that characterized that of the older established districts on the coast, provides contrasts of building tradition not to be found in any other part of the country.

The Greek Revival Style

After 1830 western Pennsylvania shared in the common unifying effects of the Greek Revival style, which achieved great significance in America. According to Kimball, "The prevailing belief has been that the most characteristic American architecture was the colonial work of the eighteenth century ... on the contrary ... A truly American contribution to architectural style appeared only after the Revolution, and then it assumed a historic importance which has been little recognized."

The Greek Revival style flourished in western Pennsylvania between 1830 and 1850 and became the prevailing medium of architectural expression in buildings large and small, public and private. The population "went Greek" with a vengeance. Among laymen and builders alike that quality known as the "Grecian Gusto" was recognized in the more elaborate manifestations of the style. In some districts, however, the Greek character was confined to the moldings and minor details applied on a building of fundamentally Colonial character, particularly in the southwestern counties below the Ohio, where the earlier traditional forms were most deeply rooted. In northwestern Pennsylvania, settled largely during the height of the Greek style and adjacent to

New York State, where this mode achieved one of its most distinguished interpretations, there was a more complete acceptance of the style.

The Greek style has positive characteristics by which it is easily recognized, its Doric, Ionic, and Corinthian orders being readily identifiable even by those only slightly familiar with architectural design. With slavish exactitude the profiles of moldings were reproduced in wood, stone, and plaster from the delicately engraved plates of the handbooks. These works, to be more fully discussed later, recorded the elements of antique form and line with a faithfulness to the originals that has never been surpassed. Even the application of the principles of conic sections was shown in these books, and the country carpenter ground the knives of his molding planes to catch the subtle lines of ellipse and parabola.

Primarily adapted to monumental effects in stone, this style achieved its most striking successes in public buildings of that material; in fact, where brick was used the wall was frequently plastered to simulate stone. The country carpenter struggled with the problem of adapting to the scale of a small wooden house the ponderous Greek forms and ornament originally designed for marble two thousand years earlier by another race on the other side of the world. What a tribute to the immortal genius of Ictinus was this picture of a rural craftsman endeavoring patiently to bring the "glory that was Greece" to a story-and-a-half frame house in young western Pennsylvania!

The Gothic Revival, which appeared in western Pennsylvania between 1850 and 1860, left few examples from that decade, and these are confined almost entirely to ecclesiastical structures. With but rare exceptions they have little intrinsic merit and are outside the primary interest of this record.

Buildings Without Traditional Style

A particularly characteristic phase of early architecture in western Pennsylvania is illustrated by the large number of simple buildings, erected chiefly in rural districts before 1830, that contain almost no traces of formal style. These must be counted among the most interesting architectural remains of the district. Their quiet lines and excellent mass are wholly satisfying. It seems that in the essential qualities of architectural design their builders, curiously enough, were capable of doing no wrong; and instinctive good taste is demonstrated in the thoughtful choice of site and the placing of the building with relationship to its surroundings. The clumps

of evergreens and other planting that have been maintained show a feeling for elementary landscaping. The seeming indifference of the builders to current fads prevented them from being led into many of the pretenses and inconsistencies that often marred the homes of their more ambitious neighbors. In this humble architecture, expressed in the local vernacular, is recorded the hard living of the descendants of the first settlers. With some measure of release from peril and drudgery their principal endeavor was to build more substantially but, in conformity with their lives, without ornamentation or display.

Review of Periods in Western Pennsylvania

Thus the development of architectural styles in western Pennsylvania may be divided approximately into four periods: first, the pioneer period, ending in 1785, chiefly represented by log and masonry buildings without definite style; second, the Post-Colonial period, between 1785 and 1830, in which the buildings reflected the characteristics of the so-called "Colonial" style represented by the Georgian as well as by the Classic Revival, or Federal, style, together with direct influences from Europe; third, the period of the Greek Revival style, from 1830 to 1850, during which the architecture of the district achieved a measure of uniformity in character; fourth, the Gothic Revival period, from 1850 to 1860, of little importance architecturally and heralding a world-wide decline in architectural taste and vitality. But throughout these periods simple unpretentious buildings without definite style characteristics continued to appear, and in them a truly local idiom in architectural expression is preserved.

The Influence of Handbooks

The parallel progress of these styles in England and America, particularly before the establishment of the Greek Revival in this country after 1830, was due in large measure to the wide circulation of builders' handbooks. Through the medium of this practical architectural literature, the simultaneous introduction of a new style throughout the civilized world was made possible for the first time. As the number and use of these books increased, provincial, localized development in isolated communities became less and less common. The origin and development of styles is readily traced in their successive editions. Through the dissemination of the handbook the guiding spirit of the architect was made effective even though he belonged to a profession limited in number and though his work was confined largely to the cities.

The first handbooks, published in England in 1715, were translations of Palladio's work and new interpretations of the ancient Roman authority, Vitruvius. Sir Christopher Wren, Inigo Jones, and James Gibbs, early leaders among English architects, designed buildings based upon these classic principles. Drawings of these buildings became material for new handbooks that contained desirable adaptations to the new conditions and requirements. A typical handbook, and one of great importance, was that published in London in 1741 by Batty and Thomas Langley. It bears this formidable title page:

The
BUILDER'S JEWEL:
or, the
YOUTH'S INSTRUCTOR
and
WORKMAN'S REMEMBRANCER.
Explaining
Short and Easy Rules,
Made familiar to the meanest Capacity,
for DRAWING and WORKING.

This 124-page book, measuring four by five and a half inches, contains one hundred plates from copper engravings of great beauty and legibility. It presents the five orders, their adaptations and rules for proportioning, profiles of moldings and their application, exterior and interior details and features, together with the solution of various geometrical and structural problems. Like many other works of its kind, it was reprinted in Europe several times and was imported in quantities to America, where it became a "best seller."

With the arrival of the nineteenth century, American handbooks prepared by American architects and carpenter-builders first began to appear. They proclaimed as their aim the adaptation of architectural forms and rules to American conditions and needs. *The Young Carpenter's Assistant* by Owen Biddle, "House Carpenter and Teacher of Architectural Drawing," was "adapted to the Style of Building in the United States." This book was advertised for sale by Zadok Cramer in Pittsburgh in 1810. America's most noted architect-publisher, Asher Benjamin, brought out in 1806 his second book, entitled *The American Builder's Companion; or, A New System of Architecture: Particularly Adapted to the Present Style of Building in the United States of America*. He states in his preface that "not more than one third of the contents of the European publications . . . are of any use to the American artist in directing him in the practical part of his business . . . Old fashioned workmen, who have for many years followed the footsteps of Palladio and Langley, will, no doubt, leave their old path with great reluctance . . . a reform in some parts of the system of Architecture is loudly demanded."

Benjamin published four later works, the last in 1833. But he was never in full sympathy with the new rage, the Greek Revival style, which at that time was taking the country by storm. His place as a leader among builders' advisers was taken by such able interpreters of the "Grecian Gusto" as Minard Lafever. Lafever's famous *Builder's Guide* owed much, as did all American publications pertaining to the Greek style, to the English works of Stuart and Revett, whose publication *The Antiquities of Athens* is still a valuable book in the architect's library. Lafever not only presented the orders and elements of Greek architecture, lifted almost verbatim from English publications, but also suggested Grecian designs for doorways, windows, and various decorative features. Complete elevations, plans, and sections of private and public buildings, some of them of American buildings then in existence, were reproduced. In the later publications on Greek work, plates dealing with Gothic designs began to appear, largely based on the works of Pugin, published in England in 1833. The joint presentation of these diametrically opposed styles resulted in an unfortunate mixture of Greek and Gothic forms in many houses of the mid-century.

Chapter III

THE EARLY BUILDERS—MATERIALS AND METHODS

THE simple construction of the early log dwellings in western Pennsylvania demanded little technical knowledge, and in the pressing need for shelter and protection architectural expression could receive scant attention. Although the self-sufficient pioneer was usually his own builder, he was assisted by his neighbors, some of them men who, having natural aptitude or previous experience in construction, formed the nucleus of the young building profession. As building became more extensive and more permanent in character, these men were joined by other craftsmen who came from the East to seek employment; and to these carpenters and masons goes the credit for the design and construction of most of the examples of our early architecture. Each district had outstanding craftsmen, such as George Marietta in northern Fayette County, who, according to a contemporary, could "go to the woods and take from the stump every timber needed for a house, hew it out, mortise and tenon every piece, and when hauled to the ground where it was to be erected put it up without a failure in one piece." In the construction of the more ambitious buildings, even in early times, it was customary to contract for the work with experienced builders. For example, an advertisement in the *Pittsburgh Gazette* of December 15, 1787, read as follows: "On the plantation of Mr. John Barr, Mingo Creek, Washington County, will be built, a square log Meeting House, forty six feet by thirty, & twelve feet high in the clear. Any person inclining to undertake said building, will meet with encouragement by applying to the undernamed Trustees, or by their attendance at Mr. Barr's on the 1st day of January next, being the day appointed to ratify a contract for the above-mentioned purpose."

The Craftsman-Builders

The most commanding figure among these first craftsman-architects was Adam Wilson, who designed and built the house of Isaac Meason in Fayette County in 1802. He was brought from England by Meason for this express purpose. An expert carpenter and stonemason, Wilson also was a landscape designer. That he was able to erect this elaborate structure in such a remote location, handicapped by the limited facilities and the backward condition of the times, is a high tribute to his resourcefulness as a builder. With the exception of this building and a house for Isaac Meason, Jr. (now altered beyond recognition) in New Haven, the town across the Youghiogheny from Connellsville, there is no record of any other buildings designed by Wilson. A wooden model that he made for the second bridge across the Youghiogheny at New Haven was sold by his executors in 1826. His last years he spent in his home in New Haven in the solitude of his remarkable garden, which was surrounded by a solid fence. It was said that "a peep through the fence into his inclosure was like getting a glimpse of the Garden of Eden, but very few ever entered its gate." He remained a bachelor until his death in 1824. It is regrettable that we do not know more about Wilson; but if the spirit and quality of his one remaining work, the Meason House, are any true reflection of the man, he was a person of rare good taste, who conceived his scheme in "the grand manner" and executed its detail with exquisite refinement. It must have given him great satisfaction to create in the western wilderness this mansion, which deserves a place in the first rank of early American architecture.

About the time of Wilson's death an Irish immigrant of Scotch parentage, named Hugh Graham, landed in Philadelphia with ten guineas, a chest of tools, and a knowledge of the carpenter's trade. After working there for two years for Stephen Girard, he walked to Pittsburgh. As he passed Jacob Black's farm near Uniontown his unkempt appearance, after five days on the road, brought a laugh from the farmer's daughter, Margaret. Graham however, had the last laugh, for he later married the girl and acquired the farm. He died there in 1890. The house of Jacob Black in which he lived is shown on page 88. Hugh Graham carried on an extensive building practice in the Uniontown district. Among his more important works were the stone addition to Gallatin's house and houses for Colonel Samuel Evans and Judge Nathaniel Ewing.

Frederick Rapp, whose name before his adoption

by George Rapp, leader of the religious group known as the Harmony Society, was Frederick Reichert, and who learned the stonemason's trade before leaving Germany, was presumably responsible for the architecture of the Harmony Society in Pennsylvania and in Indiana. The progressive development in design of the buildings of the three successive colonies of the society (Harmony, Pennsylvania; New Harmony, Indiana; and Economy, Pennsylvania) shows the interesting process by which Rapp absorbed a feeling for native American forms without entirely sacrificing his German traditions. He died in Economy in 1834 at the age of fifty-nine.

To the names of Wilson, Graham, and Rapp, all European immigrants, may be added that of John McGowen, cabinetmaker, who was brought by Isaac Manchester from Philadelphia about 1800 to work on Manchester's house in Washington County; and the name of Mordecai van Horn, also from Philadelphia, who did the modeling and carving in the Croghan House in Pittsburgh. But the names of the great majority of the craftsmen who conceived and executed the early buildings have not been recorded.

These builders, with a fine feeling for the limitations of their materials, exercised an economy of effort that the modern architect would do well to emulate. Excellent proportion and superb craftsmanship are invariably associated with their work. The rule-of-thumb knowledge that was passed from one generation of craftsmen to the next was gradually refined and amplified by the increasing use of handbooks on building design and construction. The carpenter-builder became the carpenter-architect, conversant with the vocabulary of traditional form and detail and equipped with a growing appreciation of scale and style. But the practice of architecture as it is known today was just taking form. At the beginning of the nineteenth century there were few architects, even in the East, and their work was largely confined to public buildings in the larger cities. Asher Benjamin states in his *Practice of Architecture*, published in 1833, "The time has been, within my own recollection, when New England did not contain a single professed Architect."

The First Architects

The first purely professional architect of national reputation to practice in America was Benjamin Henry Latrobe, who came to Philadelphia from England in 1796. Until his death in 1820 he was the dominating force in American architecture. To him and to his distinguished pupils, William Strickland and Robert Mills, are ascribed almost all the important public buildings in America between 1800 and 1830. Originally appointed by Jefferson, Latrobe had charge of the construction of the United States Capitol between 1803 and 1817. While in charge of this work in Washington he also executed other commissions, among them the Allegheny Arsenal, built by the Federal government in Lawrenceville, now a part of Pittsburgh. Latrobe lived in Pittsburgh between 1813 and 1815 while planning the arsenal, the drawings for which are dated 1814. It is recorded that while in Pittsburgh he also designed a house for a Mr. Robertson in 1815, and in 1816 he made alterations for the church of the Reverend Mr. Herron.

Pittsburgh's most noted architect before 1860 was John Chislett. He was born in England in 1800, served his apprenticeship in the city of Bath, and migrated to Pittsburgh early in the nineteenth century. He designed Burke's Building on Fourth Avenue (see page 273) about 1835 for Robert and Andrew Burke. This structure possesses the simplicity and restraint of the buildings known to Chislett in his student days in Bath. Chislett also designed Philo Hall for William M. Irwin. This building, which was burned in 1845, stood across from Burke's Building and several doors east on Fourth Avenue. He is also credited with the design of several unidentified bank buildings in Pittsburgh. But his great achievement was the second Allegheny County Courthouse, built in 1842, the most monumental building erected in western Pennsylvania before 1860. Its massive portico with double rows of Greek Doric sandstone columns dominated downtown Pittsburgh until its destruction by fire in 1882. Chislett served as superintendent, architect, and landscape designer for the Allegheny Cemetery from 1844 until his death in 1869. The general layout and original planting of the cemetery, as well as the gateway on Butler Street (still standing) and a large receiving vault (rebuilt on the original design), are known to be his work. The buildings Chislett produced in Pittsburgh were, as a contemporary English critic put it, "great ornaments to the town, and do honour to his talents."

The branch of the United States Bank of Pennsylvania at Erie, mistakenly ascribed to William Strickland, was designed by William Kelly, of whom we have no record but that he achieved in this structure one of the most successful Greek temple adaptations in America. Among other architects who designed buildings in western Pennsylvania before 1860 were Evans, Kerrins, Joseph W. Kerr, Richard Dewhurst, the Reverend Rea Long, John Nottman, and Barr and Moser.

Engineers and Contractors

There was little distinction made between architect and engineer in the period before 1860, and one man frequently performed the functions of both professions. Latrobe held positions as state engineer in Virginia and city engineer in Philadelphia. Robert Mills, his pupil, wrote several treatises on canals, signing himself "Engineer & Architect." Military engineers, such as Le Mercier with the French and Harry Gordon with the English, designed the military fortifications in western Pennsylvania. To General G. W. Cullum of the United States army, builder of Fort Sumter, is ascribed the design of the Meadville Congregational Church in 1830. "S. Lothrop, Architect," designed the first Pennsylvania Canal aqueduct at Pittsburgh in 1829. Buildings and bridges did not then possess the complications of mechanical and structural features that have since resulted in a definite separation of these two professions.

The functions of contractor and architect were also sometimes combined. Kinkead, Beck & Evans, contractors, were responsible for both the design and the construction of the impressive bridges on the National Pike, and they also produced the stone tavern at Somerfield, Somerset County, of which James Kinkead was first proprietor. Samuel and John Bryan of Harrisburg were contractors for, and presumably designers of, the courthouses of Fayette and Greene counties. Harrold Church (1815) and Brush Creek Church (1816-20) in Westmoreland County were designed and erected by a group of four German contractors. In the pediment of the quaintly simplified Greek portico at each end of the Sewickley Creek covered bridge in Westmoreland County (see page 191) appears the inscription: "Daniel McCain, Architect and Contractor." Among the best-known early contractors in western Pennsylvania who executed buildings designed by architects were Hannen and Fairman, S. J. Calahan, Coltart and Dilworth, and James Eassieman.

The Ornamental Crafts

The carving of ornamental details required skilled craftsmen of a type not common in this district. David G. Blythe of Uniontown, who became famous in the town as a portrait painter, caricaturist, and poet, and whose paintings are occasionally assembled for exhibition today, got his training in woodworking as a ship's carpenter in the navy. In 1847 he carved the statue of Lafayette for the Fayette County Courthouse. Bradley Mahanna executed the wooden statue of General Greene for the courthouse in Waynesburg; and that of General Washington on the Washington County Courthouse was produced by James B. Millard in 1842. Joseph Woodwell of Pittsburgh, a wood carver by profession, executed the wooden vases for the Garden Pavilion at Economy. In almost every community there was a stone carver who produced tombstones; one of these was Hines, whose name is signed to many stones in Harrold Cemetery in Westmoreland County. The production of stucco ornament for decoration was a specialized trade; the iron foundries employed men expert in designing and casting iron ornaments for fire fronts, grilles, and other architectural accessories.

Amateur Architects

The practice of architecture by laymen did not always achieve the signal success notable in the work of Thomas Jefferson and Charles Bulfinch, but there were some owners in western Pennsylvania who are credited with the design of important buildings. The curious inconsistencies often found in such structures call to mind the warning of Asher Benjamin "that such persons proceed to build without any fixed system; unlooked for difficulties are soon encountered, which lead to expensive alterations, and the harmony of the buildings is destroyed." Among these amateur architects in western Pennsylvania were the Reverend John Hopkins, rector and designer of the second Trinity Episcopal Church in Pittsburgh in 1824; and the Reverend Timothy Alden, who, in 1820, "specified every column, every capital, each slope of roof, each towering chimney" for Bentley Hall in Meadville, of which "the plans were probably the fruitage of years of loving study."

The following contract, executed in 1843 for the construction of the Timothy Ives House, shows the prominent part sometimes played by the owner in the design and erection of his house; the confidence he places in his workmen is evidenced in the brevity of the document:

"Memorandum of agreement made and concluded upon by and between Timothy Ives, Jr. of the village of Coudersport, County of Potter and State of Pennsylvania of the first part and John Crosier and George Snyder of the Town of Cuba, Allegany Co. State of New York of the second part witnesseth —That the party of the second part agrees and binds themselves to the party of the first part to enclose a certain frame put up for a dwelling house in the village of Coudersport and known by the name of the Dike frame in the following manner (to wit) In a neat substantial manner and after the latest style agreeable to the directions of the party of the first part as the work is progressing and also to put up to the main part of building four columns or pillars of the Ionic order to be finished in first workmanlike manner. And to make and put in the front door the main entrance suitable for the building. All of said work to be completed by the first day of Sept. next. And the party of the first part hereby agrees to furnish all such suitable materials as may be necessary for said work in time to have the said work completed by the time aforesaid and to furnish the sash with the lights set therein. And to pay to the party of the second part in consideration of the above mentioned work the sum of Two Hundred and Eighty Dollars in manner following viz One hundred dollars in cash when the work is completed and the balance to be paid in goods from the store of the party of the first part or in other property if the parties can mutually agree thereon and the party of the first part is to furnish board for two men for the space of three months if it should take that length of time to finish the said work. In testimony whereof we have hereunto set our hands and seals this 13th day of April A. D. 1843."

Judge William Wilkins, inspired by buildings he had seen in Europe, sought to bring some of their grandeur to his house in Pittsburgh, which, in spite of its many faults, was one of the most imposing of its day. Searight recounts the story of "Mad" Anthony Wayne's invasion of the field of architecture. General Wayne "tarried over night with John Deford" in Monroe (now Hopwood near Uniontown). "Deford at this time was contemplating the erection of a new and more imposing edifice, and applied to his distinguished guest for a plan. It was furnished, and the present stone struc-

ture is the outcome of it, which shows plainly enough that General Wayne was a much better soldier than architect."

All the many aberrations that appeared in the early architecture, however, cannot be laid on the doorstep of the enthusiastic owner-designer. Those who claimed to be builders were often little more than amateurs in matters of design. Their handbooks furnished them with the vocabulary of classic architecture, with occasional drawings of typical adaptations to modern building, but there still remained the great problem of applying them to new materials and new needs. Nevertheless, the success with which the Greek orders and details were interpreted in wood design by the country carpenters was indeed remarkable. Their blunders and naive use of established academic forms served only to emphasize the sincerity of their intentions. An odd number of columns supporting a portico is a startling sight to anyone who has even a superficial knowledge of classic rules; yet three- and five-column porticos were sometimes used. This seeking after novelty

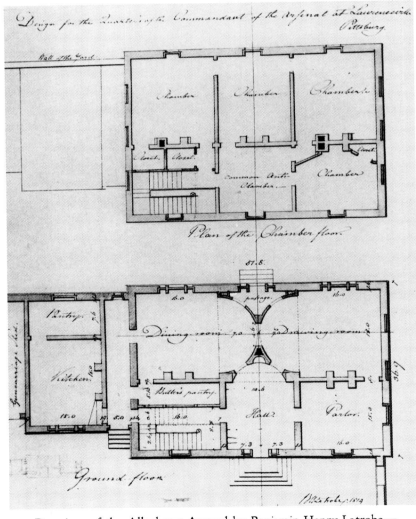

Drawings of the Allegheny Arsenal by Benjamin Henry Latrobe—

and innovation was a natural reaction to the rigidly fixed formula of classic design, particularly to that of the Greek Revival style, and it produced some incongruous and amusing effects. But as Major says, "In the hands of amateurs, precisely because of their lack of knowledge, the style developed individuality and created America's independent expression of the Greek Revival."

Designs—Handbooks, Drawings, and Accessories

The use of handbooks may be appreciated more fully by comparing their plates with actual buildings of early days. Molding profiles and such special features as mantels, stairways, and door and window details were reproduced, often with only trifling variations.

The use of drawings was not common except in designing the more elaborate residences and the public buildings. The few drawings that have been preserved are simple outline diagrams—little more than layouts of plan arrangement and occasionally of elevations and special features. Obviously, as in the case of the smaller buildings, most of the work was directed on the site as the building progressed. Hence, the development and execution of special details fell largely to the carpenter and the mason. In the accompanying illustrations are shown drawings that were probably much above the average in care and elaboration. Latrobe's studies for the commandant's headquarters and the main building of the Allegheny Arsenal, made in 1814, are his own work and show him to have been a draftsman of ability. That these designs are evidently early studies is borne out by the fact that in actual execution many revisions were made. In an effort to find a less expensive and more practical solution, the elaborately formal arrangement of monumental features of the plans apparently was discarded.

Except for the omission of the dome, the design of the Garden House at Economy, made about 1826, probably by Frederick Rapp, was carried out in the executed structure. The design for a manufacturing building illustrates the realistic, methodical manner of the Harmonites. The framing is completely shown, as well as the entire delineation of the machinery. The drawing is made on stiff paper in black drawing ink, and the various parts of the building are picked out in washes of red and yellow. Drawings such as this were made as a means to an end; they were intended primarily as instructions to workmen and not for display or effect. Joseph Kerr's drawings of the William Thaw House, made in 1852, reveal considerable progress in architectural drafting and more nearly approach the completeness and character of modern work. Of great interest are the preliminary drawings made by Thaw as a means of conveying his needs graphically to Kerr, an indication of architectural knowledge unusual in a client in any period.

There was a prevalent use of stock designs, particularly in ornamental work in composition, plaster, and metal, because of the scarcity of specially trained craftsmen and the expense of production. Until craftsmen in the East

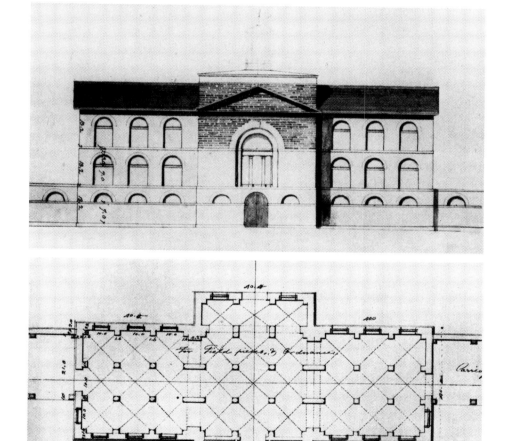

Reproduced from the Originals in the Library of Congress

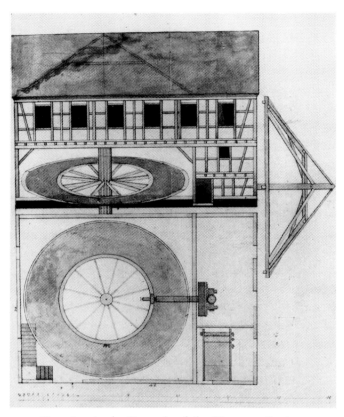

Drawing in the Records of the Harmony Society

succeeded in furnishing such stock designs for sale, composition mantel ornament was imported from England. One of the first American stucco composition workers was Robert Wellford in Philadelphia. His signature appears in the central ornament of a mantel shown on page 164. The plaster ceiling design of the Wilkins House is almost the same as that in the Shoenberger House (now the Pittsburgh Club). Door knockers were sold in various designs; that on the Anderson House in Bedford is a duplicate of the one on the Brewer House in Pittsburgh. Most of the iron furnaces in western Pennsylvania advertised various stock patterns of cast-iron fire fronts profusely ornamented with mythological or Biblical scenes. Burke's Building in Pittsburgh and the Wray House in Beaver contain identical fire fronts.

The Craftsman and His Materials

Building materials of unusual variety and quality were available to the early builder in great abundance throughout western Pennsylvania. In the use of these materials, the builder's sense of fitness and his directness of expression are reflected on every hand in the weatherbeaten structures whose substantial construction has withstood the destructive forces of a century and a half. Within the limitations of his knowledge he strove, above all, to build as substantially and as permanently as he

could. The craftsman treated his simple materials with loving care, delighting in the clean white wood shavings that curled from his hand plane, and patiently working his stones to the minutely textured finish that he so much desired. Haste and carelessness or mechanical interference had not yet appeared to smother the craftsman's pride in his skillful metamorphosis of the stones, trees, and clay he found in such plenty about him. Nothing in old buildings speaks to us more directly than does this reflection of a personal touch in the materials, which were to the craftsman what the palette is to a painter.

In structural timbers and log construction requiring great strength, oak was most commonly used; but the clear, soft-grained white pine, so easy to cut and work, was the wood most widely employed for all other purposes. For interior trim—stair newels and railings, mantels, window casings, and furniture —there was an abundance of maple, cherry, walnut, and chestnut. Other woods frequently used were hemlock, butternut, poplar, yellow pine, ash, fir, and spruce. These woods, taken from clear first-growth trees, intelligently cut and thoroughly seasoned, had remarkable lasting qualities. Suited to an infinite variety of uses, this material was the most important in building construction.

The most distinctly characteristic building material in western Pennsylvania is its sandstone, which weathers to a most beautiful variegation in color because of its conglomerate nature. Many buildings that possess no other architectural virtues attract attention because of the striking beauty of color and pattern in their stone walls. Native sandstone occurs generally throughout the district in varying degrees of color and hardness. It was

Original Study for Garden Pavilion at Economy

easily split to any desired size and dressed to the flat surface and pleasing texture that marked the front elevations of even the earliest buildings. It was not often suitable for carved ornament, but such work may be seen in signature stones, lintels and keystones, tombstones, and occasionally as architectural ornament such as that on the pediment of the Meason House. Numerous outcroppings of limestone occur in the southern and northern areas of this district and they predominate in the eastern part, mainly in Blair and Bedford counties, where sandstone also is found. Limestone spalled easily under the mason's chisel; the sharp ridges produced thereby are natural to this material. It was also valuable in the production of lime for mortar and as flux in the iron furnaces.

Much of the stone used in early building was accumulated when the fields were first cleared for cultivation, and natural quarries were to be found in many loose ledges and outcroppings. Almost every stone house illustrated in this book was built of stone taken from the owner's farm or from the immediate vicinity. In densely settled communities large quarries furnished the bulk of this material for general use, and certain districts, such as Beaver and Freeport, became celebrated for the qualities of their particular stone. Sandstone from these places was shipped by river to Pittsburgh in the later years. Building marble was not to be found in western Pennsylvania, and it was rarely imported for exterior use. The United States Bank in Erie, constructed of Vermont marble, is an important exception.

Inasmuch as brick was easily manufactured from the vast resources of excellent clay and shale, it came to be a most popular building material in western Pennsylvania. Even as early as the building of Fort Pitt, bricks were used, and more than a million were required in its construction. Because of the exorbitant cost of transportation, the existence of superior ingredients, and the general knowledge of brick manufacture in this region, it is unreasonable to assume that any bricks were brought over the mountains to western Pennsylvania. Made from the excellent clay and shale available everywhere, bricks were burned in temporary kilns set up on the building site. They were formed by pressing clay into wood molds by hand. Fired at much lower temperatures than are modern bricks, they were comparatively soft, but weathered well. Their pleasant color, texture, and slightly varying shapes are unsurpassed by most modern brick for domestic use. Brickyards were established in the larger

towns and cities where great demand and short haulage justified their existence.

Shortly before the end of the eighteenth century Albert Gallatin established his glassworks at New Geneva, and about the same time James O'Hara and Isaac Craig set up their plant on the South Side, opposite "The Point." Glass was made by both manufactories up to the size of eighteen by twenty-four inches—larger than any produced in the East—a great advance over the tiny panes, seldom larger than six by eight inches, which had been so laboriously carried over the mountains. Larger panes made possible larger windows and lighter interiors. Other glass products, such as chandeliers and tableware, soon were being used by the western home owner. The development of glass manufacture continued throughout the period, until it became one of the principal industries in western Pennsylvania.

The charcoal iron industry was established in southwestern Pennsylvania during the last years of the eighteenth century, and it spread rapidly throughout the entire district. Out of the furnaces and foundries, forges, and rolling mills came every variety of building hardware and accessory, from nails and fire fronts to cast-iron capitals and metal grille work. Lead, which had been mined in Blair County during the Revolution, was occasionally used for roof and wall flashing and as covering for small decks. This rare and costly material was utilized in the Manchester, Croghan, and Baker houses. In 1849 sheet copper was rolled in Pittsburgh for the first time. Roofing slate was first brought into western Pennsylvania from eastern Pennsylvania and from Wales about 1840.

The first plasters and mortars were nothing more than clay with a binder of straw or animal hair, but with the introduction of lime kilns their quality improved greatly. The disintegration of the early masonry mortars from exposure to the weather has necessitated repointing the walls of most of the old buildings, but much of the interior plaster work has endured and is of excellent character.

Distribution of Materials by Period and District

There were definite variations in each period and district in the relative importance of the four principal types of building construction; that is, log, frame, stone, and brick. Before 1795 there was a preponderance of log buildings in all districts, although an increasing use of stone had begun as early as 1785. Brick was not nearly so common, probably because of the relative difficulty of its manufacture. Only a few frame buildings were constructed before the late 1780's. Even when sawmills were numerous and the cost of timbers, weatherboarding, and nails was reasonable, frame construction was slow in gaining a foothold except in the northwestern district, and did not come into widespread use until well after 1800. In the early decades of the nineteenth century, stone was the favorite building material, particularly in the southwestern counties, but it finally yielded in popularity to brick, which had obvious advantages in handling and cost. By 1830 brick buildings were overwhelmingly in evidence throughout the district.

The popularity of the various building materials in each district was to some extent dependent on the origin and previous building experience of its settlers. Stone was widely used in eastern Pennsylvania, brick in Virginia. In Maryland brick predominated in the eastern portion and stone in the western section. It was only natural that immigrants to southwestern Pennsylvania from these districts should utilize the vast deposits of stone and the excellent brick shales and clays. Emigrants from New York and New England settled chiefly in northwestern Pennsylvania, where there was a natural abundance of timber but a scarcity of masonry materials, and in that section there resulted a more general use of frame construction, which was the type of building most familiar to the majority of these settlers.

The Craftsman's Attitude

The chief difference between the early domestic architecture and modern work lies not in the structural principles, which are essentially unchanged in present-day practice, but in the handling of materials and the contrast between hand and machine work. Each craftsman left in the wood and stone the marks of his individuality—the record of his triumphs and his blunders. This human quality is responsible for much of the charm in the old buildings but it has led to frequent misreadings of the original builder's intention. The enormous wooden beams with their deep checks and adze marks, so picturesque to the modern eye, would probably have drawn from the builder an apology for their uncouth finish. It was an unnecessary and, therefore, an unwarranted waste of time and money to dress the timbers to a smooth finish or to cut down their size any more than was required to permit easy handling. But when milled lumber could be had less expensively, timbers were no longer chopped

and adzed, or clapboards rived by hand. And the carpenter laid aside his molding planes when machine-run moldings were to be had more cheaply. With the development of woodworking machinery about the middle of the nineteenth century a profound change was inevitable in an architecture that, for generations, had recorded the proud touch of the independent craftsman.

Log Construction in Cabins and Houses

No type of construction gave a more picturesque character than that used in log buildings. A consideration of these relics of civilization's first appearance in western Pennsylvania is worth while, though they contributed little to the architecture that followed. In the construction of his cabin the frontiersman's principal asset was his axe. "The backwoods axe, shapely, well-poised, with long haft and light head, was a servant hardly standing second even to the rifle; the two were the national weapons of the American backwoodsman, and in their use he has never been excelled," wrote Theodore Roosevelt. The complete tool kit of the day included adze, large and small axe, draw knife, gimlet, augur, hammer, frow, crosscut saws, and ripsaws.

Log Cabin of Pioneer Days

In the very first days, when the settler built for temporary protection against the elements and the savage, he built a "log cabin," as distinguished from his later and more substantial "log house." As no known examples of log cabins exist in western Pennsylvania, the accompanying woodcut, reproduced from an early issue of The American Pioneer, is used to illustrate this primitive type of dwelling. Except for the glazed sash, it conforms to contemporary descriptions.

Round, untrimmed logs were built up in horizontal tiers for the walls, and the roof covering consisted of long thin slabs, or "clapboard shingles," which were held in place by "weight poles" laid upon them and separated by triangular pieces called "knees." The few windows were low, wide openings, sawed out, like the doors, after the logs were in place. Window openings were covered with greased paper and were barricaded at night with wooden panels. Chimneys were of wood, with clay-lined flues; the floors were of dirt. The single room thus created was as large as was permitted by the length of logs that could be handled. In it, according to Henry B. Fearon, in his *Narrative of a Journey to America in 1817–18*, were conducted "all the various operations of cooking, eating, sleeping, and, upon great occasions, washing." Such buildings contained neither iron, glass, nor stone; they were truly an architecture of the forest.

When life became less precarious the settler, or his children after him, replaced this temporary dwelling with the comparatively luxurious log house, with square-hewn timbers, shingle roof, stone chimneys, and glass windows. Iron hinges replaced those of leather and wood, and the winding stair succeeded the crude ladder to the loft space, then usually enlarged to a full second floor. Floors of wide plank were laid upon halved-log sleepers or "puncheons" and walls were plastered. Such homes were, for those days, quite acceptable, and many of them have been in continuous use until modern times.

The log house was built in from one to three days, according to various contemporary accounts, and it was usually built as a community activity, as were the churches. (The Long Run Presbyterian Church is said to have been built by the assembled congregation in a single day!) In such operations, according to John N. Boucher, a Westmoreland County historian, "a sharp axe, true eye and a strong arm were the requisites of a corner man. Had he these qualifications he could very quickly notch the logs to fit on the log below and cut its upper side to fit the triangular notch of the next log. He must also keep the corner plumb, and this required more care than we might think."

Wood in Design and Construction

Log construction in schools, churches, courthouses, forts, and mills is discussed in various sections of Part II where typical surviving examples of such structures are shown.

After the era of log building, wood continued to be the most important material both for framing and for finished construction in all types of buildings. The carpenter's work included the framing of floors, partitions, stairways, and roofs; exterior door, window, and cornice trim; and interior wainscoting, mantels, and paneling. The larger floor areas were divided by an enormous "summer" beam, often left exposed in the early buildings. The roof usually lacked a ridge pole, and the trusses that supported the roof were assembled first on the ground and often were marked with crudely incised Roman numerals to insure their proper placement. It is interesting to note that in the Gallatin and the Cook houses the number XIII was omitted.

Structural joints of mortise and tenon were held in position by wooden pins or pegs, usually made from the heartwood of oak. They were thoroughly dried before using, so that any shrinkage in the timbers they held in place would tend to bind them more firmly in position. Wooden pins were likewise used for the joinery of door and window frames, sash, paneling, mantels, furniture, and the like. Nails were reserved for use where pegs were unsuitable, as in shingling, flooring, and weatherboarding. The drawings and photographs of the Frew House window indicate the varied uses of wooden pins. (See pages 50 and 51.)

Interior partitions in the very earliest buildings were either a single thickness of vertical boards or "daub and wattle," a screen of woven saplings covered with clay plaster. With the advent of milled studs, plaster was applied to hand-split lath. Intricate problems in building stairs, particularly those of curved plan, developed a special phase of carpentry requiring great skill; some handbooks devoted their entire contents to this subject.

Brick and Stone Construction

Brick, like stone, was simply and directly used. In western Pennsylvania curved brick shapes for molding courses and other ornamental uses were not common. Frequently a special effect was gained by the use of Flemish bond on the entrance wall. (For an example of *Flemish bond*, see the photograph of the Davis House doorway on page 151). Though this pattern was very decorative and made the strongest brick wall, it was laborious to produce. Hence its use was usually confined to the entrance wall, and the side and rear walls were laid up in the simpler common bond. (For an example of *common bond*, see the photograph of the Shields House doorway on page 151). "Blackburned" headers (bricks whose ends were subjected to the greatest heat in the kiln) appear much less frequently in Flemish bond work in western Pennsylvania than they do in Virginia. Their effect can be seen in the second-story belt course of the Harper House illustrated on page 46. The early builders acquired much ingenuity in devising cornices of brick to simulate corbels and dentils; but in the later period such features were frequently marred by overelaboration. Brick was often used for floor paving in public buildings.

In the early stone buildings the walls were laid up roughly on all four sides, but with the demand for more formal design, the stonework of the entrance front was customarily dressed to a finely tooled surface. "Scabbled and drafted" work, a favorite texture design, presented a narrow edge of closely spaced "draft" lines surrounding a field of innumerable pits made with the chisel point. Typical variations in texture and pattern are shown on pages 160 and 161.

The use of stone in simple structural forms was not uncommon. At Harmony there are two large stone-vaulted cellars that, like the great wine vault at Economy (also built by the Harmony Society), were penetrated by smaller intersecting vaults which admitted light from the high windows and covered the stairways. Stone-vaulted "cooling" or "root" cellars were built into hillsides. Stones of astonishing size were often used by the masons. McClellan Leonard of Uniontown, an authority on early iron furnaces, measured in Isaac Meason's Laurel Furnace a stone nine feet, two inches, in length. The enormous lintel stone over the Wray House door is a single piece carved to simulate a flat arch. (See page 163).

Heating and Lighting

Toward the middle of the nineteenth century some of the first mechanical improvements in heating, lighting, and even in soundproofing made their appearance. Central heating plants with "warm air chambers" in the cellar delivered heat through flues and floor grilles, a vast improvement over isolated fireplaces and stoves. Public buildings presented a real problem in heating. For many years churches had no heat whatever, and the introduction of stoves was objected to by many—even physicians—who claimed that such artificial heat was "unhealthy!" In 1804 the First Presbyterian Church in Pittsburgh was heated by five large "egg" stoves.

Illumination in homes was originally furnished by hand-molded candles and by fireplaces. In churches, candles were placed in tin sconces on the walls. The glass chandelier in the Croghan House, a most beautiful specimen of its kind, was illuminated by a great number of candles. It is illustrated on page 130. James O'Hara's glass plant, under the direction of William Eichbaum (a German who was said to have formerly been glass cutter to Louis XVI), produced elaborate glass chandeliers. It was said of one of these, "A six-light chandelier with prisms of his [Eichbaum's] cutting . . . the first ever cut in the United States . . . is suspended in the house of Mr. Kerr, inn-keeper of this place [Pittsburgh]." Another product of O'Hara's plant was the chandelier that he presented to the First Presbyterian Church in Pittsburgh. William G. Johnston's account of this fixture and the accessory lighting presents a fairly complete picture of the successive developments in illumination: "At night, when its double row of tall sperm candles were lighted, there was a dazzling brilliance from its myriad of crystals; and at a later day when gas was introduced, the effect was yet more striking . . . For further lighting, besides two oil lamps on the pulpit, at frequent intervals along the aisles, close to the ends of pews and reaching a few feet above them, were turned cherry posts on the tops of which were glass globes shaped like the hand lanterns which were commonly carried on the streets at night, and in these for intended illumination were candles." William Thaw's house in Pittsburgh, built in 1852, contained gas plumbing, presumably intended for illumination.

Building Costs and Financing

Records of early building costs afford no just comparison with those of the present, because of the absence of information concerning the sources and character of labor and materials, and the difference between money values then and now. Henry Wansey, in his *Journal* of 1794, states that a log house about 150 miles west of Philadelphia, "built upon a stone foundation, having four rooms, (with floors) twelve feet square each, with thorough passage, finished in the inside, in plain manner, will cost two hundred and fifty pounds currency, or one hundred and fifty pounds sterling." Fearon, in his *Narrative* of 1817, writes: "A brick house, two stories high, containing ten rooms, may be built, with good management, in the country for 4000 dollars . . . as the bricks can be made upon the land, and 'help' boarded in the house. In towns, a similar building will cost 6000 dollars . . . exclusive of the ground."

County records that have been preserved show that the first small courthouses at the turn of the century averaged $5,000 in cost. Most of these structures were replaced before the middle of the century with buildings of increased space and more substantial construction at an average cost of $30,000. The second Allegheny County Court-house was built in 1842 for the then colossal sum of $200,000. An interesting record of the Lawrence County Courthouse, built in 1852, shows that bricks were bought at $3.40 per thousand; common labor was paid from 50 to 75 cents a day; and skilled craftsmen, from 87½ cents to $1.25 a day.

Until after the beginning of the nineteenth century currency was scarce, and barter and exchange were common. John Canon donated the ground for the stone Jefferson Academy in Canonsburg, which was built in 1791 at his expense, the cost to be reimbursed to him when the citizens were able to pay. He continued to receive payments for five years, many in the form of wheat, rye, and linen. John Cunningham gave his brother, in payment for building his house in 1800, a half interest in his farm and distillery business. The first Episcopal church in Pittsburgh, built in 1805, was financed by a lottery.

Building Laws

The first building laws were brought about by the establishment of town plans by private owners of property at important centers and were intended chiefly to stimulate development and lessen fire hazards. When Thomas Brown offered lots for sale in Brownsville in 1785, he stipulated that "all dwellings erected on them were required to be equal to twenty by twenty-five feet in dimensions, sub-stantially built, and in all cases to have a chimney or chimneys of brick or stone." Hopwood, who laid out the town that bears his name, near Uniontown, further required that "unless the purchasers . . . should improve their lots by building thereon a good dwelling-house at least twenty-four feet front and sixteen feet in depth, with sufficient stone or brick chimney thereto . . . before the expiration of five years . . . the said lot or lots should be for-feited." A law was passed by the state in 1799 requiring all counties in the future construction of courthouses to use either brick or stone. Pittsburgh, by 1826, had an ordinance prohibiting the erection of wooden buildings within certain limits. In 1816 a law was passed making illegal the erection of pro-jecting or hanging signs.

Town Planning

Town plans developed by private owners were laid out to yield the greatest possible revenue. And even in the towns established by military authorities or by the state, the usual "gridiron" plan, or rectan-gular system of streets, seldom provided for future extension or, in some cases, even for immediate requirements. Unpredictable expansions of indus-trial and business centers resulted in repeated shifts of residential areas, revisions of streets, and subse-quent additions of poorly related suburbs. The original plans were either altered or submerged in later changes and improvements, so that, except for those smaller towns whose growth was arrested, the charm and unity of the early communities have been completely lost.

Pittsburgh consisted of a straggling group of crude cabins until, after their destruction in 1763 in anticipation of Indian raids, Colonel John Campbell laid out the plot bounded by Second Avenue, Market, Water, and Ferry streets. The residents of this property prevented the widening of its streets when, in 1784, George Woods enlarged the plan of Pittsburgh for the Penns to include all of "The Point" bounded by the rivers and Eleventh and Grant streets. In 1795 the state ordered the laying out of Erie, Franklin, Waterford, and Warren and provided public parks that today are distinct assets.

In refreshing contrast to modern cities are those small towns that retain some of their original flavor, such as Bedford and the "pike towns" of Hopwood and West Alexander. These are typical "shoe-string" towns of haphazard growth. The road traffic that created them ceased with the coming of the railroads, and until the advent of the automobile they changed but little. Most of these road towns had "diamonds" at the main four corners, intended as practical provision for the overnight parking of coaches, wagons, and horses, rather than for beau-tification. They were and still are the social centers of the towns.

Hidden away in the valleys are those settlements that grew up around the grist and flour mills. The following passage, quoted from Boucher's *Old and New Westmoreland*, traces the development of such communities: "These early mills in reality deter-mined the locality in a great measure of our early villages and post offices, when the latter were es-tablished. The pioneer had to go to mill perhaps more frequently than to any other place. There he waited till his grist was ground and took the flour home with him. Then a blacksmith located near him and shod the horses while the pioneer's grist was being ground. Then came the tavern and its bar, for most people of all classes regarded whisky not as a luxury but as one of the necessaries of life. The storekeeper, when his day arrived, found the vicinity of the mill a splendid place to open up a little room filled with such 'goods' as the pioneer needed and could not make himself. Then, too, the shoemaker, the tinker, the spinning-wheel maker, the cooper, all came, each to add his mite to the collection of log houses which constituted the town . . ." With the discontinuance of the mill and with the slackening of pike traffic these towns ceased to grow and they are still among the most picturesque evidences of early days.

Model plans such as that of Economy, conceived by a closed group organized for the greatest common good, were, of course, exceptions to the rule. This town, with wide tree-shaded streets, spacious yards, community buildings, and town park, has been sufficiently preserved to indicate some of its original charm. The Allegheny Arsenal was a rare example of a self-contained group plan of great impressiveness.

Landscaping and Gardening

Although the simple homesteads of the settlers revealed little conscious landscape planning, many acquired the essential effects so studiously striven for in modern times. The selection of the site, the placing of accessory buildings, walls, fences, and walks, the planting of trees, orchards, and vegetable gardens, all combined to create *ensembles* of great charm, even though frequently of accidental origin. The site of many a log house that has long since disappeared can be readily identified by the pines, arbor vitæ, and other specimen evergreens that once surrounded it.

Among the few architects of the times, Adam Wilson and John Chislett appear to have taken the most lively interest in landscape design and in horticulture. Many laymen found pleasure in the arrangement of their grounds. Dr. Felix Brunot de-

veloped Brunot's Island with great effectiveness. Fortescue Cuming wrote of it in his *Sketches* in 1807: "He has judiciously left the timber standing on the end of the island nearest Pittsburgh, through which, and a beautiful locust grove of about twelve acres, an avenue from his upper landing is led with taste and judgment about half a mile to his house . . . and an excellent garden and nursery. He has fenced his farm in such a way, as to leave a delightful promenade all round it, between the fences, and the margin of the river, which he has purposely left fringed with the native wood about sixty yards wide . . ."

The beautiful grounds of the Manchester House in Washington are still faithfully preserved, almost exactly as they were in 1815, by the granddaughters of the original builder. The Irvin House in Warren County, the LeMoyne House in Washington County, and the Shields House in Allegheny County retain in their grounds and gardens much of their original beauty. James Ross maintained the garden about the Marie House on Grant's Hill in Pittsburgh after he purchased it. Cuming's *Sketches* mentions that "on the top of an ancient Indian tumulus or barrow, is a handsome octangular summer house of lattice work, painted white, which forms a conspicuous and pleasing object." Ross later developed an extensive terraced landscape scheme about his house near Aspinwall. The garden of the Harmony Society at Economy was famous for its rare trees, planted labyrinth, winding walks and paths, flower beds, and garden buildings.

The foregoing are but a few of the many examples that show that there was among the inhabitants of the crude western country a desire for some of the amenities of pleasant living. It is regrettable that the essentially perishable nature of landscaping has prevented more general preservation of the settings that the old buildings now so sadly lack. What nature has not reabsorbed, man has destroyed. But, even without *entourage* or interior furnishing, and though thoughtlessly altered, the shells of many buildings are tangible evidence of a period of unconscious good taste, which the world is slowly and self-consciously regaining.

Chapter IV
THE PRESERVATION OF OUR EARLY BUILDINGS

AS MAY readily be seen by glancing over the illustrations that follow, the hand of man has frequently been more damaging to the appearance of the early buildings than have the effects of time. Western Pennsylvania contains many structures of importance that have been so completely changed from their original condition as to prevent their inclusion in this book. Succeeding generations of owners, with the desire to "modernize" and keep abreast of the current mode, have altered and added without reference to the character established by the first builder. Such was the fate of the exterior of the Gallatin House. The result is as unfortunate as that produced by painters who have sought to improve upon old masters by making irrelevant and inharmonious changes on the original canvas.

In towns and cities, with the encroachment of commercial centers, the disappearance of old buildings is inevitable. Even though they are not demolished, the demand for shop fronts and large entrances produces such results as may be seen in the Bradford House in Washington and in the Espy House in Bedford. Occasionally, as in the case of St. Peter's Episcopal Church in Pittsburgh, the owners have moved a building to a new location so that it might be preserved intact.

Alterations intended to lengthen the life of an old building are, of course, an absolute necessity. Roofs must be re-covered, cornices repaired, doors and sashes replaced; the early fireplaces, often drafty and dirty, must be modernized. Changing modes of living require the addition of porches and wings and internal rearrangements to accommodate modern plumbing, wiring, and heating. But it has been demonstrated that it is not necessary to depart from the materials and spirit originally established in the design in order to gain these ends.

The Intelligent Care of Old Buildings

Through the agency of interested private owners and of organizations many early buildings have been lovingly cared for and intelligently altered where circumstances have required, as in the case of the Manchester and LeMoyne houses in Washington County and the Cook House in Westmoreland County, which are still owned and occupied by descendants of the original builders. At Allegheny College in Meadville and at Washington and Jefferson College in Washington original college buildings are still in active use. They compare favorably with the buildings of later periods that surround them, thoroughly justifying the pride manifested in their preservation.

The congregations of the Meadville Congregational Church and the Presbyterian Church in Bedford have preserved these church structures intact. St. Peter's Roman Catholic Church in Brownsville is being carefully restored. St. Patrick's log church at Sugar Creek, no longer used as a meeting place, has been set aside as a shrine. The German Union Church near Schellsburg, although unused for several generations, may be visited by those who care to see the interior of one of our oldest log churches.

Outstanding buildings have been set aside in several districts in western Pennsylvania as the homes of historical organizations. The Erie County Historical Society occupies the old United States Bank of Pennsylvania, which was later the customhouse; the Blair County Historical Society is housed in the Elias Baker House in Altoona; and the Abraham Overholt House near Scottdale is preserved as the headquarters of the Westmoreland-Fayette Branch of the Historical Society of Western Pennsylvania. The Anderson House in Bedford is now a community center containing a public library and headquarters for various civic and patriotic organizations; and the Church House in Allegheny is occupied by the Logan Community Center. The John Shoenberger House, occupied by the Pittsburgh Club, and the Fahnestock House, now headquarters of the Congress of Women's Clubs in Pittsburgh, as well as the Charles M. Reed House in Erie, used by the Erie Club, are striking examples of city homes of the forties that are well suited for such modern occupancy.

Some attention has been given the preservation of military structures. The Blockhouse of Fort Pitt was restored by the Daughters of the American Revolution; and reconstructions have been made of

31

Fort Necessity in Fayette County and of the Presque Isle Blockhouse at Erie. The United States Allegheny Arsenal has been permitted to pass into commercial hands, and its interesting buildings are rapidly being altered or demolished by industrial establishments. The movement to preserve the Guardhouse of the Arsenal is to be commended, although this structure, built at a much later date and distinctly of inferior design, was not one of the original Arsenal buildings.

The rebuilding of the highways has obliterated most of the picturesque covered bridges. Juniata Crossings Bridge was carried away in the flood of 1936. Many of the original stone bridges on the National Pike have been destroyed or, like the old "S" bridge west of Washington, have been disfigured by partial destruction. In the case of the "S" bridge, as in that of the brick tollhouse just west of Uniontown, a slight change in the course of the new road would have preserved it unspoiled with little or no expense. The stone tollhouse at Addison, fortunately, has been preserved by the Daughters of the American Revolution, who intend to restore it to its original condition.

The skew arch that carried the Northern Turnpike (now the William Penn Highway) over plane number six of the Portage Railway near Cresson has been preserved by the state as a memorial. The state has likewise assisted local organizations in the preservation of the old buildings of the Harmony Society at Economy. Unfortunately, similar care has not been taken of the earlier structures of that organization in Harmony and they are rapidly disappearing.

The Field for Future Activity

There still is much that could be done in the restoration and preservation of the old architecture of the region. One of the most interesting structures and certainly one with obvious sentimental appeal, George Washington's Mill, near Perryopolis, has collapsed into almost complete ruin within the past few years for lack of attention. Efforts by individuals and groups have failed to arouse sufficient interest to obtain funds for its preservation. It is remarkable, however, that no one has restored this historic shrine to exploit its commercial possibilities through paid admissions. The Meason House, near Uniontown, should have been set aside long ago through public or private initiative for its superb architectural qualities and the historical associations of its neighborhood with Braddock, Washington, and Gist.

Even where patriotic, commercial, or historical motives for preserving the early houses are lacking, there is a growing realization of the possibility of remodeling them for modern living, now that they are made accessible by the automobile. Many log houses have recently been converted with great success for use as summer homes or as quaint accessory buildings on estates.

There has been too little realization of the intrinsic architectural merit of the early buildings. Their preservation has been due almost entirely to their association with prominent families, historical episodes, and military events. If such distinguished visitors as Lafayette and Washington did not happen to grace them by their presence, they have lapsed into obscurity and disrepair. Unless the appreciation for the early work becomes more widespread, many of those simple, unpretentious buildings that have no distinction beyond their architectural charm will be lost.

The Purpose of the Survey

One of the main purposes of this book is to bring acutely to the attention of the modern western Pennsylvanian the fact that his region contains many structures, hitherto unknown or ignored, that are comparable with the famous early buildings of the Atlantic seaboard. There is probably no district of equal importance in the early history of America where so little documentary record of the early architecture has heretofore been made or where so slight an appreciation of the need for such a record has been aroused. Much remains to be done in the preservation of the early buildings of the region, when the general public has learned to appreciate these buildings for their inherent architectural value as well as for their historical significance.

PART TWO

—

DRAWINGS AND PHOTOGRAPHS

THE buildings shown in Part Two are the tangible evidence of architectural development in western Pennsylvania from the earliest times up to 1860. Although the photographs, with few exceptions, are confined to structures now in existence, they present a comprehensive and representative record. The buildings have been arranged according to type, in seven sections. Section One has been divided into three parts, making a total of nine groups of illustrations. Preceding each of these groups is a descriptive text outlining the course of architectural progress as exemplified by the buildings shown.

Within the three parts of Section One (log, Post-Colonial, and Greek Revival houses) the illustrations are grouped according to three districts—southwestern, eastern, and northern—and a rough chronological order has been maintained.

The photograph captions give (1) the date of completion; (2) the name of the original owner; (3) the general location; and (4) the county in which the building is situated and the key number.

Many buildings in this book required several years or more to construct. The date of the beginning of a building operation is not only more difficult to ascertain than the time of its completion but is of less significance. Therefore only dates of completion are given.

All structures are identified by the names of the individuals or organizations responsible for their creation. The names of subsequent owners, however intimately associated with the history and the preservation of the structure, are omitted as irrelevant in a source record.

Approximate locations of buildings may be obtained from the illustration captions and the map inside the back cover. Exact locations are shown on United States Geological Survey maps in the permanent records file in the Pennsylvania Room of the Carnegie Library, Pittsburgh, where all materials accumulated by the Survey are accessible to the public. The county key number, given with each example, is essential in referring to the records.

The 416 photographs in this book were selected from 1,940 preserved in the Survey files. Their selection was governed by a desire to present a broad picture of early architecture in the district before 1860, rather than to focus attention upon particular buildings because of their historical or sentimental associations. Thus space has been made available for those examples of lesser architectural significance which are, however, characteristic of a type prevailing in a particular period or district.

As supplements to the photographs, the measured drawings are invaluable in showing the buildings in their original condition, ignoring alterations made after 1860 and restoring such details as window sash, shutters, cornices, roofs, and the like. These drawings furnish sufficient evidence, in most instances, to permit the reconstruction of the building, if desired. The 81 drawings published were chosen from 105 made under the direction of the Survey Committee.

Floor plans of each building are shown—an essential too often omitted from measured drawings. Profiles of moldings and ornamentation are given in single-line silhouette. Such details of special interest as signature stones, hardware, and the like have been included in order to convey some of the quality of the early craftsman's work. Stone joining has, in all cases, been faithfully drawn, joint for joint, to record the charm of the old wall patterns. The size of the drawings as published is about half that of the originals.

In selecting and arranging the illustrations, the object has been to use as many examples as possible in the space available rather than to feature the outstanding buildings. With this point in mind, as much material was condensed in the measured drawings as legibility would permit; and the photographs were taken not primarily for pictorial effect but to display the architecture as completely and effectively as possible. Thus these illustrations present a very complete documentary record of the best source material assembled by the Western Pennsylvania Architectural Survey.

Section One

DOMESTIC ARCHITECTURE

A. Log Houses

ALTHOUGH most of the existing log houses in western Pennsylvania were not built until the frontier days had passed, their rude, simple character is symbolic of the pioneer's primitive mode of life. About these venerable and picturesque structures are woven countless legends of peril and toil in the conquest of the virgin forest, the actual timber of which is preserved in their rough-hewn logs.

The early settler's significant distinction between the log *house* and the log *cabin* has been observed throughout this book, even though in popular modern terminology all log dwellings are log "cabins." No existing examples of the log cabin in western Pennsylvania are known to the Survey. This makeshift shelter of the frontier, described on pages 26 and 27, was superseded by the comparatively luxurious log house just as soon as conditions permitted.

Many of the most famous log houses of early days are now but a memory. The home of John Frazier at the mouth of Turtle Creek, where George Washington stopped in 1753, and "Croghan's Castle," an elaborate log residence near the site of modern Lawrenceville where Washington was entertained in 1770 by George Croghan, have not been recorded even by adequate description. Another renowned log building, mentioned by Washington in his diary as "Semple's Tavern," stood at Water and Ferry Streets. It was the first residence of pretentious character in Pittsburgh. Originally built as the home of George Morgan in 1765, it was demolished in 1913. Records indicate that John Neville's log home, built in 1794 on the island which now bears his name, was a structure of unusual size and elaboration.

Log taverns are shown in the section with log houses because both types were quite similar in construction and appearance; in fact, most of the log inns were originally built as residences. In those days any home was easily adapted to tavern uses by the addition of a long, low porch, a room for public entertainment, usually a taproom, and additional rooms for lodging.

Most of the nineteen log houses and taverns illustrated on pages 36 to 42 are in the southwestern area where the first settlements were made. It appears that the house of Robert Neal, built on ground purchased by him in 1787, is the oldest of the group. It is the log house in its simplest form, a single room with only a loft above, reached by a ladder, and with no cellar beneath. The large chimney of field stone laid up in clay mortar serves two fireplaces. Except for the missing door and sash, and the roof of later date, it is well preserved. A movement to restore the house is now on foot.

The Nixon Tavern, in contrast with the Neal House, is a multiple log house which grew in size to suit changing needs and uses. When it was transformed into a tavern, the story-and-a-half unit containing the taproom was built a short distance from the original cabin, and its roof was extended to cover the space between. By thus separating the new and old log walls, a difficult problem—the joining of the logs—was avoided. The enormous stone chimneys provide fireplaces for cooking and heating on both floors, and are of better construction and finish than those in the Neal House. Winding stairways by the chimney breasts lead to the second floor, where the rude loft is supplanted by a full-height plastered room with plank floors. This building and the Hereline House are noteworthy among log houses in the Survey records for their unspoiled character.

The log house near Greensburg (like the Nixon Tavern near Fairchance) demonstrates the combination of original log house and additions made at several different periods. (See page 42). The low central section was built some time before 1800. The story-and-a-half portion to the left was presumably added later, with the upper tiers of logs extending over the small original building for greater structural bond. As has been stated, there was no successful solution to the problem of joining two cabins by butting the logs together; to avoid this difficulty and to furnish a through passage or porch the two-story portion added about 1830 was therefore set some distance from the original building. This porch, as in many other instances, was later boarded up and made to serve as a small room.

The other log houses illustrated in this section are variations of the two foregoing types. The application of weatherboarding to the logs at some later date (see examples on page 39) obviated replacement of chinking and reduced the penetration of rain and cold. Sometimes, as in the instances of the log house near Sewickley and the Halfway House, weatherboarding was applied on the weather side only. But even when concealed by weatherboards, the log house is detected by the experienced eye because of the high stilted proportion produced by single-log width. This characteristic shape is especially evident in the Hereline House. By reason of the limited size in which logs could be obtained and handled with ease, the width of log cabins was seldom great enough to permit of two full-sized rooms. In the early one-room types, privacy was furnished at first by cloth or skin hangings and later by plank partitions. But even in the larger log buildings, space was at a premium and stair halls were a rarity. It was many years before a builder was so venturesome as to add a full second story. The first two-story cabin near Uniontown was long known as the "tall house." Foundations were usually inadequate, frequently resulting in the uneven settlement of the walls.

Builders of log houses necessarily ignored or, perhaps, were unacquainted with traditional architectural forms; occasionally, however, some effort was made to gain a special effect, as in the log house near Canonsburg. Its boxed cornice returning on the gable end, its molded trim, and its regular fenestration give this building an air of distinction. The log house was almost always pleasantly placed in relation to its particular landscape and was further set off by specimen evergreens, fruit trees, vegetable and flower gardens, and stone retaining walls. The original surroundings of the log houses near Sewickley and Elizabeth are very well preserved.

Log houses were built quickly, but they also aged prematurely, acquiring the appearance of hoary antiquity long before equally old buildings of masonry or even of frame construction. Perhaps it is for this reason that there have grown up about them so many stories of early days to confirm the popular association of these picturesque structures with the beginnings of civilization in western Pennsylvania. This quality has contributed to the difficulty of determining the dates of their erection except in the rare instances where valid records are available. It is, furthermore, hazardous to assign an approximate date, as may be done with houses of definite style tendencies, because there was little or no change in principles of construction and detail over the long period in which log houses were built.

On page 41 are presented various examples of log construction, the technique of which was fairly uniform throughout the district, the diamondwise treatment of the log ends in Fort Gaddis being unique in the Survey's records. Chinking was accomplished with either heartwood chips or small flat stones, plastered or "mudded" over with clay strengthened with straw or animal hair. The remarkable stone chimney near Eau Claire (all vestiges of the building itself have disappeared) is a perfect example of early masonry construction. Good workmanship and proportion compensate for lack of elaboration. Outside chimneys were not as common as those built within the structures, for joints exposed to the weather continually required repointing.

The log house was easily adapted to many uses of the early community, serving as the prototype of the first schools, churches, courthouses, stores, and even that grim essential, the settlers' blockhouse. The Survey found no log houses that show evidence of having been designed for defense. Although legends associated with many log houses state that they were used as "forts," there were found no loopholes such as would have been required for firing from within—although, of course, a portion of the chinking might have been removed temporarily for the purpose. (The only authentic loopholed structure in the region is the brick Blockhouse of Fort Pitt. See page 263). With the coming of peaceful times, the long, low, barricaded windows were replaced by larger ones with glazed sash, and the heavy plank door by the lighter paneled variety, such as may be seen in the examples illustrated in the pages following.

For many years after the general discontinuance of log construction—in fact until the middle of the nineteenth century—the log house remained the poor man's solution of the building problem, particularly in remote districts abounding in good timber. The enduring quality of log construction is attested by the fact that most of these structures have been continuously occupied to the present day, and many of those which for years have been abandoned can be reconditioned with but little effort and expense.

Date Unknown   *Allegheny 36*

A Log House near Sewickley

Before 1810   *Fayette 69*

The Nixon Tavern in Fairchance

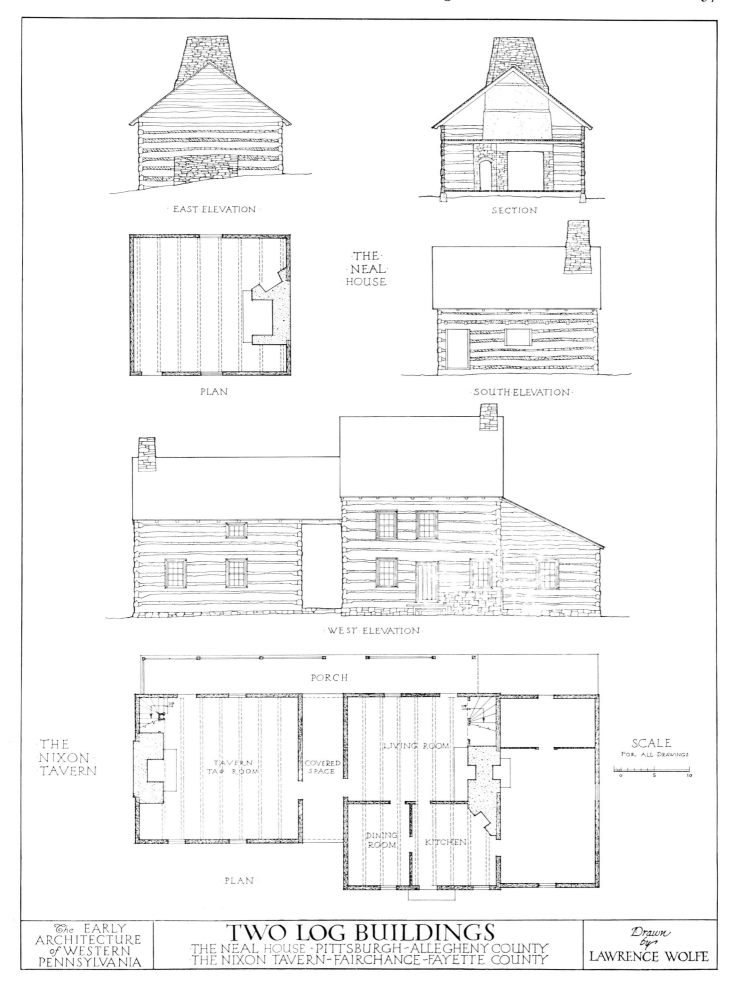

EAST ELEVATION

SECTION

THE
·NEAL·
HOUSE

PLAN

SOUTH·ELEVATION·

WEST·ELEVATION·

PORCH

THE
·NIXON·
TAVERN

TAVERN
TAP·ROOM

COVERED
SPACE

LIVING·ROOM

DINING
ROOM

KITCHEN

SCALE
FOR ALL DRAWINGS

0   5   10

PLAN

The EARLY
ARCHITECTURE
of WESTERN
PENNSYLVANIA

TWO LOG BUILDINGS
THE NEAL HOUSE · PITTSBURGH · ALLEGHENY COUNTY
THE NIXON TAVERN · FAIRCHANCE · FAYETTE COUNTY

Drawn
by
LAWRENCE WOLFE

Allegheny 36

A Log House near Sewickley

Date Unknown

Washington 109

A Log House near Canonsburg

Before 1800

Allegheny 170

The Robert Neal House in Pittsburgh

About 1787

Allegheny 37

The Daniel Willoughby House near Ingomar

Before 1823

Allegheny 121

A Log House near Elizabeth

Date Unknown

Bedford 77

The Jacob Krichbaum House in Bedford

Date Unknown

Crawford 46

The Patrick McGill House in Saegerstown

1796

Allegheny 92

The Henry Morrow House near Wilkinsburg

1819

Date Unknown *Bedford 80*

The John Hereline House near Mann's Choice

Date Unknown *Butler 44*

Chimney near Eau Claire

Date Unknown *Butler 44*

Fireplace Detail

Washington 28

Dr. John McMillan's School in Canonsburg

Fayette 107

Fort Gaddis near Uniontown

Westmoreland 102

A House near Smithton

Allegheny 138

The Rhodes House near McKeesport

Washington 96

A Springhouse near Washington

Cambria 10

A Barn near Vinco

Date Unknown   *Westmoreland 84*

The "Half-way House" near Blairsville

Before 1800 (High Portion Added 1830)   *Westmoreland 103*

A Log House near Greensburg

DOMESTIC ARCHITECTURE

B. The Post-Colonial Period

THE Post-Colonial period of the architecture of western Pennsylvania extended approximately from 1785 to 1830. Of the houses shown on pages 46 to 107, only two were built before the first date and but four after the last. The most celebrated houses of the period were built within the quarter of a century following the establishment of peace by the Greenville Treaty in 1795. The year 1815 was particularly significant. By that time the Meason, Roberts, Daily, and Ross houses had been built, and in that same year the Manchester, Johnston, Royer, and Anderson houses were completed. In these buildings are discernible various phases of the Georgian style, introduced from the eastern United States and England.

Few of the houses possessed the elegance of their eastern contemporaries, but in the process of transplanting the style beyond the mountains they acquired a rugged character, massive proportions, and a freedom from ornamentation. The simple requirements of the settler, combined with an architectural knowledge imperfectly remembered from his native surroundings, prohibited an elaboration that he could seldom afford or obtain.

The Power of Precedent

The natural desire of the immigrants to build according to their native traditional forms brought into western Pennsylvania a constantly vitalizing influence during the Post-Colonial period. Variation from these forms was, of course, limited by the bounds of the accepted English building traditions as modified to suit their new American interpretations. Thus Colonel Edward Cook built in the vernacular of the eastern Pennsylvania farmhouse, whereas Joseph Dorsey faithfully reproduced the type of house still to be seen in his birthplace, Ellicott City, Maryland. The house of Presley Neville betrayed his Virginia origin, and there could be no doubt of Isaac Manchester's New England ancestry, for "Plantation Plenty" is faithful even in the smallest detail to the character of the buildings in his native Newport. Amos Judson built his house after the manner of those he remembered in his birthplace, Woodbury, Connecticut. James White, born in Washington County, lived

for a time in northern Ohio as a medical student—an experience that undoubtedly prompted his desire to have his house in Crawford County designed after the model of those he saw in the Western Reserve, where the New England influence had been firmly implanted.

And yet the recollection of the owner's native district did not necessarily determine the design of his house, for the background of the builder was also a contributing force. Thus, Isaac Meason, a Virginian by birth, imported the architect Adam Wilson from England expressly to execute his house. In its design is revealed the subtle hand of one well versed in the best English building tradition—the likely explanation of its resemblance to the buildings of the Colonial chain in Fairmont Park, Philadelphia, which also adhered closely to the contemporary English mode.

Many other architects and carpenter-builders of western Pennsylvania were foreign-born. Among them were the Englishmen, Benjamin Henry Latrobe and John Chislett; the German, Frederick Rapp; and the Irishman, Hugh Graham. James Stewart, who came directly from Scotland, brought with him a stonemason, Charles Nelson, who built for him a house resembling those in Scotch seaport towns. In the buildings of the Harmony Society at Harmony the heavy German hand is obvious, and even in the architecture of the Society's later settlement at Economy, the American sojourn had not entirely eradicated evidence of a Teutonic origin. When Alexander Johnston of Westmoreland County sought to reproduce his old homestead in County Tyrone, Ireland, he was unable to ignore the influence of American building tradition in the design of his house.

Although these divergent architectural influences brought into western Pennsylvania from the outside world during the Post-Colonial period gave its buildings a most interesting variety of expression, they prevented the development of a distinctive local style such as occurred in Annapolis, Germantown, and the James River district. Any such evolution of a local version of the Georgian style by the assimilation of these varied influences was interrupted in western Pennsylvania by the introduction, shortly after 1830, of the Greek Revival style. This new fashion, received with universal enthusiasm, imposed its exotic and formal character on all architecture.

The illustrations representing the Post-Colonial period are grouped according to three districts. The populous southwestern area is represented by houses from Allegheny, Fayette, Greene, Washington, and Westmoreland counties, shown on pages 46 to 92. Houses belonging to the eastern district beyond the Allegheny Ridge, comprising Blair and Bedford counties, are shown on pages 93 to 101. The northern district, settled much later than the first two, contains but few outstanding examples built in the Post-Colonial period. Houses from Erie and Crawford counties are presented on pages 102 to 107. The photographs and drawings of houses in these three regions show representative examples not only of the large buildings but also of the more numerous, less pretentious dwellings, which best portray the social condition of western Pennsylvania. Contrasting vividly with the large estates and manor houses of Virginia or the spacious farmhouses of eastern Pennsylvania, these smaller houses illustrate the most characteristic western Pennsylvania type.

Local Characteristics in House Design

One of the best preserved examples of indigenous domestic architecture is the farmhouse of the Miller family in South Park, Allegheny County. Of similar significance, because of their local quality, are the Frew, Chambers, Jackson, and Ludwick houses. The building of these houses was governed by a shrewd consideration of their site and an intelligent use of materials available in the immediate vicinity. Their handsome stone walls seem literally to grow out of the ground. Simple plans and details of charming directness show that their builders were not hampered by any self-conscious effort or by dependence upon traditional form.

Brick city houses like those on Watson and Spring streets in Pittsburgh have little connection with architectural precedent. The Harris, Hill, and Black houses make only the slightest concessions to historic building forms. One of the best examples of independent architectural thought is the design of the typical small brick house (see page 210) erected by the Harmony Society at Economy, which combines the utmost simplicity of design with a fine appreciation of the limitations of the materials used. In the design of such notable buildings as the

Johnston and Royer houses can be seen many characteristics peculiar to the district. Even though they represent the living requirements of another age, their homelike quality holds an emotional appeal for modern western Pennsylvanians.

The owners of the more pretentious houses were men of means, usually industrial leaders or men in professional and business life, who introduced into the western country some of the culture of the seaboard states, and whose homes contrasted with the simple character of most of the other houses in the district. The Manchester and Meason houses stand out even today in their respective districts as extremely unusual accomplishments. When the undeveloped nature of their original surroundings is visualized, it becomes easy to imagine how magnificent they must have seemed.

The Evolution of the House Plan

The first effort to progress beyond the log house is well illustrated in the Dinsmore House. To the original building, constructed of logs cut on the property, has been added a one-room wing with walls of stone taken from the local fields. Both old and new buildings are of elementary plan and construction. The original stone portion of the Frew House has but one room in the basement and on the first floor, and only two on the second. The Jackson and Patterson houses merely repeat the space requirement of the log house, enclosed with walls of more enduring character. The plans of such simple houses seldom afforded space for a separate stair hall, and windows were few and small.

The stair hall of the Dorsey House, placed at the side of the building, affords access to comparatively spacious rooms on both floors. The McConnell, Moore, Roberts, and Espy houses all present this identical arrangement, so often used throughout the district during the first half of the Post-Colonial period. These houses are nearly square in plan and their proportions are therefore conspicuously high. It is strange to see this plan used in country districts, for it was derived from the city house with blind party walls. In the houses mentioned above, the windows are confined to the front and rear walls, with small windows in the gable ends to light the attic space. The entrance fronts are elaborately treated with special jointing and surfacing of the stone work, and ornamentation of cornice, doors, and windows; whereas the windowless side walls are roughly laid up, and the gable cornices are reduced to a single narrow board.

By far the commonest plan was the center-hall type, which was well suited to the living requirements and formal design of the Post-Colonial period. As wealth increased, so did the number of rooms. It often became necessary to attach ells and side wings to provide sufficient space. These were either symmetrically disposed, as in the Meason House, for architectural effect, or unsymmetrically attached to the rear, as in the Anderson House. As time went on, windows were enlarged, interiors became lighter and more spacious, and provision was made for the accommodation of servants within the house. A separate servants' stair was included in the Manchester and Anderson houses.

In northwestern Pennsylvania the White and Judson houses not only reflected the character of the New England Colonial but anticipated the Greek Revival house based on the temple motif. This turned the gable to the front, making possible the classic pediment motif with full-height pilasters, a feature almost unknown to the Post-Colonial period in western Pennsylvania.

Characteristics of the Post-Colonial House

As houses became more elaborate and spacious, the large cooking fireplace, which had originally been the center of household life, was relegated to the cellar or kitchen wing, eventually being replaced by the cooking stove. The general use of coal resulted in smaller fireplaces and greater emphasis on the wood mantel as a decoration. The separate stair hall placed more emphasis on the stairway. Scrolled rail terminations, turned balusters, and ornamented step ends were found even in small houses. Circular stairs were occasionally used, and considerable importance was given to the lightness and delicacy of their construction.

Good plasters were developed at an early date, when lime became accessible. Smooth finish was the rule, and plaster walls were remarkably true. Cramer, in Pittsburgh, advertised a "large stock of hanging or wall papers." Stairs and walls were occasionally decorated with painted designs. Wainscoting of wood, when applied full height, was always confined to the end of the room containing the fireplace, as in the Dorsey, Gallatin, Cunningham, and Daily houses. However, the chair rail and cornice treatment exemplified in the living room of the Neville House was more common.

Exterior ornamentation, when used at all, was judiciously placed where it would be most effective —in doorways, cornices, and, occasionally, in windows. Carved ornament in stone was quite rare. The stone pediment ornament of the Meason House is unique in western Pennsylvania. The delicacy of design and execution in this raised ornament is truly remarkable. Carved exterior woodwork was largely confined to cornices and doorways. Windows were almost invariably double-hung, with molded wood trim brought out to the face of the masonry and with sash rails and muntins of remarkably light section. The replacement of the many-paned old windows with modern sash, usually with a single vertical division, has reduced the housewife's cleaning problem but has detracted greatly from the character of many old houses.

Porches were seldom used on the original Georgian houses. The first porches in western Pennsylvania, introduced late in the Post-Colonial period, were of the type seen on the Wright and the Royer houses. The porch on the Anderson House appears to have been added at a later date. The two-story porch on the Quail House, a curious interpretation of a familiar Virginia motif, is unusual in the district. Dormers were fairly common in the city (see the Russell and the Anderson houses), but rather uncommon in the country, the Neville and the Barclay houses being exceptions. The attic space depended for light upon the characteristically small, square gable windows.

Roofs in the Post-Colonial period rarely exceeded a thirty-degree pitch. Ridge roofs were almost invariably used. Hip roofs were a rarity, and the truncated gable roof of the Great House in Economy was unique. Flat roofs were never used because of weatherproofing problems. The small deck on the roof of the Manchester House was covered with sheet lead, a most expensive and unusual treatment. The roof projection at the gable was usually sufficient only to cover the single board forming the cornice; but there was considerable projection in the front if the full classic cornice was used. Chimneys were usually placed at the gable ends, and only in such early types as the house on Spring Street in Pittsburgh were they combined in a single central stack. As many fireplaces as possible were combined in one chimney, for they were the only source of heat. (Observe the enormous triangular stack in the Neville House.) Double-gable chimneys were occasionally connected with a horizontal parapet wall, but the application of parapets on the sloping gable walls, as in the Russell and the Stewart houses, was quite uncommon except in city houses with party walls. The horizontal return of the cornice at the gable end, as shown in the Roberts and the Ross houses, was unusual, the cornice more often being returned on itself a short distance from the corner.

Alteration and Preservation

Almost all the houses demonstrate the more or less disastrous effort of successive generations to improve the original design by alterations and additions. Changes made before the fatal decline of 1860 were generally unobjectionable, such as the brick addition to the Frew House, the various additions to the Miller and the Royer houses, the ell attached to the Johnston House when it was converted into a tavern, and the porches added to the Neville House. But the changes of modern times—the addition of "front" porches, the removal of original sash, shutters, doors, and the like—made without proper regard for the original character of the building, are most regrettable. And it is to be hoped that more intelligent care will attend future changes that may become necessary.

The Meason House, even in its present dilapi-

dated state, still preserves the grace and dignity of the "grand manner," although the imagination must supply the trees that originally lined the entrance drive; the flowers and shrubs, which once contrasted with the rugged stone walls of the great circle; the missing shutters; and the many little marks of care and attention now so sadly lacking. A full appreciation of this loss can be grasped only when one sees an example like the Manchester House, which, together with the grounds, has been so cherished that even now it looks as it did the day it was finished. The very farming implements and building tools have been preserved by the three granddaughters of Isaac Manchester, who still occupy the house. It is interesting to speculate on the thoughts of Isaac Manchester as he stood on the "captain's walk" of the roof, supervising the cutting of his initials and the date in the stone parapet (see page 163) at the conclusion of his venture. What faith he must have had to cast his fortunes with the western country, surrounded on all sides by forest-clad hills and valleys, many hundreds of miles from his beloved ocean.

About 1800   *Greene 24*
The Samuel Harper House near Carmichaels

1805   *Washington 111*
The Alexander McConnell House near Bishop

Allegheny 157

The Dinsmore House near New Kensington

Date Unknown

Allegheny 157

The Dinsmore House—Fireplace detail

Date Unknown

Washington 86

A House near West Brownsville

Date Unknown

Allegheny 97

The Hugh Jackson House near Mt. Lebanon

1808

The Colonel Edward Cook House near Fayette City

1772–76

Front View of the Cook House

1772–76

The John Hegarty House in Houston

1805

Fayette 71

Side View of the Cook House

1772–76

Westmoreland 60

The Samuel Ludwick House near New Kensington

Date Unknown

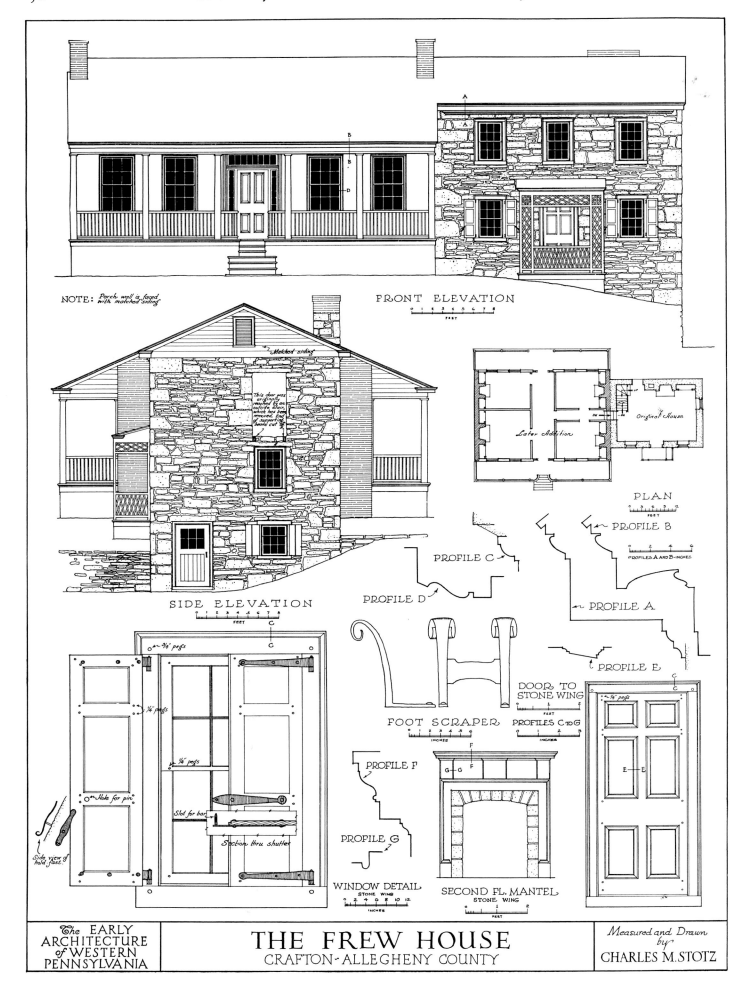

NOTE: *Porch wall is faced with matched siding*

FRONT ELEVATION

SIDE ELEVATION

Matched siding

This door was originally reached by an outside stair, which has been removed. End of support beams cut off

PLAN

PROFILE B

PROFILES A AND B-INCHES

PROFILE C

PROFILE D

PROFILE A

PROFILE E

¾" pegs

¼" pegs

¼" pegs

Hole for pin

Slot for bar

Section thru shutter

Side view of hold fast

DOOR TO STONE WING

FOOT SCRAPER   PROFILES C TO G

PROFILE F

PROFILE G

WINDOW DETAIL
STONE WING

SECOND FL. MANTEL
STONE WING

¾" pegs

The EARLY
ARCHITECTURE
of WESTERN
PENNSYLVANIA

THE FREW HOUSE
CRAFTON-ALLEGHENY COUNTY

Measured and Drawn by
CHARLES M. STOTZ

Window Detail of the Frew House

Allegheny 17

Before 1800

The John Frew House in Crafton

Allegheny 17

Before 1800

The Frew Springhouse

Allegheny 17

Before 1800

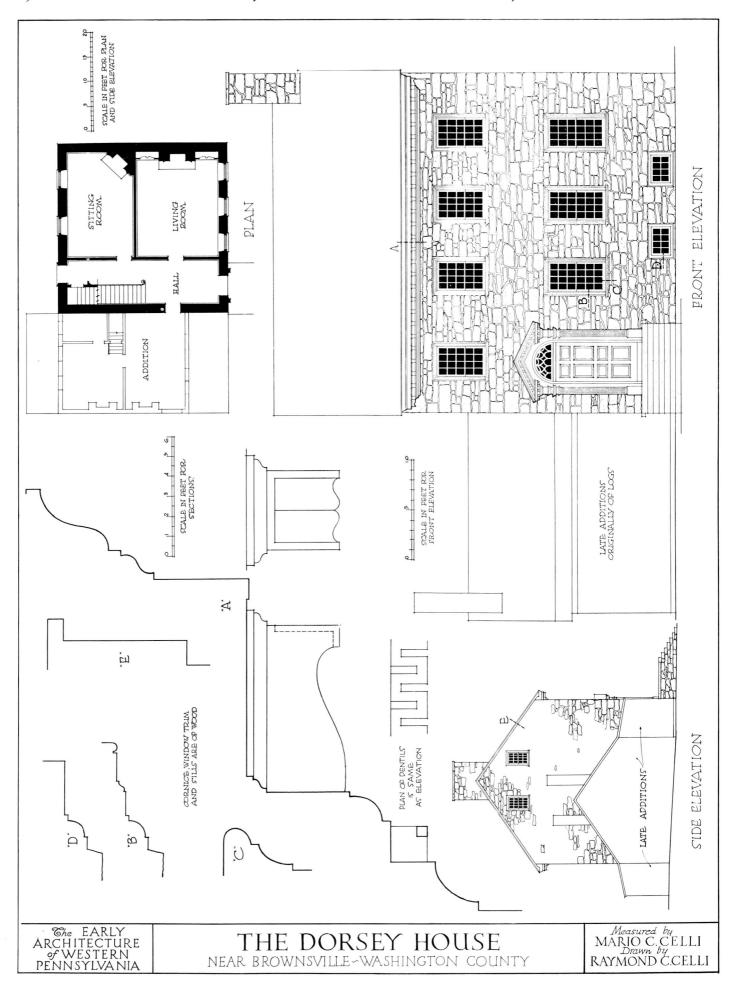

SCALE IN FEET FOR PLAN AND SIDE ELEVATION

PLAN

SITTING ROOM

LIVING ROOM

HALL

ADDITION

FRONT ELEVATION

SCALE IN FEET FOR SECTIONS

SCALE IN FEET FOR FRONT ELEVATION

LATE ADDITIONS ORIGINALLY OF LOGS

CORNICE, WINDOW TRIM AND SILLS ARE OF WOOD

PLAN OF DENTILS IS SAME AS ELEVATION

LATE ADDITIONS

SIDE ELEVATION

The EARLY ARCHITECTURE of WESTERN PENNSYLVANIA

THE DORSEY HOUSE
NEAR BROWNSVILLE — WASHINGTON COUNTY

Measured by
MARIO C. CELLI
Drawn by
RAYMOND C. CELLI

The Joseph Dorsey House near Brownsville

Door Detail of the Dorsey House

Main Entrance of the Dorsey House

PANELED END OF LIVING ROOM

SCALE IN FEET FOR PLAN AND ELEVATIONS.

THREE SHELVES IN CUPBOARD.

PLAN

SCALE IN INCHES FOR SECTIONS.

LIVING ROOM
HALF ELEVATION OF FENESTRATED SIDE

The EARLY ARCHITECTURE of WESTERN PENNSYLVANIA

THE DORSEY HOUSE
NEAR BROWNSVILLE ~ WASHINGTON COUNTY

Measured by
MARIO C. CELLI
Drawn by
RAYMOND C. CELLI

"A"

A

"Y"

"V" "U"

"C"

B

C

"B"

"Z"

D

"W"

MOLDING ON
DOOR PANELS SAME

"X"

SCALE IN INCHES
FOR SECTIONS

"D"

ENTRANCE DOOR
WOOD

PLAN

SCALE IN FEET FOR PLANS
AND ELEVATIONS

THREE SHELVES
IN CUPBOARDS

U

V

Y

Z

W

X

BED ROOM

The EARLY
ARCHITECTURE
of WESTERN
PENNSYLVANIA

THE DORSEY HOUSE
NEAR BROWNSVILLE—WASHINGTON COUNTY

Measured by
MARIO C. CELLI
Drawn by
RAYMOND C CELLI

About 1787

Washington 88

Rear View of the Dorsey House

About 1787   *Washington 88*

Bedroom Closet in the Dorsey House

About 1787   *Washington 88*

Living Room Detail in the Dorsey House

The Presley Neville House near Woodville

End View of the Neville House

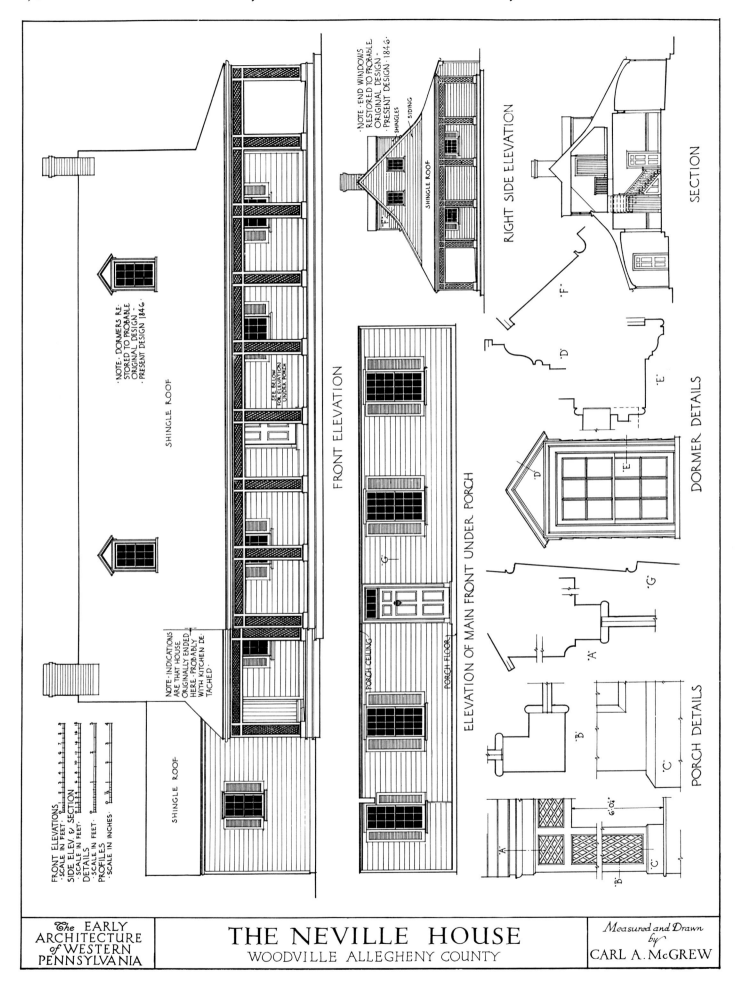

·NOTE· DORMERS RE-
STORED TO PROBABLE
ORIGINAL DESIGN·
·PRESENT DESIGN 1846·

SHINGLE ROOF

·NOTE· END WINDOWS
RESTORED TO PROBABLE
ORIGINAL DESIGN·
·PRESENT DESIGN ·1846·

SHINGLES
SIDING

SHINGLE ROOF

RIGHT SIDE ELEVATION

SECTION

SEE BELOW
FOR ELEVATION
UNDER PORCH

FRONT ELEVATION

·NOTE· INDICATIONS
ARE THAT HOUSE
ORIGINALLY ENDED
HERE· PROBABLY
WITH KITCHEN DE-
TACHED·

SHINGLE ROOF

PORCH CEILING
PORCH FLOOR

ELEVATION OF MAIN FRONT UNDER PORCH

DORMER DETAILS

PORCH DETAILS

FRONT ELEVATIONS
·SCALE IN FEET·
SIDE ELEV· & SECTION
·SCALE IN FEET·
DETAILS
·SCALE IN FEET·
PROFILES
·SCALE IN INCHES·

The EARLY
ARCHITECTURE
of WESTERN
PENNSYLVANIA

THE NEVILLE HOUSE
WOODVILLE ALLEGHENY COUNTY

Measured and Drawn
by
CARL A. McGREW

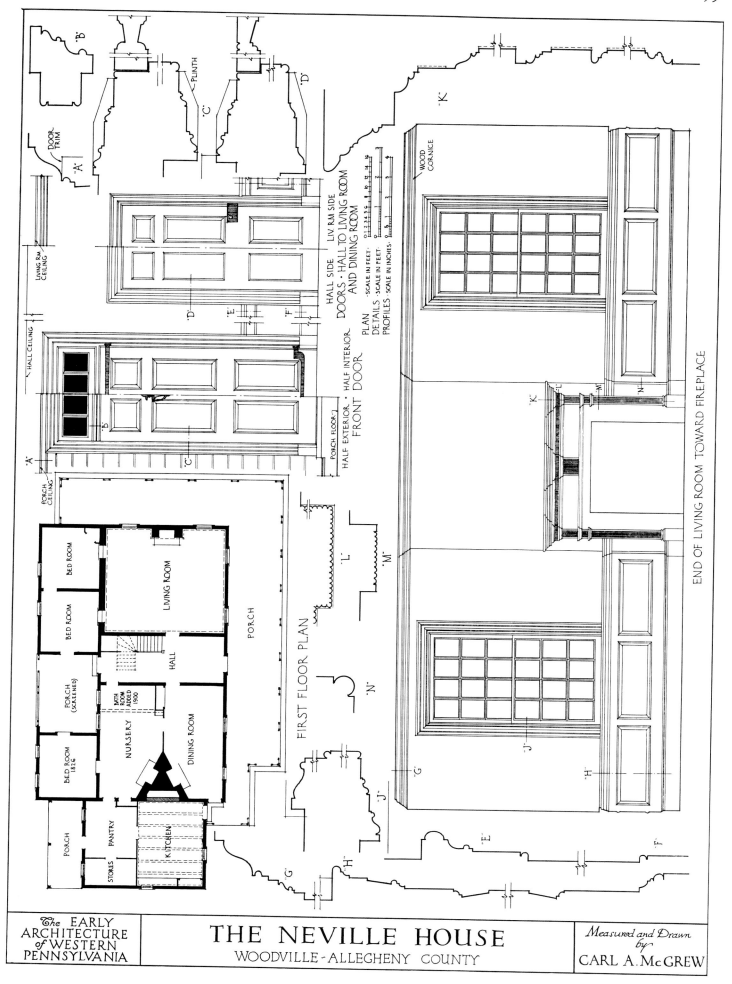

DOOR TRIM

"A"

PLINTH

"C"

"D"

DOOR TRIM

LIVING RM CEILING

HALL CEILING

"A"

PORCH CEILING

HALL SIDE · LIV RM SIDE
DOORS · HALL TO LIVING ROOM
AND DINING ROOM

"D"

"E"

"F"

HALF INTERIOR · HALF EXTERIOR
FRONT DOOR

"B"

"C"

PORCH FLOOR

PLAN · SCALE IN FEET·
DETAILS · SCALE IN FEET·
PROFILES · SCALE IN INCHES·

WOOD CORNICE

"K"

END OF LIVING ROOM TOWARD FIREPLACE

"K"

"M"

"N"

"J"

"G"

"H"

"E"

"F"

FIRST FLOOR PLAN

"L"

"M"

"N"

"G"

"H"

"J"

BED ROOM

BED ROOM

LIVING ROOM

PORCH (SCREENED)

HALL

BATH ROOM ADDED 1900

BED ROOM 1826

NURSERY

DINING ROOM

PORCH

STORES

PANTRY

KITCHEN

PORCH

The EARLY
ARCHITECTURE
of WESTERN
PENNSYLVANIA

THE NEVILLE HOUSE
WOODVILLE—ALLEGHENY COUNTY

Measured and Drawn
by
CARL A. McGREW

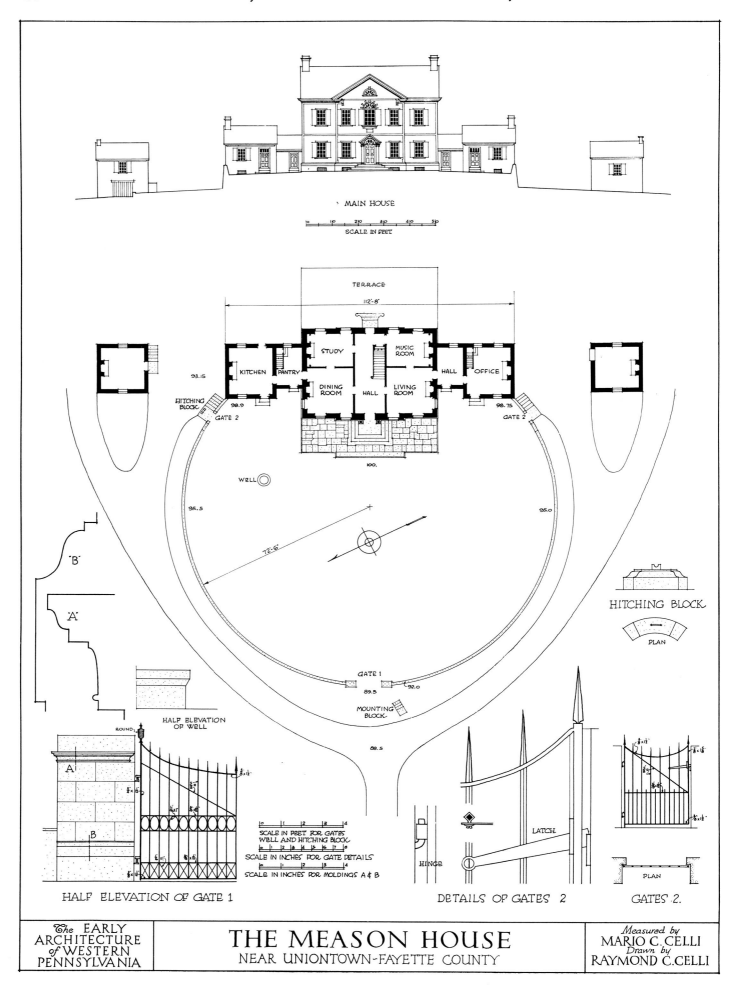

MAIN HOUSE

SCALE IN FEET

TERRACE

112'-8"

93.15

KITCHEN PANTRY   STUDY   MUSIC ROOM   HALL   OFFICE

DINING ROOM   HALL   LIVING ROOM

HITCHING BLOCK

98.9   GATE 2

98.75   GATE 2

100.

WELL

95.5

95.0

72'-6"

HITCHING BLOCK

PLAN

"B"

"A"

GATE 1

89.5   92.0

MOUNTING BLOCK

88.5

HALF ELEVATION OF WELL

ROUND

A

B

SCALE IN FEET FOR GATES
WELL AND HITCHING BLOCK

SCALE IN INCHES FOR GATE DETAILS

SCALE IN INCHES FOR MOLDINGS A & B

LATCH

HINGE

PLAN

HALF ELEVATION OF GATE 1   DETAILS OF GATES 2   GATES 2.

| The EARLY ARCHITECTURE of WESTERN PENNSYLVANIA | THE MEASON HOUSE
NEAR UNIONTOWN-FAYETTE COUNTY | Measured by
MARIO C. CELLI
Drawn by
RAYMOND C. CELLI |

1802

"Mt. Braddock," the Isaac Meason House near Uniontown

Fayette 2

1802

General View of the Meason House

Fayette 2

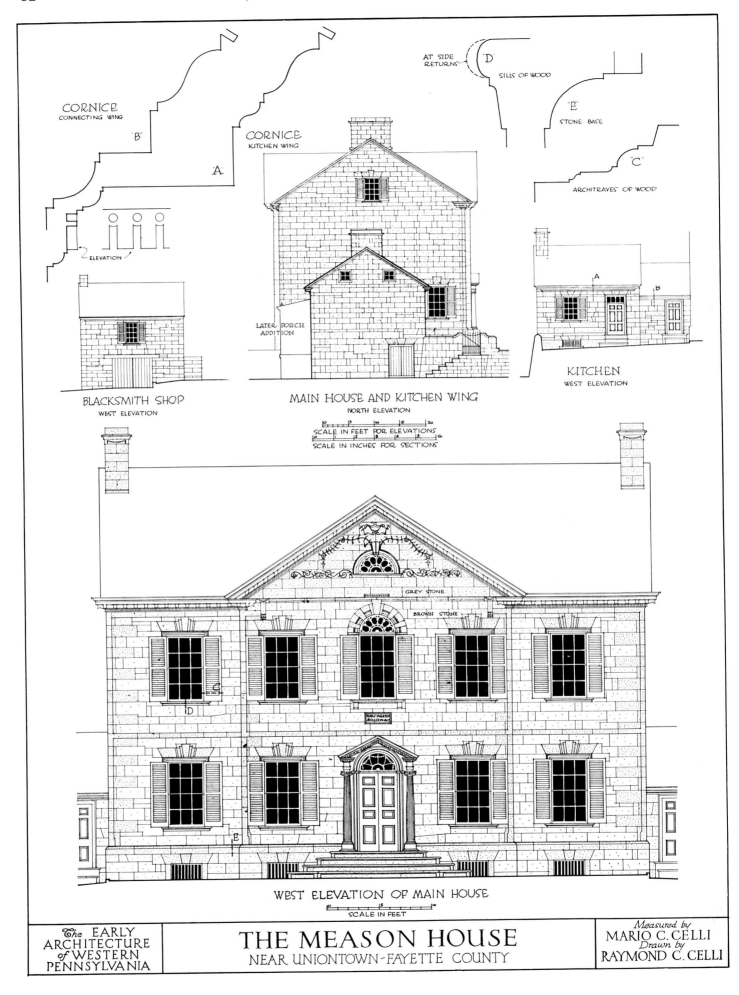

CORNICE
CONNECTING WING
'B'
'A'
ELEVATION

CORNICE
KITCHEN WING

AT SIDE
RETURNS   'D'
SILLS OF WOOD

'E'
STONE BASE

'C'
ARCHITRAVES OF WOOD

LATER PORCH
ADDITION

KITCHEN
WEST ELEVATION

BLACKSMITH SHOP
WEST ELEVATION

MAIN HOUSE AND KITCHEN WING
NORTH ELEVATION

SCALE IN FEET FOR ELEVATIONS
SCALE IN INCHES FOR SECTIONS

GREY STONE

BROWN STONE

WEST ELEVATION OF MAIN HOUSE
SCALE IN FEET

The EARLY
ARCHITECTURE
of WESTERN
PENNSYLVANIA

THE MEASON HOUSE
NEAR UNIONTOWN-FAYETTE COUNTY

Measured by
MARIO C. CELLI
Drawn by
RAYMOND C. CELLI

1802 Cornice Detail of the Meason House *Fayette 2*   *1802* Pediment Detail of the Meason House *Fayette 2*

1802 Window Detail of the Meason House *Fayette 2*   *1802* Gable End of the Meason House *Fayette 2*

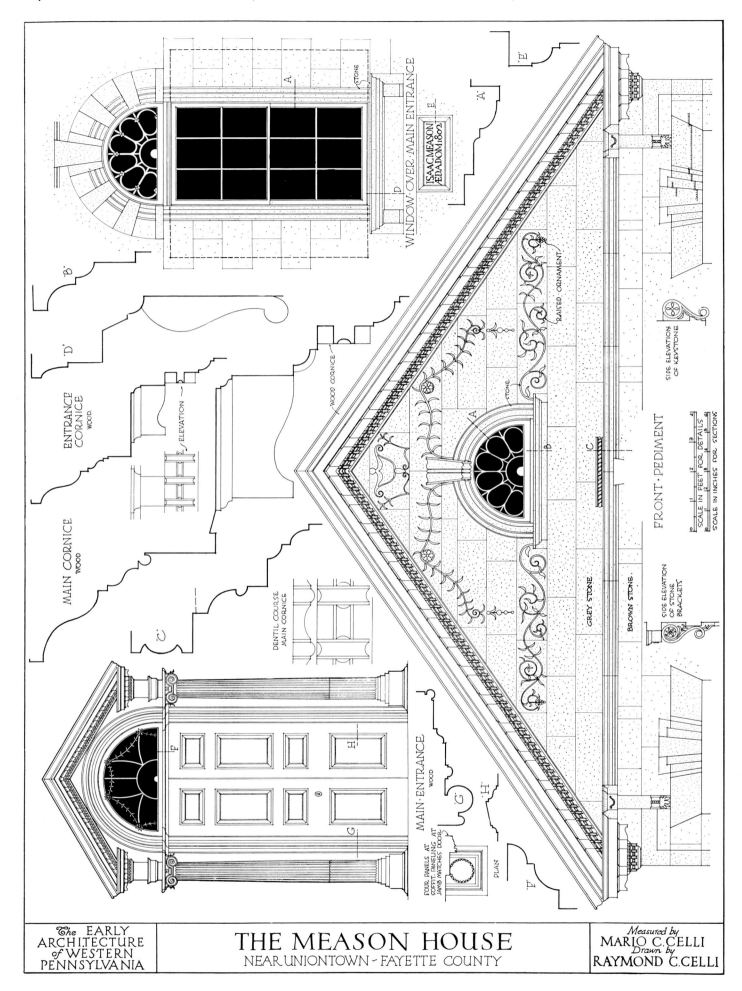

WINDOW·OVER·MAIN ENTRANCE

ISAAC MEASON AEDADOM 1802

ENTRANCE CORNICE WOOD.

ELEVATION

WOOD CORNICE

MAIN CORNICE WOOD

DENTIL COURSE MAIN CORNICE

RAISED ORNAMENT

FRONT·PEDIMENT

SIDE ELEVATION OF KEYSTONE

GREY STONE.

BROWN STONE.

SIDE ELEVATION OF STONE BRACKETS

SCALE IN FEET FOR DETAILS

SCALE IN INCHES FOR SECTIONS

MAIN·ENTRANCE WOOD

FOUR PANELS AT COFFIT. PANELING AT JAMB MATCHES DOOR.

PLAN

The EARLY ARCHITECTURE of WESTERN PENNSYLVANIA

THE MEASON HOUSE
NEAR UNIONTOWN - FAYETTE COUNTY

Measured by
MARIO C. CELLI
Drawn by
RAYMOND C. CELLI

Entrance Doorway Detail of the Meason House

Fayette 2

1802

Entrance Doorway of the Meason House

Fayette 2

1802

MANTEL
IN DINING ROOM

MANTEL
IN OFFICE

SCALE IN FEET FOR
ALL MANTELS

MANTEL
IN BED ROOM

COMPOSITION ORNAMENT IN HALL

SCALE IN INCHES

"F"

"G"

"D"

"E"

"F"

ELEVATION

INTERIOR DOORS

FIRST FLOOR   2ND FL.

SCALE IN FEET

"A"

"X"
WOOD CORNICE
IN HALL

"X"
WOOD CORNICE
IN DINING ROOM

"B"

"H"

"C"

DOOR TRIM
FIRST FLOOR

PLINTH

REAR DOOR

DOOR TRIM
SECOND FLOOR

DADO
FIRST FLOOR

DOOR SECTION
FIRST FLOOR

ONE HALF PLAN

SCALE IN FEET FOR PLAN
AND ELEVATION

DOOR SECTION
SECOND FLOOR

HALL DADO
SECOND FLOOR

BASE
FIRST FLOOR

BASE
SECOND FLOOR

"X"
ROOM DADO
SECOND
FLOOR

"X"
SECONDARY
TRIM
SECOND FLOOR

SCALE IN INCHES FOR ALL LETTERED SECTIONS

SCALE IN INCHES FOR ALL OTHER SECTIONS

The EARLY
ARCHITECTURE
of WESTERN
PENNSYLVANIA

THE MEASON HOUSE
NEAR UNIONTOWN-FAYETTE COUNTY

Measured by
MARIO C CELLI
Drawn by
RAYMOND C. CELLI

An Out-building of the Meason House

Fayette 2

1802

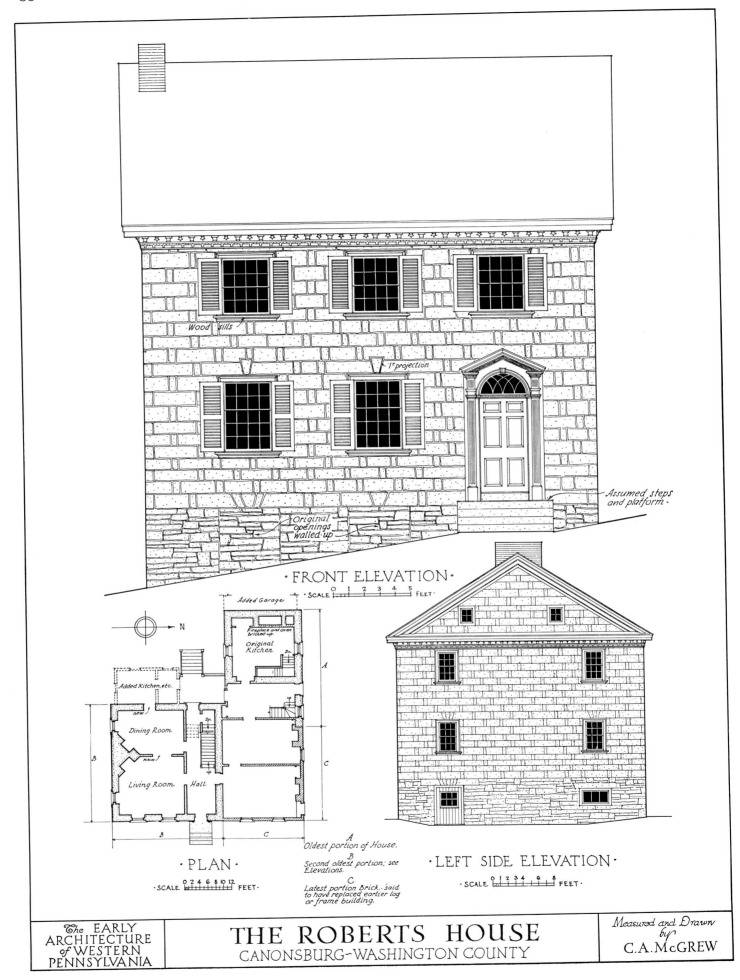

Wood sills

1" projection

Assumed steps
and platform·

Original
openings
walled·up·

·FRONT ELEVATION·

·SCALE· 0 1 2 3 4 5 FEET·

Added Garage

Fireplace and oven
bricked·up·

Original
Kitchen

Dn.

N

Added Kitchen, etc.

new!

Dining Room

new!

Up

Dn

Living Room   Hall

A

C

B

B   C

·PLAN·

·SCALE· 0 2 4 6 8 10 12 FEET·

A
Oldest portion of House.

B
Second oldest portion; see
Elevations.

C
Latest portion Brick,- said
to have replaced earlier log
or frame building.

·LEFT SIDE ELEVATION·

·SCALE· 0 1 2 3 4 6 8 FEET·

The EARLY
ARCHITECTURE
of WESTERN
PENNSYLVANIA

THE ROBERTS HOUSE
CANONSBURG-WASHINGTON COUNTY

Measured and Drawn
by
C.A. McGREW

Washington 29

1804

Doorway in the Roberts House

Washington 29

The John Roberts House in Canonsburg

1804

·SECTION·

·MAIN ENTRANCE DETAILS·

SCALES

·INTERIOR·

Face of stone step

"C"

"D"-"D"

"E"-"E"

"F"-"F"

DETAIL AT "A"

DETAIL AT "B"

The EARLY ARCHITECTURE of WESTERN PENNSYLVANIA

THE ROBERTS HOUSE
CANONSBURG·WASHINGTON COUNTY

Measured and Drawn by
C. A. McGREW

· SCALES ·

ELEVATIONS
EXCEPT CORNICE

DETAILS
AND CORNICE

PROFILES

TYPICAL WINDOW
IN LIVING ROOM

STAIR.

CORNICE
SECTIONS

"A-A"   "B-B"   "C-C"   "D-D"

CORNICE ELEVATION

"E-E"

DINING ROOM MANTEL

DETAIL AT "M"   LIVING ROOM MANTEL   DETAIL AT "N"

The EARLY
ARCHITECTURE
of WESTERN
PENNSYLVANIA

THE ROBERTS HOUSE
CANONSBURG - WASHINGTON COUNTY

Measured and Drawn
by
C.A.McGREW

About 1808   *Allegheny 2*

The James Miller House in South Park

1830   *Allegheny 111*   *About 1798*   *Fayette 93*
Shepherd's House, James Patterson Farm near Dravosburg   The Jacob Harris House near Perryopolis

Fayette 92

The Richard Hill House near Upper Middletown

About 1820

Westmoreland 70

"Mansion House," The John Daily House near Webster

About 1797

Allegheny 164

House on Spring Street, Pittsburgh

Date Unknown

Allegheny 34

"The Meadows," the James Ross House near Aspinwall

About 1810 (Demolished)

About 1797

Bedroom Wall in the Daily House

About 1797   *Westmoreland 70*

Mantel Detail of the Daily House

About 1797   *Westmoreland 70*

Trim Detail of the Daily House

About 1797   Living Room Closet in the Daily House

About 1797   Entrance Doorway of the Daily House

SCALE IN FEET

THIS SPACE
REACHED FROM
2ND. FLOOR
CLOSET.

SECTION A·A   SLIDING
SHELF.

SCALE OF INCHES FOR DETAILS
MARKED · F. T. G. S. N. R. H.

PLAN AT Z.

ELEVATION · &·
DETAILS of MANTEL
& CUPBOARDS.

SCALE OF INCHES FOR
DETAILS MARKED
A. B. D. K. M. Z.

The EARLY
ARCHITECTURE
of WESTERN
PENNSYLVANIA

THE DAILY HOUSE
WEBSTER·WESTMORELAND COUNTY

Measured and Drawn
by
N.D.KUTCHUKIAN

SECTION A.

A.
MAIN ELEVATION
SCALE OF FEET

ONE HALF
INTERIOR ELEV.

DETAILS
OF DOORWAY.
SCALE OF INCHES FOR
C·D·H·J AND DETAILS
IN FAN LIGHT

WOOD   WOOD

SCALE OF INCHES FOR·
B·M·F·K· AND E·

The EARLY
ARCHITECTURE
of WESTERN
PENNSYLVANIA

THE DAILY HOUSE
WEBSTER·WESTMORELAND COUNTY

Measured and Drawn
by
N·D·KUTCHUKIAN

1815   *Washington 36*

"Plantation Plenty," the Isaac Manchester House near West Middletown

1815   *Washington 36*

Front View of the Manchester House

1815

End View of the Manchester House

Washington 36

1815

Washington 36

An Out-building of the Manchester House

1815

Washington 36

Gable Detail of the Manchester House

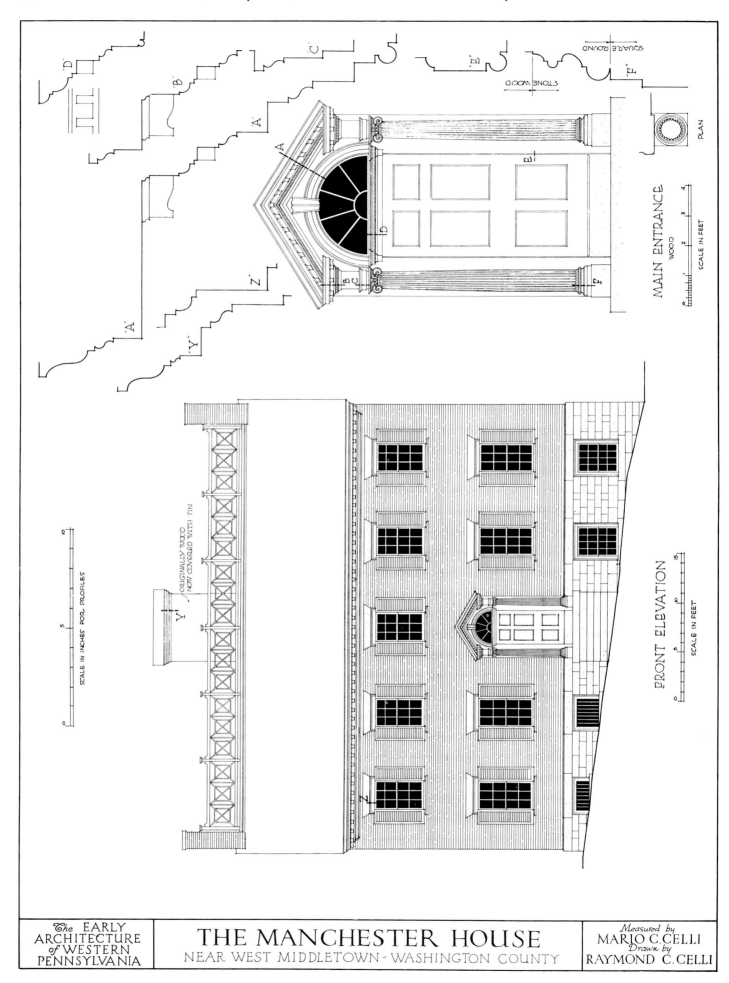

MAIN ENTRANCE

WOOD

SCALE IN FEET

PLAN

SQUARE ROUND

STONE WOOD

PROFILES

SCALE IN INCHES FOR PROFILES

ORIGINALLY WOOD
NOW COVERED WITH TIN

FRONT ELEVATION

SCALE IN FEET

THE MANCHESTER HOUSE
NEAR WEST MIDDLETOWN - WASHINGTON COUNTY

Measured by
MARIO C. CELLI
Drawn by
RAYMOND C. CELLI

Door Detail of the Manchester House

1815

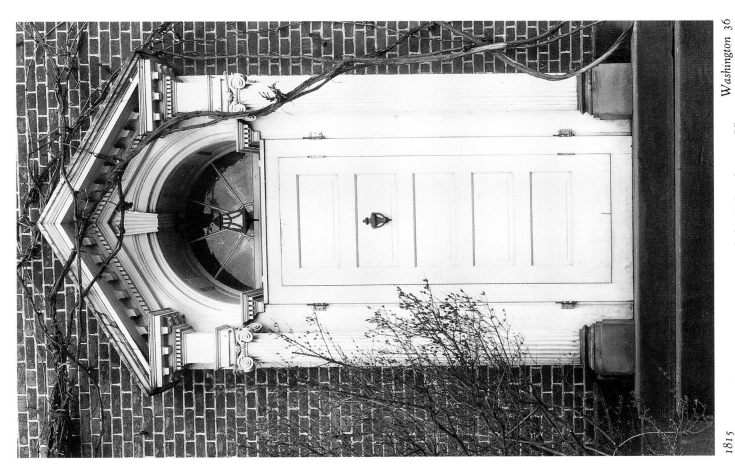

Entrance Doorway of the Manchester House

1815

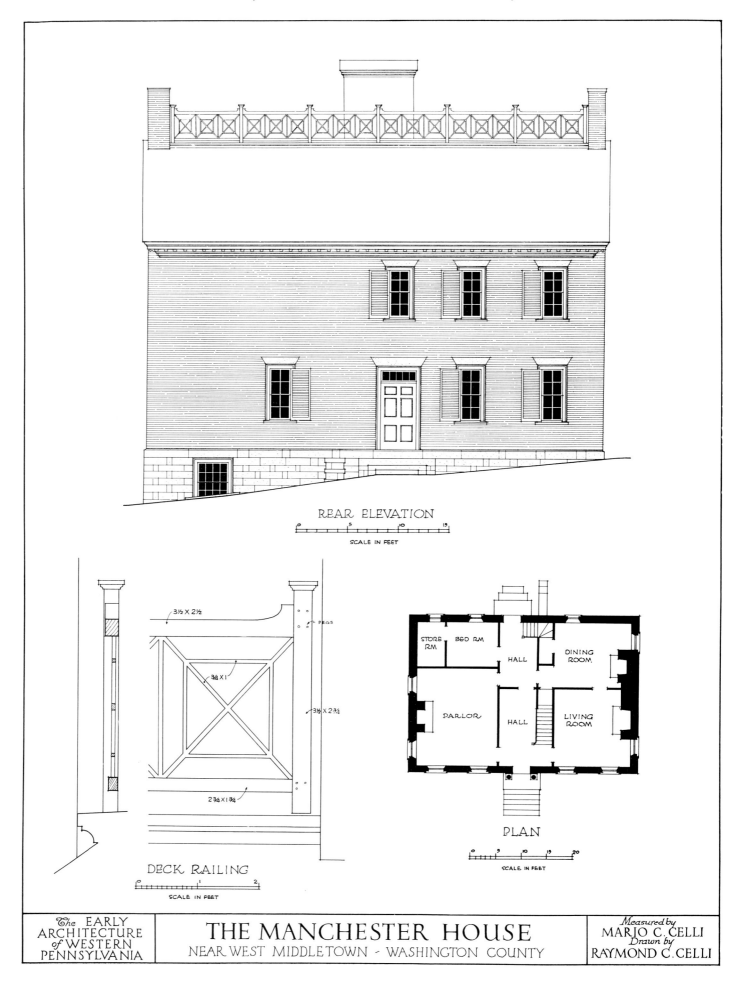

REAR ELEVATION

SCALE IN FEET

DECK RAILING

SCALE IN FEET

PLAN

SCALE IN FEET

STORE RM

BED RM

HALL

DINING ROOM.

PARLOR

HALL

LIVING ROOM

3½ X 2½

PEGS

¾ X 1

3½ X 2¾

2¾ X 1¾

The EARLY ARCHITECTURE of WESTERN PENNSYLVANIA

THE MANCHESTER HOUSE
NEAR WEST MIDDLETOWN · WASHINGTON COUNTY

Measured by
MARIO C. CELLI
Drawn by
RAYMOND C. CELLI

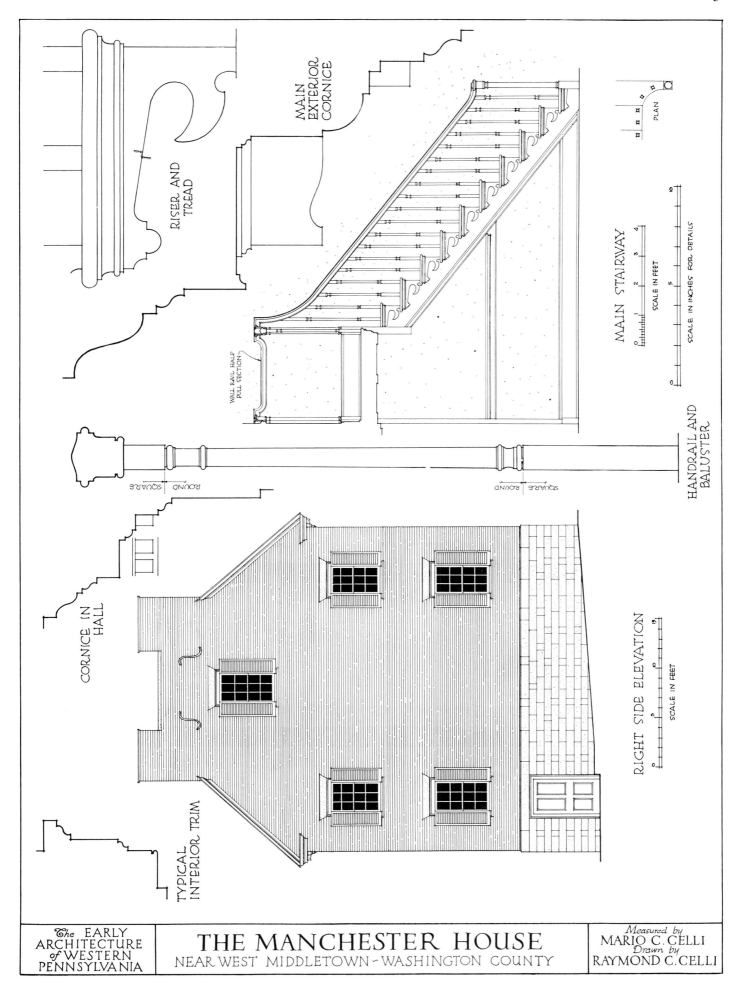

RISER AND TREAD

MAIN EXTERIOR CORNICE

PLAN

WALL RAIL HALF FULL SECTION

MAIN STAIRWAY

SCALE IN FEET

SCALE IN INCHES FOR DETAILS

ROUND | SQUARE

SQUARE | ROUND

HANDRAIL AND BALUSTER

CORNICE IN HALL

TYPICAL INTERIOR TRIM

RIGHT SIDE ELEVATION

SCALE IN FEET

The EARLY ARCHITECTURE of WESTERN PENNSYLVANIA

THE MANCHESTER HOUSE
NEAR WEST MIDDLETOWN - WASHINGTON COUNTY

Measured by
MARIO C. CELLI
Drawn by
RAYMOND C. CELLI

1815

"Kingston House," the Alexander Johnston House near Latrobe

1815   *Westmoreland 28*

Porch Detail of the Johnston House

1815   *Westmoreland 28*

Entrance Doorway of the Johnston House

Westmoreland 28

Left Side View of the Johnston House

1815

Westmoreland 28

Outside Oven of the Johnston House

1815

Westmoreland 28

Side Porch of the Johnston House

1815

Westmoreland 28

Rear Porch of the Johnston House

1815

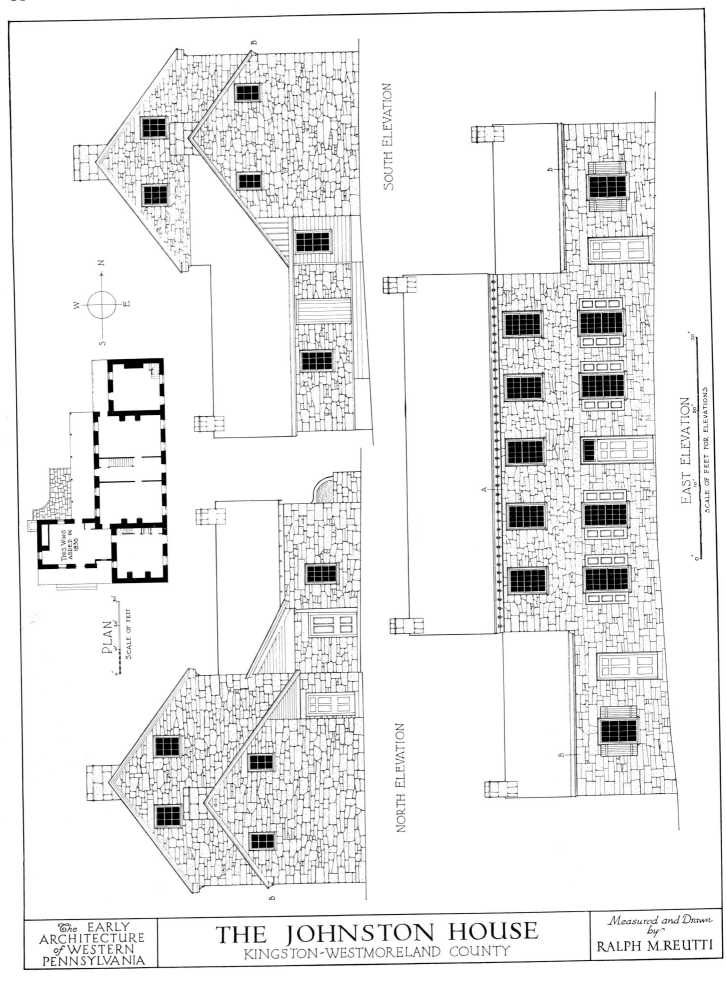

SOUTH ELEVATION

N

W E

S

PLAN

SCALE OF FEET

THIS WING
ADDED IN
1830

NORTH ELEVATION

EAST ELEVATION

SCALE OF FEET FOR ELEVATIONS

THE JOHNSTON HOUSE
KINGSTON-WESTMORELAND COUNTY

Measured and Drawn
by
RALPH M. REUTTI

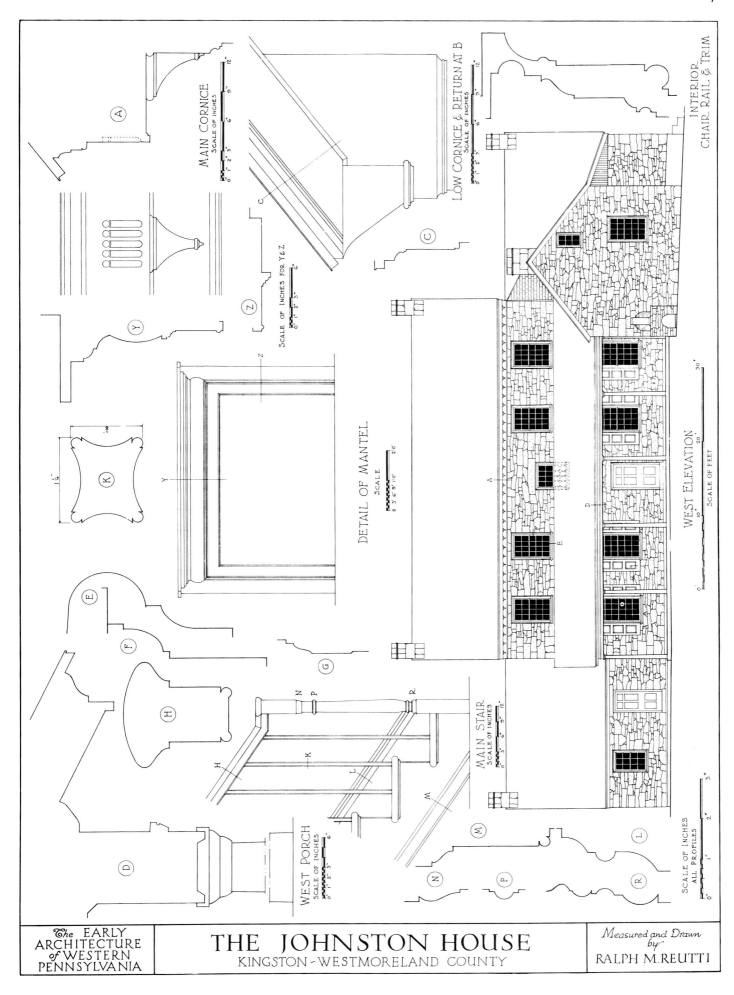

MAIN CORNICE
SCALE OF INCHES

LOW CORNICE & RETURN AT B
SCALE OF INCHES

INTERIOR
CHAIR RAIL & TRIM

SCALE OF INCHES FOR Y&Z

DETAIL OF MANTEL
SCALE

WEST ELEVATION
SCALE OF FEET

MAIN STAIR
SCALE OF INCHES

WEST PORCH
SCALE OF INCHES

SCALE OF INCHES
ALL PROFILES

The EARLY
ARCHITECTURE
of WESTERN
PENNSYLVANIA

THE JOHNSTON HOUSE
KINGSTON - WESTMORELAND COUNTY

Measured and Drawn
by
RALPH M. REUTTI

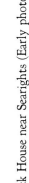

Washington 9

The William M. Quail House near Canonsburg

1832

Fayette 532

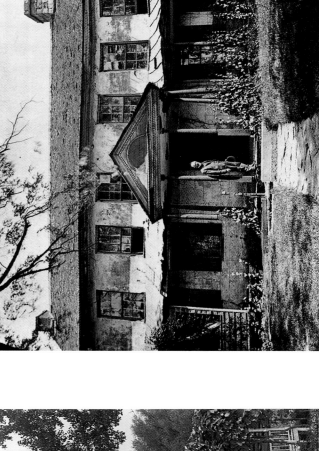

The Jacob Black House near Searights (Early photo)

About 1795

Washington 62

The Joshua Wright House near Finleyville

About 1821

Westmoreland 23

The Peter Waugaman House near Delmont

About 1830

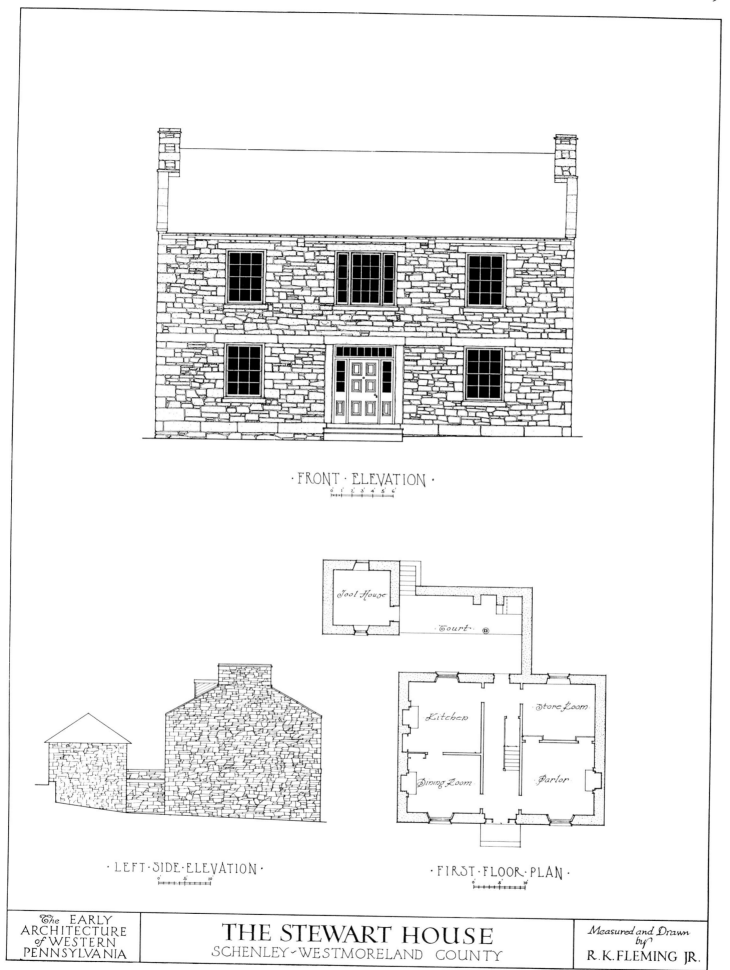

· FRONT · ELEVATION ·

· LEFT · SIDE · ELEVATION ·

· FIRST · FLOOR · PLAN ·

Tool House

· *Court* ·

Kitchen

Store Room

Dining Room

Parlor

The EARLY
ARCHITECTURE
of WESTERN
PENNSYLVANIA

THE STEWART HOUSE
SCHENLEY~WESTMORELAND COUNTY

Measured and Drawn
by
R.K. FLEMING JR.

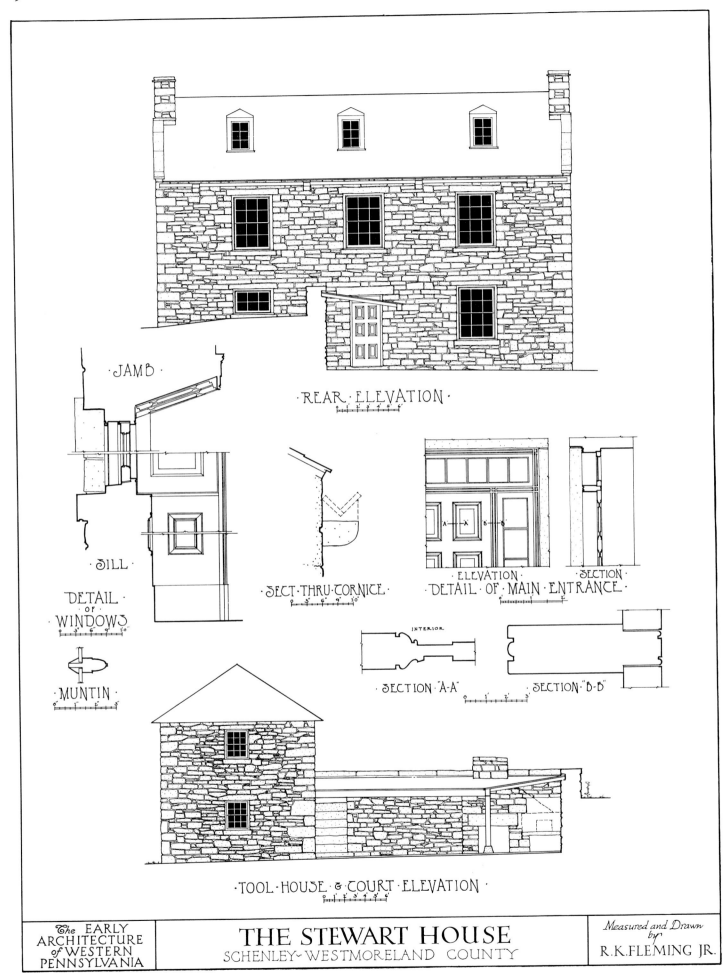

· JAMB ·

· SILL ·

DETAIL
OF
WINDOWS

· MUNTIN ·

· REAR · ELEVATION ·

· SECT · THRU · CORNICE ·

INTERIOR

SECTION "A-A"

· ELEVATION ·
· DETAIL · OF · MAIN · ENTRANCE ·

· SECTION ·

SECTION "B-B"

· TOOL · HOUSE · & · COURT · ELEVATION ·

| The EARLY ARCHITECTURE of WESTERN PENNSYLVANIA | THE STEWART HOUSE SCHENLEY~WESTMORELAND COUNTY | Measured and Drawn by R.K. FLEMING JR. |

1844   *Westmoreland 2*

"The King of Scotland's House," the John Stewart House near Schenley

1844   *Westmoreland 2*   1844   *Westmoreland 2*

Toolhouse of the Stewart House   Entrance Doorway of the Stewart House

Washington 85

The Hiram Smith House in Centerville

1830

Allegheny 15

A House on Watson Street, Pittsburgh

Date Unknown

Allegheny 150

House on Canal Street, Sharpsburg

About 1835

Washington 98

The Chambers House at Chambers Dam

1823

Blair 12

The Hileman House in Frankstown

About 1795

Bedford 17

The Hugh Barclay House in Bedford

1796

Bedford 63

The Noble House near New Enterprise

Date Unknown

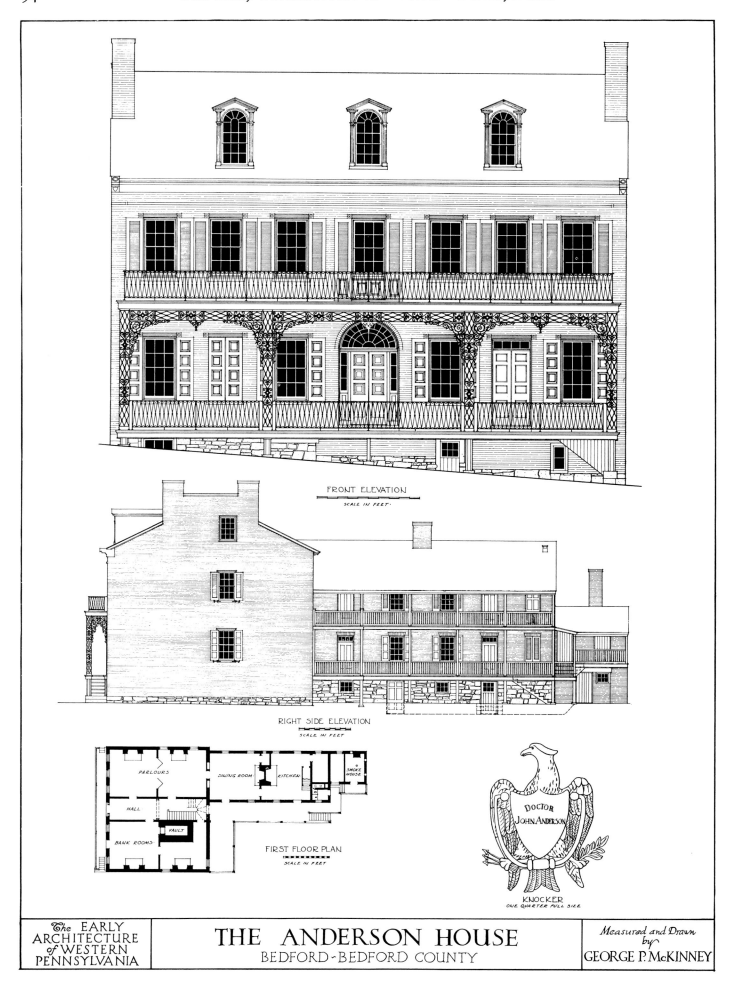

FRONT ELEVATION

SCALE IN FEET

RIGHT SIDE ELEVATION

SCALE IN FEET

PARLOURS

DINING ROOM

KITCHEN

SMOKE HOUSE

HALL

VAULT

BANK ROOMS

FIRST FLOOR PLAN

SCALE IN FEET

DOCTOR JOHN ANDERSON

KNOCKER
ONE QUARTER FULL SIZE

The EARLY ARCHITECTURE of WESTERN PENNSYLVANIA

THE ANDERSON HOUSE
BEDFORD - BEDFORD COUNTY

Measured and Drawn by
GEORGE P. McKINNEY

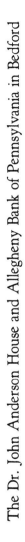

Bedford 29

The Dr. John Anderson House and Allegheny Bank of Pennsylvania in Bedford

1815

DORMER. ORNAMENT

CAST IRON PORCH ORNAMENT

DORMER.

PROFILE C

MAIN CORNICE OF FRONT ELEVATION.

SLATE

·D·

CAP

·E·

BASE

DORMER PROFILES·

SCALE OF ALL PROFILES·

MAIN ENTRANCE·

PORCH RAIL

The EARLY
ARCHITECTURE
of WESTERN
PENNSYLVANIA

THE ANDERSON HOUSE
BEDFORD~BEDFORD COUNTY

Measured and Drawn
by
GEORGE P. McKINNEY

1816   *Bedford 33*

The James Russell House in Bedford

About 1800   *Blair 21*   *1770*   *Bedford 14*

The Moore House near Frankstown   The Colonel Espy House in Bedford

1815   *Blair 18*

The Daniel Royer House near Williamsburg

1815   *Blair 18*

End View of the Royer House

1815   *Blair 18*

Log Wing of the Royer House

1815   *Blair 18*   1815   *Blair 18*

Porch Detail of the Royer House   Wall Detail of the Royer House

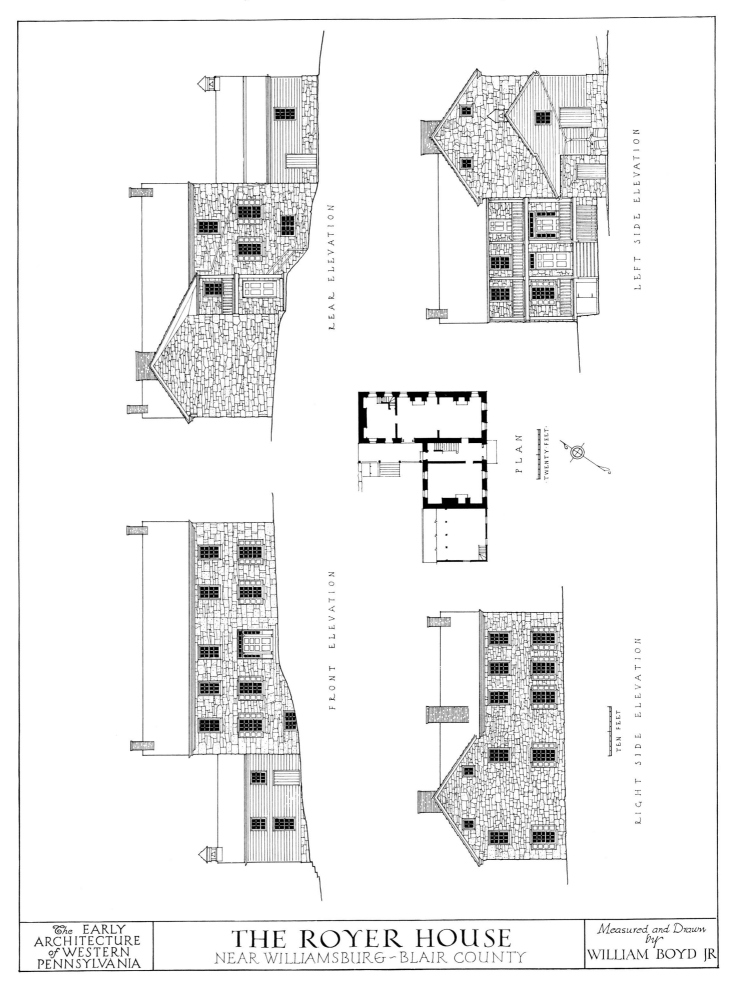

REAR ELEVATION

LEFT SIDE ELEVATION

PLAN

TWENTY FEET

FRONT ELEVATION

TEN FEET

RIGHT SIDE ELEVATION

The EARLY
ARCHITECTURE
of WESTERN
PENNSYLVANIA

THE ROYER HOUSE
NEAR WILLIAMSBURG - BLAIR COUNTY

Measured and Drawn
by
WILLIAM BOYD JR

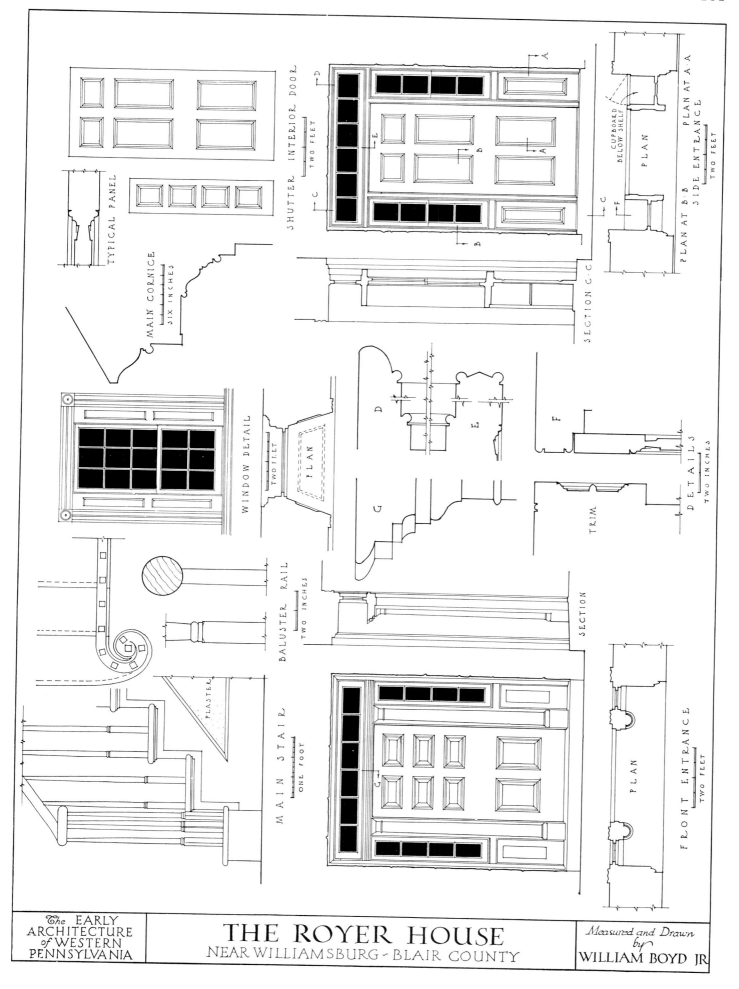

TYPICAL PANEL

MAIN CORNICE
SIX INCHES

SHUTTER INTERIOR DOOR
TWO FEET

SECTION C-C

PLAN AT B-B   PLAN
SIDE ENTRANCE
TWO FEET

PLAN AT A-A
CUPBOARD BELOW SHELF

WINDOW DETAIL
TWO FEET

PLAN

D   E   F

G   TRIM

DETAILS
TWO INCHES

BALUSTER RAIL
TWO INCHES

SECTION

MAIN STAIR
ONE FOOT

PLASTER

FRONT ENTRANCE
TWO FEET

PLAN

The EARLY ARCHITECTURE of WESTERN PENNSYLVANIA

THE ROYER HOUSE
NEAR WILLIAMSBURG - BLAIR COUNTY

Measured and Drawn by
WILLIAM BOYD JR

1820

The Amos Judson House in Waterford

1820   Erie 15   1820   Erie 15

Stair Detail of the Judson House   Cornice Detail of the Judson House

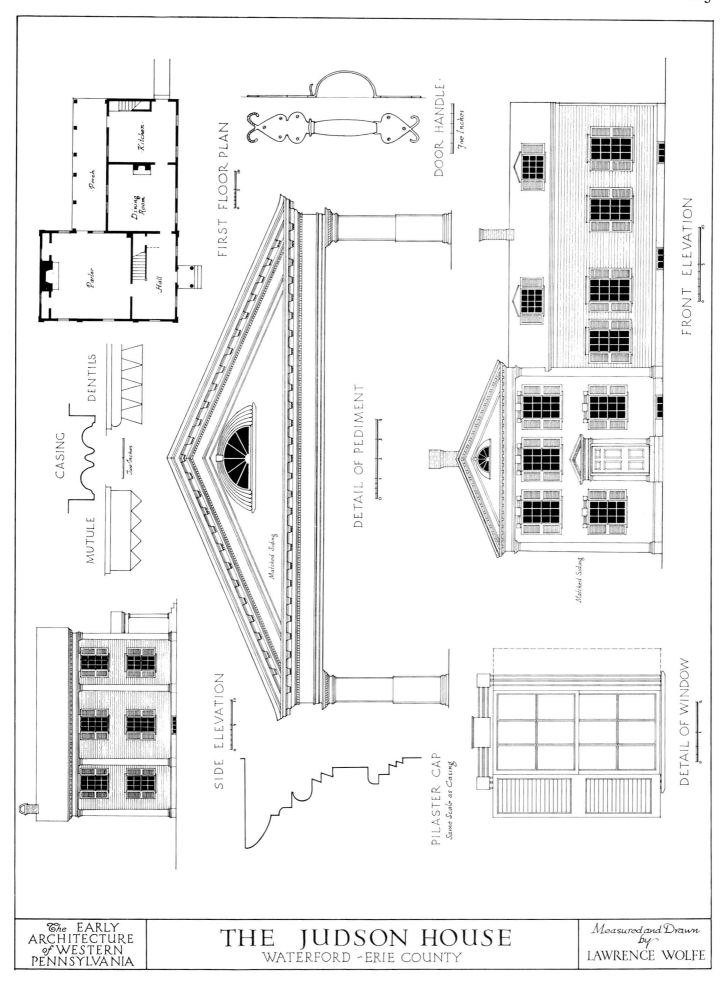

FIRST FLOOR PLAN

Porch

Kitchen

Dining Room

Parlor

Hall

DOOR HANDLE.
Five Inches

CASING

DENTILS
Two Inches

MUTULE

DETAIL OF PEDIMENT

Matched Siding

FRONT ELEVATION

Matched Siding

SIDE ELEVATION

PILASTER CAP
Same Scale as Casing

DETAIL OF WINDOW

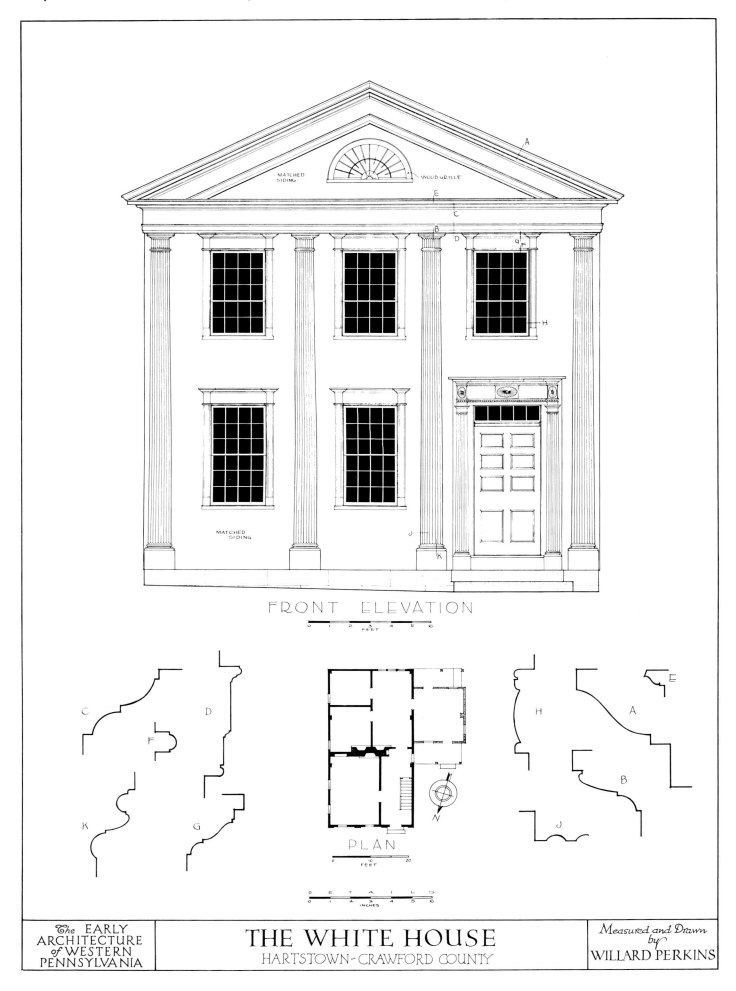

FRONT ELEVATION

PLAN

DETAIL

THE EARLY ARCHITECTURE of WESTERN PENNSYLVANIA

THE WHITE HOUSE
HARTSTOWN-CRAWFORD COUNTY

Measured and Drawn
by
WILLARD PERKINS

Crawford 37

The Dr. James White House in Hartstown

1835

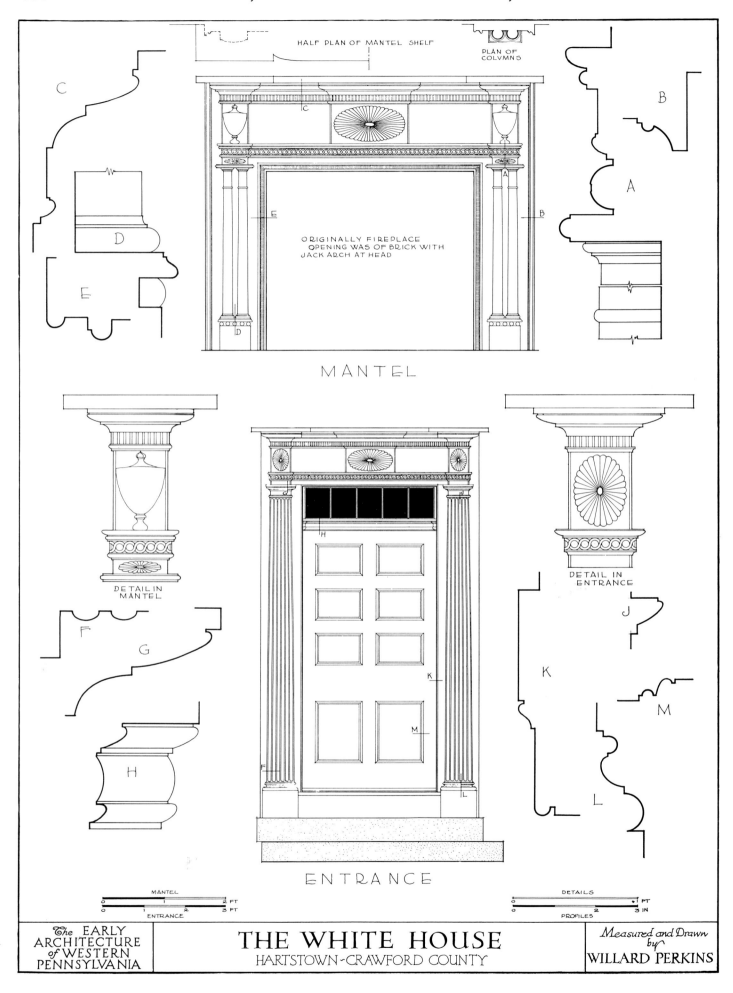

HALF PLAN OF MANTEL SHELF

PLAN OF COLUMNS

ORIGINALLY FIREPLACE
OPENING WAS OF BRICK WITH
JACK ARCH AT HEAD

MANTEL

DETAIL IN MANTEL

DETAIL IN ENTRANCE

ENTRANCE

MANTEL

ENTRANCE

DETAILS

PROFILES

The EARLY
ARCHITECTURE
of WESTERN
PENNSYLVANIA

THE WHITE HOUSE
HARTSTOWN–CRAWFORD COUNTY

Measured and Drawn
by
WILLARD PERKINS

Crawford 37

Entrance Doorway of the White House

1835

Crawford 37

Living Room Mantel of the White House

1835

Crawford 37

Gable Detail of the White House

1835

DOMESTIC ARCHITECTURE

C. The Greek Revival

WHEN the Greek Revival style appeared in western Pennsylvania the district had finally achieved a degree of maturity and prosperity, and building practice was well established. Hence the young country west of the Allegheny Mountains was now ready to share in the full career of this new style, whereas it had known only the after-glow of the Colonial styles in its earlier archi-tecture. Although influences from the Post-Colonial period lingered for many years after 1830 in western Pennsylvania, particularly in the southwestern counties, the overwhelming popularity of the Greek Revival style dominated architectural design throughout the 1830's and 1840's and left its austere mark on houses erected as late as Civil War days.

Ancient Greek architecture was conspicuous more for its refinement and subtlety than for its variety of forms. A votive architecture, expressed in its highest development by the temple, it was the result of many centuries of intense emphasis upon a single type of building. It was an architecture of masonry construction, adapted to a warm, sunny climate.

Problems Peculiar to the Style

Thus it at once becomes obvious that conditions governing residential design in nineteenth-century America scarcely suited the Greek style for revival. The older heads among the builder-designers, such as Asher Benjamin, resented its intrusion upon well-established practices. Benjamin grudgingly recog-nized the style in his handbooks, but, as popular enthusiasm grew, plates illustrating forms of Georgian origin were rapidly supplanted in later editions by surprisingly faithful delineations of building remains in Greece and her colonies.

In applying these ancient marble temple forms to American wood house construction the carpenter was obliged to work out his own salvation and, surprisingly often, came off with honors. The formal porticoes, usually of wood, presented such difficul-ties in execution as the shallow fluting and subtle entasis of the Doric shaft, the involved spirals of the Ionic capital, and the undercutting required to produce the crisp delicacy of the original moldings. The manufacture of stock capitals, bases, ornament,

and the like solved these problems only partially. Not until the later editions of the handbooks did the carpenter have access to plates of designs and details of construction indicating how he might adapt his methods to the exigencies of the style.

Eberlein properly contends that the Greek Re-vival style was a "gigantic exhibition of architec-tural archaeology," but a sympathetic study of this curious phenomenon brings to light many houses of rare grace and dignity. At any rate, the Greek Revival style, as applied to domestic architecture, was a unique development in America and almost unknown in Europe; it was our first distinctly national style.

Regional Differences in the Style

In the twenty-three examples reproduced on pages 111 to 143 may be seen a representative group of houses in western Pennsylvania which show the full range of the style, from the little Hendryx House of wood to the monumental Baker House of stone. There was a much closer bond in design during this period than in the Post-Colonial era, although definite regional differences can be detected.

In the northern district there was a whole-hearted acceptance of the style; for this section, like central and western New York, was still in the settlement stage when the style was introduced. The majority of the houses of the northern area shown on pages 136 to 143 are of frame. In contrast with them, the buildings of the southwestern area, illustrated on pages 111 to 131 are almost all of masonry construc-tion. The lingering effects of the Post-Colonial period are most apparent in Washington, Fayette, and Greene counties. It is interesting to compare the Cunningham and Gordon houses with a pure Greek Revival example such as the Ives House in Potter County, in which the Greek elements have been assimilated and adapted to their new uses and materials.

Four distinguished examples in Allegheny County —the Shoenberger, Church, Wilkins, and Croghan houses—demonstrate the style in its most ambitious expression, but the contemporaneous Way and Lightner houses, though among the most delightful residences built during any period in the district, reflect but slight acquaintance with Greek influence. East of the Allegheny Ridge are two excellent products of the "grand manner" in Greek design—the Baker and Lyon houses.

The Portico

The glory of the Greek Revival house was its free-standing portico with four or six columns in one of the three orders, surmounted by a pediment or, less often, by a horizontal parapet. This feature, with its variations and adaptations, remained the chief problem in the rendition of the style.

The portico was more easily applied to the narrow end of the house, since the gable could serve as pediment (see the Baker and Mann houses); sometimes with wings at one or both sides, as in the Church and Ives houses. To simulate the stone originals, the pediments were treated as plain surfaces and rarely contained windows; when made of wood they were usually surfaced with matched flush board to eliminate the horizontal shadows of weatherboarding. In frame houses the wall face behind the portico also was treated in this way. Brick walls were frequently plastered to produce the effect of stone masonry, as in the Shoenberger and Reed houses.

The effect of placing the portico on the narrow end was to make an elaborate frontispiece of the entrance elevation, leaving the long barren side elevations practically devoid of architectural treatment. But this departure from precedent was accepted as an inevitable consequence of practical requirements. The portico was sometimes applied to the long elevation, as in the Reed House, where, if not an integral part of the house structure, it had a more logical relationship to the plan than did the cumbersome portico of the Wilkins House. In this instance, the portico is placed on the garden elevation purely for its external effect and, lacking the usual entrance, the three double-hung windows are extended to the floor.

Temple-front designs varied from such literal versions as the Wilkins House, in which the original stone forms were slavishly reproduced in wood and brick, to their more graceful interpretation in the Church House, or to such rational designs as the Ives House, where the essential elements of the Greek formula were adapted to the low scale and technique of a small house of wood construction.

The portico of the Baker House, marred only by its oversized Ionic capitals, is most imposing on its hilltop site. The rear portico of square stone piers is both impressive and refreshing in its contrast with the usual order treatment. This house conforms closely to its antique prototype, the masonry "cella" of unbroken rectangular shape. Such monumental quality is gained at the expense of domestic expression; in fact, with the addition of a cupola this building might easily be mistaken for a courthouse of the period. The portico with one-story order as expressed in the Way, Mulvanen, and Lightner houses was not common. These are transitional types, which happily combined in their designs the grace of the Georgian style with a pleasing restraint in the use of Greek moldings and detail.

Houses Without Porticoes

The application of orders and classic detail to the very small frame house—the rural American metamorphosis of the "temple"—produced such quaint anachronisms as the Hendryx House. In the anthemion of the pilasters and door head the carpenter produced a wooden jig-saw version of the antique marble ornament. Undaunted by the necessity of exposing the nail heads, he arranged them as a part of the pattern. The horizontal entablature is characteristically broken on the entrance front to permit the introduction of the second-story windows. The house in Wattsburg is another interesting diminutive rendering of the monumental Greek forms. The ingenious adaptation of the Ionic capital to square wooden piers is noteworthy. The jig-saw cornice board is probably of later vintage.

Even when two-story columns or pilasters were not employed, the entablature was proportioned to suit the absent members, as in the Lyon and Shoenberger houses. Because the entablature usually extended through most of the third story, windows were placed in the frieze to light this otherwise dark space. Because of their location close to the floor, they became known as "lie-on-your-stomach" windows. They were usually ornamented with grilles of wood or cast iron set in front of the glass, as in the Shoenberger, Church, and Baker houses. Those in the Lyon House have been removed.

Entrance doorways almost invariably were square-headed and usually had side lights and transoms. The door was framed either by pilasters or by a pair of columns surmounted by a pedimented hood, beautifully exemplified in the Irvin House. The three-story entrance design of the Playford House is unique in the district. Sometimes the entrance was protected by a one-story porch running the full length of the building, as in the Linn House. This might be considered the forerunner of the modern "front porch." The Saeger House, with recessed second-story porch opening on the pediment front, is most interesting. This building shows that a considerable degree of independence and judgment was exercised, particularly in the superimposed order of square wood posts and the generous proportion of the whole and its parts.

The use of ornament during the Greek Revival period was much more general than in the Post-Colonial period. It was executed in wood for exterior work, and in wood, plaster, and composition within the house. Cast-iron ornament was used for capitals, lintels, fences, and window and porch grilles. Plaster decoration was used in "stock" patterns, that of the Wilkins House ceiling, for instance, being identical with the pattern used in the Shoenberger House. Ornament reproduced in plaster and wood from the copious plates of designs in the handbooks required great skill, and special craftsmen were trained in this work. Mordecai van Horn, one of the ornamental workers, came to Pittsburgh from Philadelphia to execute the remarkable wood and plaster ornament profusely employed in the Croghan House interior.

Plan Arrangements

The favorite plan of the Greek Revival period was the center-hall house, with main entrance at the center of the narrower side. When the width of the house did not permit a center hall, the entrance was placed off center, as in the Mann and Ives houses. However, in many cases, as in the Lyon House, the plan arrangement differs little from those of the Post-Colonial period.

A plan arrangement of great interest was developed in the type of the Lightner, Way, and Mulvanen houses. The "English basement," brought halfway out of ground, is lighted by large windows, and contains a kitchen and dining room. These houses are most livable, containing light, airy interiors and room arrangements adapted to modern use.

In some cases, requirements of symmetry and regularity demanded by the Greek exterior led to the use of windows undesirably located for the plan arrangement. Thus, as in the Baker and Gordon houses, false window frames, differing from the others in that their shutters were permanently closed, were built in shallow masonry recesses.

The most fascinating and unusual plan of all is that of the early stone portion of the Croghan House, which appears to have been built in the late thirties. Its extremely plain exterior is completely dominated by the larger undistinguished three-story brick addition, which presumably was added later in anticipation of the return from England of William Croghan's daughter Mary and her husband, Major Schenley. The encircling porch, with an ingenious fret ornament in its frieze, was evidently continued around the brick portion when that was added. The stair hall of the new building was laid out on the same axis as that of the ballroom, oval room, and original entrance vestibule in the old building, but the low connecting doorway beneath the new stairway destroys the effectiveness of the vista through the rooms. The interiors of the stone building are among the most distinguished in the Greek Revival.

The character and arrangement of the rooms in the stone building indicates that they were intended for entertainment. The original name, "Picnic House," tends to confirm this assumption. The principal room is the ballroom, which, except for a heavy scale in the plaster ceiling ornament, is consistently excellent in character. The wooden Corinthian capitals are exquisitely carved. Each wall presents a pleasing composition, particularly the entrance elevation with carved doorway, free-standing columns, and mirrored walls. The exterior windows are repeated on the opposite wall by false windows. As shown in the photograph on page 131, the lower sash slides into the wall, revealing the hinged doors of the neighboring bedrooms.

The somewhat oversized crystal and bronze chandelier was fitted for candles and must have created an effect of dazzling magnificence. The presence of an oval room, with niches and curved doorways, was most unusual in plans of the district. This room led on one side into an anteroom with a painted groined vault leading to the porch, and on another side to the original entrance vestibule with quaint lead-dome skylight. The plan is reminiscent of Classic Revival schemes of Jefferson and Latrobe.

Much remains to be known about the Croghan House—the exact dates of erection of its two parts, the designer or architect, and the intention of the owner. This building has been kept in an excellent state of preservation by the family estate. It is to be hoped that at least the interiors of the stone building will be preserved for posterity as the outstanding achievement of the Greek Revival style in western Pennsylvania, and as one of the most distinguished interiors of the style to be found in the United States.

The Dr. John Julius LeMoyne House in Washington

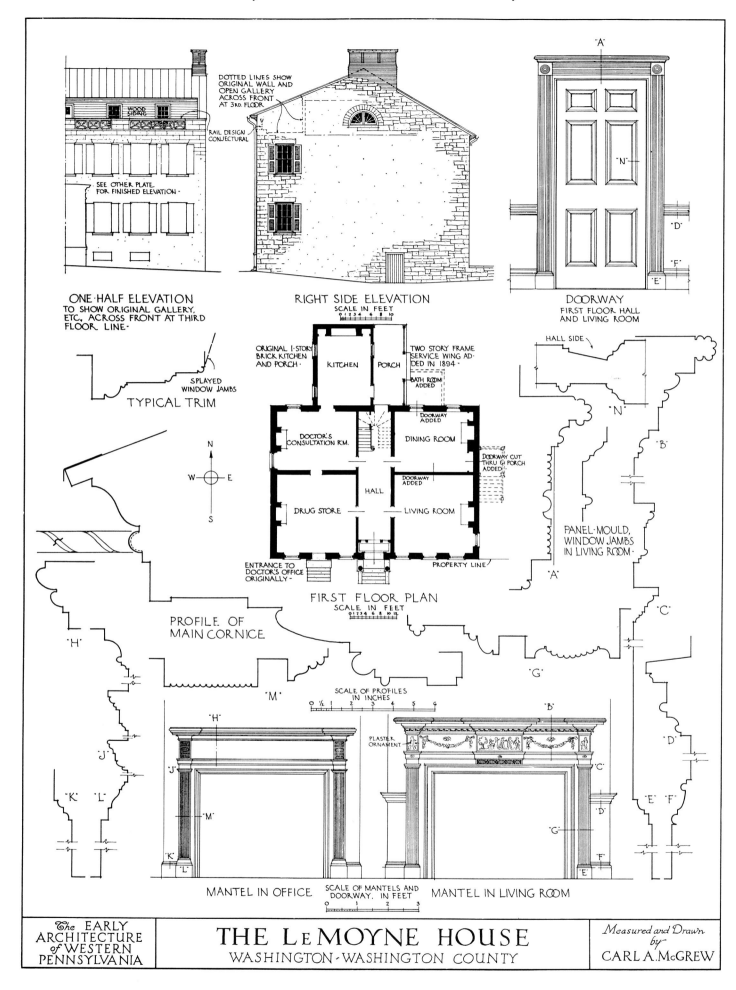

ONE-HALF ELEVATION
TO SHOW ORIGINAL GALLERY,
ETC., ACROSS FRONT AT THIRD
FLOOR LINE-

DOTTED LINES SHOW
ORIGINAL WALL AND
OPEN GALLERY
ACROSS FRONT
AT 3RD. FLOOR.

RAIL DESIGN
CONJECTURAL

WOOD SIDING

SEE OTHER PLATE
FOR FINISHED ELEVATION -

RIGHT SIDE ELEVATION
SCALE IN FEET

DOORWAY
FIRST FLOOR HALL
AND LIVING ROOM

"A"
"N"
"D"
"F"
"E"

TYPICAL TRIM

SPLAYED
WINDOW JAMBS

FIRST FLOOR PLAN
SCALE IN FEET

ORIGINAL 1-STORY
BRICK KITCHEN
AND PORCH -

KITCHEN   PORCH

TWO STORY FRAME
SERVICE WING AD-
DED IN 1894 -

BATH ROOM
ADDED

DOORWAY
ADDED

DOCTOR'S
CONSULTATION RM.

DINING ROOM

DOORWAY CUT
THRU S. PORCH
ADDED

HALL

DOORWAY
ADDED

DRUG STORE   LIVING ROOM

ENTRANCE TO
DOCTOR'S OFFICE
ORIGINALLY -

PROPERTY LINE

HALL SIDE

"N"

PANEL-MOULD,
WINDOW JAMBS
IN LIVING ROOM -

"A"
"B"
"C"
"D"
"E" "F"
"G"

PROFILE OF
MAIN CORNICE

"H"
"J"
"K" "L"
"M"

SCALE OF PROFILES
IN INCHES

PLASTER
ORNAMENT

"H"
"J"
"M"
"K"
"L"

MANTEL IN OFFICE

"B"
"C"
"D"
"G"
"E"

SCALE OF MANTELS AND
DOORWAY, IN FEET

MANTEL IN LIVING ROOM

The EARLY
ARCHITECTURE
of WESTERN
PENNSYLVANIA

THE LeMOYNE HOUSE
WASHINGTON-WASHINGTON COUNTY

Measured and Drawn
by
CARL A. McGREW

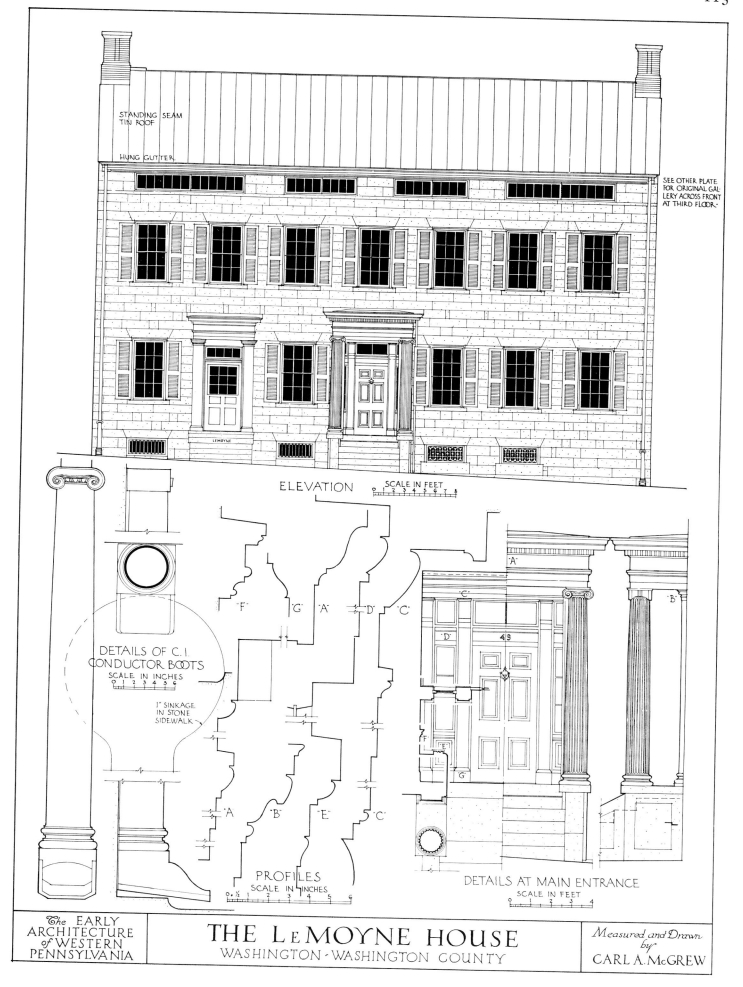

STANDING SEAM
TIN ROOF

HUNG GUTTER

SEE OTHER PLATE
FOR ORIGINAL GAL-
LERY ACROSS FRONT
AT THIRD FLOOR.

LEMOYNE

ELEVATION   SCALE IN FEET
0 1 2 3 4 5 6 7 8

DETAILS OF C. I.
CONDUCTOR BOOTS
SCALE IN INCHES
0 1 2 3 4 5 6

1" SINKAGE
IN STONE
SIDEWALK

F   G   A   D   C

'A'   'B'   'E'   'C'

'A'

'C'   'B'

'D'   49

F   E

G

PROFILES
SCALE IN INCHES
0 ½ 1   2   3   4   5   6

DETAILS AT MAIN ENTRANCE
SCALE IN FEET
0 1 2 3 4

The EARLY
ARCHITECTURE
of WESTERN
PENNSYLVANIA

THE LeMOYNE HOUSE
WASHINGTON · WASHINGTON COUNTY

Measured and Drawn
by
CARL A. McGREW

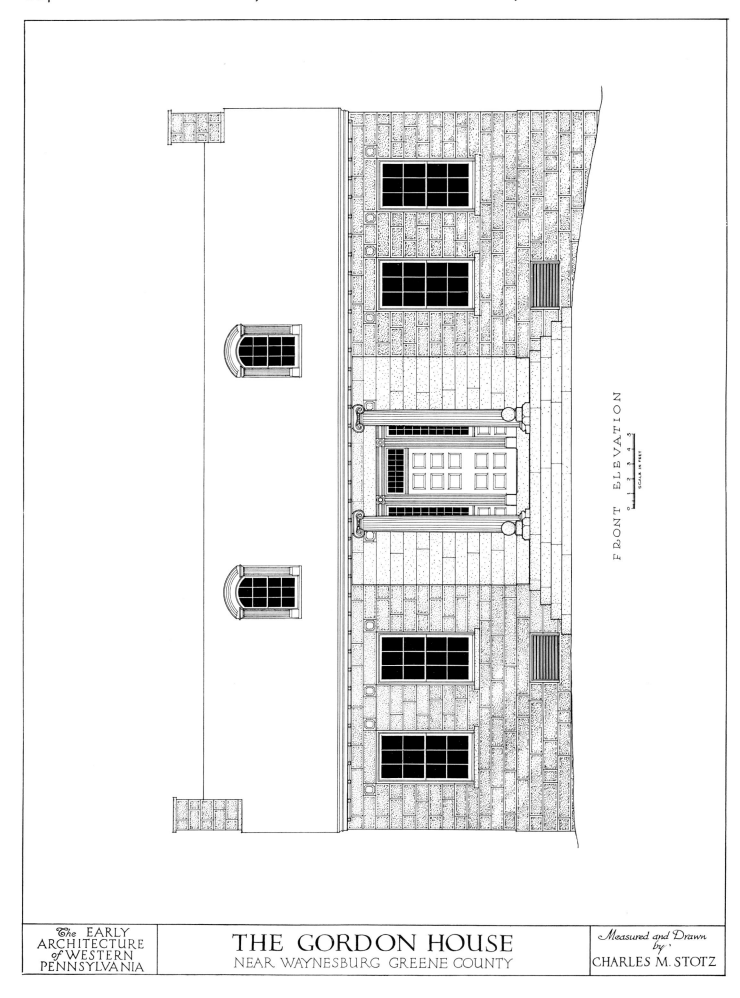

FRONT ELEVATION

SCALE IN FEET

THE GORDON HOUSE
NEAR WAYNESBURG GREENE COUNTY

Measured and Drawn
by
CHARLES M. STOTZ

Greene 1

The John B. Gordon House near Waynesburg

1843

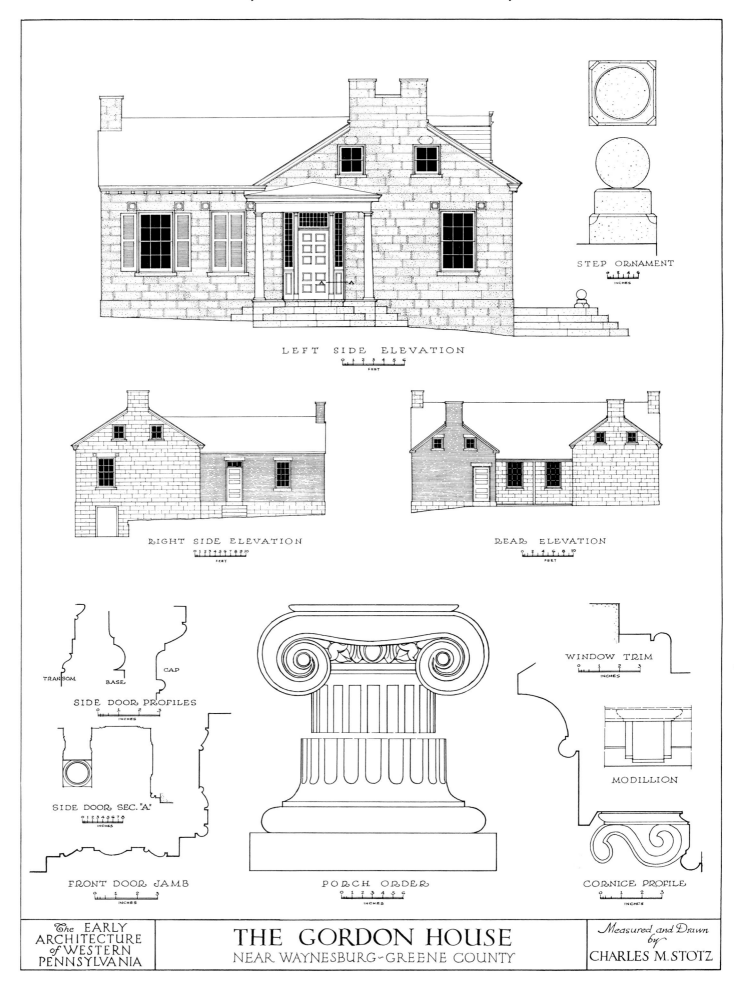

STEP ORNAMENT
INCHES

LEFT SIDE ELEVATION
FEET

RIGHT SIDE ELEVATION
FEET

REAR ELEVATION
FEET

TRANSOM   BASE   CAP
SIDE DOOR PROFILES
INCHES

SIDE DOOR SEC. "A"
INCHES

FRONT DOOR JAMB
INCHES

PORCH ORDER
INCHES

WINDOW TRIM
INCHES

MODILLION

CORNICE PROFILE
INCHES

The EARLY ARCHITECTURE of WESTERN PENNSYLVANIA

THE GORDON HOUSE
NEAR WAYNESBURG~GREENE COUNTY

Measured and Drawn by
CHARLES M. STOTZ

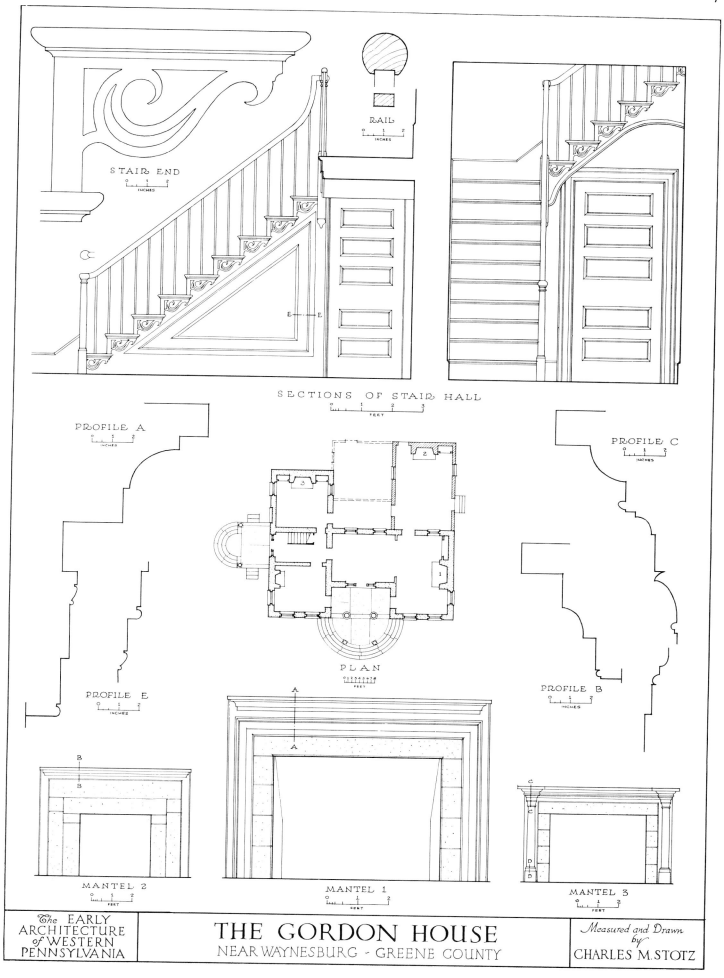

STAIR END

RAIL

SECTIONS OF STAIR HALL

PROFILE A

PROFILE C

PROFILE E

PLAN

PROFILE B

MANTEL 2

MANTEL 1

MANTEL 3

The EARLY
ARCHITECTURE
of WESTERN
PENNSYLVANIA

THE GORDON HOUSE
NEAR WAYNESBURG - GREENE COUNTY

Measured and Drawn
by
CHARLES M. STOTZ

Greene 1

Gable End of the Gordon House

1843

Greene 1

Entrance Porch of the Gordon House

1843

1838

Allegheny 51

The Nicholas Way House in Sewickley

1847

Beaver 11

The Patrick Mulvanen House near Beaver

1848

Washington 71

The Linn House near Washington

Allegheny 129

Porch Detail of the Lightner House

1833

Allegheny 129

The Isaac Lightner House near Glenshaw

1833

Allegheny 129

Smokehouse of the Lightner House

1833

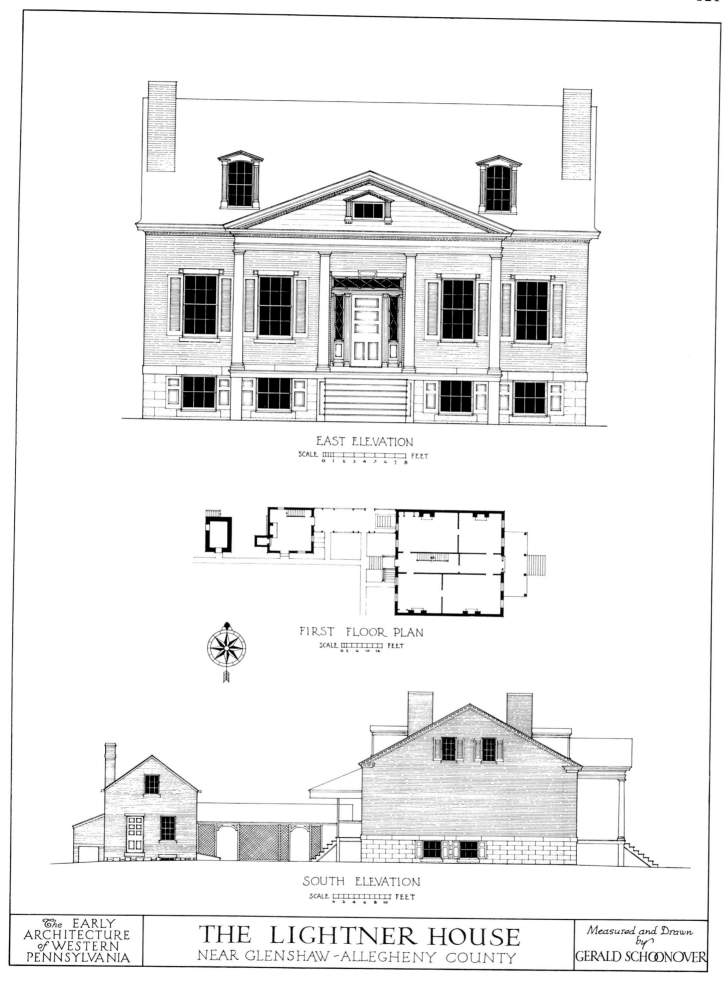

EAST ELEVATION

SCALE |||||||||||||| FEET
0 1 2 3 4 5 6 7 8

FIRST FLOOR PLAN

SCALE |||||||||| FEET
0 2 6 10 14

SOUTH ELEVATION

SCALE |||||||||| FEET
0 2 4 6 8 10

The EARLY ARCHITECTURE of WESTERN PENNSYLVANIA

THE LIGHTNER HOUSE
NEAR GLENSHAW—ALLEGHENY COUNTY

Measured and Drawn by
GERALD SCHOONOVER

SMOKE HOUSE
END VIEW
SCALE IN FEET

WINDOW IN GABLE

SMOKE HOUSE
SIDE VIEW
SCALE IN FEET

WOOD STAIR

BRICK CORNICE

DORMER WINDOW

WOOD CORNICE

G

H

COLUMN BASE

PORCH
CORNICE

CORNICE AT
PORCH
CEILING

C

COLUMN CAP

G

A

B

H

D

INSIDE TRIM

E

F

SCALE IN INCHES FOR PROFILES

c

D   A

F

D

E

MAIN ENTRANCE
SCALE IN FEET FOR DETAILS

The EARLY
ARCHITECTURE
of WESTERN
PENNSYLVANIA

THE LIGHTNER HOUSE
NEAR GLENSHAW ~ ALLEGHENY COUNTY

Measured and Drawn
by
GERALD SCHOONOVER

1835 (Razed 1924)   *Allegheny 583*

"Homewood," the Judge William Wilkins House in Pittsburgh

1837   *Washington 43*

The David Cunningham House in Washington

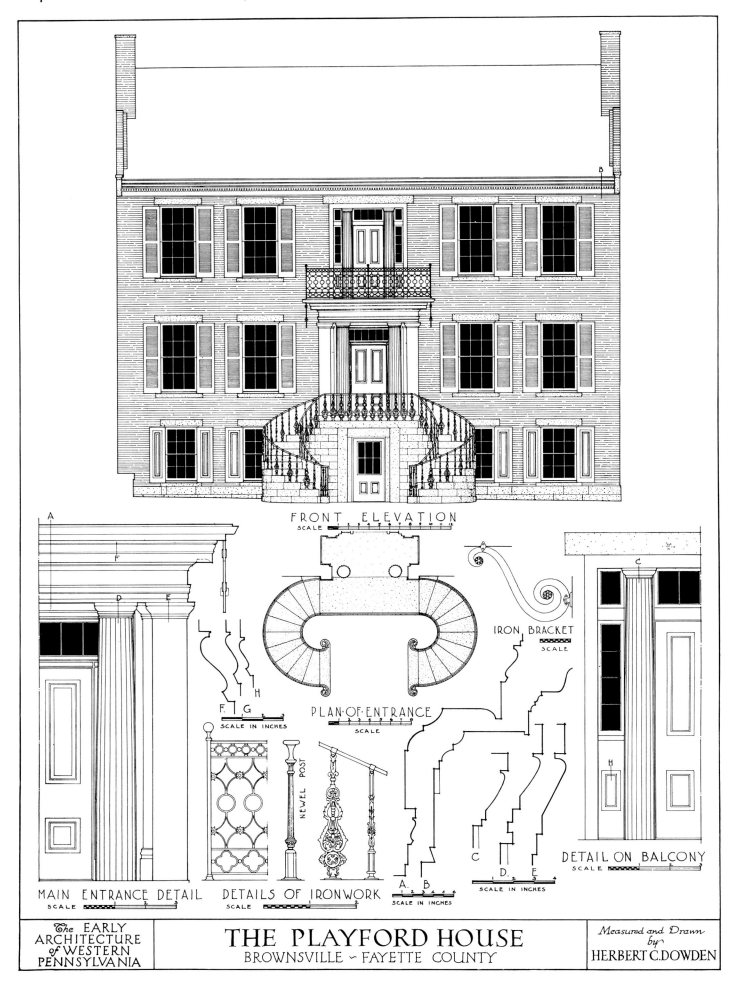

FRONT ELEVATION
SCALE

A

F

D   E

F   G
SCALE IN INCHES

PLAN·OF·ENTRANCE
SCALE

IRON BRACKET
SCALE

NEWEL POST

C
D   E
SCALE IN INCHES

A.   B
SCALE IN INCHES

H

DETAIL ON BALCONY
SCALE

MAIN ENTRANCE DETAIL
SCALE

DETAILS OF IRONWORK
SCALE

The EARLY ARCHITECTURE of WESTERN PENNSYLVANIA

THE PLAYFORD HOUSE
BROWNSVILLE ~ FAYETTE COUNTY

Measured and Drawn by
HERBERT C. DOWDEN

1833

"Woodlawn," the Samuel Church House in Pittsburgh

Allegheny 7

About 1847

The John H. Shoenberger House in Pittsburgh

Allegheny 13

1833

Pediment Detail of the Church House

Allegheny 7

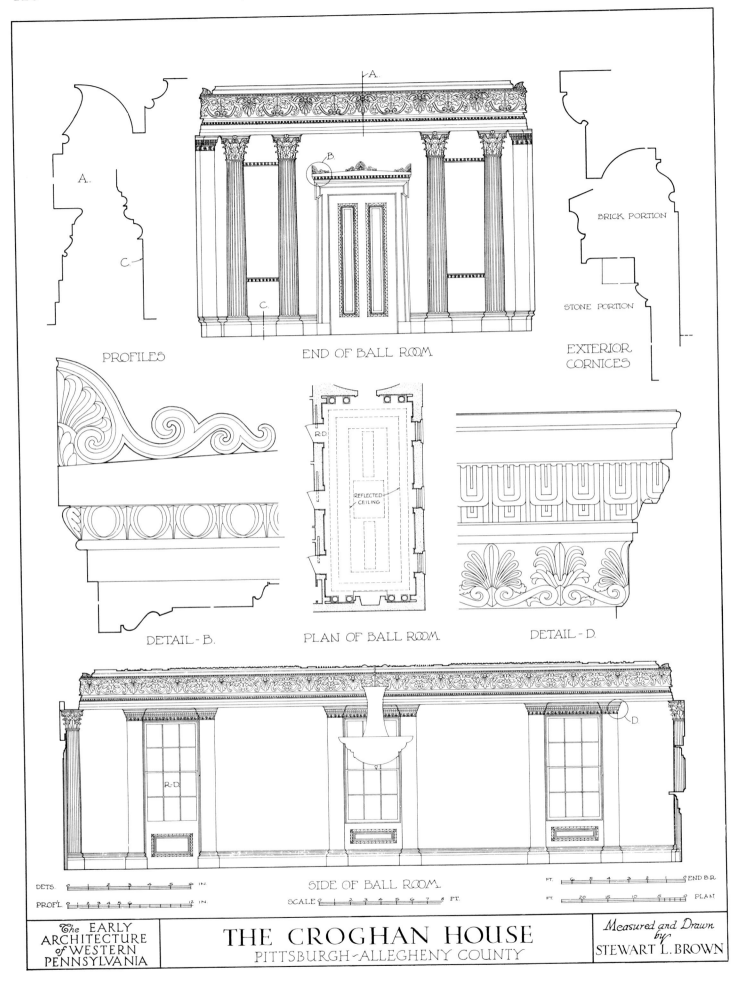

PROFILES

END OF BALL ROOM

EXTERIOR CORNICES

BRICK PORTION

STONE PORTION

DETAIL - B.

PLAN OF BALL ROOM.

REFLECTED CEILING

DETAIL - D.

SIDE OF BALL ROOM.

DETS.   IN.

PROF'L.   12 IN.

SCALE   FT.

FT.   END B.R.

FT.   PLAN

The EARLY ARCHITECTURE of WESTERN PENNSYLVANIA

THE CROGHAN HOUSE
PITTSBURGH-ALLEGHENY COUNTY

Measured and Drawn by
STEWART L. BROWN

"Picnic House," the William Croghan House in Pittsburgh—Entrance End of Ballroom

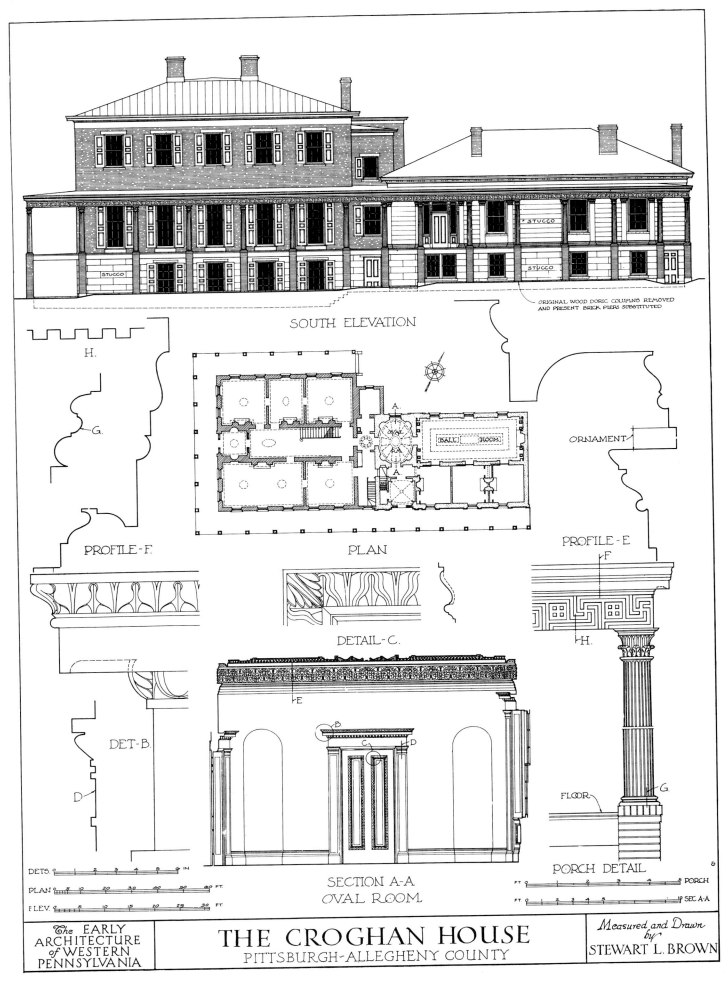

SOUTH ELEVATION

ORIGINAL WOOD DORIC COLUMNS REMOVED
AND PRESENT BRICK PIERS SUBSTITUTED

H.

G.

PROFILE-F.

DET-B.

D

ORNAMENT

PROFILE-E

PLAN

DETAIL-C.

F

H.

FLOOR

G.

PORCH DETAIL

SECTION A-A
OVAL ROOM

DETS.
PLAN
F.ELEV.

FT.   PORCH
FT.   SEC A-A

The EARLY
ARCHITECTURE
of WESTERN
PENNSYLVANIA

THE CROGHAN HOUSE
PITTSBURGH-ALLEGHENY COUNTY

Measured and Drawn
by
STEWART L. BROWN

About 1835

Mantel End of Ballroom of the Croghan House

Ballroom Chandelier of the Croghan House

About 1835

Oval Room Entrance Detail of the Croghan House

About 1835

Ballroom Entrance Detail of the Croghan House

About 1835

Ballroom Frieze of the Croghan House

About 1835

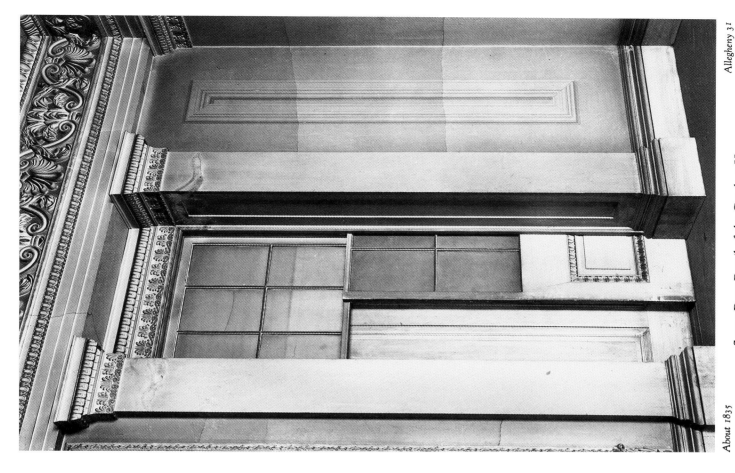

About 1835 Secret Door Detail of the Croghan House

Allegheny 31

About 1835 Original Stone Portion of the Croghan House

Allegheny 31

About 1835 Porch Cornice Detail of the Croghan House

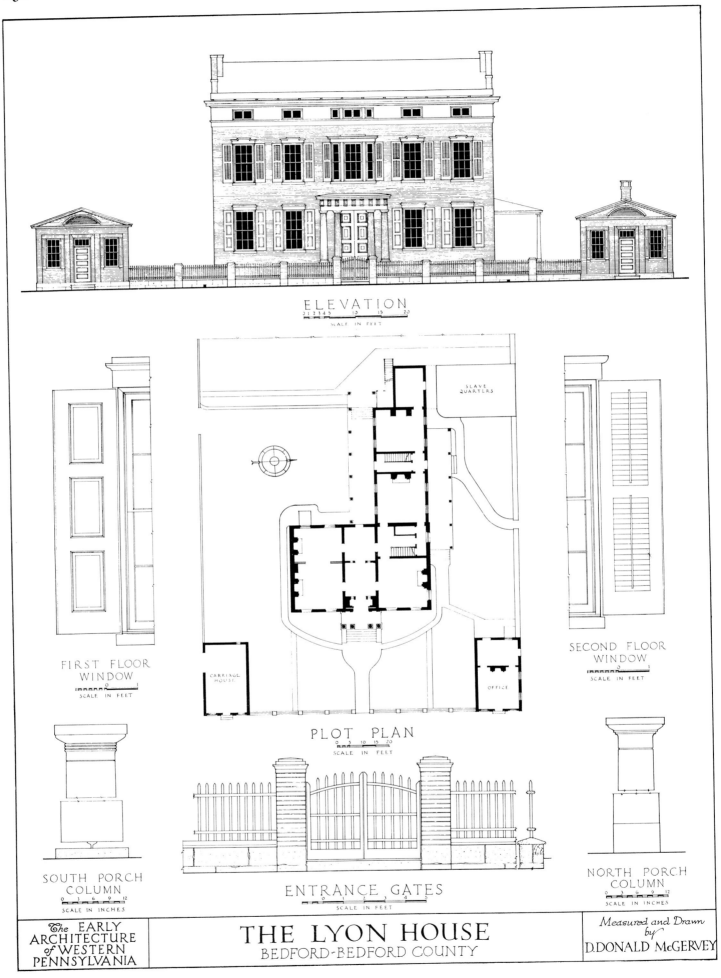

ELEVATION

SCALE IN FEET

FIRST FLOOR
WINDOW
SCALE IN FEET

SECOND FLOOR
WINDOW
SCALE IN FEET

PLOT PLAN
SCALE IN FEET

SLAVE
QUARTERS

CARRIAGE
HOUSE

OFFICE

SOUTH PORCH
COLUMN
SCALE IN INCHES

ENTRANCE GATES
SCALE IN FEET

NORTH PORCH
COLUMN
SCALE IN INCHES

The EARLY
ARCHITECTURE
of WESTERN
PENNSYLVANIA

THE LYON HOUSE
BEDFORD-BEDFORD COUNTY

Measured and Drawn
by
D. DONALD McGERVEY

The William Lyon House in Bedford

Office of the Lyon House

Porch Detail of the Lyon House

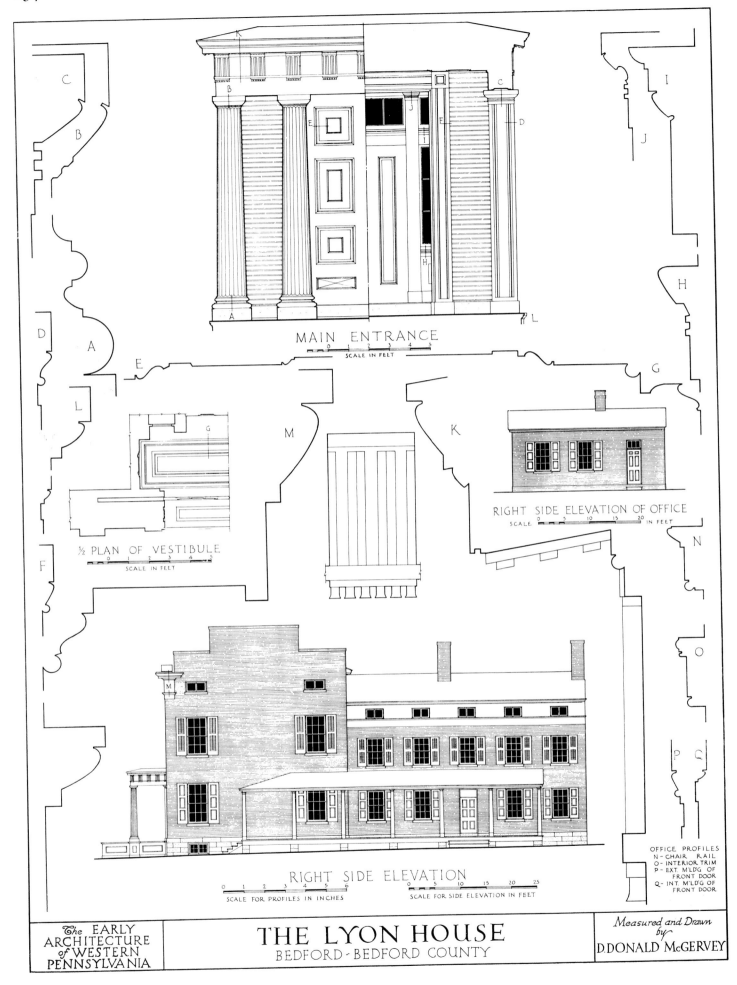

MAIN ENTRANCE

SCALE IN FEET

½ PLAN OF VESTIBULE

SCALE IN FEET

RIGHT SIDE ELEVATION OF OFFICE

SCALE   IN FEET

RIGHT SIDE ELEVATION

SCALE FOR PROFILES IN INCHES   SCALE FOR SIDE ELEVATION IN FEET

OFFICE PROFILES
N - CHAIR RAIL
O - INTERIOR TRIM
P - EXT. M'LD'G OF
FRONT DOOR
Q - INT. M'LD'G OF
FRONT DOOR

The EARLY ARCHITECTURE of WESTERN PENNSYLVANIA

THE LYON HOUSE
BEDFORD - BEDFORD COUNTY

Measured and Drawn by
D. DONALD McGERVEY

1844   Blair 1

The Elias Baker House in Altoona

1844   Blair 1

Interior Detail of the Baker House

1844   Blair 1

Side View of the Baker House

1844   Blair 1

Rear Portico of the Baker House

1834   *Warren 27*

The Guy C. Irvin House near Warren

1834   *Warren 27*   1834   *Warren 27*

Entrance Portico of the Irvin House   Stair Detail of the Irvin House

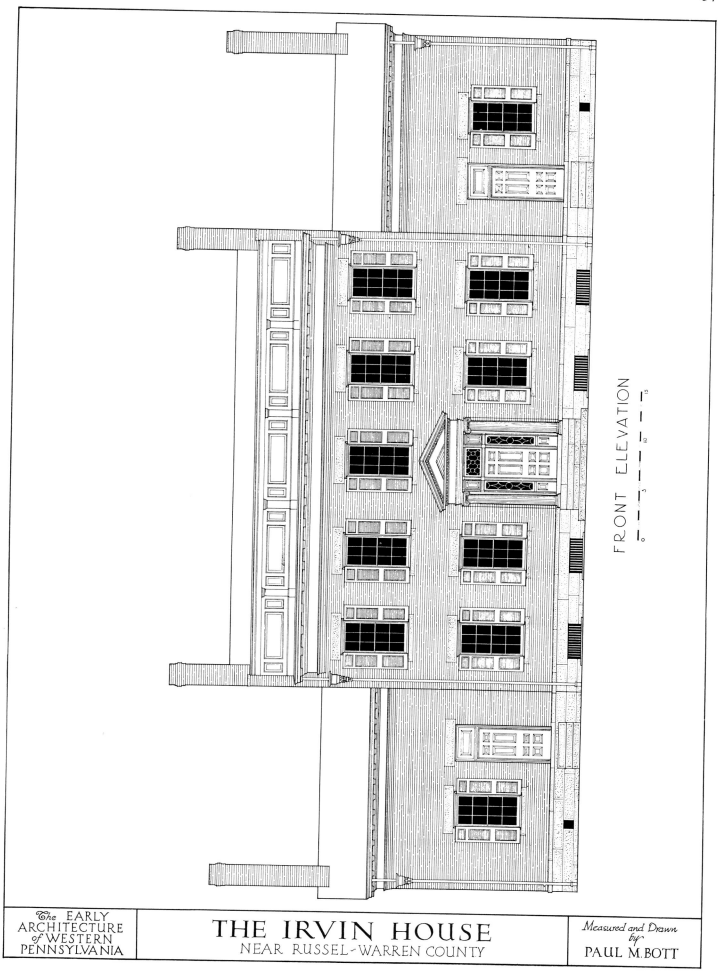

FRONT ELEVATION

THE IRVIN HOUSE

NEAR RUSSEL~WARREN COUNTY

Measured and Drawn by PAUL M. BOTT

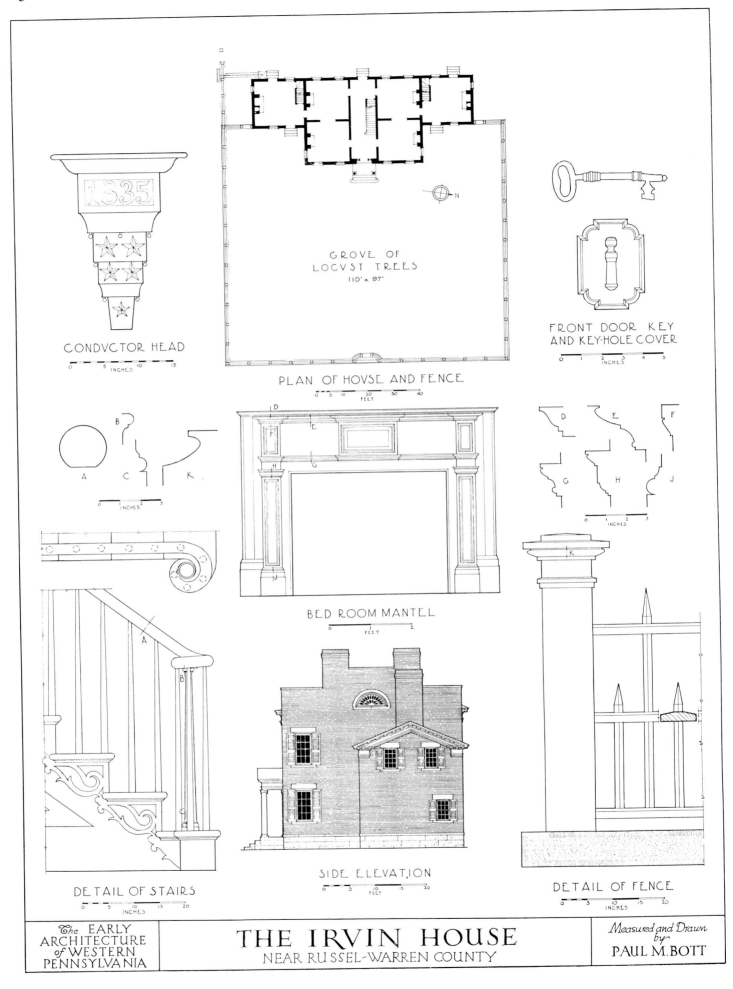

CONDVCTOR HEAD

GROVE OF
LOCVST TREES
110' x 97'

PLAN OF HOVSE AND FENCE

FRONT DOOR KEY
AND KEY·HOLE COVER

BED ROOM MANTEL

DETAIL OF STAIRS

SIDE ELEVATION

DETAIL OF FENCE

The EARLY
ARCHITECTURE
of WESTERN
PENNSYLVANIA

THE IRVIN HOUSE
NEAR RUSSEL-WARREN COUNTY

Measured and Drawn
by
PAUL M. BOTT

MAIN ENTRANCE

MAIN ENTABLATVRE

ENTABLATVRE
OF END WINGS

WINDOW HEAD

LEAD ORNAMENT
IN TRANSOM·

DOOR KNOCKER

DETAIL OF COLVMN

LEAD ORNAMENT
IN SIDE LIGHTS

ENTABLATVRE OF
MAIN ENTRANCE

The EARLY
ARCHITECTURE
of WESTERN
PENNSYLVANIA

THE IRVIN HOUSE
NEAR RUSSEL-WARREN COUNTY

Measured and Drawn
by
PAUL M. BOTT

SCALE FOR PROFILES

PARTIAL FRONT ELEVATION

SCALE FOR ORNAMENT

PLAN

CORNICE & PILASTER

MAIN DOORWAY

WINDOW & SHUTTER

SLAT   MUNTIN

FRONT ELEVATION

The EARLY ARCHITECTURE of WESTERN PENNSYLVANIA

THE HENDRIX HOUSE
RICEVILLE ~ CRAWFORD COUNTY

Measured and Drawn by
ROBERT W. SCHMERTZ

Crawford 28

Door Detail of the Hendryx House

1852

Crawford 28

The Dr. H. E. Hendryx House in Riceville

1852

1842   *Potter 1*

The Timothy Ives, Jr., House in Coudersport

1854   *Mercer 8*   *Date Unknown*   *McKean 1*

The Robert Mann House in Greenville   A House near Smethport

Crawford 47

The Edward Saeger House in Saegerstown

1843

Erie 54

The Charles M. Reed House in Erie

1849

Erie 63

A House in Wattsburg

Date Unknown

Erie 57

The John Dickson House near North Girard

1842

Section Two

ACCESSORY BUILDINGS AND DETAILS

MUCH of the appeal in our early farmhouses lies in the grouping of the accessory buildings about them. These minor structures seem to have escaped the devastating alterations which have so often spoiled the main building. In exterior and interior details the early craftman's handiwork is most effectively displayed. Ornament was used sparingly and with restraint, materials with an admirable appreciation of their limitations.

Barns (Pages 146-147)

The pioneer log barn consisted of two entirely separate log units built some distance apart but connected by a common roof. The central space had a log wall in the rear and an entrance for the wagons in the front. The Crumrine barn, like many of its time, had a roof of rye straw, composed of many small bundles secured by bark withes. Most of the log barns extant have been reroofed and their walls have been covered with weatherboarding.

The log barns, as well as the later barns of stone, brick, and frame, were usually placed on sloping ground, affording an entrance for the wagons on an upper level and access for the animals below. These "bank barns" usually had a cantilevered extension running their full length, which served as weather protection for the lower entrances and as additional storage space above. Ventilation in log barns was obtained by omitting the chinking. In later types, louvered windows, vertical slits in the stonework, or a pattern of openings in the brickwork acted as ventilators.

Spring-, Smoke-, and Washhouses (147-149)

As important to the farmer as his barn, the springhouse served as protection for the indispensable water supply and contained the tubs in which his dairy products were stored. Springhouses, like the barns, were usually built on a slope to gain a separate entrance to the upper story, which served as a storage room and, sometimes, as living quarters. Stone was the favorite material.

The smokehouse adjacent to the Cook House (see page 48) has been in continuous use since its erection and is typical of these simple structures.

The Lightner smokehouse (see page 120) with its outside ladder, sheltered by an overhanging roof, is of particular interest.

The washhouse was either connected to the main building by a roofed porch (see Lightner House), or was a free-standing structure (see Cook House). It contained a large fireplace with heavy cranes.

Doorways (150-155)

The entrance doorway was usually the focus of attention in house design and often the only detail to receive any special treatment. Although some of the doorways in the early houses of western Pennsylvania followed the conventional Georgian formula (see Passavant, Dorsey, Meason, Roberts, Daily, and Manchester houses), most of them were of simple design. Lead muntins and ornament, as used in the Dickson House doorway, were not common, but during the Greek Revival period there was a more general use of carved wood ornament. The wide variety of style forms in western Pennsylvania is nowhere better illustrated than in the photographs of these early doorways.

Porches (156-157) and Windows (158)

Porches were not common in early Georgian architecture in America and, except for the taverns, were almost never seen in western Pennsylvania before 1815. Many houses, in later times, have been disfigured by the addition of porches, with little or no regard for the original design. The house porch was often incorporated within the structure of the house, as with the cantilevered porches of the Sill and Kaddoo houses, the recessed second-story porch of the Saeger House, or the graceful enclosed porch of the Washabaugh House. The two-story gallery porch probably originated with the tavern, where it served as a second-floor corridor to private rooms and was reached by an outside stair (see Defibaugh Tavern). An early form of the double porch is seen in the Ludwick House with its quaint curved headboard, chamfered posts, and plain board rails. The two-story porch of the Royer House is typical of the later farmhouses in the eastern district. The unique arched recess enclosing the pump in the Stewart House is both useful and decorative.

Casement windows were quite rare in the early buildings and were used only under special circumstances; double-hung windows were the rule. In spacing, proportion and craftsmanship they reflected much credit on the early builder. Since glass was available in rather limited sizes, the normal window contained no less than twelve panes, and often as many as thirty. Muntins and rails were characteristically slender in section and, like the molded wood casing around the window, were joined by wooden pins. (See drawing of the Frew House window on page 50). The wood casing or trim was almost always brought to the face of the masonry, in contrast with the modern practice of recessing the weight box in the wall.

Stone Walls and Textures (159-161)

The native sandstone of western Pennsylvania, obtainable in a wide range of sizes and lending itself to a great variety of surface treatments, was used with marked success by the early masons. At first the stone was used just as it came from the field or quarry, with little or no attempt to dress it flat with the tool; but later work shows that a smooth surface was considered desirable. Tool marks were left as a definite part of the pattern. A favorite treatment was known as "scabbled and drafted work" (see the Wetmore, Gordon, and Wray houses), in which a field of pits made by the chisel point is surrounded by a narrow margin of closely drafted scorings. The tooled lines in the work at Harmony shown on pages 195 to 199 are most effectively used for their textural value.

Limestone was not as common as sandstone. It spalled too easily to permit the same variety of textures and it did not weather to the same range of color and tone. The limestone in the Royer House is left in a fairly rough state, but in the Baker House it is worked to a perfectly smooth finish.

The corners of the house were strengthened by bonding with larger stones, as can be observed in the Royer, Chambers, Frew, and Ludwick houses. In the Irvine Church and the Wetmore House they are given a special shape as quoins, or rustications.

Signature Stones (162-163)

Until about the middle of the nineteenth century it was customary for the owner to place in the gable or over the door a signature stone bearing the date of completion, his name or initials and, sometimes, those of his wife. Occasionally the signature stone was set low, at a corner of the house, or in such an unexpected place as the back of the coping stone in the roof parapet (see the Manchester House). Public buildings often bore similar designating marks, such as the cast-iron plaque of the Arsenal at Pittsburgh, which once hung over the entrance of the main building (now demolished).

Mantels (164-167) and Paneling (168-169)

The complicated ornamental details portrayed in the handbooks were ingeniously simplified by the country carpenter to suit the limitations of his tool kit. He made frequent use of his gouge to form continuous ornamental lines or figures. Mantels with tasteful profiles and good proportions, on which this homemade ornament was applied, were often more attractive than many elaborate mantels of conventional design, such as those shown on pages 164 and 165. In these the ornament is of composition and was originally imported from England. A craftsman in Philadelphia, Robert Wellford, first produced domestic ornament of this character for general sale. The mantel from an inn at Bedford bears his signature. As may be readily detected in the photograph, this mantel was altered to suit the larger fireplace opening of a later location. It is restored to its original dimensions in the drawing.

The earliest fireplaces, which served for cooking as well as heating, were seldom elaborately designed. (See the Patterson, Dinsmore, and Neal houses.)

Again, the mantel was sometimes so glorified that it became the central feature of a paneled room end (see the Dorsey, Neville, Daily, and Croghan houses). Two excellent examples are shown here in the Cunningham and Gallatin houses. Such elaboration, however, was rare in the district.

Stairways (170-171) and Interior Details (172)

The stairway was usually the first detail of interest seen upon entering the house. The commonest form was that of the straight run, as used in the Wray House, interrupted in its ascent by a landing the width of the hall. Occasionally it was of curved plan, as in the Baird House stairway. It was the custom to embellish the stair with spiral rail terminations, turned balusters, and scrolled brackets on the stair ends.

Ceilings such as that in the Shoenberger House, designed from handbooks and cast by specially trained workmen, were used in the finer houses. The carved wood capitals in the Shoenberger House rival those in the Croghan House.

Washington 20

The Baker Barn near West Brownsville

1820

Blair 14

A Barn near Williamsburg

1834

Bedford 69

The Hartley Barn near Everett

Date Unknown

Fayette 89

The Newmeyer Barn near Pennsville

About 1796

A Springhouse near Washington

Washington 96

Date Unknown

The Beazell Springhouse near Webster

Westmoreland 108

Date Unknown

The Crumrine Barn near Zollarsville

Washington 102

1805

The Snoeberger Springhouse near New Enterprise

Bedford 62

Date Unknown

1830   *Allegheny 139*

The Risher Springhouse in Hays

Date Unknown   *Westmoreland 94*

The Stoner Barn near Scottdale

Date Unknown   *Fayette 71*

The Cook Wash-house near Fayette City

Greene 24

The Harper Springhouse near Carmichaels

About 1800

Greene 36

The Sayer Smokehouse near Waynesburg

1822

Blair 11

The Lowry Springhouse near Frankstown

1785

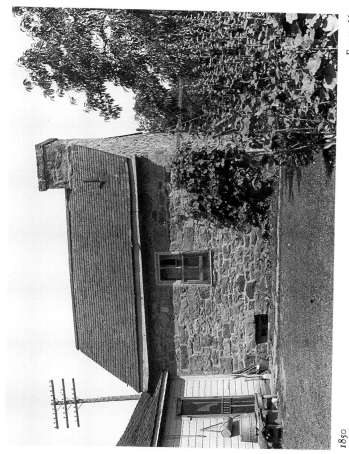

Fayette 66

The Hayden Smokehouse in Hopwood

1850

1828   *Bedford 56*

The Danaker House in Schellsburg

1830   *Cambria 12*

The Lemon Inn near Cresson

1826   *Erie 13*

The Eagle Hotel in Waterford

About 1795   *Blair 12*

The Hileman House in Frankstown

1838

The Overholt Springhouse near Scottdale

Westmoreland 62

About 1820

A Store at Florence

Washington 72

1816

The Shields House in Shields

Allegheny 53

1805

The Davis House near Ruffsdale

Westmoreland 92

1842   *Erie 59*

The Dickson House near North Girard

1842   *Erie 59*

Door Detail of the Dickson House

1835   *Bedford 78*

The Washabaugh House in Bedford

Date Unknown   *Beaver 30*

The McLaughlin House in Hookstown

1833

The Metz House in Williamsburg   *Blair 17*

1805

The Stauffer House near Harmony   *Butler 40*

Date Unknown

Doorway at Pleasant Unity   *Westmoreland 78*

1796

The Brashear Tavern in Brownsville   *Fayette 76*

Date Unknown   Allegheny 149
The Ferry House near Etna

1855   *Crawford 15*
Ruter Hall, Allegheny College, in Meadville

Date Unknown   Westmoreland 76
A House at Adamsburg

1840   *Erie 55*
The Hoskinson House in Erie

About 1814

The Phillippe Louis Passavant House in Zelienople

Butler 38

Date Unknown   *Bedford 1*
The Defibaugh Tavern near Everett

1843   *Crawford 47*
The Saeger House in Saegerstown

1836   *Westmoreland 99*
The Stewart House in New Alexandria

Date Unknown   *Westmoreland 60*
The Ludwick House near New Kensington

Westmoreland 99

The James Stewart House in New Alexandria

1836

Allegheny 116

The Kaddoo House near Finleyville

Date Unknown

Bedford 78

The Washabaugh House in Bedford

1835

Bedford 81

The Sill House near Bedford

1823

Date Unknown   *Westmoreland 60*
The Ludwick House near New Kensington

1815   *Blair 18*
The Royer House near Williamsburg

1826   *Beaver 38*
The Great House in Economy

1815   *Washington 36*
The Manchester House near West Middletown

Butler 37

1825

The Mennonite Church near Harmony

Washington 36

1815

The Manchester House near West Middletown

Bedford 48

1833

The Lyon House in Bedford

Beaver 20

1835

The Wray House near Beaver

160   The Early Architecture of Western Pennsylvania

1815   *Blair 18*
The Royer House near Williamsburg

1823   *Washington 98*
The Chambers House at Chambers Dam

1837   *Warren 12*
The Irvine Presbyterian Church in Irvine

1839   *Warren 65*
The Wetmore House near Warren

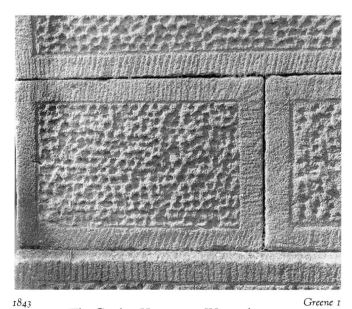

1843   *Greene 1*
The Gordon House near Waynesburg

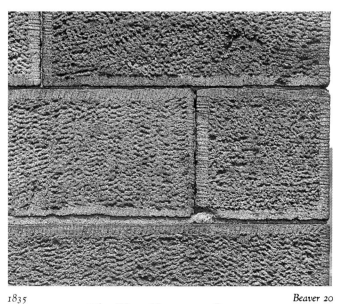

1835   *Beaver 20*
The Wray House near Beaver

1797   *Bedford 19*

Naugle's Mill near Bedford

1833   *Blair 6*

Portage Railway Skew Arch near Cresson

1832   *Allegheny 79*

The Williams Springhouse near Mt. Lebanon

1844   *Fayette 1*

St. Peters Church in Brownsville

About 1808   *Allegheny 2*

The Miller House in South Park

1814   *Washington 100*

The Gantz House near Lone Pine

1826   *Erie 13*

The Eagle Hotel in Waterford

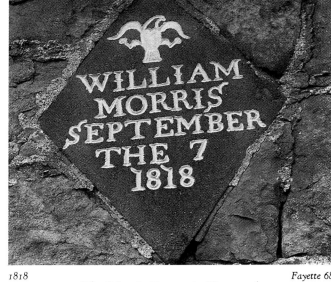

1818   *Fayette 68*

The Morris Tavern in Hopwood

1830   *Allegheny 139*

The Risher Springhouse in Hays

1764   *Allegheny 41*

The Blockhouse in Pittsburgh

1814   *Washington 100*

The Gantz House near Lone Pine

1802   *Fayette 2*

The Meason House near Uniontown

The U. S. Allegheny Arsenal in Pittsburgh

1814

Malden Tavern near West Brownsville

1830

The Manchester House near West Middletown

1815

The Wray House near Beaver

1835

MANTEL-A.

MANTEL-B

0 2 4 6 8 10 12
SCALE IN INCHES

| The EARLY ARCHITECTURE of WESTERN PENNSYLVANIA | TWO MANTELS
A - MOVED FROM INN AT BEDFORD TO HOUSE IN SCHELLSBURG
B - MOVED FROM HOUSE AT BRADDOCK TO HOUSE NEAR INDIANA | Measured and Drawn by GEORGE P. McKINNEY |

Date Unknown

Mantel moved from Inn at Bedford to House in Schellsburg

Bedford 60

Date Unknown

Mantel moved from House at Braddock to House near Indiana

Indiana 63

Allegheny 176

Mantel in the Bigham House in Chatham Village, Pittsburgh

1844

Fayette 88

A House on First Street in Connellsville

Date Unknown

Washington 6

The LeMoyne House in Washington

1812

Beaver 20

The Wray House near Beaver

1835

Washington 74

The Patterson House near Avella

1794

Allegheny 86

The U. S. Allegheny Arsenal in Pittsburgh

1814

Allegheny 24

The Neville House in Woodville

1785

Westmoreland 73

The Guthrie House near Slickville

1809

Fayette 3

The Gallatin House near New Geneva

1789

Fayette 97

The Cunningham House near Merrittstown

1808

Fayette 3

Dining Room of the Albert Gallatin House near New Geneva

1814   The Baird House in Washington   *Washington 67*

1835   The Wray House near Beaver   *Beaver 20*

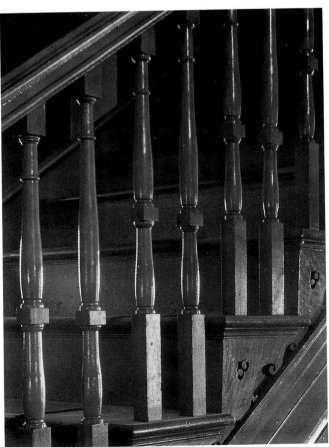

1843   The Gordon House near Waynesburg   *Greene 1*

1820   The Brush Creek Church near Adamsburg   *Westmoreland 5*

1808

The Cunningham House near Merrittstown

Fayette 97

1808

The Cunningham House near Merrittstown

Fayette 97

1787

The Dorsey House near Brownsville

Washington 88

About 1797

The Daily House near Webster

Westmoreland 70

About 1830

The Brewer House in Pittsburgh

Allegheny 10

1814

The Baird House in Washington

Washington 67

Greene 24

The Harper House near Carmichaels

About 1800

Allegheny 13

Capital Detail of the Shoenberger House in Pittsburgh

About 1847

Washington 72

A Store in Florence

About 1820

Allegheny 13

Ceiling Detail of the Shoenberger House in Pittsburgh

About 1847

Section Three
THE ARCHITECTURE OF TRANSPORTATION

ALTHOUGH the main highways in western Pennsylvania today follow practically the same routes that were used during the golden era of the turnpike (1815 to 1830), the modern motorist finds little to recall the dramatic atmosphere of their earlier days. The hum of automotive traffic has replaced the blast of the coachman's horn, the shouts of the drover and the teamster, the rumbling and creaking of the wagons, and the chorus of complaint from the great herds rising above the thunder of their hooves on the dusty pike. The only tangible reminders of this memorable era are the few taverns and bridges that have survived the modern reconstruction of the highways and have not been altered beyond recognition.

Taverns

The taverns, illustrated on pages 177 to 185, are located in country districts. Originally they were divided into two general types, one catering to stagecoach passengers and the other to teamsters and drovers. The great number of stage houses, wagon stands, and drovers' taverns that once dotted the roads is truly surprising. They appeared with even greater frequency in the mountain regions, where hauls were necessarily shorter. Most of those illustrated are on the National Pike, which carried the heaviest traffic. The best types of taverns were the coach stands, which were usually under the supervision of private companies, who vied with each other in the quality of service and appointments. They often included post offices and stores. Here relays of fresh horses were stabled and passengers obtained their meals. Ewing's Tavern on the Good Intent line near Fort Necessity served as many as seventy-two guests at breakfast.

The taverns did not materially differ in appearance from private houses, and their design in the various districts followed the same style trends as those discussed in Section One. In fact, many taverns originally were private homes adapted to accommodate the evergrowing business of the road. Such were the Way Tavern, built in 1810 as a private residence, and enlarged in 1820; the Nixon Tavern, which received a taproom addition when put to public use; and the Kingston House, originally the private home of Alexander Johnston, to which was appended a rear porch and an ell wing of appropriate characters. (See pages 183, 36, and 84).

The enlargements made to accommodate the increasing traffic are obvious in most of the taverns illustrated in this book. In 1820 a stone section was joined to the original log Compass Inn of 1799; "Malden," built in 1822, was enlarged in 1830, when the owner optimistically placed the stone (see page 163) that proclaimed the establishment of "Kreppsville," a town that never materialized. Additions are also apparent in the Moxley Tavern, the Halfway House, and others. As ells attached in the rear, these extensions are often hidden from the road, so that the enormous size of many of these old taverns is not readily apparent. The Eagle Hotel was a large establishment for its time; the Lemon Inn is five stories high in the rear; and the Smith Tavern, near New Enterprise, once had five tiers of gallery porches extending across its massive stone front. Many of the inns (see the Leet, Johnson, and Weaverling taverns), stripped of their signs and other identifications, cannot now be distinguished in either size or character from private homes.

The principal feature of the tavern was its full-length porch, usually of shallow width and often two tiers high. The lower porch afforded weather protection for the guests and loafers or hangers-on, and the upper porch gave access to the bedrooms. Usually an outside stairway led to the upper level.

The early taverns were of logs, as exemplified by the Halfway House, the Nixon Tavern, and the left half of the Compass Inn. In later times the advantages of stone and brick construction prompted the general use of these materials for the better taverns.

The tavern proclaimed its identity by a large sign hung to swing freely within a wooden frame supported by a high pole. The sign bore a name, usually in gilded letters, and was often enhanced by a carved or painted representation of the insignia or namesake. The wooden eagle perched over the door of the Eagle Hotel in Waterford originally stood on a high pole near the road. The early taverns, particularly those in the cities, bore such colorful names as the Sign of the Negro, the Sheaf of Wheat, the Black Bear, the Indian Queen, the Whale and Monkey, the Cross Keys, and the Sign of the Waggon—all Pittsburgh inns.

The now-deserted tavern gives little impression of its one-time importance. Gone are the bustling activity, the confusion and excitement of arrivals and departures, the gaudy equipages and dress of the time, the beaming host, and the many other evidences of life and color described in travelers' accounts of that day. The earlier journals, however, often bitterly complained of the primitive board and lodging.

Missing, too, are the great yards and fields of the teamsters' and drovers' taverns, where the wagons, horses, and cattle were kept overnight. Some idea of the nature and extent of this activity may be gained from the following letter, written by a wagoner of the times and reprinted in Searight's *Old Pike*: "I have stayed overnight with William Sheets, on Nigger mountain, when there would be thirty six-horse teams on the wagon yard, one hundred Kentucky mules in an adjacent lot, one thousand hogs in other enclosures, and as many fat cattle from Illinois in adjoining fields. The music made by this large number of hogs, in eating corn on a frosty night, I will never forget." The registers of the Defibaugh Tavern for the 1840's have been preserved. In them are entered the names of the owners of the herds, the number of cattle, their destination, the cost of yard rental and feeding, and sometimes the name of the drover, who occasionally offered such casual comment as, "3 hogs died of colery last night."

The interiors of the taverns have changed even more than have the exteriors, for, with the decline and practical disappearance of road traffic after the advent of the railroad, they were put to new uses or reverted to residential needs. The original enormous dining rooms have been partitioned into smaller rooms, and almost all the barrooms, the social centers of the taverns and the wagon stands, have been altered beyond recognition. In a few, however, the original bar fittings have been preserved, as in the Defibaugh Tavern, where the counter, register desk, and cupboards for bottles and glasses are still intact. The early photograph of the interior of the White Swan barroom shows the quaint little bar, typically ornamented with fancy lattice work. Judging from the record book for 1794 of Coates Tavern in West End, Pittsburgh,

the bars enjoyed a thriving business, offering the traveler "slings," "todys," and "bounces" with a base of either "whisky," "cherry" or "jinn." At Leet Tavern, whisky was three cents a glass or two for a nickel. In the larger taverns the enormous fireplaces often contained grates seven feet long, with the capacity of an ordinary wagonload of coal. In the drovers' taverns the teamsters usually slept in the barroom. When there was a supplementary stove in the center of the room, the men arranged themselves on the floor like the spokes of a wheel, their feet toward the stove.

Many of the old taverns had a long life of activity. The White Swan offered its facilities to the public for more than ninety years, and the Hill Tavern at Scenery Hill, also on the National Pike, has been operated as an inn from 1794 to this day. It is one of the oldest on the National Pike west of Baltimore. With modern road traffic instilling new life into the highways, many of the old hostelries, such as "Malden" near West Brownsville, Lemon Inn near Cresson, and Eagle Hotel in Waterford, have been reopened.

The town and city taverns have been either razed or altered beyond identification in order to turn their valuable sites to more profitable uses. In their day they were often centers of political activity, such as Marie's Tavern on Grant's Hill in Pittsburgh and the Black Horse Tavern in Canonsburg, the latter famous for meetings of the Whisky Insurrectionists. Church services, school, and court were held in taverns as occasion required. Pittsburgh had many inns to house its vast transient population; it had twenty-four taverns as early as 1808.

Taverns sprang up along the rivers and canals to accommodate those traveling by water. The Raftsman's Tavern stood until modern times on the lower Point in Pittsburgh; the Rising Sun catered to trade from the Pennsylvania Canal near the present site of Etna; and the Lemon Inn, on the crest of Allegheny Ridge at the head of plane number six, cared for canal travelers on the Portage Railway. The Monongahela House and Semple's Tavern were favorite stopping places in Pittsburgh for river travelers.

Watering Places

Western Pennsylvania also had its "spas" where natural medicinal waters were drunk after the fashion of the times. The most celebrated was Bedford Springs, which has been in operation ever since its institution in 1824, when its first elaborate buildings were erected by Dr. John Anderson of Bedford, although the value of the springs was recognized long before that time. Even though the original buildings have been drastically altered, and some of them removed (such as "Crockford," an interesting frame building catering to the bachelor trade) the old watering place still presents a picturesque appearance in its beautiful setting. Its roster contains the names of many distinguished persons of the country for a century back. The establishment at Frankfort Springs in Beaver County was extensively patronized for many years. There is at neighboring Frankfort a large brick hotel, built in 1840, with three tiers of porches. This building accommodated two hundred guests at a time.

Bridges, Tunnels, Toll and Canal Structures

The broken topography of western Pennsylvania and its vast network of streams were natural obstacles to the development of highway transportation. The vastly greater accomplishments of twentieth-century engineering overshadow the conquest of Allegheny Ridge and the mountains east and west of it, accomplished through an expenditure of money and with a resourcefulness that once commanded the admiration of the nation. Either too narrow or too weak, most of the early bridges have not been equal to the ever increasing strain of modern traffic in town and country. After the abandonment of the canals, the stones of their aqueducts, culverts, locks, and other structures were salvaged, if not utilized by the railroads that laid their tracks on the right of way earlier traversed by the canal boats. The structures that are illustrated in this section represent only a few of the many that once existed. Their structural forms were limited chiefly to the wooden truss and the stone arch and vault. These members, despite certain variations in form and in size brought about by their incorporation in bridges and other canal and road structures, were designed according to principles familiar to the architect. Toward the end of the period the use of wire cables and iron members began to influence the character of structural forms.

Adam Wilson, architect of the Meason House, made the model for the second bridge over the Youghiogheny at Connellsville, built in 1818. S. Lothrop, architect, designed the first aqueduct to carry the Pennsylvania Canal over the Allegheny

River at Pittsburgh, constructed in 1829 at a cost of $104,000. It was replaced in 1845 by an aqueduct designed upon entirely new principles by John A. Roebling, engineer, and built at a cost of $62,000. The trough of wood, which contained the canal, averaged 15 feet in width and 8½ feet in depth. It was built in seven self-supporting spans of 160 feet each, the weight of the water within them being borne by two seven-inch multiple-wire cables strung along the sides. Another suspension-type bridge designed by Roebling, utilizing wire cables that he manufactured in neighboring Saxonburg, was the Sixth Street Bridge at Pittsburgh, erected in 1856. Roebling is best known nationally for his Brooklyn Bridge in New York.

The engineer, Sylvester Welch, was famed for his direction of the engineering work of the Portage Railway. W. Milnor Roberts, principal assistant on the eastern slope, later completed the Erie Extension of the Beaver and Erie Canal. Solomon W. Roberts, on the same project, designed the viaduct that carried the railway over the Conemaugh River eight miles east of Johnstown—a magnificent single stone arch, eighty feet in diameter. It was carried away by the Johnstown Flood of 1889, when the water beneath it rose to seventy-nine feet above normal river level.

The heavy construction and simple design of the structures erected for the Portage Railway are exemplified in the Skew Arch and the tunnel near Johnstown, which remain in a good state of preservation. The Skew Arch, or skew-vaulted culvert, shown on page 190, carried the Northern Turnpike (now the William Penn Highway) over the tracks near the foot of plane number six. The angle of the plane is indicated by the pitch of the stones forming the barrel vault, an interesting problem in stone-cutting. The same careful stone texturing is seen in the rusticated portal arch of the tunnel built in 1830 at the head of plane number one of the Portage Railway near Johnstown. It is said to be the first railway tunnel constructed through a hill in America and is 870 feet long and 20 feet high. When the Portage Railway was rebuilt, another tunnel was constructed at Gallitzin, which today covers the east-bound tracks of the Pennsylvania Railroad. Nine miles west of Blairsville a tunnel, one thousand feet in length, opened upon an enormous stone aqueduct, which carried the Pennsylvania Canal over the Conemaugh. A tunnel leading the canal from the basin at Eleventh Street to the Monongahela River was constructed under Grant's Hill in Pittsburgh in 1829. Although it cost $61,000, it was allowed to lapse into disuse soon after its completion. The basin into which this tunnel opened, on the Monongahela, was intended to join the Pennsylvania Canal and the Chesapeake and Ohio Canal, but that ill-fated venture never brought its waters beyond Cumberland.

Even though the development of the canals was cut short by the advent of the railroads, a tremendous sum had been expended on the canals. The Beaver and Lake Erie Canal contained 134 locks, 221 bridges, 13 dams, and 9 aqueducts. The locks, mostly of cut stone, averaged 80 feet in length by 15 feet in width. The Pennsylvania Canal's western division (Pittsburgh to Johnstown) contained 64 locks, 16 aqueducts, and 2 tunnels. Among the few vestiges of all these structures are a partially destroyed lock on the French Creek Canal above Franklin, a lock on the Conemaugh at Blairsville Intersection, and the Girard Locks at the mouth of the Beaver River. The Girard Locks were the most extensive in western Pennsylvania's canal system. They were large enough (25 feet by 120 feet) to admit small river steamers.

Felix Brunot, grandson of Dr. Felix Brunot of Pittsburgh's early days, was an engineer employed in the construction of locks between the towns of Girard and Erie. He designed the Walnut Creek Aqueduct in Erie County, also for the Beaver and Lake Erie Canal. It was 800 feet long and 104 feet high.

In rerouting and regrading the highways some of the original bridges have been spared. Juniata Crossings Bridge was by-passed when the modern Lincoln Highway bridge supplanted it, but it was destroyed by flood in 1936. As is true of most of the remarkable bridges on the National Pike, the Great Crossings Bridge at Somerfield is of sufficient width and strength for the requirements of modern traffic. Like the impressive single-arch bridge over the Casselman River in neighboring Maryland, it is an outstanding example of simple design in stone bridge construction.

Such simple one-lane covered bridges as the Bell's Mill Bridge over Sewickley Creek were until recent years to be found in great numbers throughout western Pennsylvania, but now are to be seen only in remote localities as yet untouched by modern road improvements. The architectural embellishment of the entrance portals of the Bell's Mill Bridge was not uncommon among such structures of bygone

days. The great stone pier of the Juniata Crossings Bridge, almost medieval in feeling, was typical of the massive construction of the time. This bridge, like that at Waynesburg, was originally a double-lane affair throughout its entire length; but when the eastern half was carried away by ice or flood about 1885, it was replaced by a single-lane span. The bridge at Everett was continuously used until its destruction by the flood of 1936.

Among the famous covered bridges no longer in existence was that over the Conemaugh at Blairsville, built in 1821, a single wooden arch with a span of 295 feet. The wooden bridge over the Monongahela River at Brownsville was used continuously from 1833 until 1910. The first bridge over the Allegheny River at Pittsburgh was built in 1818 at a cost of $92,250. It was a wooden bridge, 1,122 feet long, and was supported by six stone piers. Of even greater size was the Monongahela Bridge over the Monongahela River at Smithfield Street, constructed in 1818 by Coltart and Dilworth, and burned in 1845. It was 1,500 feet long, was supported by eight stone piers, and cost $102,450. Some of these early Pittsburgh bridges are excellently illustrated in the oil paintings made by Russell Smith in the 1830's.

In addition to the wire suspension bridges of Roebling, many notable experiments in bridge construction were first made in western Pennsylvania. The first chain suspension bridge in the United States was built in 1801 over Jacob's Creek, Westmoreland County, at a cost of $600. The first cast-iron bridge west of the Allegheny Mountains was erected over Dunlap's Creek at Brownsville in 1835 to carry the National Pike, and is still in use.

After the National Pike was turned over by the United States Government to the various states through which it passed, the Commonwealth of Pennsylvania in 1831 authorized the erection of six tollhouses within the state. Only three remain— one located at West Alexander, one near Uniontown, and one at Addison. The latter two are illustrated in this book. Originally, strong iron gates were erected at these buildings to enforce toll collection by barring the road. A table of tolls, lettered on a board set in the road face of the buildings, still announces the fee for animals, pedestrians, and for all types of vehicles. These buildings were well planned to serve their purpose; they afforded a clear view of the road in both directions and contained living quarters for the toll collector.

1826

The Eagle Hotel in Waterford

Erie 13

1826

Side View of the Eagle Hotel

Erie 13

1826

Entrance Door of the Eagle Hotel

Erie 13

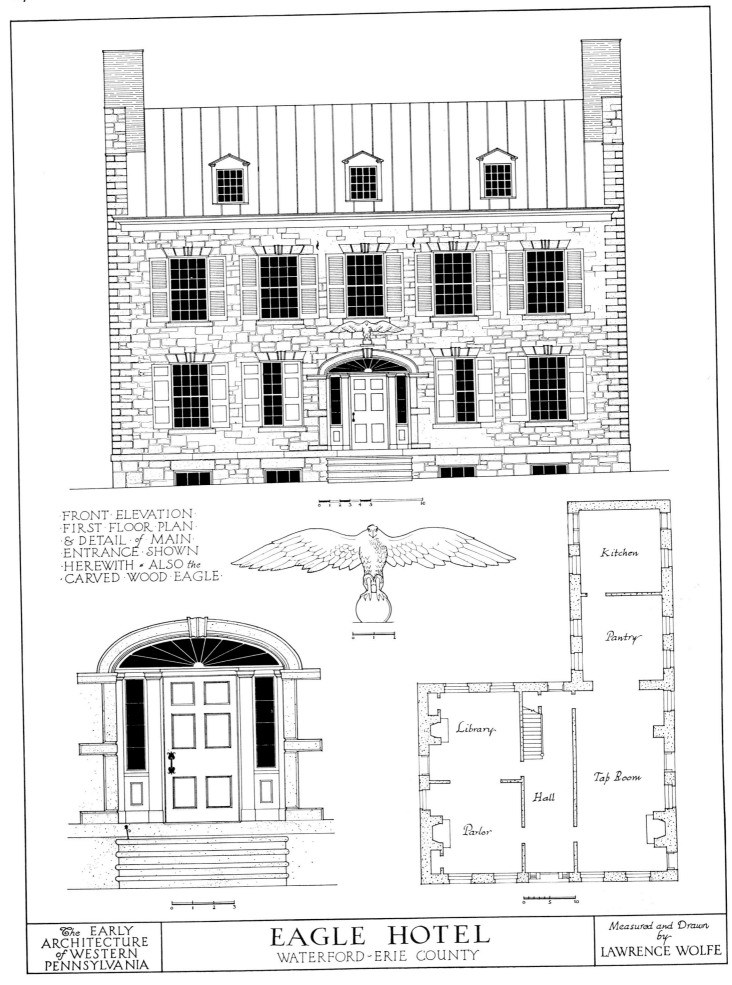

FRONT·ELEVATION·
FIRST·FLOOR·PLAN·
& DETAIL·of·MAIN·
ENTRANCE·SHOWN·
HEREWITH ⁂ ALSO the
·CARVED·WOOD·EAGLE·

Kitchen

Pantry

Library

Hall

Tap Room

Parlor

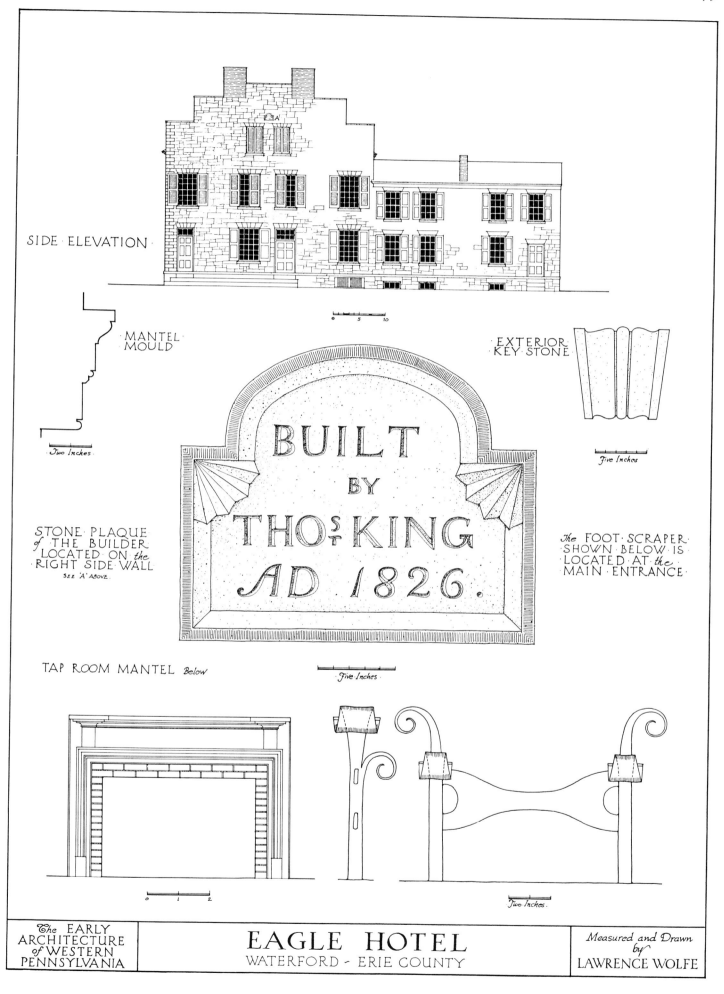

SIDE · ELEVATION ·

MANTEL MOULD

Two Inches

STONE · PLAQUE of THE · BUILDER LOCATED ON the RIGHT · SIDE · WALL SEE 'A' ABOVE.

BUILT BY THOS KING AD 1826.

EXTERIOR KEY · STONE

Five Inches

The FOOT · SCRAPER · SHOWN · BELOW · IS LOCATED · AT the MAIN · ENTRANCE ·

TAP · ROOM · MANTEL Below

Five Inches

0   1   2

Two Inches.

The EARLY ARCHITECTURE of WESTERN PENNSYLVANIA

EAGLE HOTEL
WATERFORD - ERIE COUNTY

Measured and Drawn by
LAWRENCE WOLFE

About 1800   *Allegheny 137*

A Tavern built by Major Daniel Leet in Leetsdale

About 1800   *Allegheny 137*   *About 1800*   *Allegheny 137*

Entrance Detail   The Springhouse

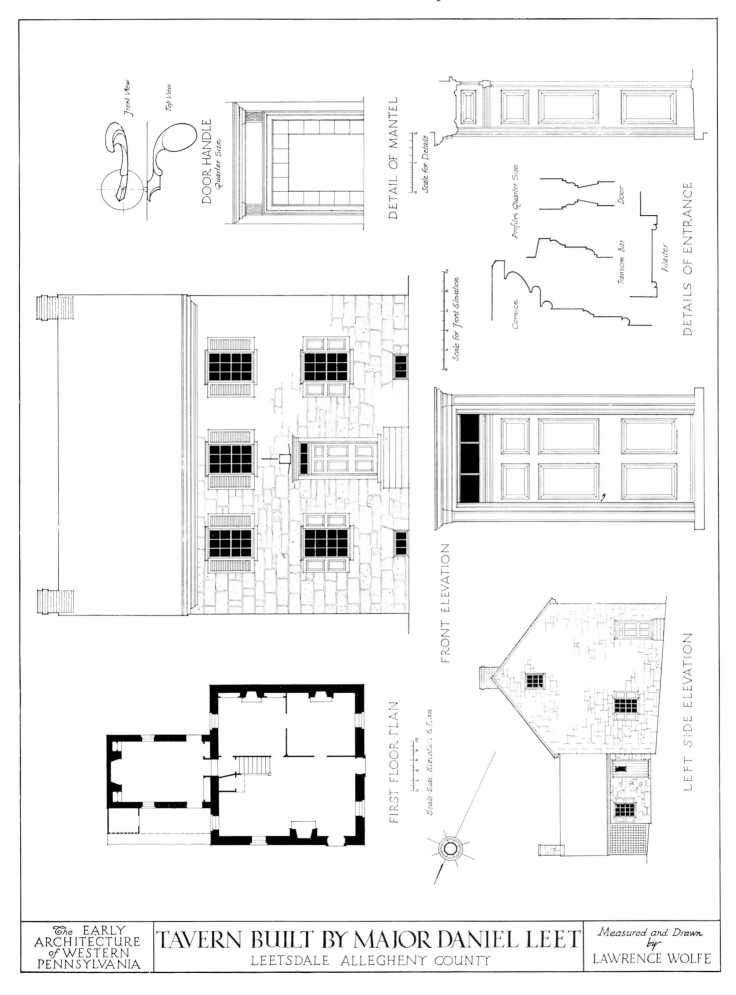

Front View

Top View

DOOR HANDLE
Quarter Size

DETAIL OF MANTEL

Scale for Details

Profiles Quarter Size

Cornice

Transom Bar

Door

Pilaster

DETAILS OF ENTRANCE

Scale for Front Elevation

FRONT ELEVATION

LEFT SIDE ELEVATION

FIRST FLOOR PLAN

Scale Side Elevation & Plan

The EARLY ARCHITECTURE of WESTERN PENNSYLVANIA

TAVERN BUILT BY MAJOR DANIEL LEET
LEETSDALE ALLEGHENY COUNTY

Measured and Drawn by
LAWRENCE WOLFE

1831　　　　　　　　　　　　　　　　　　　　　　　*Mercer 24*

The Johnson Tavern near Mercer

1831　　　　　　　　　　*Mercer 24*　　*1831*　　　　　　　　　　*Mercer 24*

Door Detail of the Johnson Tavern　　　　Entrance Door of the Johnson Tavern

1830

The Lemon Inn near Cresson

Cambria 12

1810

The Way Tavern in Edgeworth   *Allegheny 153*

1843

The Weaverling Tavern near Everett   *Bedford 67*

Fayette 533

The Moxley Tavern near Searights (Early photo)

1818

Blair 20

The Ling Tavern at Claysburg

1838

Westmoreland 27

"Compass Inn" in Laughlintown

1799

Bedford 1

The Defibaugh Tavern near Everett

Date Unknown

Fayette 45

The Searights Tavern in Searights

1819

Fayette 528

The "White Swan" Barroom in Uniontown

1805 (Demolished)

Washington 55

The Hill Tavern at Scenery Hill

1794

Washington 82

Malden Tavern near West Brownsville

1822–30

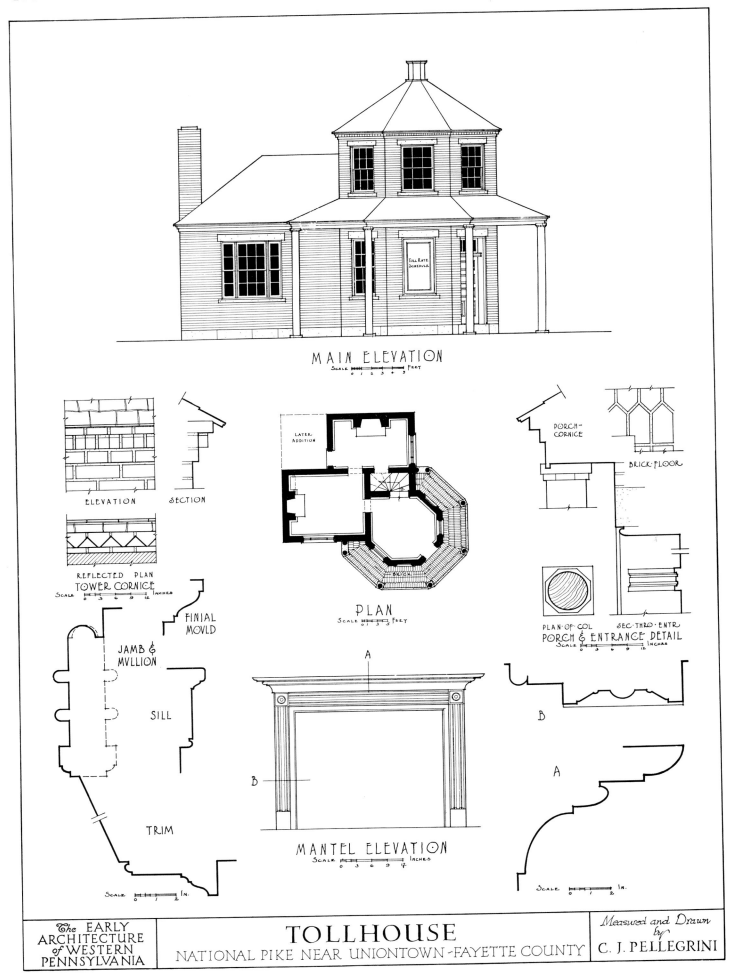

MAIN ELEVATION
Scale   Feet
0 1 2 3 4 5

ELEVATION   SECTION

REFLECTED PLAN
TOWER CORNICE
Scale   Inches
0 3 6 9 12

FINIAL MOVLD

JAMB & MVLLION

SILL

TRIM

Scale   In.
0 1 2

LATER ADDITION

PLAN
Scale   Feet
0 1 3 5

A

B

MANTEL ELEVATION
Scale   Inches
0 3 6 9 4

PORCH CORNICE

BRICK FLOOR

PLAN OF COL   SEC THRO ENTR
PORCH & ENTRANCE DETAIL
Scale   Inches
0 3 6 9 12

B

A

Scale   In.
0 1 2

TOLL RATE SCHEDULE

The EARLY
ARCHITECTURE
of WESTERN
PENNSYLVANIA

TOLLHOUSE
NATIONAL PIKE NEAR UNIONTOWN - FAYETTE COUNTY

Measured and Drawn by
C. J. PELLEGRINI

1835

A Tollhouse on the National Pike near Uniontown

Fayette 35

1835

A Tollhouse on the National Pike at Addison

Somerset 22

1818 Great Crossings Bridge over the Youghiogheny River at Somerfield

1818 Center Arch of the Great Crossings Bridge

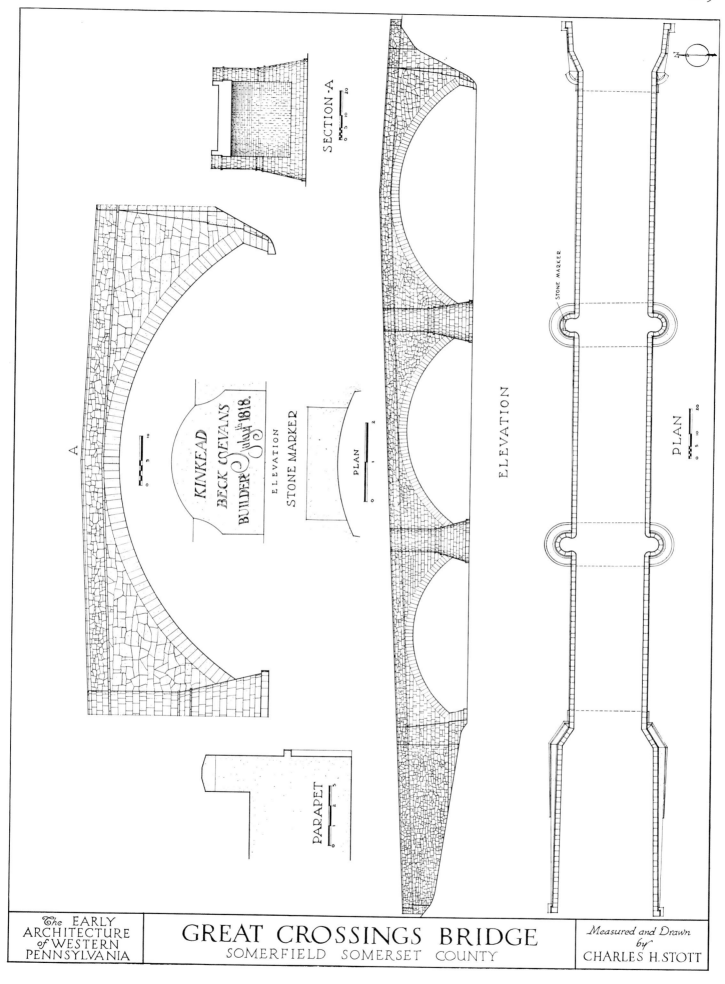

SECTION·A

A

SECTION·A

KINKEAD
BECK & EVANS
BUILDER July 4th 1818.

ELEVATION
STONE MARKER

PLAN

PARAPET

ELEVATION

STONE MARKER

PLAN

GREAT CROSSINGS BRIDGE
SOMERFIELD SOMERSET COUNTY

Measured and Drawn
by
CHARLES H. STOTT

Blair 6

1833

Portage Railway Skew Arch over Plane Number Six near Cresson

1833   Skew Arch Detail   *Blair 6*   1833   Buttress Detail   *Blair 6*

Westmoreland 51

Portal Detail of Bell's Mill Bridge

1850

Greene 29

Bridge over Ten Mile Creek in Waynesburg

Date Unknown

Westmoreland 51

Bell's Mill Bridge over Sewickley Creek

1850

Cambria 14

Portage Railway Tunnel near Johnstown

1830

Bedford 42

1818 (Demolished 1936)   Juniata Crossings Bridge near Everett

Bedford 82

Date Unknown (Demolished 1936)
Bridge over the Juniata River at Everett

Bedford 42

1818 (Demolished 1936)
General View of the Juniata Crossings Bridge

Section Four

THE HARMONY SOCIETY

THE Harmony Society existed independently within the scheme of economics and architecture in western Pennsylvania. Because of its self-contained character it was little affected by contemporary environment, as the pronounced individuality of its buildings in Harmony and Economy so convincingly bear witness. Today these buildings are the only remnants of a remarkable social experiment conducted in western Pennsylvania.

In 1803 George Rapp purchased five thousand acres in and about Zelienople, Butler County. In 1804, a small company of his followers erected 46 log houses, each 18 by 24 feet, to accommodate the 135 families who arrived from Germany in February of the following year when the Harmony Society was finally organized as a communistic theocracy with George Rapp as its acknowledged temporal and spiritual leader.

Among the Harmonites were many skilled craftsmen and mechanics. The surrounding wilderness was soon cleared, and great strides were made toward the establishment of agriculture and industry. Four thousand additional acres were purchased; and, by 1814, 130 buildings had been erected in and about Harmony. The few that remain today have undergone extensive alterations. In 1853 a disastrous windstorm played havoc with a great number of the buildings. In 1858 fire took a heavy toll. The church has been drastically altered and extended with a new front section; the few original log houses that remain are disguised by later weatherboarding and alterations.

The Survey drawings and photographs of the buildings at Harmony are confined to doorways, some of which are well preserved. They are all from brick buildings which, so far as can be ascertained, were devoted to public or industrial use—storerooms, weaving and shoemaking establishments, schools, libraries, taverns, and the like. These doors are outstanding in the district because of their distinctly German flavor and their elaborately carved stone ornament, which has a robust vigor and a rich, decorative quality. The marks of the mason's tool have been ingeniously incorporated into the pattern of the designs. Presumably, Frederick Rapp,

an expert stone mason, directed this work. There has been much conflicting speculation concerning the significance of the angel head with bow tie and apoplectic expression.

The house that contained the double doorway has been demolished. The left half of the doorway is now utilized as an entrance of the new church. The lintel stone of the right half of the doorway is incorporated in a stone retaining wall on the Perry Highway near by.

The buildings that have the doorways with the angel head and the diamond pattern contain stone-vaulted wine cellars similar to the one shown from Economy, and of even more careful construction. The house ascribed to Frederick Rapp, with its "Philadelphia" door (surprisingly like that of the Passavant House in neighboring Zelienople) and its Flemish bond brickwork, differs completely in character from the other buildings in the community.

A short distance south of the town is the Harmonites' stone-fenced cemetery erected in 1869, long after the establishment of Economy. Elias Zeigler was retained to erect the stone gate and fence for the sum of $7,000. The masonry work, both in its character and its soundness of construction, is reminiscent of the original stonework of the Harmonites. The stone gate, though it weighs more than a ton, still revolves easily on its metal pin.

The rules of the Society did not permit headstones but the cemetery contains one stone, that of Johannes Rapp, who died in 1812. He was the only son of George Rapp, who, it is said, permitted the stone to remain on the grounds but not over the grave. It is broken and its delicate lettering was disfigured by a recent attempt to restore its legibility by rechiseling.

In 1814 the Harmony Society, seeking adequate transportation facilities and better grape country, sold their entire holdings to Abraham Zeigler for the then large sum of $100,000 and moved to the banks of the Wabash in Indiana. There they established the town of New Harmony, with many buildings of even more pretentious character, among them a remarkable church of Greek-cross plan.

After ten years in Indiana the Society returned

to western Pennsylvania and purchased a tract of thirty-five thousand acres, which extended five miles along the Ohio river and one mile inland. Here they established Economy. The story of the Society's new successes in agriculture, industry, and finance has been told by others; this account must be confined to the truly remarkable buildings that remain from this, the Society's last venture. Though there have been alterations in roofs, cornices, and in minor details, these buildings stand today almost exactly as they were built; and through the foresight of those who secured the patronage of the State Historical Commission, they are now assured many more years of preservation.

In the design of these buildings there is a noticeable degree of assimilation of American influence; but, as in the Moravian buildings in eastern Pennsylvania, an Old World quality is apparent.

The town plan comprises two unusually wide streets parallel to the river and four streets at right angles to it. The plan was admirably adapted to its purpose, affording generous space for gardens and pasturage around each individual house. The one and only door opened upon this private yard rather than onto the street—a pleasing arrangement, which appealed to the Harmonites' desire for economy as well as privacy. These simple, well-proportioned dwellings, surrounded by trees, ample yards, and gardens bordered with fences and shady streets, expressed their desire for good living.

The industrial activities of the Harmonites required many elaborate buildings. They built a cotton and a woolen mill, a silk factory, a cabinet shop, a brewery, a distillery, brickyards and tanyards, warehouses, and a flouring mill. They also erected administration buildings, a meeting hall, a hotel, a church, shops, and other structures. These buildings were methodically planned with an eye to their efficient use, structural soundness, and external effect. Many drawings of machinery and structural layouts have been preserved to indicate this thorough consideration of their architectural problems. Two of the drawings are reproduced on page 24.

Of the buildings which remain, the Great House, the Feast Hall, and the Church are most noteworthy. It is reasonable to assume, in the absence of definite authority, that Frederick Rapp was responsible for the architectural design of these buildings—they are obviously by the same hand.

The Great House, or Executive Mansion, served as the home of George Rapp and his adopted son Frederick, and as a meeting place for the Board of Elders and other groups. It is in reality two distinct buildings, joined together, and increased in size by later additions. The original condition of the roof, with truncated gables, is shown in the drawings. The interiors, which have suffered some alteration, are not comparable with the finely executed details of the exterior doors, porches, and other woodwork. The Great House has an interesting two-story porch on its rear elevation facing the community garden, which once was celebrated for its intricately planned plot of geometric pattern and its many rare trees, shrubs, and flowers.

The Garden Pavilion, a drawing of which is reproduced on page 24, is a pure exercise in architectural design. It was the principal ornament of the garden. Despite the severe weathering of the stone, it is fairly well preserved. Although its keystone is dated 1831, it was really not completed until after the death of Frederick Rapp in 1834. The wooden vases shown in the drawing are now in possession of Johanna K. W. Hailman, granddaughter of Joseph Woodwell, who carved them. Although they show no evidence of exposure to the weather, they were reputedly designed for this use, perhaps as a substitute for the dome shown in the drawing.

On the ground floor of the Feast Hall rooms were devoted to printing, drawing, school, library, offices, and a museum of natural history. The space above provided for an auditorium with an entrance vestibule. Here were celebrated the established "feasts" and gatherings of the Society. The quaint wall treatment with pilasters between windows is dominated by a huge elliptical vaulted ceiling of plaster. Grape vines were trained upon metal grilles on the walls of the Feast Hall and other buildings.

An impressive tower, with brick base and octagonal wooden cupola bearing one-handed clock dials, is the outstanding feature of the Church. The drawings show these cornices, rails, and roof pitches as they appeared before they were altered.

Beneath the shop containing the quarters for the tailor, milliner, and shoemaker was the huge stone-vaulted wine cellar, where many 600- and 1,000-gallon barrels were kept cool.

The social or economic importance that may be attached to the experiment of the Harmony Society is of rather less concern in this particular record than is the fact that they established in western Pennsylvania the only truly homogeneous community of which any tangible evidence remains.

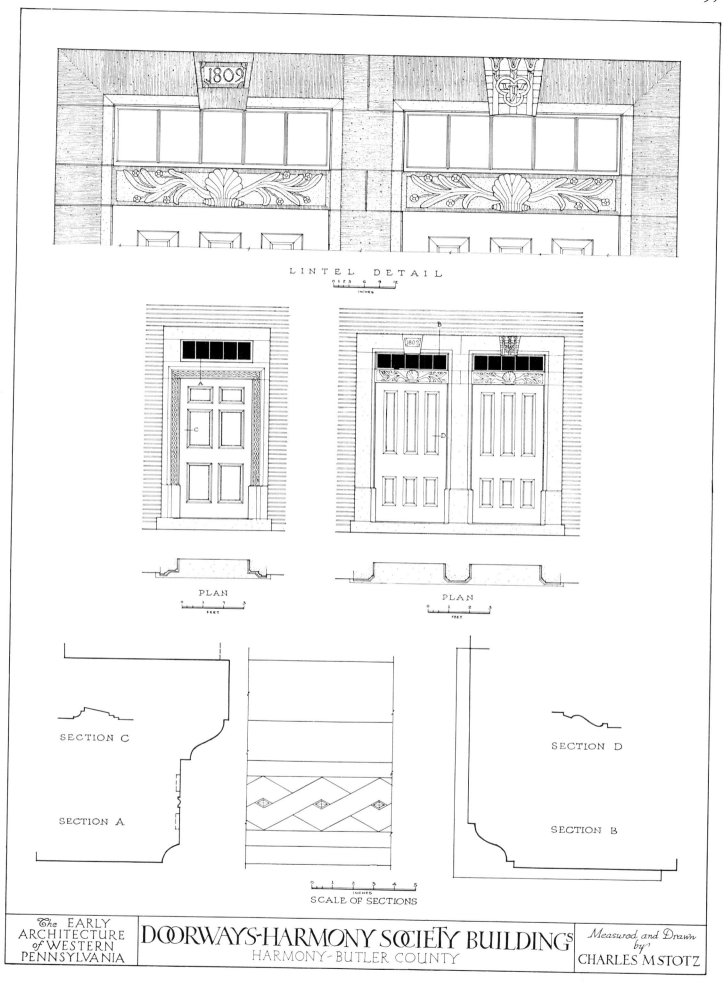

LINTEL DETAIL

0 1 2 3 6 9 12
INCHES

PLAN

0 1 2 3
FEET

PLAN

0 1 2 3
FEET

SECTION C

SECTION A

SECTION D

SECTION B

0 1 2 3 4 5
INCHES
SCALE OF SECTIONS

The EARLY
ARCHITECTURE
of WESTERN
PENNSYLVANIA

DOORWAYS-HARMONY SOCIETY BUILDINGS
HARMONY-BUTLER COUNTY

Measured and Drawn
by
CHARLES M STOTZ

About 1811   *Butler 30*

Lintel from a Doorway in Harmony

1811   *Butler 35*

Doorway in Harmony

About 1809   *Butler 47*

Doorway in Harmony

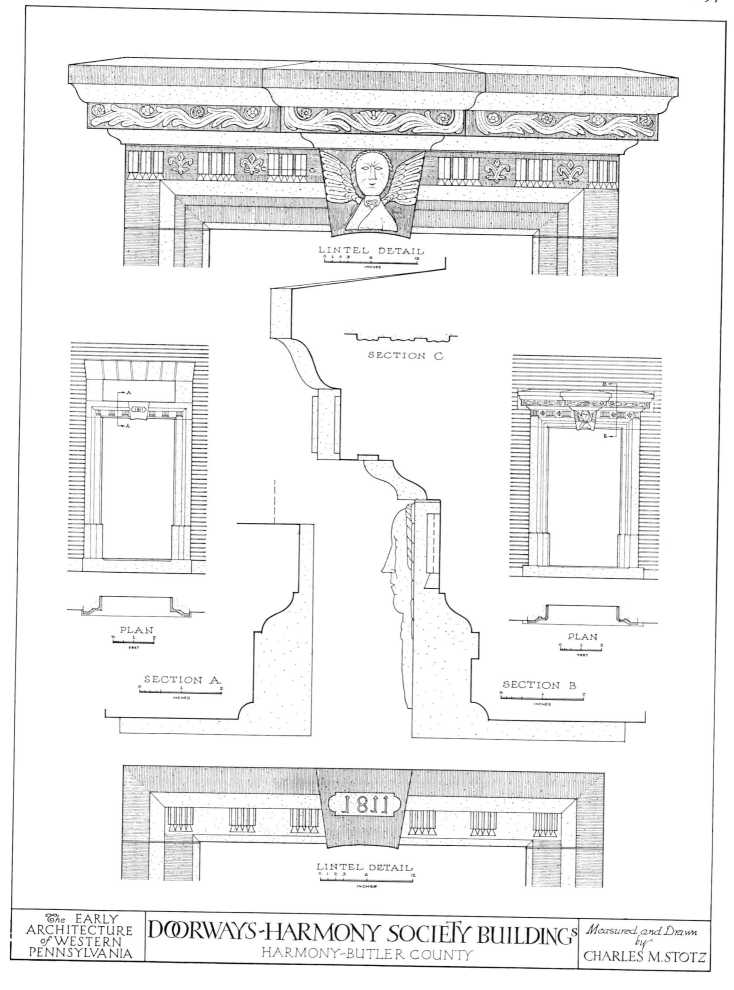

LINTEL DETAIL

SECTION C

PLAN

SECTION A

PLAN

SECTION B

1811

LINTEL DETAIL

Butler 29

1869   The Entrance to the Harmonites' Cemetery in Harmony

1869   Detail of the Cemetery Gate in Harmony   *Butler 29*

1809   Keystone from a Doorway in Harmony   *Butler 49*

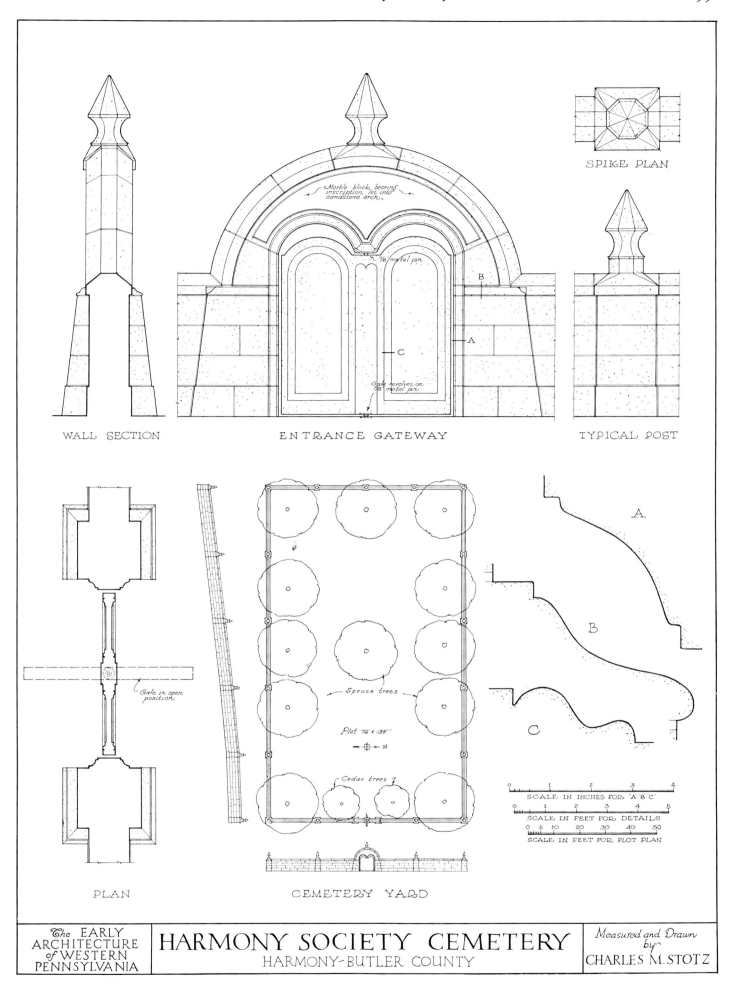

WALL SECTION   ENTRANCE GATEWAY   TYPICAL POST

SPIKE PLAN

Marble block, bearing inscription, let into sandstone arch.

7/8" metal pin

Gate revolves on 7/8" metal pin

A

B

C

PLAN

Gate in open position

CEMETERY YARD

Spruce trees

Plot 76' x 135'

N

Cedar trees

SCALE IN INCHES FOR 'A' 'B' 'C'

SCALE IN FEET FOR DETAILS

SCALE IN FEET FOR PLOT PLAN

The EARLY ARCHITECTURE of WESTERN PENNSYLVANIA

HARMONY SOCIETY CEMETERY
HARMONY-BUTLER COUNTY

Measured and Drawn by
CHARLES M. STOTZ

FRONT ELEVATION

SIDE ELEVATION

THE FEAST HALL
ECONOMY-BEAVER COUNTY

Measured and Drawn
by
THOMAS PRINGLE

SIDE ELEVATION.

WEATHER VANE

END ELEVATION.
INTERIORS OF FESTIVAL HALL.

·E·

·A·

·L·

·D·

·H·

·H·

·F·

FRONT ENTRANCE.

C:
SCALE FOR DETAILS.

SCALE FOR INTERIORS.

G
SCALE FOR ENTRANCE.

| The EARLY ARCHITECTURE of WESTERN PENNSYLVANIA | THE FEAST HALL ECONOMY-BEAVER COUNTY | Measured and Drawn by THOMAS PRINGLE |

1828   *Beaver 36*

The Feast Hall in Economy

                                                                        Beaver 42
1826

The Storehouse and Granary at Economy

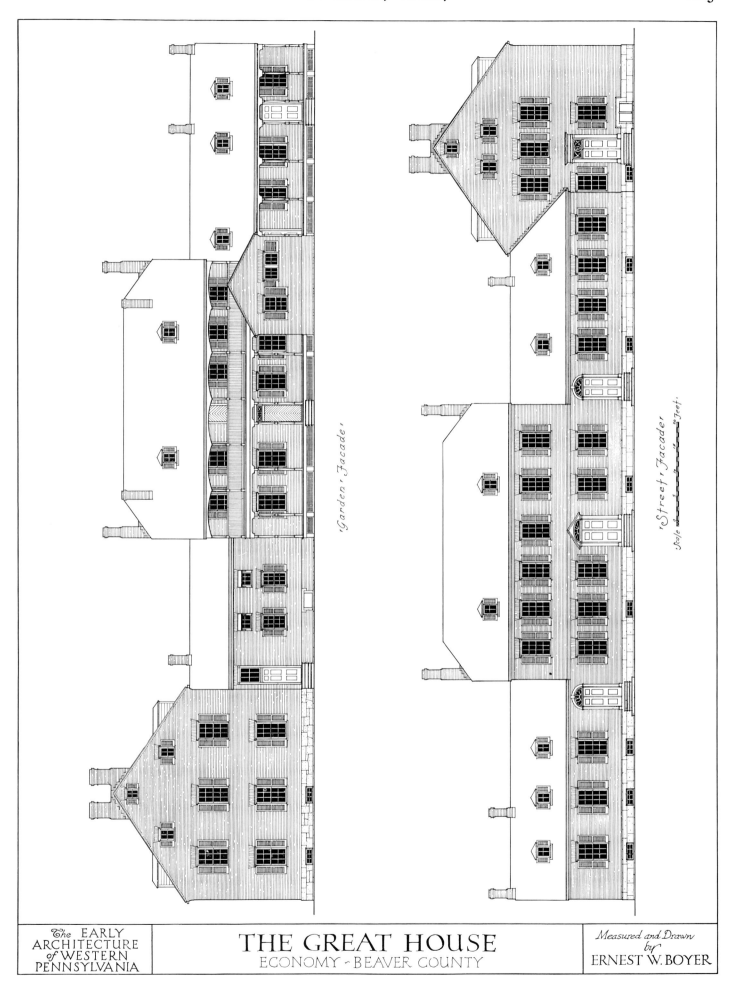

'Garden·Facade'

'Street·Facade'

Scale

THE EARLY
ARCHITECTURE
of WESTERN
PENNSYLVANIA

THE GREAT HOUSE
ECONOMY · BEAVER COUNTY

Measured and Drawn
by
ERNEST W. BOYER

1826   *Beaver 38*

The Great House at Economy

1826   *Beaver 38*   *1826*   *Beaver 38*

Doorway of the Great House   Doorway of the Great House

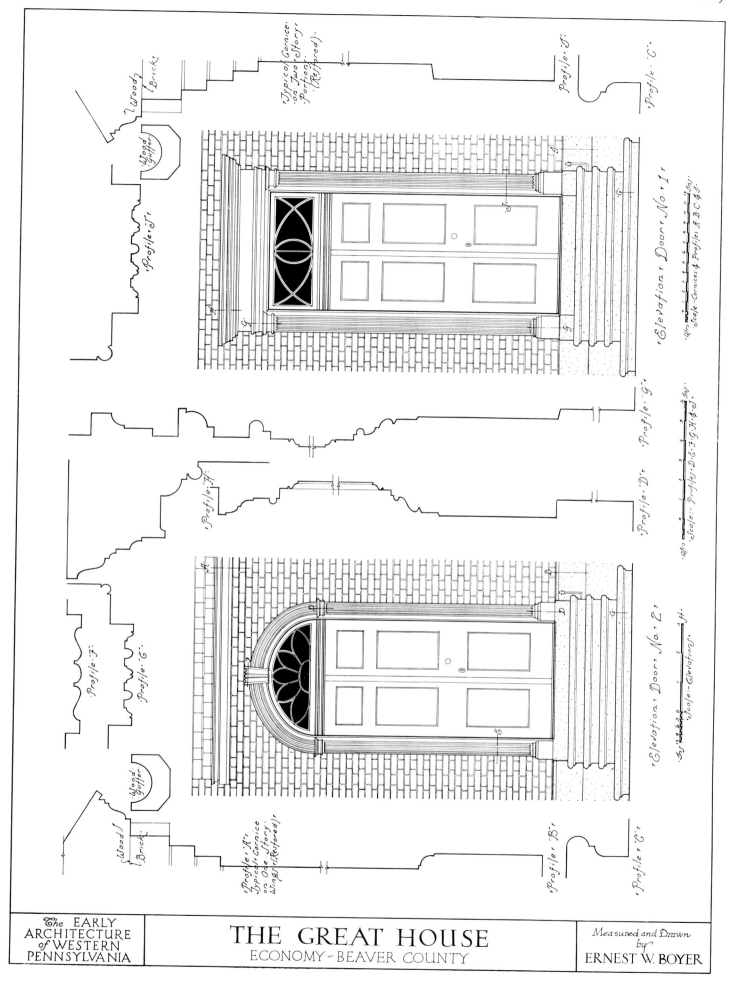

The EARLY
ARCHITECTURE
of WESTERN
PENNSYLVANIA

THE GREAT HOUSE
ECONOMY - BEAVER COUNTY

Measured and Drawn
by
ERNEST W. BOYER

1826   *Beaver 38*
Garden Front of the Great House

1831   *Beaver 41*   *1831*   *Beaver 41*
Vase from the Garden Pavilion at Economy   Detail of Vase Carving

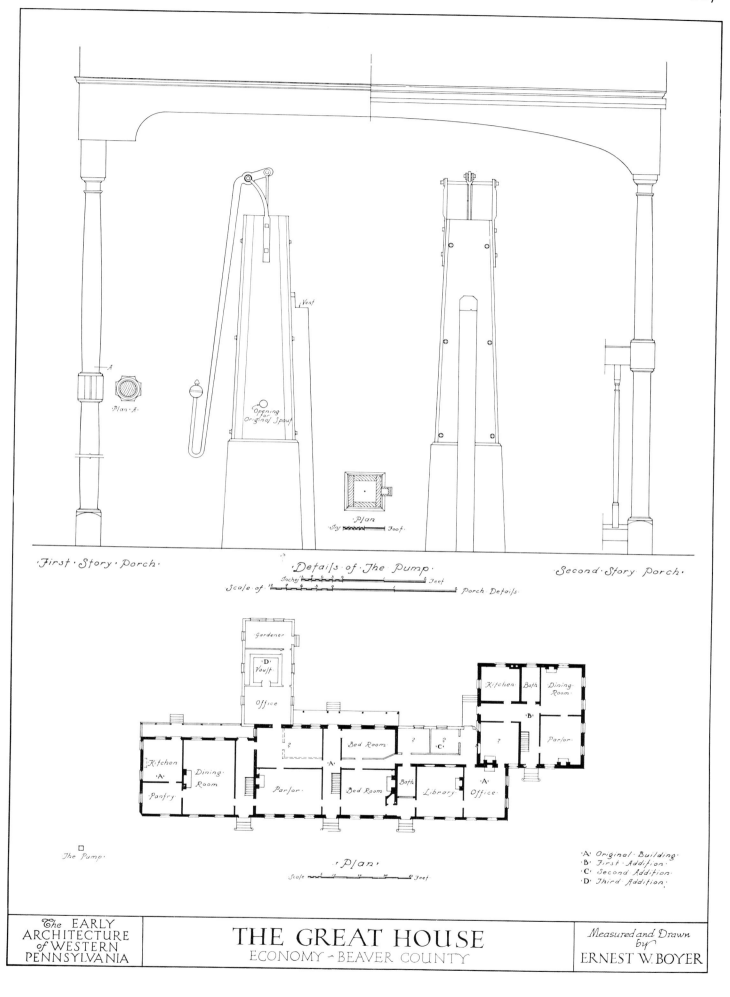

·First·Story·Porch·

·Details·of·The·Pump·

·Second·Story·Porch·

Scale of Porch Details·

·Plan·A·

Vent

Opening for Original Spout

·Plan·

Gardener

·D· Vault

Office

Kitchen Bath Dining Room

·B·

Parlor

Kitchen ·A· Dining Room

Pantry

Parlor

Bed Room

·A·

·C·

Bed Room

Bath

Library

Office ·A·

Parlor

The Pump·

·Plan·

Scale of Feet

·A· Original·Building·
·B· First·Addition·
·C· Second·Addition·
·D· Third·Addition·

Beaver 41   Garden Pavilion at Economy

1831

Beaver 38   Pump Beside the Great House in Economy

1826

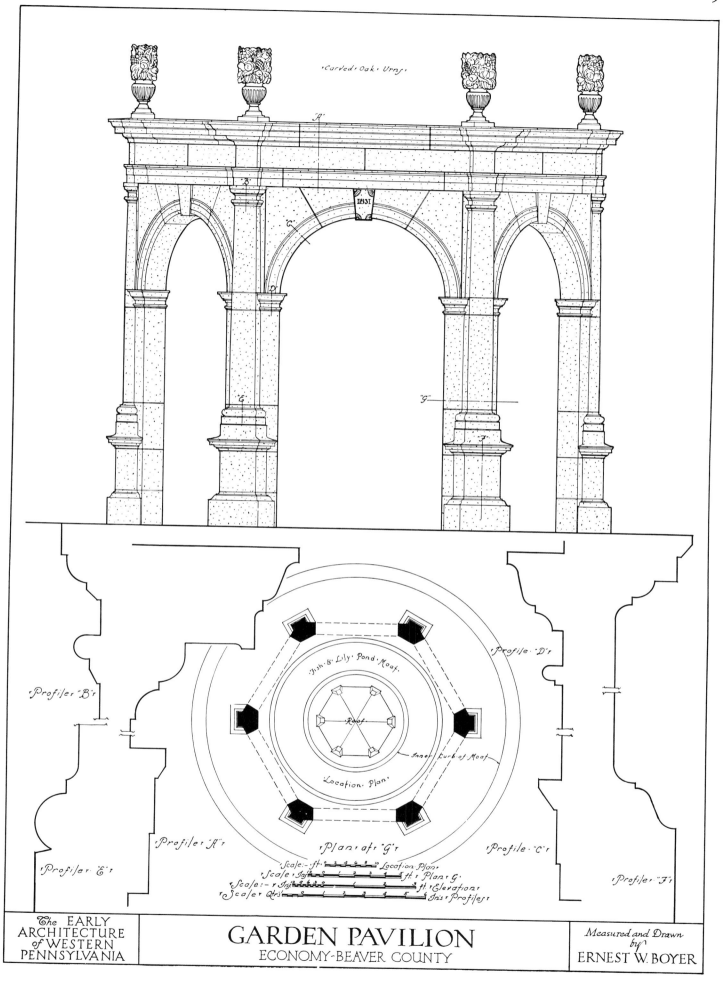

Carved Oak Urns.

Fish & Lily Pond Moat.

Roof

Inner Kurb of Moat

Location Plan.

Plan at "G"

Profile "B"

Profile "D"

Profile "A"

Profile "C"

Profile "E"

Profile "F"

Scale: ft. Location Plan.
Scale: Ins. ft. Plan G.
Scale: Ins. ft. Elevation.
Scale: Qtrs. Ins. Profiles.

The EARLY ARCHITECTURE of WESTERN PENNSYLVANIA

GARDEN PAVILION
ECONOMY-BEAVER COUNTY

Measured and Drawn by
ERNEST W. BOYER

The Church of the Harmony Society in Economy

Beaver 39

1832

A Typical House in Economy

Beaver 40

1826

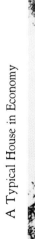

A Street Scene in Economy (Early photo)

Beaver 39

WEST ELEVATION

FEET 5   0   5   10   15   20   25 FEET

ST. JOHN'S CHURCH
ECONOMY-BEAVER COUNTY

Measured and Drawn
by
THOMAS PRINGLE

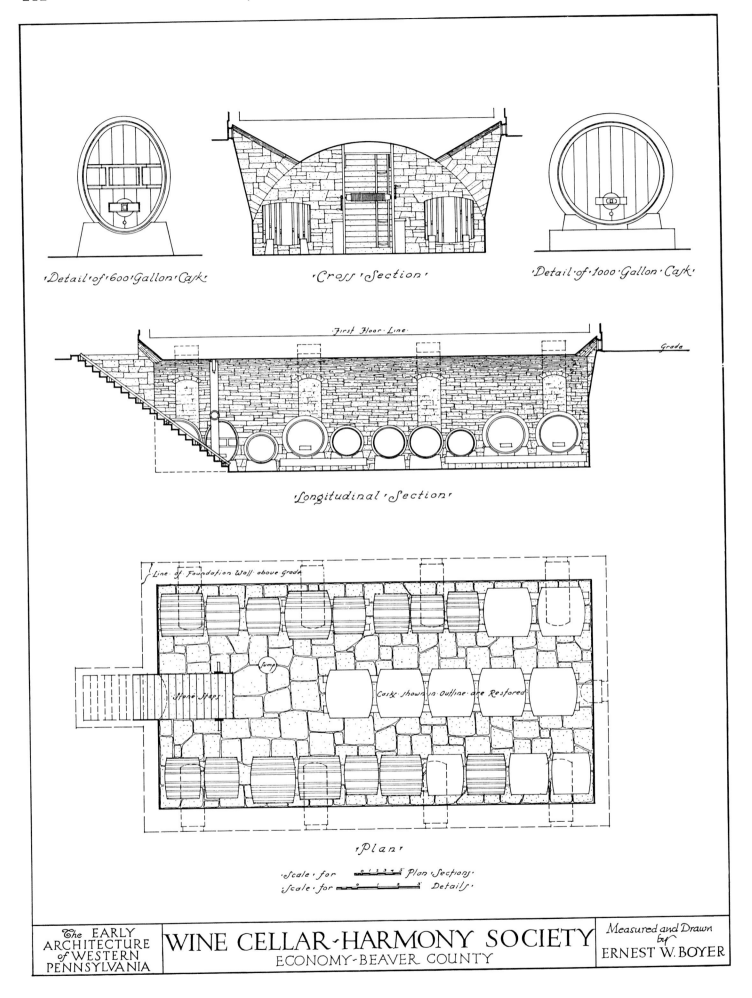

·Detail·of·600·Gallon·Cask·   ·Cross·Section·   ·Detail·of·1000·Gallon·Cask·

·Longitudinal·Section·

·Plan·

·Scale·for· ——— ·Plan·Sections·
·Scale·for· ——— ·Details·

The EARLY ARCHITECTURE of WESTERN PENNSYLVANIA	WINE CELLAR·HARMONY SOCIETY ECONOMY·BEAVER COUNTY	Measured and Drawn by ERNEST W. BOYER

1826
Detail of the Granary in Economy
Beaver 42

1826
The Great House in Economy
Beaver 38

1826
Entrance of a Shop in Economy
Beaver 35

1826
Wine Cellar under Shop in Economy
Beaver 35

Section Five

INSTITUTIONAL ARCHITECTURE

THE first schoolhouses and church buildings differed from the simple cabins and log houses of their day only in the arrangement of their interiors.

Schools

A frontier school, located on the James Hays farm, is portrayed in the *History of Butler County*: "Professor Matthews, who studied therein, described it as being constructed of hewn logs, while most of the others in the county were built of round logs. In the center was a fire-place, with a hearth eight feet square. At the corners of the hearth were posts, which supported the flue—a thing of poles and clay. To the posts, below the ceiling, boards were nailed on each side, extending downward from the ceiling about four feet, to lead the smoke into the flue, whenever the ordinary draft failed to do so. Oak shingles formed the roof, while slabs formed the ceiling. The front and rear were weatherboarded, but, for some reason, the gables were not so protected. The door was like an ordinary stable door, the floor laid with loose boards, the desks were rough boards, resting on wooden pins driven into the walls, while the puncheon seats were of the backless variety. The presence of glass in the two windows of this cabin gave to it an air of respectability which was not accorded to houses with greased paper wi[n]dows."

The original log house in which Dr. John McMillan conducted school on his farm near Hill Church was moved in recent years to Canonsburg, Washington County, to be preserved for the sake of its associations. This building, shown on page 223, was presumably like the "classical and mathematical" school built by the Reverend Thaddeus Dodd on his farm at Ten-Mile in 1782, and the school established by the Reverend Joseph Smith at Buffalo in 1785—both in Washington County.

There were six such log school buildings in Snowden Township, Allegheny County, in 1805. Most of the rural schools of later date were built of more substantial materials, but were often no larger in size. The brick school at New Geneva was built in 1810 by public subscription, the name of Albert Gallatin, who lived near by at "Friendship Hill," heading the list of subscribers. The stone Concord School near Rostraver, Westmoreland County, built in 1830, also exhibits the extreme simplicity that characterized the much later schools. Even today, the district is dotted with hundreds of simple rectangular schools of brick, frame, and stone, seldom of more than four rooms, in which the rudiments of education were taught—and some of them are still in use.

The school at Cherry Tree, typical of the frame construction and Greek Revival trimmings of the northern counties, is unusually elaborate.

These unpretentious beginnings led to the establishment of most of the large institutions of learning in western Pennsylvania today. The log school of Dr. McMillan was the forerunner of Canonsburg Academy, the first stone building of which was financed by John Canon in 1791. Of this institution, later known as Jefferson College, but one building, erected 1829-32, now stands in Canonsburg.

Similarly, the school first held on the second floor of the early log courthouse in Washington moved in 1793 into the stone building that is today the central unit of the Administration Building of Washington and Jefferson College at Washington. The brick wings, added in 1816, were originally used as dormitories. This institution, first known as Washington Academy, acquired its present title when Jefferson College merged with it in 1869.

Although the first actual school in Pittsburgh was held in 1761, the present University of Pittsburgh had its beginning in the Pittsburgh Academy, chartered in 1787. The Academy had a small log building on a plot granted by the Penns on Third Avenue between Smithfield and Grant streets. It was supplemented by a building of brick in 1790. On the same property the first building of the Western University of Pennsylvania appeared in 1830. This impressive structure, bearing a portico of four free-standing Ionic columns superimposed upon a rusticated stone base, burned in 1845.

Two other institutions of learning of architectural importance in the Pittsburgh district were the Western Theological Seminary, erected on Seminary (now Monument) Hill in 1831 at a cost of more than

$25,000, and the Edgeworth Female Seminary, built in 1836. Both were destroyed by fire, the former in 1854, the latter in 1865.

Waterford Academy in Erie County, opened in 1826, is excellently preserved. The treatment of the false pediment, heavy doorway, and graceful cupola is quite unexpected in the district, and the stone-work of the building is executed with great care and precision.

The most impressive school building remaining from early days in western Pennsylvania is Bentley Hall at Allegheny College, Meadville. Except for interior alterations it is unchanged. This building was conceived and its construction directed largely by the first president, the Reverend Timothy Alden. The cornerstone was laid in 1820 and the roof was finished in 1824, but the many obstacles that beset this determined man delayed its completion until the year 1835. This building departs from academic rule in many details, such as the atten-uated Greek Doric columns and abnormally low entablature of the porch wings; the brick pilasters, stepped back at each floor, with their curiously simplified Ionic capitals; and the odd relationship between these pilasters and the central pediment. But these architectural eccentricities do not detract from the effectiveness of the design; they rather lend to it a definite individuality. The cupola is particularly well proportioned and beautifully de-tailed. The New England Colonial character is quaintly intermingled with Greek Revival forms, which were at that time beginning to permeate architectural expression.

Churches

The chapels built by the French within their various forts of the mid-eighteenth century were the first church structures to be erected in western Pennsylvania, but no descriptions of them survive. The path that led from Fort Duquesne to the burial plot near the present location of Sixth Avenue and Wood Street in Pittsburgh was known as *l'Allée de la Vierge*, later Anglicized as Virgin Alley. It is unfortunate that this oldest street name in Pitts-burgh should have been discarded.

The first church services of the pioneers were of necessity held in their log cabins. The early churches were also of log construction. They were of simple rectangular shape, sometimes containing a gallery. St. Thomas' Church, seven miles from Brownsville, built in the 1770's, was, to quote from Alfred Creigh, "almost square, being thirty feet long by

twenty-six feet or twenty-seven feet in width, and was two stories in height with a gallery inside for the slaves, which went around three sides of the building." This description agrees with the general character of the Union Church near Schellsburg, illustrated on page 225, built in 1806, measuring 25 by 30 feet. Although the exterior was later weatherboarded, the interior is remarkably well preserved. The wineglass pulpit was crudely pat-terned after those so elegantly executed in the churches of the eastern states. The gallery benches are uncomfortable beyond belief, with narrow seats and high straight backs.

St. Patrick's Sugar Creek Church, built of logs in 1806, has been restored and preserved as a memorial to the first congregation there. It is a simple rectangle containing a narrow gallery across the entrance front, and the altar space is raised the height of one log. Its wide low windows are quite close to the floor.

The larger churches were built in three log units under a common roof. The central unit, slightly wider than the others, projected front and rear to provide an entrance vestibule on one side and a pulpit recess on the other. The pulpit was some-what elevated and usually had a sounding board over it. The Salem Presbyterian Church in West-moreland County was of this triple-cabin type. According to Boucher in his *Old and New West-moreland:* "It was seventy by forty feet . . . there were . . . seventy-one log seats in it and from six to eight hundred people could be accommodated in it."

The Poke Run Presbyterian Church, built in 1789 of the same log type, measured 70 by 30 feet. The next year in the same county (Westmoreland) the Fairfield Presbyterian Church, or White Meet-inghouse, was likewise built of three units.

The Fairfield Church succeeded a log *tent* on the same site. This interesting device, described in Joseph Smith's *Old Redstone*, was designed to per-mit open-air services when the congregation was too large to be accommodated in the church. It consisted of a lean-to shed of boards erected on an elevated platform at the base of a hill. The open side faced the sloping ground, upon which were arranged logs or slabs for seats. At right angles to these seats, and extending through them up the hillside from the tent, was a line of logs hewn on the upper side and laid end to end. They were covered with linen and, being somewhat elevated, served as tables for the communicants who sat on lower logs on either side. Thus the name of the

Tent Presbyterian Church near Uniontown was derived from a log tent that once occupied its site.

Few of the churches illustrated in this book were the first to be erected on their sites. Loss by fire and the growing needs of the congregations caused churches to be replaced periodically by others of larger size and more substantial construction. For this reason many of the most interesting, particularly the pioneer log churches, have long ceased to exist.

The first building of Trinity Church in Pittsburgh was a singular brick structure of octagonal shape, known as "Old Round Church." It was built in 1805 on the triangular plot bounded by Sixth Avenue, Liberty Avenue, and Wood Street. Sketches showing its original state prove that it was of excellent architectural character. The rector of this church, the Reverend John H. Hopkins, designed the second church, built about 1825 on the site later occupied by the present Trinity Church. In spite of its mediocre English Gothic character, it must have been most impressive in its day.

One of the most pretentious churches constructed in western Pennsylvania was St. Paul's Roman Catholic Church, built between 1829 and 1834 on Grant's Hill, Pittsburgh. It was constructed of brick in the Gothic style. Among the largest churches of its time in the United States, it measured 175 by 76 feet, contained three aisles, and could seat 1,800 persons. It was replaced, after its destruction by fire in 1851, by another Gothic building of brick, second in size only to St. Patrick's Cathedral in New York. This building was demolished in 1901.

In marked contrast to the elaborate adaptation of the Gothic style in these two churches is the utter simplicity of St. Peter's Roman Catholic Church at Brownsville, built in 1844 and extensively restored in recent years. This building, according to legend, was patterned after a village church in Ireland from which many of the parishioners had emigrated. Its Old World flavor is evident in details such as the winding stone staircase and the baptismal font. There are no moldings on the exterior; traditional label molds over the arches are simulated by straight flat sections of stone. St. Peter's enjoys an imposing site overlooking the Monongahela River valley.

The use of Gothic forms in western Pennsylvania was confined almost entirely to churches and cemetery structures; and in most instances these forms were but superficially followed. St. Luke's Episcopal Church at Woodville, built in 1853, differs little, except for its pointed windows, from the usual rectangular meetinghouse. The Tent Presbyterian Church, typical of the vast majority of the churches built in western Pennsylvania (particularly the southwestern portion, during the first half of the nineteenth century) was the simplest answer to the problem and was properly termed a *meeting house*. The Pleasant Grove Church in Westmoreland County shows the stone version of this type, somewhat larger and provided with two entrances. In the pleasant surroundings of this church, accentuated by the broad reaches of the old cemetery, there has been preserved the charm of the early rural church setting.

The Quaker Church near Perryopolis was rebuilt in 1893 from the material of, and on the same design as, the original church constructed in 1795. To the casual observer it would pass without question as the original building. The Mennonite Church near Harmony is likewise of simple lines but has carefully dressed stonework. The interior view shows the trestles arranged in four sections for men, women, boys, and girls. The Irvine Presbyterian Church in Irvine, Warren County, in contrast with these churches, is of extremely refined design and of a character unique in western Pennsylvania. It was built in 1837 by Dr. William A. Irvine on property owned by the family since Revolutionary days. Dr. Irvine is credited with having directed the execution of the work. The severity of form and the simple classic lines are relieved by the delicate detail of the windows, which merits careful attention. The two front windows are false. The shutters, closing on a blank masonry recess, were deemed necessary to achieve the desired symmetry.

The Brush Creek Salems Church was designed and built by the same workmen who constructed the Harrold's Church and the "Beehive" Church in Greensburg for the German Lutheran congregations. Were it not for the unfortunate, stilted proportion resulting from the excessive height required to accommodate the balcony, the Brush Creek Church, the only remaining one of the three, would be comparable with much of the work done in the East. The delicately ornamented doorways and the interior woodwork are notable in workmanship and design. Much of this ornament was executed with the gouge and other simple tools. It is particularly effective in the detail of the balcony front and the supporting post terminations. The original wineglass pulpit was replaced in 1864 by one of inharmonious Greek Revival design.

Compared with the foregoing examples, the character of the churches of the northern district show marked points of divergence. The builders, who seized upon the Greek Revival style as their favorite medium of expression, reveal that they were strongly influenced by this style as it was used in New York State and New England. Although many of the churches, like the Covenanter Church (now a stable) near Adamsville, were small and simple in plan, they carried the full architectural regalia of the Greek temple. The larger churches usually had spires or cupolas, as in the Pleasantville Free Baptist Church, the Coudersport Presbyterian Church, and the Riceville Congregational Church. All have the pedimented front with shallow pilasters of various types. The pilasters in the Riceville Church have full Ionic capitals and flutes executed from a board but seven-eighths of an inch thick. This church was erected by Dowd, the same carpenter-builder who built the Hendryx House, also in Riceville.

One of the most distinguished churches of the northern counties is the Independent Congregational (Unitarian) Church at Meadville. The Greek Revival style is skillfully applied here, both inside and out. The exterior openings have been kept in large scale and design to conform with the Doric columns of the portico. The entrance front contains but one opening, which was made higher than the actual entrance doorway in order to maintain a proper relationship with the design as a whole. The detail photograph of the entablature and column capital shows the flush joints of the wood construction which form a smooth surface to simulate the masonry prototype. The interior detail is lighter and, like the exterior, has been carefully preserved in its original state. The designer of this building was General G. W. Cullum of the United States Army (famous also for his plans of Fort Sumter). Its design is based on a Unitarian church in Philadelphia. The Greek Revival style, then popular in church building, was justified by a writer in the *Christian Register* of November 15, 1845: "Gothic architecture belongs to the Trinitarian Church, and the severe majesty of the Doric would better suit the simplicity of the Unitarian faith." Light was originally furnished by a chandelier of whale-oil lamps hung in the center of the room, and heat by two large wood-burning stoves in the rear corners.

Tombstones

On pages 248 to 251 are illustrated tombstones of various periods and from many parts of western Pennsylvania. Their treatment throughout the period, from the simple to the elaborate, developed hand in hand with architectural design. Of all the handiwork remaining from early days, the tombstone has changed least.

It is difficult to reconcile the illiteracy and the carelessness in spacing and arrangement with the excellence of the design and carving of the letters on these stones. This is best illustrated in the stones from the Union Church Cemetery near Schellsburg.

The naive charm of the stone at Donegal and that of Mary Ann Kelly in Hill Church Cemetery, the oldest stone (1783) in Washington County, with the childlike drawing of their ornamental designs, makes them even more impressive than later and more conventionally ornate stones. The lettering of the stones to John Riggs and Coonrod Stiffy in the Salem Church Cemetery, Westmoreland County, recalls the best carved lettering of ancient Roman inscriptions.

Tombstones occasionally derived their inspiration from architectural forms, as is evident in the stone in Sewickley Church Cemetery, Westmoreland County, and the cenotaph in the graveyard at Mercer, both obviously reflections of the Greek Revival mode then current.

The monument to Dr. Nathaniel Bedford, one-time surgeon at Fort Pitt, was for its time an unusually elaborate example of the mason's art. Originally erected by his widow on the Bedford property in old Birmingham on the South Side, the stone was removed to the churchyard of Trinity Cathedral, Pittsburgh, in 1909. The sandstone has disintegrated so far as to make the curious carving of the Masonic emblems now almost indistinguishable.

The stone found on Peter's Creek not far from its juncture with the Monongahela River has aroused much speculation. Some authorities have maintained that it was left by Céloron on his famous voyage. For proof they pointed to the partially destroyed stone molding at the base, which might have framed one of the lead plates deposited at the mouths of important streams to claim the territory for the King of France. Although it is known that Céloron did not deviate from his route down the Allegheny and Ohio rivers, the design of the ornamental cross seems to be of French origin. The stone is now on the property of Dr. L. W. Hoon in Monongahela.

1820

Crawford 1

Bentley Hall, Allegheny College, in Meadville

1820   *Crawford 1*

Rear View of Bentley Hall

1820   *Crawford 1*

Porch Detail of Bentley Hall

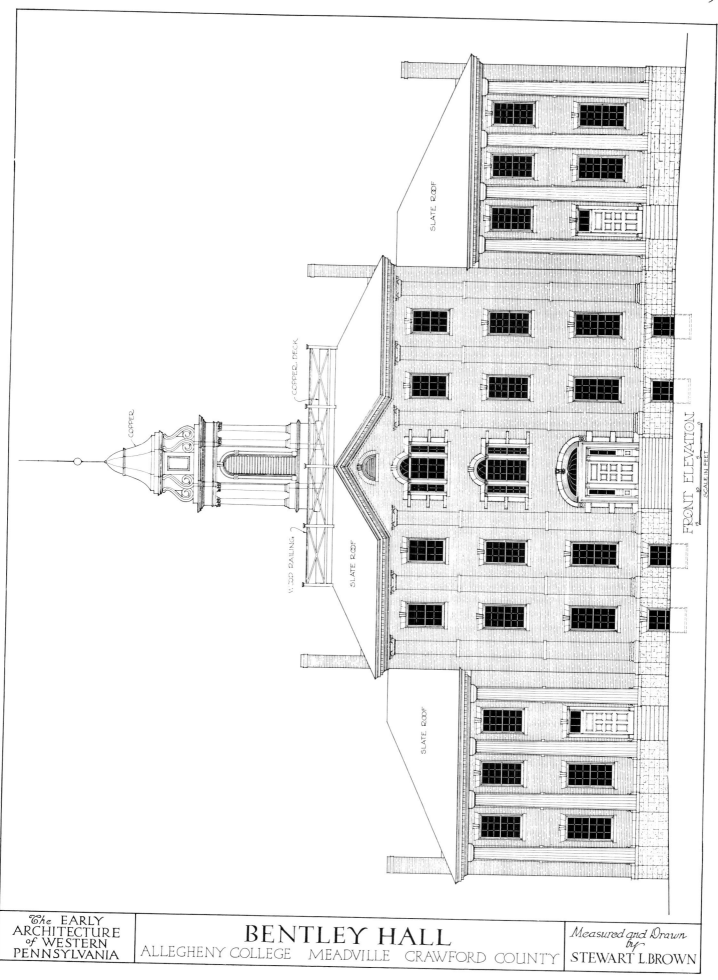

FRONT ELEVATION

SCALE IN FEET

COPPER

COPPER DECK

WOOD RAILING

SLATE ROOF

SLATE ROOF

SLATE ROOF

The EARLY
ARCHITECTURE
of WESTERN
PENNSYLVANIA

BENTLEY HALL

ALLEGHENY COLLEGE   MEADVILLE   CRAWFORD COUNTY

Measured and Drawn
by
STEWART L. BROWN

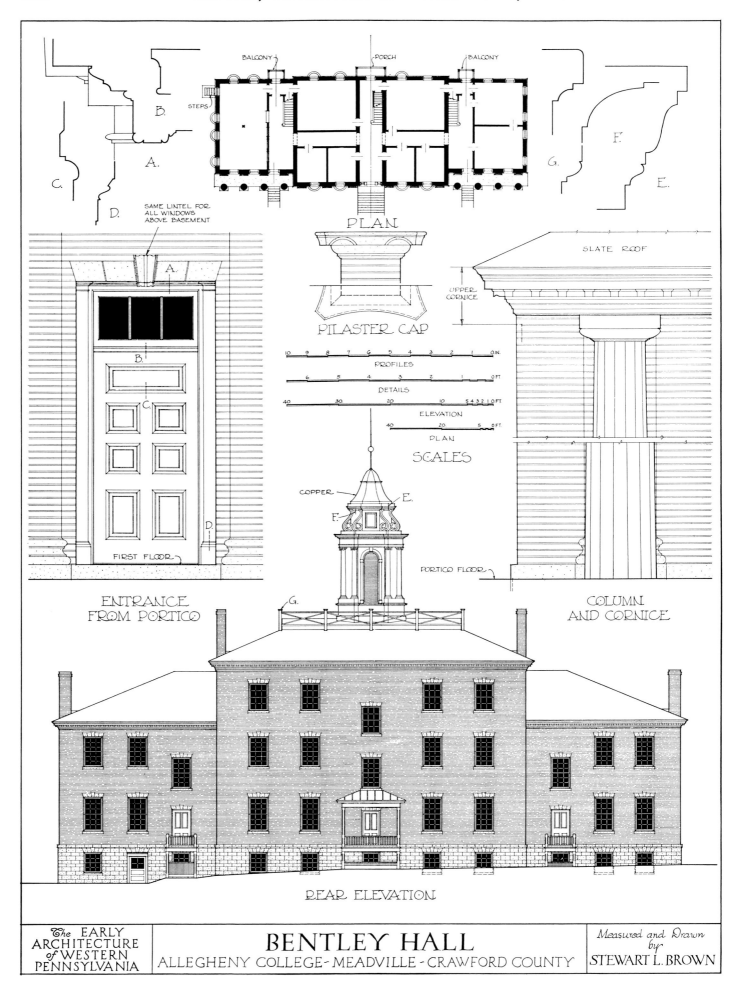

BENTLEY HALL
ALLEGHENY COLLEGE - MEADVILLE - CRAWFORD COUNTY

The EARLY ARCHITECTURE of WESTERN PENNSYLVANIA

Measured and Drawn by
STEWART L. BROWN

WOOD
SPLAY

WOOD

½ INTERIOR 3rd.
FLOOR WINDOW

MAIN ENTRANCE MOTIVE

K L

COMPOSITE
DETAIL OF
CUPOLA
ORDER

SCALES

J. L. K. M. N.

CEILING

DETAILS
PROFILES
ELEVATION

M.

N.

SLATE ROOF

J.

WOOD

½ INTERIOR 2nd.
FLOOR WINDOW

RIGHT SIDE ELEVATION

½ EXTERIOR 2nd.
FLOOR WINDOW

The EARLY
ARCHITECTURE
of WESTERN
PENNSYLVANIA

BENTLEY HALL
ALLEGHENY COLLEGE~MEADVILLE~CRAWFORD COUNTY

Measured and Drawn
by
STEWART L. BROWN

1793–1816   *Washington 8*

Administration Building, Washington & Jefferson College, in Washington

Date Unknown   *Venango 30*   *1810*   *Fayette 47*

A Public School in Cherry Tree   A School in New Geneva

Erie 14

1822

Waterford Academy in Waterford

Westmoreland 100

1830

Concord School in Rostraver

Washington 28

1780

Dr. John McMillan's School in Canonsburg

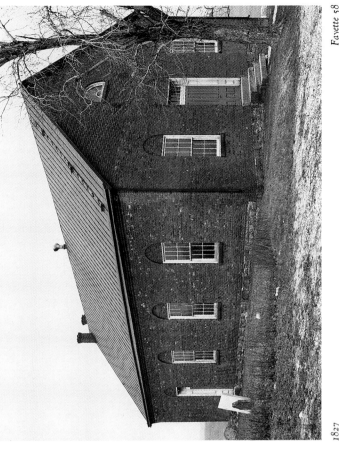

Fayette 58

The Tent Presbyterian Church near Fairchance

1827

Fayette 7

Quaker Church near Perryopolis

1795 *(Rebuilt in 1893)*

Crawford 39

The Covenanter Church in Adamsville

Date Unknown

Westmoreland 38

Pleasant Grove Presbyterian Church near Stahlstown

1832

1806

Interior of Union Log Church near Schellsburg

Bedford 15

PULPIT

ALTAR

BAPTISMAL FONT

STONE STAIR

WEST FRONT

Scale: 0   5   10

Scale   of   Details

0   1   2   3

The EARLY
ARCHITECTURE
of WESTERN
PENNSYLVANIA

ST. PETER'S CHURCH
BROWNSVILLE - FAYETTE COUNTY

Measured and Drawn
by
RAYMOND M. MARLIER

1844

St. Peter's Church in Brownsville

Fayette I

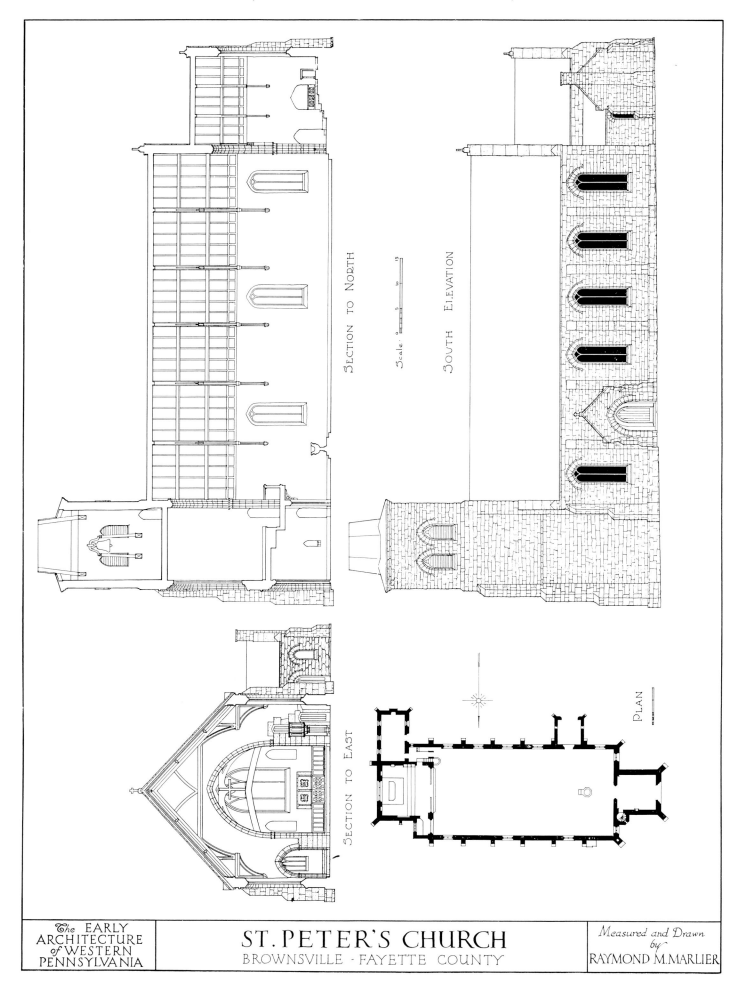

SECTION TO NORTH

Scale. 0 5 10 15

SOUTH ELEVATION

SECTION TO EAST

PLAN

ST. PETER'S CHURCH
BROWNSVILLE · FAYETTE COUNTY

Measured and Drawn
by
RAYMOND M. MARLIER

1844

Nave of St. Peter's Church

Fayette 1

1844

Baptismal Font, St. Peter's Church

Fayette 1

1844

Tower Detail, St. Peter's Church

Fayette 1

Exterior Detail, St. Peter's Church

Side Entrance, St. Peter's Church

Tower Stair, St. Peter's Church

Sacristy Entrance, St. Peter's Church

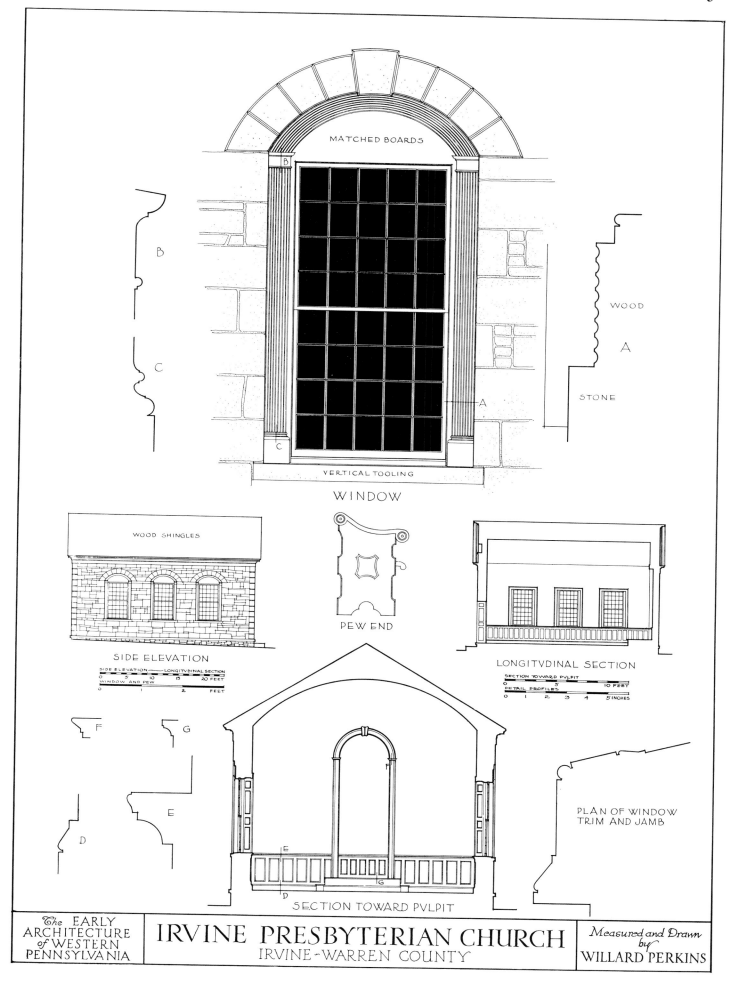

MATCHED BOARDS

B

B

C

A

WOOD

A

STONE

VERTICAL TOOLING

WINDOW

WOOD SHINGLES

SIDE ELEVATION

SIDE ELEVATION—LONGITVDINAL SECTION
0   5   10   15   20 FEET
WINDOW AND PEW
0   1   2   FEET

PEW END

LONGITVDINAL SECTION

SECTION TOWARD PVLPIT
0   5   10 FEET
DETAIL PROFILES
0   1   2   3   4   5 INCHES

F

G

E

D

E

D

G

PLAN OF WINDOW
TRIM AND JAMB

SECTION TOWARD PVLPIT

The EARLY
ARCHITECTURE
of WESTERN
PENNSYLVANIA

IRVINE PRESBYTERIAN CHURCH
IRVINE-WARREN COUNTY

Measured and Drawn
by
WILLARD PERKINS

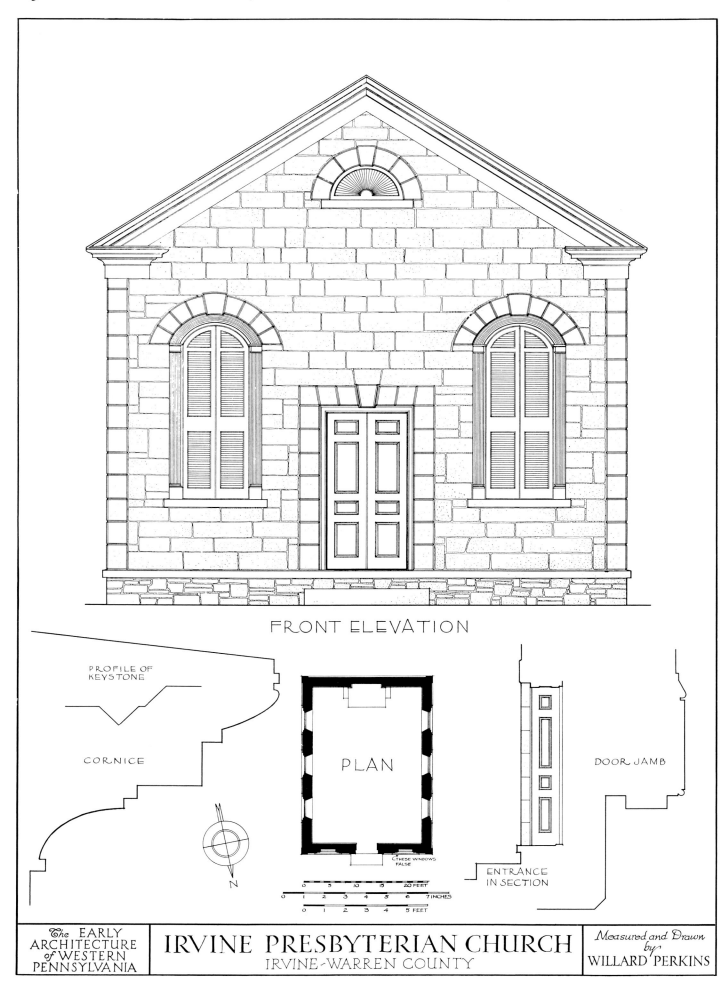

FRONT ELEVATION

PROFILE OF
KEYSTONE

CORNICE

PLAN

THESE WINDOWS
FALSE

N

DOOR JAMB

ENTRANCE
IN SECTION

0 5 10 15 20 FEET

0 1 2 3 4 5 6 7 INCHES

0 1 2 3 4 5 FEET

The EARLY
ARCHITECTURE
of WESTERN
PENNSYLVANIA

IRVINE PRESBYTERIAN CHURCH
IRVINE-WARREN COUNTY

Measured and Drawn
by
WILLARD PERKINS

The Irvine Presbyterian Church in Irvine

Warren 12

Rear View of the Irvine Presbyterian Church

Warren 12

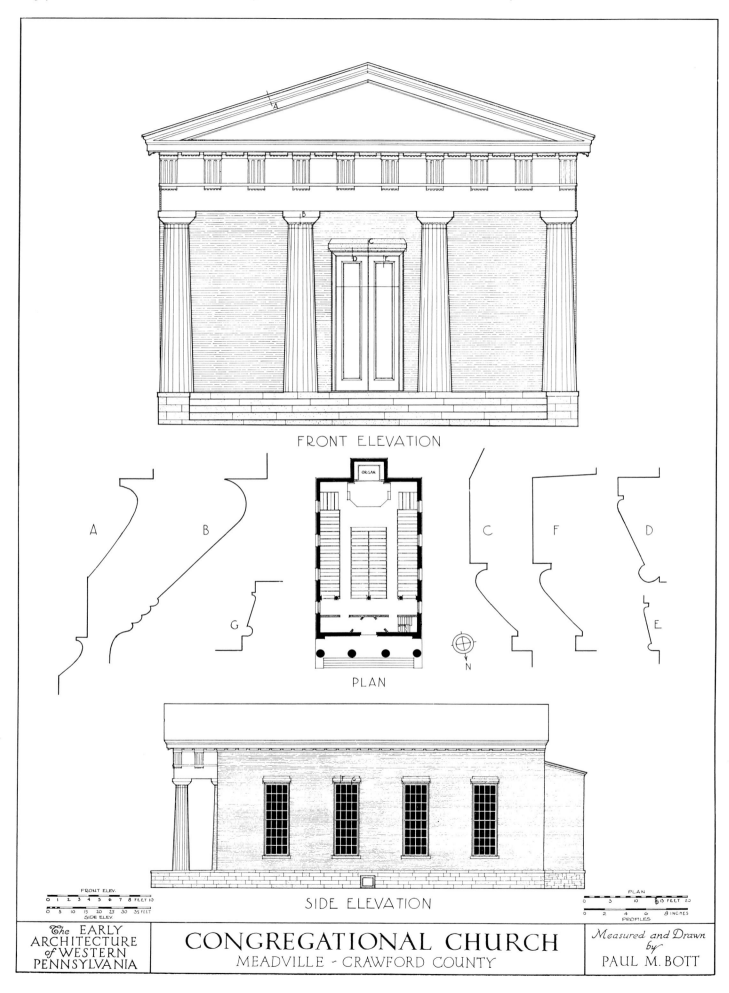

FRONT ELEVATION

PLAN

SIDE ELEVATION

CONGREGATIONAL CHURCH
MEADVILLE · CRAWFORD COUNTY

Measured and Drawn
by
PAUL M. BOTT

Crawford 16

1830 Interior View of the Congregational Church

Crawford 16

1830 Independent Congregational Church (Unitarian), Meadville

Crawford 16

1830 Pediment Detail of the Congregational Church

REAR ELEVATION

FRONT ELEVATION

SIDE ELEVATION

ORDER UNDER BALCONY

DETAIL OF PEWS

ORDER BEHIND PULPIT

The EARLY ARCHITECTURE of WESTERN PENNSYLVANIA

CONGREGATIONAL CHURCH
MEADVILLE - CRAWFORD COUNTY

Measured and Drawn by
PAUL M. BOTT

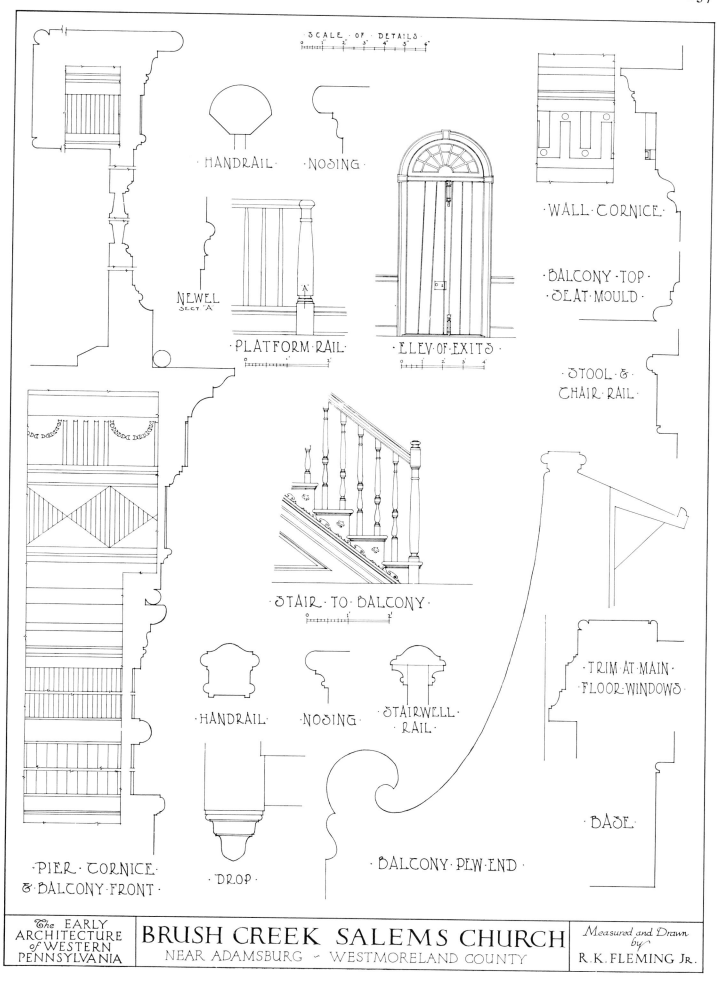

· SCALE · OF · DETAILS ·

· HANDRAIL ·   · NOSING ·

· NEWEL ·
SECT "A"

· PLATFORM · RAIL ·   · ELEV · OF · EXITS ·

· WALL · CORNICE ·

· BALCONY · TOP ·
· SEAT · MOULD ·

· STOOL · &
· CHAIR · RAIL ·

· STAIR · TO · BALCONY ·

· HANDRAIL ·   · NOSING ·   · STAIRWELL ·
· RAIL ·

· TRIM · AT · MAIN ·
· FLOOR · WINDOWS ·

· PIER · CORNICE ·
& · BALCONY · FRONT ·   · DROP ·   · BALCONY · PEW · END ·   · BASE ·

The EARLY
ARCHITECTURE
of WESTERN
PENNSYLVANIA

BRUSH CREEK SALEMS CHURCH
NEAR ADAMSBURG - WESTMORELAND COUNTY

Measured and Drawn
by
R.K. FLEMING Jr.

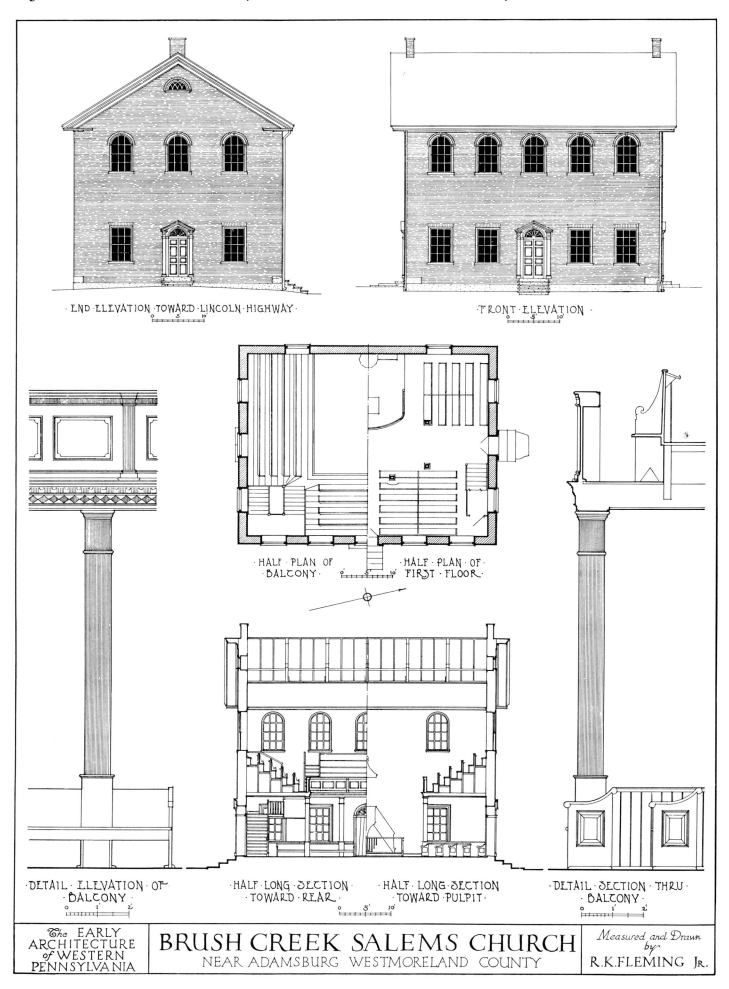

· END · ELEVATION · TOWARD · LINCOLN · HIGHWAY ·

· FRONT · ELEVATION ·

· HALF · PLAN · OF · BALCONY ·   · HALF · PLAN · OF · FIRST · FLOOR ·

· DETAIL · ELEVATION · OF · BALCONY ·

· HALF · LONG · SECTION · TOWARD · REAR ·

· HALF · LONG · SECTION · TOWARD · PULPIT ·

· DETAIL · SECTION · THRU · BALCONY ·

The EARLY ARCHITECTURE of WESTERN PENNSYLVANIA

BRUSH CREEK SALEMS CHURCH
NEAR ADAMSBURG WESTMORELAND COUNTY

Measured and Drawn by
R.K. FLEMING Jr.

Westmoreland 5

1820

The Brush Creek Salems Church near Adamsburg

Westmoreland 5

1820

Entrance Door of the Brush Creek Salems Church

· ATTIC · WINDOW ·

· ROSETTE ·

· CORNICE ·

"A"

"B"

"C"

"D"

SCALE · OF · SECTIONS

· ELEVATION ·

· MAIN · ENTRANCE ·

· SECTION ·

· ENTRANCE · KEYSTONE ·

· KEYSTONE ·

· BALCONY · WINDOW ·

· JAMB ·

· PLAN · AT · MAIN · ENTRANCE ·

The EARLY ARCHITECTURE of WESTERN PENNSYLVANIA

BRUSH CREEK SALEMS CHURCH
NEAR ADAMSBURG · WESTMORELAND COUNTY

Measured and Drawn by
R.K. FLEMING Jr.

Door Detail of the Brush Creek Salems Church

1820

Balcony Detail of the Brush Creek Salems Church

1820

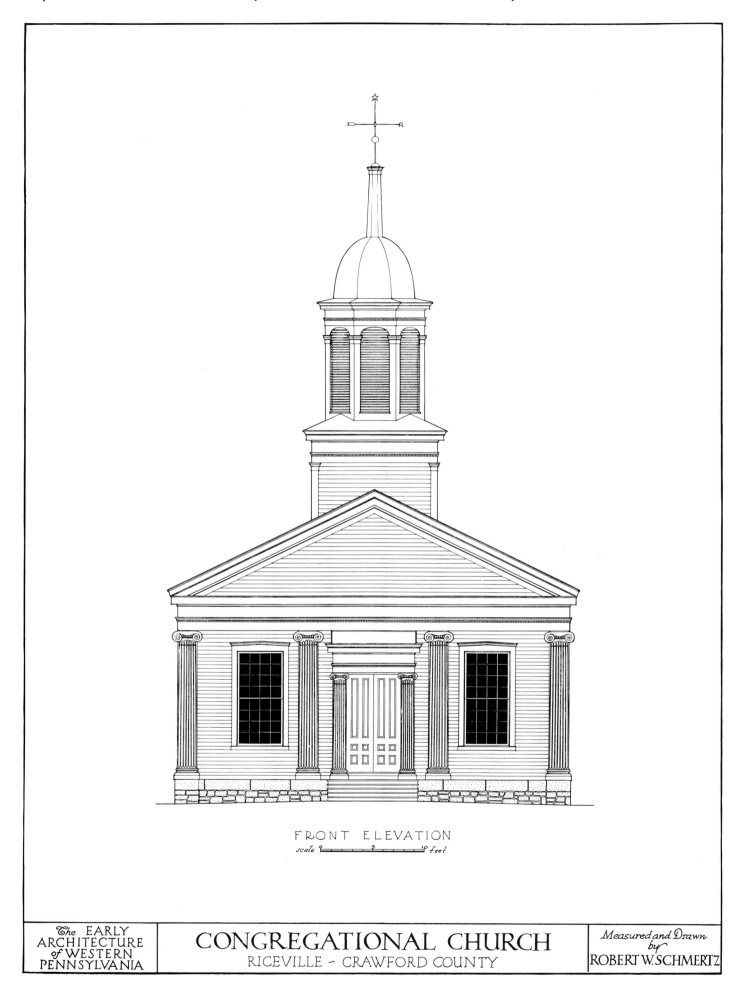

FRONT ELEVATION
scale feet

The EARLY ARCHITECTURE of WESTERN PENNSYLVANIA

CONGREGATIONAL CHURCH
RICEVILLE ~ CRAWFORD COUNTY

Measured and Drawn
by
ROBERT W. SCHMERTZ

Crawford 24

1858

Entrance of the Congregational Church

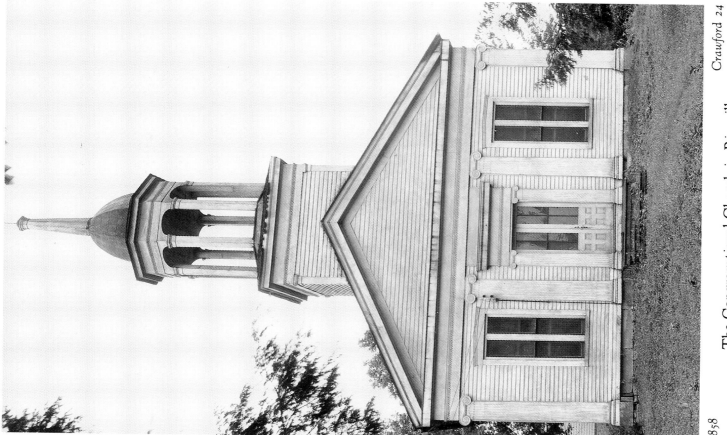

Crawford 24

1858

The Congregational Church in Riceville

PROFILES

scale |_____| inches

PLAN OF BELFRY

scale |_____| feet

DOOR

scale |_____| feet

UPPER PANELS RESTORED

PLAN

scale |_____| feet

MAIN PILASTER & CORNICE

scale |_____| feet

SIDE ELEVATION

scale |_____| feet

LOUVRES RESTORED

WINDOWS RESTORED

The EARLY ARCHITECTURE of WESTERN PENNSYLVANIA

CONGREGATIONAL CHURCH
RICEVILLE ~ CRAWFORD COUNTY

Measured and Drawn by
ROBERT W SCHMERTZ

1825

The Mennonite Church near Harmony

Butler 37

1825

Interior of the Mennonite Church

Butler 37

1825

Entrance Door of the Mennonite Church

Butler 37

1805   *Armstrong 14*

St. Patrick's Sugar Creek Church near Millerstown

Date Unknown   *Venango 38*

The Free Baptist Church in Pleasantville

1849   *Potter 3*

The Presbyterian Church in Coudersport

Entrance of the Pleasant Grove Church

Westmoreland 38

St. Luke`s Church in Woodville

Allegheny 27

1852

Westmoreland 50

Entrance of Sewickley Church near West Newton

Date Unknown

Gate of the Cross Creek Cemetery

Washington 93

1790   *Westmoreland 26*
From Salem Church Cemetery near New Derry

Date Unknown   *Westmoreland 109*
From a Cemetery at Donegal

1808   *Washington 93*
From Cross Creek Cemetery

1828   *Westmoreland 26*
From Salem Church Cemetery near New Derry

About 1818　　　　　　　　　　　　　　*Allegheny 181*
Dr. Nathaniel Bedford Monument, Trinity Church, Pittsburgh

About 1818　　　　　　　　　　　　　　*Allegheny 181*
Detail of Bedford Monument, Trinity Church

Date Unknown　　　　　　　　　　　　　*Allegheny 171*
Stone found on Peters Creek near Clairton

About 1837　　　　　　　　　　　　　　*Mercer 25*
Cenotaph in Cemetery at Mercer

1830   *Westmoreland 50*   1816   *Washington 93*
From Sewickley Church Cemetery near West Newton   From Cross Creek Cemetery

1827   *Westmoreland 107*   1836   *Bedford 15*
From Fels Church Cemetery near Webster   From Union Church Cemetery near Schellsburg

Washington 2

From Hill Church Cemetery near Canonsburg

1783

Westmoreland 26

From Salem Church Cemetery near New Derry

1795

Bedford 15

From Union Church Cemetery near Schellsburg

1836

Bedford 15

From Union Church Cemetery near Schellsburg

1836

Section Six

GOVERNMENTAL AND MILITARY ARCHITECTURE

WITH the annexation of new land, the spread of population, and the division of the early counties into smaller units, courthouses increased in number in western Pennsylvania. Local pride dictated that the county seat should be marked by a building of distinction, both in size and character; hence from early days the courthouse was a conspicuous structure. And each courthouse, as it became outmoded or inadequate in size or fell a victim to fire, was supplanted by a new and more pretentious one.

Three eras of courthouse building occurred which were more or less contemporaneous with the style periods of early architecture—the log period before 1800, the Post-Colonial period before 1830, and the Greek Revival between 1830 and 1860. Thus, before 1860, most of the older counties had built three courthouses; the younger ones, two. With each successive period, size, elaborateness, and cost increased. A fourth wave of courthouse building occurred before 1900 and still another, after that date. Only a few courthouses remain from the period covered by this book (up to 1860), and these are of the last, or Greek Revival period.

The first log courthouses, hardly distinguishable from the log houses of the times, reflected the poverty and unsettled conditions of the western country. In Westmoreland County, court was held for a time in the log home of Robert Hanna in Hannastown, near Greensburg. Virginia laid claim to western Pennsylvania, included it within her District of West Augusta, and held court separately in Pittsburgh in defiance of Pennsylvania's authority. In 1777 a log courthouse was built on the farm of Andrew Heath, on the Monongahela River near the present Washington County line, as the seat of Virginia's newly established Yohogania County.

A second log courthouse for Westmoreland County was erected in 1786 in Greensburg. But this building proved so unsatisfactory, after six years' use, that court was held in taverns of the village. The log courthouse built in Washington in 1783 provided quarters on the second floor for the Washington Academy. It cost 701 pounds, 8 shillings, 9¾ pence, which expense included 102 gallons of whisky, undoubtedly for the workmen.

The second era is typified by the first Allegheny County Courthouse, erected shortly before 1800 on Market Street Diamond in Pittsburgh. Excellent lithographs and engravings of it are preserved. Built of brick, it was nearly square in plan, and its roof terminated in a slender spire. The rather ornate doorway, together with descriptions of the interior, indicates the Georgian ancestry of its design. The portico with full-length order was conspicuously absent. The somewhat similar first Fayette County Courthouse, erected in 1796, had "a belfry over the center of the building supported by eight turned columns and surmounted by a weather vane." During this Post-Colonial period Washington County had a handsome courthouse, and the one completed in Erie in 1825 was for many years famous as the most elegant in northwestern Pennsylvania.

The earliest courthouse of substantial character in the district was built (by authority of an act of 1771) in Bedford of blue limestone. It so commanded the admiration of the town that when the court declared it a "nuisance" and ordered its demolition, a storm of protest was aroused. When the new courthouse (see page 260) was built in 1828, it was described as "deforming what is otherwise one of the most beautiful town parks in the Commonwealth." Although this building, of transitional design, may lack an academic purity of form, it hardly seems to have deserved such violent abuse. The lingering effects of the Post-Colonial period are evident in the pediment, fanlight, and circular lobby stair, while the dawning of the Greek Revival style in the district was expressed in the Doric columns and entablature.

The contracts and other records of the Post-Colonial period indicate that the cost of the courthouses then ranged from $1,362.53 (in Fayette County) to $8,000 (in Washington County).

The "grand manner" in courthouse design actually began with the Greek Revival style, an ideal medium for these dignified and imposing buildings. Within the 1840's and 1850's courthouses were erected in Allegheny, Clarion, Washington, Elk,

McKean, Fayette, Venango, Lawrence, Greene, Somerset, Westmoreland, Armstrong, and Clearfield counties. These buildings were all of brick except those in Elk and McKean counties, where frame construction extended even to public buildings; and those in Lawrence and Allegheny Counties, where stone was used. In all but a few, a monumental portico was the distinguishing feature. Six-column porticoes of Ionic, the most popular order, were applied to the Washington, Lawrence, Butler, and Somerset courthouses; there were four-column Corinthian porticoes on the Fayette, Westmoreland, and Armstrong courthouses; and the Greene County Courthouse had a six-column Corinthian portico.

Such buildings often occupied a prominent site on an elevation overlooking the city; and, occasionally, as in the case of the Armstrong County Courthouse, terminated the axis of a main street. Their dominance was further enhanced by cupolas that rose above their roofs. The cupolas often contained clocks or bells and were usually surmounted by carved wooden figures. Thus General Butler, General Greene, Marquis Lafayette, George Washington, and other famous patriots contemplated from their lofty positions the rolling countryside of the counties that bore their names.

Of these wooden figures, two have been preserved and are shown in the accompanying illustrations. The figure of Lafayette was carved by David Blythe, who is recognized today as one of the leading genre painters of his time. He was a most versatile and interesting personality and undertook this unusual and difficult task for a fee of $125, raised by popular subscription. The figure was carved from a block of wood built up from two-inch poplar planks. Descriptions from memory and portrait engravings of Lafayette were Blythe's only guides in making a good likeness.

By requesting the "exorbitant" sum of $300 for the work, Blythe lost the opportunity to execute General Greene's statue for the Greene County Courthouse. The statue was eventually carved by Bradley Mahanna of Waynesburg. The figure of Washington was carved by James P. Millard. In addition to the figure of General Butler on the cupola, the Butler County Courthouse had several carved figures in the tympanum of the pediment.

The Greene County Courthouse is perfectly preserved, except for the cupola, which was burned and replaced in 1926. It is one of the finest examples of the Greek Revival type. The drawing of the cupola and figure in this book is based on a photograph taken some years before the fire. The community is justly proud of this handsome building, which serves its purpose adequately even today.

The commissioners of Greene County required in their building contract that this courthouse conform to "the general plan, style and materials of the Courthouse of Fayette County," with the stipulation that if "cast-iron caps can be procured, the Corinthian capitols are to be adopted." The graceful detail and form of these "capitols" fully justified the change from Ionic. The builders, Samuel and John Bryan of Harrisburg, who also built the Fayette County Courthouse, were to be paid under the terms of the contract $6,000 upon completion of the building, $5,000 one year from that date, $5,000 two years from that time, and a final $500 three years after completion—scarcely a happy arrangement for the contractors.

The Armstrong County Courthouse reveals in its design, particularly in the dome and second-floor windows, the tendencies that toward the mid-century had begun to undermine the academic purity of the Greek Revival style. However, the portico and the arcaded stone base have considerable distinction, and the position of the building at the upper termination of a wide, rising street is most effective.

The cost of a Greek Revival courthouse averaged about $20,000, but a few cost much more. The one in Butler County cost $37,000, with an extra cost of $40,000 for additions. By far the most massive and costly county building in western Pennsylvania before 1860 was the second Allegheny County Courthouse, built in 1842 by Coltart and Dilworth, after the plans of the architect, John Chislett, at a cost of nearly $200,000. The portico, a double row of six Doric columns of large diameter, had no pediment. The entire building, measuring 100 by 165 feet, was of sandstone. A dome surmounted the whole, rising 148 feet above the pavement. The dome was an incongruity that was not uncommon in contemporaneous public buildings of the Greek style in various parts of the country. This building, destroyed by fire in 1882, had attracted much favorable comment both at home and abroad.

The Fortifications of the Settler

Of the many log fortifications erected by settlers in the eighteenth century for protection against the Indians, none is in existence today, although several are known to have been standing as late as the end

of the nineteenth century. The conflicting terminology in written descriptions of these fortifications
makes it somewhat difficult to segregate the various
types, but in general they consisted of fortified
cabins, blockhouses, or stockades. The more important forts were combinations of these elements.

Although every log cabin or house was built to
resist surprise attacks, more effective defense was
soon provided at strategically located centers of
population. This was sometimes a blockhouse,
which, according to Boucher, "was not considered
very secure. It was made of heavy logs, and in its
general construction did not differ greatly from the
log houses . . . The logs of a blockhouse were heavier
and often unhewn. . . . The first story was made
from eight to ten feet high. . . . the logs of the second
story extended from two to four feet beyond the
lower story. . . . The upper story was made six or
seven feet high and had port holes in its walls . . ."

The most effective protection was afforded by the
stockaded fort, such as that described by Doddridge
in his *Notes*: "The fort consisted of cabins, blockhouses, and stockades. A range of cabins commonly
formed one side, at least, of the fort. Divisions or
partitions of logs separated the cabins from each
other. The walls on the outside were ten or twelve
feet high, the slope of the roof being turned wholly
inward. A very few of these cabins had puncheon
floors, the greater part were earthen . . . The stockades, bastions, cabins, and blockhouse walls, were
furnished with port holes at proper heights and
distances. The whole of the outside was made
completely bullet proof."

The Fortifications of the Armies

The early fortresses were of rough construction,
principally of log and earth, but they were carefully
laid out and supervised by experienced army engineers. Diagrammatic plans of the forts constructed
by the English are today in the British War Office,
and those of the American forts are in the War
Department at Washington.

Le Mercier laid out the French forts. The first,
at Presque Isle (now Erie), built in 1753, had
fifteen-foot walls of chestnut logs enclosing a space
approximately 120 feet square, with a blockhouse of
logs at each corner. Similar forts were also constructed at Le Bœuf (Waterford) and at Venango
(Franklin). Fort Duquesne, built at the forks of the
Ohio in 1754, was of even larger size, measuring
about 120 by 150 feet. It housed a garrison of five
hundred. The walls on the river side were of

stockade; those facing the land were double log
walls separated by an earth filling, twelve feet wide.
Outside this wall a ditch, with a log stockade in
front of it, extended between the rivers. At the
corners were bastions, which mounted small guns.
The buildings within the enclosure were "covered
with boards, as well the roof as the sides that look
inside the fort, which they saw there by hand."

The principal English fortresses in western Pennsylvania were Fort Bedford (probably 1757), Fort
Ligonier (1758), and Fort Pitt (1758). There were
lesser forts throughout the district—Fort Burd,
Fort Hand, and others. All, except Fort Pitt, were
of similar character, and varied only in size and
equipment. They consisted of log stockades, usually
square in plan, with projecting bastions at the
corners, mounting guns that could sweep the walls
of the fort. Within this stockade were the officers'
quarters, magazines, storehouses, and the like. To
make it more difficult to scale the stockade, more
ditches were dug in front of them and the earth
was banked up against the walls. Firing platforms,
with loopholes for the rifles, were built behind the
stockades.

Fort Pitt was the most complete stronghold in
the district. "The fort proper was located on the
bank of the Monongahela beginning about six
hundred feet from the point and extending about
an equal distance along the river and two thirds of
the distance across to the Allegheny. It was in the
shape of an irregular pentagon with bastions at the
corners, and it covered about eight acres. The
western walls were revetted with brick, and the
others were wooden stockades banked with earth.
Around the fort was a broad moat, which was
connected with the Allegheny River. Beyond the
moat and running across the point from river to
river was a broad glacis or earthwork, and along the
river banks within the inclosed area was a light
parapet with three bastions . . . The fort was designed to house a garrison of about a thousand men,
and its cost to the British government was probably
in the neighborhood of six thousand pounds."
(Description by Dr. Solon J. Buck.) At the time of
the demolition of Fort Pitt more than a million bricks
and a large number of structural timbers were
itemized. James Kenny in his *Journal* of 1761 mentions: "A fine large Stone House, a Building in ye
S. E. Corner of ye fort for a Governor's House,
Stone quarrying & Squairing for the House, quarrying for Lime and Burning ye Same, Making &
Burning Brick, . . ." From brick purchased at the

razing of the Fort, a number of houses were constructed on Market Street.

The blockhouse was erected by Colonel Bouquet in 1764. According to Annie Clark Miller: "There is a division of opinion as to the relation of the Block House to the fort. It was thought for many years to have been an outpost for riflemen to defend the fort when water in the surrounding ditch was low. More recent authorities believe the redoubt was not outside the fort, but part of the stronghold, and most likely stood on the north bastion." At any rate, it is the last surviving relic of warfare in western Pennsylvania, and the oldest building of any sort of verified date in the district. Fortunately it has been restored and set aside by the Daughters of the American Revolution as a permanent historical monument. It is five-sided in plan and is of simple construction. (See page 263.) Inside, a crooked stairway leads to an upper firing level. Two tiers of hewn logs, built into the wall, contain loopholes. Over the doorway is a plaque (see page 162) bearing the inscription: AD 1764 Coll Bouquet.

Headquarters for the western army of the United States were transferred in 1778 to the newly finished Fort McIntosh on the present site of Beaver. This fort housed a garrison of about 1,300. Inside its walls of squared logs closely fitted together were a number of log buildings with shingled roofs and glass windows. It was laid out by a military engineer—Le Chevalier de Cambray.

The last fort to be constructed in Pittsburgh has been almost forgotten—Fort Lafayette, built in 1792, on the plot bounded by Ninth and Tenth streets, Penn Avenue, and the river. It was an elaborate fortification containing bastions, blockhouses, barracks, and accessory structures. Fort Lafayette was erected as a precautionary measure after the defeat of St. Clair because Fort Pitt had already been demolished, leaving Pittsburgh without any fortification. This new site was considered more effective strategically than that of Fort Pitt.

Arsenals

The United States Allegheny Arsenal erected on the site of Lawrenceville, Pittsburgh, between 1812 and 1820, was one of the most extensive in the country. The description of this group of buildings in Israel Rupp's *Early History of Western Pennsylvania*, published in 1846, indicates the importance of the Arsenal:

"Among the active measures of the Administration at the commencement of the war of 1812, and among the most necessary and useful too, was the selection of suitable sites for the establishment of large National Arsenals."

"As a position whence supplies may be sent to our north-western frontier, the posts on the great tributaries of the Mississippi, New Orleans, the fortresses that protect that great city, and to the chain of permanent defences on the coast of the Gulf of Mexico the Allegheny Arsenal can have no equal, . . ."

"As a structure, this Arsenal possesses no particular architectural merit, although its style is peculiar; while it presents an appearance of strength, it does not possess any power of defence against an attack. Its high connecting walls forming a square with sides of about 600 feet, give to the place, from the exterior, a stern, and cheerless aspect, which however, is dissipated immediately on entering the Arsenal yard, towards which, all the buildings forming the square present a handsome plain front.

"The arrangement of the public buildings is a judicious and convenient one, and they have been constructed upon a capacious scale, calculated for the extensive operations of a state of war, . . ."

"The cost of the Allegheny Arsenal, including about thirty-seven acres of land . . . has been little short of $300,000 . . . "

Rupp's architectural appraisal of the Arsenal buildings was well taken. The "handsome plain front" of the buildings and the "judicious and convenient" arrangement of the group as a whole are descriptions that applied generally to the work of the architect, Benjamin Henry Latrobe, who designed the Arsenal. The dominating figure of the architectural profession in the early 1800's, Latrobe was equally well known for his engineering skill. He served as city engineer in Philadelphia and as state engineer for Virginia. Glenn Brown in his *History of the Capitol* states that his drawings show "fondness for construction rather than artistic feeling."

Six of Latrobe's studies for the Arsenal buildings, now in the Library of Congress, were made, presumably, during his two years' stay in Pittsburgh between 1812 and 1814. Latrobe's studies reveal that he was influenced by the then popular classic revival school, so ably headed by Thomas Jefferson, which stressed the circular-plan forms of Roman origin. However, most of these forms seen in the preliminary sketches reproduced on pages 22 and 23 were later discarded, as an examination of the existing buildings reveals. In keeping with the utilitarian purpose of the buildings, all exterior ornamental detail was consistently omitted.

The large square stone building on the southwest corner of the quadrangle housed the officers; a corresponding building of similar design, on the southeast corner, was the commandant's quarters (see page 265), where Lafayette was entertained in 1828 during his triumphal tour. These buildings are almost square in plan. The stone is carefully dressed, and doors and windows are framed with massive stone architraves. The cornices have simple stone brackets occurring in pairs. The buildings have been much disfigured by reroofing, addition of porches, removal of original sash and shutters, and revision of the interiors. The brick wings containing the elliptical door and window heads, evidently of

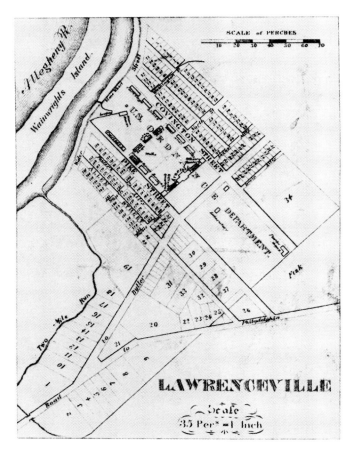

The United States Allegheny Arsenal—
from *Map of Pittsburgh and Environs*, 1830

somewhat later date, do not appear in the plan reproduced herewith. This plan was taken from a map of Pittsburgh of 1830.

The two corner buildings just described were connected by carriage sheds (since demolished). These formed a high barricade across the southern side of the quadrangle on both sides of the main Arsenal building (see page 266), which once stood

in the center of the property. Over its entrance hung the cast-iron plaque illustrated on page 163. This prisonlike structure, with small square windows and great expanses of stone masonry, dominated the Arsenal grounds, commanding the attention of the traveler passing on the Butler Road.

Extending along the east and west walls from the officers' quarters are interesting brick buildings, some of which have arcaded open corridors on the yard side. Here were the noncommissioned officers' quarters, the hospital, and other rooms for the personnel. The central building on the northern side of the quadrangle contained a celebrated steam engine which was installed in 1828 at a cost of $12,000.

Between the quadrangle and the river stands the storehouse. Its unusually thick walls, carefully dressed ashlaring, and simple cornice contribute to the austerity of the architectural effect. The stone wall surrounding the property is broken at several points by wrought-iron gates hung from stone piers of good design. One of these is illustrated on page 265.

The powder house, a curious, L-shaped structure on the southern half of the property, is half buried in the ground. Beneath its timber roof is a barrel vault of masonry. The laboratory, also shown on the map of 1830, has been destroyed.

The small guardhouse, which now stands in the center of the grounds on Butler Street, has frequently been mistaken for one of the original Arsenal buildings. Its absence from the map of 1830 shows that it was built after that date. Its Gothic Revival style would indicate that it was built shortly before the Civil War. Other additions were made to the original Arsenal buildings, including the interesting Greek Revival buildings north of the quadrangle, which were used as workshops. They were partially demolished when the approach to the Washington Crossing Bridge was constructed.

The Arsenal was an active government post until 1926, when it was sold at public auction. Since that time many of its buildings have been drastically altered, and a number of large shops and warehouses have been erected. But enough remains for one to visualize the one-time impressiveness of the whole. A few details of interior ornamentation, such as stairways and mantels (see page 167), have escaped alteration. Plans have recently been completed to preserve the relatively unimportant guardhouse on Butler Street, now accepted as the symbol of the Arsenal; but the original buildings are fast yielding to the encroachment of industrial developments.

Portico of Greene County Courthouse

Greene 3

1850

The Greene County Courthouse in Waynesburg

Greene 3

1850

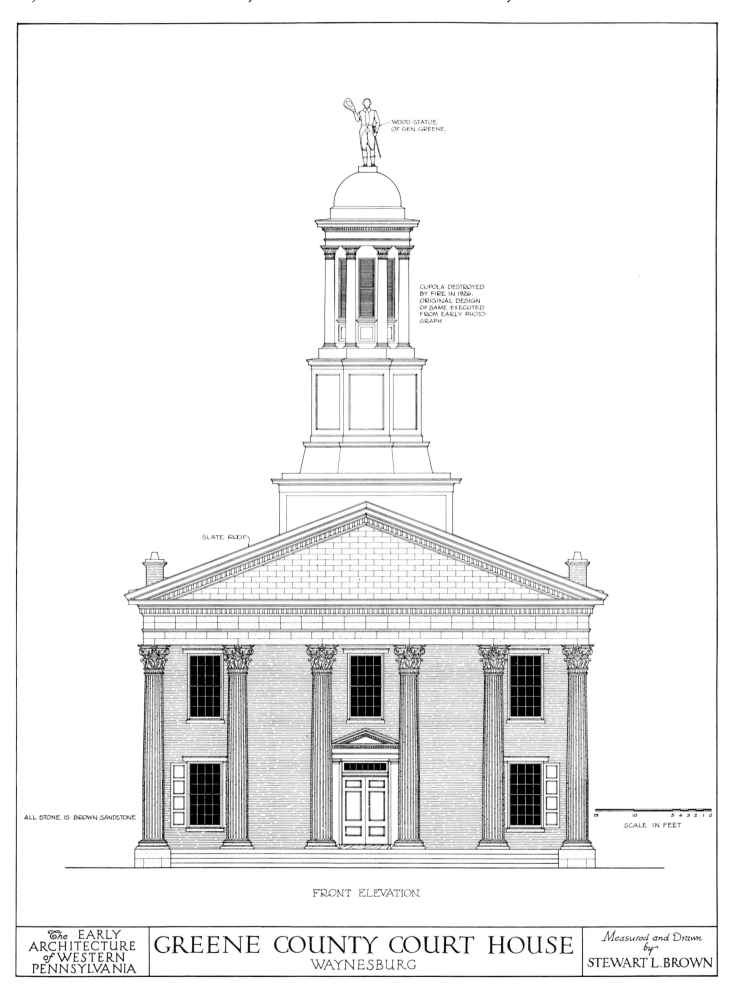

WOOD STATUE
OF GEN. GREENE

CUPOLA DESTROYED
BY FIRE IN 1926.
ORIGINAL DESIGN
OF SAME EXECUTED
FROM EARLY PHOTO-
GRAPH

SLATE ROOF

ALL STONE IS BROWN SANDSTONE.

SCALE IN FEET

FRONT ELEVATION

The EARLY
ARCHITECTURE
of WESTERN
PENNSYLVANIA

GREENE COUNTY COURT HOUSE
WAYNESBURG

Measured and Drawn
by
STEWART L. BROWN

SLATE ROOF

WOOD

C.

B.

A.

ONE HALF
PILASTER
CAP

CAST IRON

STONE

ENTABLATURE
AND COLUMN

ENTRANCE MOTIF

0
1
2
3
4
5
6
INCHES

B.

C.

A.

D.

DETAILS
5   4   3   2   1   0

PLAN
30   20   15   10   543210

SIDE ELEVATION
50   30   20   10   543210

SCALE IN FEET

PLAN OF PORTICO

SIDE ELEVATION

The EARLY
ARCHITECTURE
of WESTERN
PENNSYLVANIA | GREENE COUNTY COURT HOUSE
WAYNESBURG | *Measured and Drawn*
by
STEWART L. BROWN

Armstrong 4

The Armstrong County Courthouse in Kittanning

1860

Bedford 49

The Bedford County Courthouse in Bedford

1828

1847 (Building demolished)
Statue of Lafayette from Fayette County Courthouse

Fayette 99

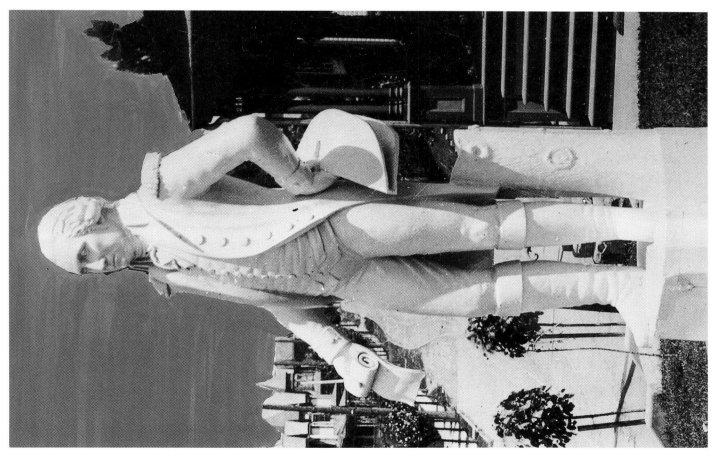

1842 (Building demolished)
Statue of Washington from Washington County Courthouse

Washington 505

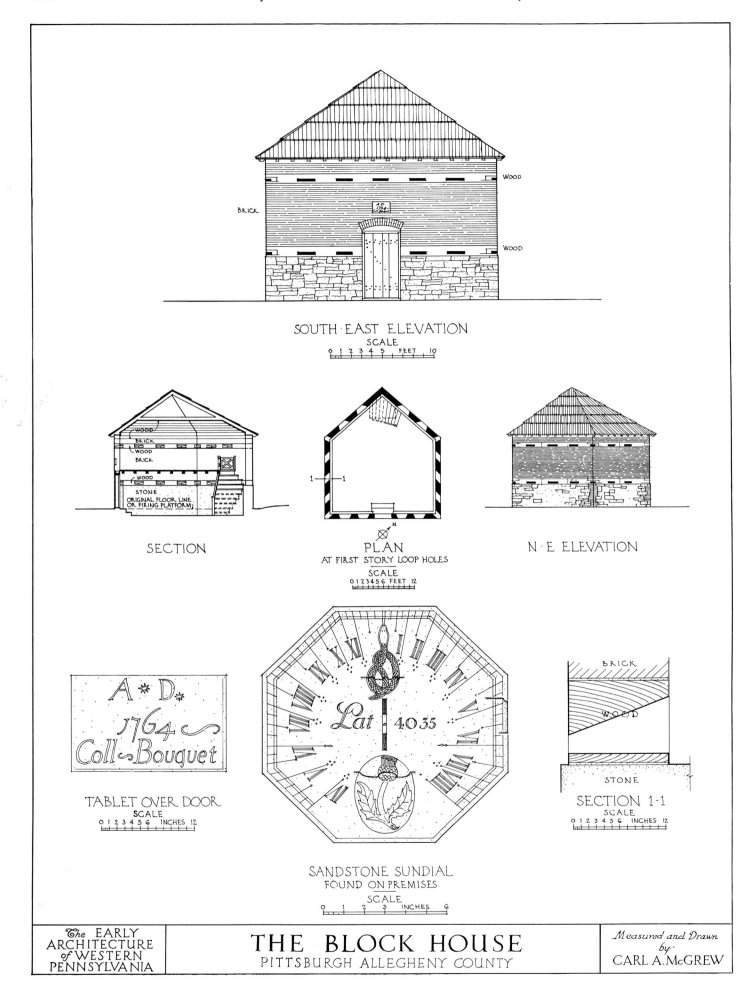

SOUTH·EAST ELEVATION
SCALE
0 1 2 3 4 5 FEET 10

SECTION

PLAN
AT FIRST STORY LOOP HOLES
SCALE
0 1 2 3 4 5 6 FEET 12

N·E ELEVATION

A·D·
1764
Coll Bouquet

TABLET OVER DOOR
SCALE
0 1 2 3 4 5 6 INCHES 12

Lat 40·35

SANDSTONE SUNDIAL
FOUND ON PREMISES
SCALE
0 1 2 3 INCHES 6

SECTION 1-1
SCALE
0 1 2 3 4 5 6 INCHES 12

The EARLY ARCHITECTURE of WESTERN PENNSYLVANIA

THE BLOCK HOUSE
PITTSBURGH ALLEGHENY COUNTY

Measured and Drawn by
CARL A. McGREW

The Blockhouse of Fort Pitt in Pittsburgh

Allegheny 41

1764

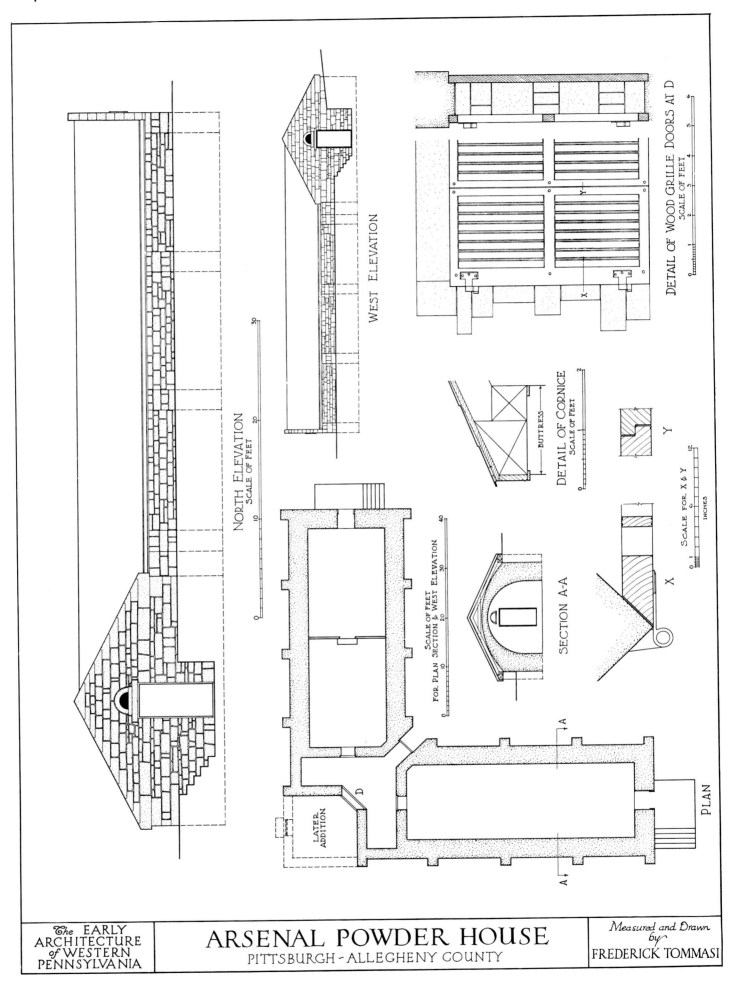

NORTH ELEVATION
SCALE OF FEET

WEST ELEVATION

DETAIL OF WOOD GRILLE DOORS AT D
SCALE OF FEET

DETAIL OF CORNICE
SCALE OF FEET

BUTTRESS

SECTION A-A

SCALE OF FEET
FOR PLAN SECTION & WEST ELEVATION

SCALE FOR X & Y
INCHES

X

Y

LATER
ADDITION

D

A

A

PLAN

ARSENAL POWDER HOUSE
PITTSBURGH - ALLEGHENY COUNTY

Measured and Drawn
by
FREDERICK TOMMASI

1814–20

The Powder House of the U. S. Allegheny Arsenal in Pittsburgh

1814–20   Allegheny 86
Side Entrance of the Allegheny Arsenal

1814–20   Allegheny 86
Commandant's Quarters of the Allegheny Arsenal

Allegheny 86

Officers' Quarters of the Allegheny Arsenal

1814–20

Allegheny 86

Storehouse of the Allegheny Arsenal

1814–20

Allegheny 86

Officers' Quarters of the Allegheny Arsenal

1814–20

Allegheny 86

Main Building of the Allegheny Arsenal

1814–20 (Demolished)

Section Seven

COMMERCIAL AND INDUSTRIAL ARCHITECTURE

AT FIRST business and professional activities were conducted in private homes or outbuildings attached to them but as the district expanded separate buildings were devoted to these purposes, which took on a distinctive character all their own. The growth of the cities, in which the greater part of such buildings were located, has brought about the destruction of the vast majority of this type of building.

Banks

The first bank established west of the Allegheny Mountains, the Pittsburgh Branch of the Bank of Pennsylvania, was installed in 1805 in a stone house, built in 1787, on the north side of Second Avenue below Chancery Lane. The Allegheny Bank of Pennsylvania, chartered in 1814, likewise occupied quarters in a residence—that of Dr. John Anderson (see page 95)—built in Bedford in 1815 for this dual purpose. The banking-room entrance and the original bank vault can be seen on the plan.

In 1810 the Bank of Pittsburgh built an imposing building, with a six-column Ionic portico, on Fourth Avenue. The design of this building inspired James Logan to add a similar portico to the house he had purchased in Allegheny in 1843 from Samuel Church (illustrated on page 125). The Merchants and Manufacturers Bank, also on Fourth Avenue, was designed by the architect, John Chislett, in 1834 and, with the Bank of Pittsburgh, was lost in the Fire of 1845.

The most impressive early banking structure in western Pennsylvania, and one of the most celebrated buildings of the Greek Revival style, was the Erie branch of the United States Bank of Pennsylvania, built in 1839, of Vermont marble—the only front of this material in the district before 1860. The name of the architect, William Kelly, is carved in the portico. Montgomery Schuyler, an authority on the Greek Revival style, wrote: ". . . the branch bank at Erie, Pa., now [1911], like the parent bank in Philadelphia, a custom house, and, like that a Doric temple, only hexastyle instead of octastyle and of modest size, being only 50 feet by 70 feet in plan. In spite of these diminutive

dimensions, it is a more effective reproduction than the older and larger building, the material being here also marble, but the proportions and detail much more 'correctly' and successfully adjusted."

The Erie Bank shows what can be accomplished in the Greek style, when the design is executed on monumental scale in marble—the material best suited to its subtle lines. As in the Meadville Congregational Church, the entrance door of normal size is concealed within a larger door, which is adjusted in scale to the requirements of the design. The forms are literally and faithfully executed to conform with the Greek prototype, with the sound knowledge and sympathy for the style so essential in such adaptations. The side walls of brick were plastered to resemble the marble front.

After the failure of the bank, the building was sold to the United States Government in 1849 for $29,000, and was converted into a customhouse. Now the permanent quarters of the Erie County Historical Society, its preservation is assured.

Stores

In 1795 Amos Judson was authorized by Holme and Herrioh of Pittsburgh to act as their agent in setting up a trading post at Le Bœuf, now Waterford, in Erie County. Judson did so well that he bought out his employers and opened a "general store" of his own. For this purpose he added a story-and-a-half wing to his house (see page 102), which opened, in the rear, onto a large storage yard enclosed by a high fence. The large front room served as public space.

The first stores were, like Judson's, usually included within the house of the proprietor, who often also acted as postmaster. He was often a person of considerable importance in his community.

Colonel Edward Cook, shortly after his arrival in Fayette County in 1770, erected a log cabin in which he conducted a store. In 1784 Albert Gallatin constructed a log house in New Geneva for the same purpose. John Roberts conducted a post office in his house (illustrated on page 69), as did David Shields in his large house, completed in 1815 and still standing, in Shields, Allegheny County.

267

The large front room was a post office and store combined. The small door at the left of the main entrance of the Daily House, illustrated on page 73, led to the public store conducted by John Daily. Dr. J. J. LeMoyne incorporated a drug store in his house, a separate entrance being reserved for the public (see photograph on page 111).

Three illustrations in this section show detached store buildings. Although they contain living quarters for the proprietor, they none the less express the character that later came to be associated with the "country store." Samuel Black, who came to Monongahela, Washington County, in 1796, opened a store and, later, in 1815, built on Main Street the charming little store with bowed windows, which is here reproduced from a photograph made before its demolition. The store at Florence, Washington County, was built shortly after the completion of the Steubenville Pike. Its low, dimly lit interior, filled to overflowing with merchandise arranged between the many posts that support the heavily loaded second floor, and the shallow front porch with its display of wares, possess an atmosphere distinctly suggesting another era. A very interesting old mantel, illustrated on page 172, is contained in one of the ground-floor rooms now used for storage. The Drake Hotel and Store at Little Cooley, Crawford County, grew out of several separate building operations. Initially only a store, it was enlarged to include hotel quarters and a dance hall 26 by 70 feet. It is a typical commercial building of the Greek Revival period. The unusually large windows are separated by flat wooden pilasters, and the whole building is crowned by a heavy entablature.

The stores and buildings located in the larger towns and in the cities have, of course, been entirely lost by alteration and replacement. Pittsburgh —the "Emporium of the West"—was the outfitting point for travelers en route to the interior and contained all varieties of mercantile establishments. As early as 1803 Pittsburgh had 49 stores and shops.

Offices

The first offices were incorporated within the owner's residence or were contained in small buildings located on the same property and designed to conform with the house, as with the law offices of the William Lyon House in Bedford and the Charles Reed Residence in Erie. Sometimes they were isolated structures, such as those of Cessna and Samuel Barclay in Bedford.

Burke's Building was one of the very first office buildings in Pittsburgh and is so used today. At one time it contained banking quarters. It was built in 1836 by Robert and Andrew Burke on property on Fourth Avenue off Market Street, which was purchased from the Irwin family. The architect, John Chislett, achieved in its design the chaste restraint that distinguishes the better buildings of the Greek Revival period. The stone front has since been painted, and very little of the original finish inside the building has been preserved. The replacement of the original sash and frames and the present unsightly litter of signs detract from the dignity of the facade.

Mills

In western Pennsylvania today the deserted grist- and flour mill is a familiar sight—its dam broken, its wheel gone, and its grinding stones carried away by relic seekers. Though a few of the old gristmills are still in operation, these picturesque structures have outlived their importance in the economic life of their districts. Many rural communities still bear the names of the mills that determined their location. The following passage from Boucher's *Old and New Westmoreland* gives a remarkably vivid picture of the early mill:

"The first water-power mills were operated by water wheels known as the tub-mill wheel, which gave its name frequently to the stream [such as "Tub-Mill Run"] which turned it. The tub-mill wheel was in a round enclosure that resembled a large tub. The water falling on it made it revolve, and thus the perpendicular shaft to which it was fastened was turned, and by gearing, made the mill stones revolve, or ran a saw, as the occasion might be. This wheel gave place to the paddle wheel, the under-shot wheel and, finally, the over-shot wheel, which was then regarded as the greatest improvement possible.

"These mills and the embryo towns were located on streams that would not turn a mill now. The little mills required less water than the mills of today. . . . The removal of the timber . . . has diminished the streams all over the country."

Of the many mills the Survey visited, only one today retains its outside wheel of wood, for most of the wooden wheels have been replaced by metal ones, and mill wheels were usually contained within the structure. Whether the mill was of log, frame, or brick construction, the first-story walls were almost always of stone in order to bear the weight of the grinding stones and machinery on the main floor. Great skill in joinery and craftsmanship is exhibited in wooden machinery. Graceful touches of ornamentation, as in the turning of the legs that supported the wooden hoods over the stones, present a striking contrast to the severe lines of modern mechanical apparatus.

The mills had remarkably long lives. Henry Beeson built a flour mill in Uniontown in 1772 and replaced it with another that was operated as a flour mill until 1866, and as a cement mill from then to 1890. The log mill erected by John White on Raccoon Creek in 1789 was operated by water power until 1911, when high water destroyed its dam. A steam boiler was then installed—a common substitute for diminishing water supply in later days. The great oak logs can now be seen where the weatherboarding has been removed.

One of the oldest mills in western Pennsylvania was built near the present town of Perryopolis under the direction of George Washington on land that he purchased in what is now Fayette County. The building was begun before the Revolution, but its completion was delayed, chiefly by border warfare, until 1776. Washington sent a workman named Gilbert Simpson to superintend the work. A letter from his local agent, Valentine Crawford, dated July 27, 1774, states, "I sold Peter Miller and John Wood to Edward Cook for forty-five pounds, the money to be applied to building your mill." Valentine Crawford wrote Washington in September 20, 1776: "I think it the best mill I ever saw anywhere. If you remember you saw some rocks at the mill seat. These are as fine mill stone grit as any in America. The mill right told me the stones he got for your mill there are equal to English burr." The mill, however, did not turn out to be a profitable investment for Washington, who, after leasing it for a while, put it up for sale; but it was not sold until after his death. The mill was still in operation in 1901. Since that time it has been allowed to fall into disrepair, and in recent years its frame has partially collapsed. The photograph shows it when still in fairly good condition with the outside overshot wooden wheel intact. Despite the historical associations of this mill and its value as evidence of Washington's confidence in the future of western Pennsylvania, all efforts to preserve this building have thus far failed.

The quaint little mill built by Samuel Milligan on Little Puckety Creek near New Kensington, Westmoreland County, is in excellent condition today, both inside and out. Its outside wooden wheel is the only one in the Survey records. The mill, built in 1825, saw active service until 1892, but the failure of water supply in later times curtailed its operation to not more than a few months in the year.

Naugle's Mill near Bedford, erected in 1797, and Way's Mill at Weyant north of Bedford, are both of the same type, with rough stone walls and projecting gables equipped with hooks and pulleys for raising the grain to the upper floor. Both mills take advantage of sloping ground to afford an entrance on the upper floor.

Chambers' Mill, one of the largest in Washington County, was constructed by Robert and William Chambers, whose father, an Irish immigrant, came to the district in 1797. This sturdy building (1823) is of particular interest because of the texture and color of its stone and brick masonry. The original mill pond serves as a recreational center today, and it is hoped that the building will be preserved.

Perhaps the most remarkable log mill ever constructed in western Pennsylvania was built in 1806 (or earlier) by Simon Hay, in Somerset County. The logs on the long side of Hay's Mill measure 54 feet, 9 inches. The enormous size of these timbers must have presented to the pioneer unusually difficult problems. Allowance for taper in the logs was made by laying them with the butt ends alternating in courses. The stonework was done by an Irish mason, Thomas Short. The photographs of the interior show the interesting bins, chutes, and wooden machinery. Notwithstanding its great age, the building is in good condition although the rotting shingles freely admit the weather. There is another mill—almost a replica of the one just described—at Roxbury, also in Somerset County, originally owned by John Grover.

Furnaces

Western Pennsylvania today contains a great number of abandoned charcoal iron furnaces. Of these nothing remains but the pyramidal stone stacks, reminiscent of Mayan temple ruins, and overgrown with vines and shrubbery. The superstructures and adjoining buildings necessary to their operation have long since disappeared.

The location of these furnaces was determined by the proximity of certain natural resources: a stream to furnish water power, an area of dense forest to supply timber for making charcoal, limestone for the necessary flux, and accessible ore deposits. Because of these diverse requirements, they are usually located in isolated districts, which today makes it the more difficult to visualize the intense activity that once surrounded them.

A complete picture of these early industrial plants is graphically portrayed in Boucher's *Old and New Westmoreland:*

"In selecting a furnace site, a level place close to a stream of water and near a high bluff was preferred, so that a bridge could be built from the bluff to the top of the furnace stack. Over this bridge they could readily haul the ore, limestone and charcoal, ready for dumping into the furnace stack. The base of the stack must not be too high above the stream, for water power was essential in making the blast ... by double bellows, worked by a beam, pinioned in its center, each end of which worked up and down, and thus alternately forced a continuous blast of air into the furnace. In more modern furnaces, the bellows was supplanted by fans propelled by water wheel. ... From the base of the furnace there must necessarily be some level ground upon which to build a casting house and upon which to lay out sand beds. These extended to the outlet of the furnace. The molten metal, which by its weight readily dropped to the bottom, was drawn out and through a small ditch of molder's sand, which had outlets or pockets at each side. When ... filled with metal, it was allowed to cool off and the vent of the furnace was closed up again. ...

"Burning charcoal was an important work in old furnace days. Generally about three hundred fifty bushels of charcoal was used in smelting one ton of ore ... All over the furnace section of the country can be seen the level places which were originally used as charcoal beds. ...

"The early furnaces of this country were all made of stone and varied in size from twenty feet square at the base and about twenty feet high, tapering towards the top, to forty feet square at the base and perhaps thirty feet high ... [this, called the stack] was hollow from top to bottom, the cavity ... about eight feet in diameter. [Washington Furnace] Into this cavity the ore, the charcoal and a small amount of limestone to flux the ore, was dumped from the top of the stack. Wood for kindling was placed at the bottom at first. Charcoal, when properly blown by the fans, produced an intense heat, so great indeed that the stone and all the materials in the ore were readily converted into a molten mass. For this reason the inside of the furnace was lined with firebrick and needed fre-

quent renewal. [The brick lining of the Valley Furnace is shown on page 279.] When the furnace was in blast it made a roaring noise which could be heard a long distance, its mouth emitting a continuous stream of sparks. ... It required three to five tons of ore to make one ton of pig metal."

The transportation of ore, limestone, and timber by wagon was extremely costly, but the canals lowered the price of these basic materials. Then came the railroads, which made available the richer ore from the West; and when, about 1859, coke replaced charcoal, the modern iron and steel industry began. Thenceforward it was centralized in populous districts, chiefly about Pittsburgh.

The first iron made from western Pennsylvania ore is attributed to John Hayden of Fayette County in 1789. This county, utilizing the excellent ore at the base of Chestnut Ridge, came to be the center of the early iron industry. At one time it contained eighteen furnaces. However, furnaces were also scattered throughout many other counties in the district, and the enthusiasm that accompanied them is well expressed in a letter written by a Philip Biers to an iron producer in Philadelphia in 1814. Boucher reviews this letter as follows: "The iron business 'was all the rage in Westmoreland County' and, in that day in his [Biers'] judgment, it would be but a few years until there would be scarcely a stream furnishing a favorable site for a furnace or a forge, which would not be thus occupied."

Many fortunes were made and lost in these enterprises. Outstanding among the few men who became conspicuously wealthy was Isaac Meason, who had large investments in the iron industry. The outlet for his products and for those of most of the other operators was "down the river." Great quantities of his sugar and salt kettles, Dutch ovens, and other castings were shipped each year by flat boat to Louisiana. The Mt. Vernon Furnace (see page 278) in Fayette County, built in 1798 and reconstructed in 1801, was one of Meason's most successful ventures. This furnace, operated by Isaac Meason, Jr., furnished employment to sixty men. By the time it was blown out in 1830, the second growth of timber had been cut for charcoal manufacture.

Iron masters of means held commanding positions in the early communities. Usually they built a "mansion house," near their furnaces. And among these are some of the finest residences in western Pennsylvania, such as those built by Isaac Meason, Elias Baker, and Daniel Royer.

Erie 3

The United States Bank of Pennsylvania in Erie

1839

Bedford 31

The Barclay Office in Bedford

1830

Washington 72

A Store in Florence

About 1820

Crawford 44

The Drake Store and Hotel in Little Cooley

About 1859

Washington 507

The Store and House of Samuel Black in Monongahela

1815 (Demolished)

"Burke's Building" in Pittsburgh

Allegheny 3

About 1836

Office adjoining the Reed Mansion in Erie

Erie 54

1846

Office adjoining the Cessna House in Bedford

Bedford 74

1799

1774-76   *Fayette 6*

A Mill built for George Washington near Perryopolis (Early photo)

About 1825   *Westmoreland 45*
Milligan's Mill in Milligantown

About 1825   *Westmoreland 45*
Wheel of Milligan's Mill

1807

Way's Mill in Weyant

Bedford 12

1789

White's Mill near Murdocksville

Beaver 17

1823

Chambers' Mill at Chambers' Dam

Washington 97

1806

Hay's Mill near Meyersdale

1806   Somerset 12   1806   Somerset 12
Interior View of Hay's Mill   Entrance Doorway of Hay's Mill

Somerset 12

Machinery in Hay's Mill

1806

Somerset 12

Gable End of Hay's Mill

1806

Bedford 19

Naugle's Mill near Bedford Springs

1797

Fayette 33

1837   The Wharton Furnace near the National Pike on Laurel Hill

Fayette 34

1798–1801   The Mt. Vernon Furnace near Wooddale

1837 *Fayette 33*

Detail of the Wharton Furnace

1844 *Butler 7*

A Furnace near Bruin

1855 *Westmoreland 80*

Interior of Valley Furnace near Waterford

Date Unknown *Westmoreland 106*

The Ross Mountain Furnace in Ross Mountain Park

PART THREE

—

THE STORY OF THE SURVEY

IN RETROSPECT, the Western Pennsylvania Architectural Survey appears to have been a curious natural compensation, whereby an unprecedented economic depression was made to yield dividends that may be measured in both material and spiritual values. Originating in a desire to turn enforced leisure within the architectural profession to a useful end, the Survey was, to those who participated in it, the extension of a hobby, carried on with all the enthusiasm of a serious avocation. It was in no sense a relief measure. The costs of operation and publication were defrayed by grants from The Buhl Foundation.

The Western Pennsylvania Architectural Survey is not to be confused with the Historic American Buildings Survey, organized some eighteen months later under the public works program of the Federal Government. The Federal project, having similar aims, operated in western Pennsylvania under the direction of the same chairman and with much the same personnel as the Western Pennsylvania Architectural Survey. Thus, much duplication of effort was avoided and the vastly greater resources and the trail-blazing of the local survey were made available to the governmental project.

The quotations in the following paragraphs, taken from an announcement distributed throughout western Pennsylvania in 1932, define the purpose and scope of the Survey:

"The Western Pennsylvania Architectural Survey has been established for the purpose (1) of locating buildings erected in this section before 1860, insofar as these buildings are of importance architecturally and historically; (2) of compiling and collecting available pictures, drawings and historical information of these existing buildings and any that have been demolished; (3) of making measured drawings and photographs of a representative selection of these buildings for ultimate publication, together with historical studies of the buildings and of the development of architecture in the region . . . By 'western Pennsylvania' is meant all the territory west of and including Potter, Cameron, Clearfield,

Blair, and Bedford counties . . . The work treated in this Survey will not be confined to residences. Of fully equal interest are public buildings, barns, mills, manufactories, furnaces, bridges, canal structures, tollhouses, and fortifications."

The Survey's accomplishments are represented in this volume and in the permanent records on file in the Pennsylvania Room of the Carnegie Library in Pittsburgh.

Origin

The Western Pennsylvania Architectural Survey grew out of the Committee for the Preservation of Historic Monuments of the Pittsburgh Chapter, American Institute of Architects. In 1930 this committee consisted of Sidney H. Brown, Robert W. Schmertz, and Charles M. Stotz, chairman. The annual report of this committee, covering the year 1931, concluded as follows: ". . . a little investigation during the past year has revealed a great many buildings that should be recorded. The intention is to formulate a definite scheme of activity for the coming year." But the committee realized that no extensive program could be undertaken unless money were found to cover operating expenses. After permission had been obtained from the Pittsburgh Chapter, a petition for funds for the work was prepared and presented to The Buhl Foundation by the Historic Monuments Committee. The financial problem was solved in October, 1932, when the Foundation made a grant of $6,500 for a survey and the preparation of its materials for publication. The publication of the book was assured by another grant made eighteen months later.

Personnel

To the original committee mentioned above, the chairman, by authority granted from the Chapter, added Ralph E. Griswold, then president of the Pittsburgh Architectural Club, and Rody Patterson. This Executive Committee of five was made responsible for the organization and direction of the work. The secretary, Rody Patterson, who was required to establish a Survey headquarters, perform all routine office work, and maintain the records, was allowed a modest salary. His contribution was a very great one; his unfailing collaboration with the chairman in all matters from the beginning to the end of the Survey is gratefully acknowledged, as is the generous cooperation of the other members of the Executive Committee.

An Advisory Committee was set up, consisting of Louis Stevens, Frederick Bigger, Charles T. Ingham, and the late James M. Macqueen, whose death in 1934 prevented him from seeing the final accomplishment of a work that engaged his liveliest interest. This group, to whom were referred matters of policy, was supplemented by Dr. Solon J. Buck, then director of the Western Pennsylvania Historical Survey. The mature judgment of these men was invaluable in guiding the Executive Committee in the many decisions occurring in the course of the work.

The enlarged committee of ten decided, for the purposes of the work to be done under the grant of The Buhl Foundation, to adopt a new title; the Western Pennsylvania Architectural Survey. Responsibilities were defined, methods of operations determined, and the actual work undertaken before the end of 1932. The work of the Survey extended through the terms of three Chapter presidents: Press C. Dowler (193233), Harvey M. Schwab (193435), and Raymond M. Marlier (1936).

Procedure

The Western Pennsylvania Architectural Survey functioned as an independent, selfcontained body and was given full authority in the expenditure of the Survey funds. The difficulties in devising a program were multiplied because no precedent existed for an exhaustive architectural survey of a territory as large as western Pennsylvania, which includes some twentytwo thousand square miles. Nor were the district's full resources in early architecture known to the committee or indicated in any records or books then in existence. In other words, the Survey had to begin by answering many questions before they could be asked.

Publicity

Early in 1932, 2,500 fourpage announcements, presenting the aims and scope of the Survey and appealing for information on locations of buildings erected before 1860, were mailed to persons and organizations thought to be interested in such matters,

as well as to schools and libraries. News stories were printed by some 250 daily and weekly newspapers throughout western Pennsylvania, and several radio announcements were broadcast from Pittsburgh stations. The results of this solicitation were most gratifying. Within a few weeks data on some 600 buildings were received and added to the list of buildings already known to the Survey Committee.

Field Work

The investigation of the field by automobile proved to be the most entertaining and colorful phase of the work. Each trip was an adventure in discovery, for the territory was far richer than had been supposed. In this firsthand experience the influence of the early routes of transportation upon architecture was strikingly apparent. Sectional differences in architectural character were likewise obvious, and these observations were later, in great part, to determine the chairman's conception of the text. Six thousand miles were traveled in twentynine trips, each occupying from one to four days. Almost every township in the twentyseven western counties was entered, some on several occasions. Trips were made usually at weekends, so that they might not conflict with private practice. Of the several thousand buildings seen, 542 were recorded by photographs and data in the permanent records. At least one third of the examples recorded were discovered en route. Because of repetition in type or insufficient architectural interest, many of the buildings first reported were rejected. Records of 312 demolished buildings were made, many of them being added during later library research.

All trips were made by the chairman and secretary, sometimes accompanied by one or more members of the Executive Committee. An approximate route was charted for each trip in order to include all reported examples in the counties visited and to traverse the district as thoroughly as possible in search of unreported buildings. Since only twenty buildings could be fully recorded and photographed in a day, a fixed routine was established to insure minimum loss of time. The route of the car was marked in red pencil on Government maps, and each building selected was assigned a map number.

The procedure followed by the chairman and secretary soon resolved itself into a pattern. Upon alighting from the automobile the secretary, alert for the dreaded watchdog, proceeded to the door while the chairman set up the photographic equip ment. The secretary would engage the occupant in conversation, recording data on the Survey questionnaire and deftly side-stepping subjects digressing from the business in hand. After giving the signal to photograph, the secretary would enter the house to see if there were any mantels, stairways, or other details worthy of record. His diplomacy was then taxed to its limit to contrive a gracious retreat before the family could bring out old flintlocks, parchment deeds, chromo portraits, and other interesting but unarchitectural mementos. Counties were large and time was fleeting.

As might be expected, many of the old buildings —usually occupied by complaining tenants—were in a pitifully dilapidated condition. And many owners, even descendants of the original builder, expressed a desire to plaster over a beautiful stone wall and strike it off in artificial joints, discard an old doorway in favor of a "front porch," or, if they had not already done so, break up a carved mantel for kindling wood and install a "modern" one. In one old house rich in hand-carved mantels of amazing originality and grace, the owner expressed great wonder at the admiration they aroused. Admitting that the mantels might be really splendid, he insisted that he "would much rather own a coal mine, a field of wheat, or even a good pile of manure." On the other hand, a number of owners were not only proud of their old homes but had shown rare taste in preserving them and in making necessary changes.

Many trips extended until darkness, and, as all buildings recorded were photographed, many pictures were made late in the evening. The photograph of the Harper Springhouse (see page 149) was made with an exposure lasting from 8:30 to 9:00 P. M. The exactions of time in completing the work outlined for each field trip, as well as unforeseen delays in recording unreported structures en route, resulted in many late homecomings and full acknowledgment is hereby given to the long sufferance of the "Survey widows."

Through misunderstanding, many persons sent in reports of buildings no longer in existence—a fact that often did not become known to the chairman and secretary until they arrived at the spot. For instance, half a day of arduous travel over an almost impassable mountain road to the top of Chestnut Ridge ended at a marker on the site of a house that had been burned some fifty years before. Another wild-goose chase over an endless road through Pymatuning Swamp in search of a "beauti-

ful old home" revealed an atrocious Victorian farmhouse of no possible interest to the Survey.

Special Photographs

The selection of a photographer to supplement the field work was simplified by the appearance on the scene of a photographer with no small measure of national prominence, an intense interest in the objectives of the Survey, and a determination to take a hand in the work. Needless to say, his ability and enthusiasm were welcomed; and although the name of Luke Swank does not appear on the committee, his contribution deserves that recognition. It was arranged that he revisit and rephotograph outstanding buildings selected for special attention. His photographs are grouped with most of the measured drawings in the book. He also enlarged 244 illustrations appearing in this volume from the small negatives made in the field by the chairman.

A few early photographs of excellent buildings, now so dilapidated as to be unsuitable for photography, as well as photographs of buildings long demolished, were contributed by such interested persons as Earle Forrest, of Washington, and McClellan Leonard, of Uniontown, who also assisted greatly in obtaining data on old buildings in their districts. John Duss of Economy kindly made available The Harmony Society drawings of the Garden Pavilion and manufacturing building on page 24.

Measured Drawings

In the spring of 1933 the program of making measured drawings was begun. Some thirty architects and draftsmen were engaged by the Survey to measure the outstanding structures throughout the district. A nominal fee was established to cover expenses and a modest compensation. The men were chosen for their ability to produce work of the standard set for the book. The best talent was available, and the intense interest displayed by those who participated put financial consideration in secondary place. The names of these architects appear on the drawings; the thanks of the Survey are extended to them for their vital contribution in producing these important documents.

The Executive Committee met twice a week for some eleven months while this work was in progress, and all measured drawings were minutely scrutinized, from the first rough penciled layouts to the final ink drawings. In behalf of uniformity, titles for all drawings were lettered by Lawrence Wolfe, selected for his outstanding ability in this work. He also drew the map in the back of the book from drafts prepared by the Survey from field records.

A real problem encountered in measuring large buildings in the field was the physical difficulty and danger involved in gaining exterior access to the upper stories. The services of local fire companies were enlisted in measuring courthouses in Waynesburg and Bedford, where the draftsmen were raised on extension ladders to the cornices and column capitals.

The Text

It had been intended to complete the text by the early part of 1934, but the task proved to be so enormous that the chairman, who had been authorized to write it, being also occupied with the direction of the Survey as well as a moderate amount of private practice, found it impossible to hold to the original schedule. There was available no reference material dealing primarily with architecture in the district, and such records as did exist were scattered and fragmentary. Through the co-operation of the Historical Society of Western Pennsylvania and the staff of the Pennsylvania Room of the Carnegie Library of Pittsburgh some two hundred books and periodicals, as well as hundreds of newspaper clippings, were examined. In addition to conducting purely architectural investigation, the chairman found it necessary to make a study of the economic, social, and industrial background of the district before 1860. More than 150 letters were written to obtain records of original owners, dates, architects, builders, drawings, and other data necessary to complete the records for publication.

In its various stages the text was submitted to members of the Survey Committee for comment. Matters of style were referred to Emily Alter Werkheiser and Elizabeth Mellon Sellers.

Permanent Records

In the permanent records deposited in the Pennsylvania Room of the Carnegie Library, persons desiring information on any particular structure may obtain access to all data, photographs, and maps accumulated by the Western Pennsylvania Architectural Survey. Much of the material is related to architectural examples shown in this volume. The balance refers to buildings omitted because of duplication of building types and lack of space. The public is asked to assist in further building up these files by contributions. Of particular desirability are photographic negatives and prints of buildings contained in these records depicting them in a still earlier state, or buildings that have been inadvertently overlooked in Survey trips or have been demolished. Engravings, woodcuts, sketches, and other graphic representations of early architecture also are welcome. Equally desirable are data pertaining to builders or architects who practiced in western Pennsylvania before 1860, and letters that indicate their method of working, contracts or plans pertaining to buildings, bills of materials, specifications, and other related records.

Conclusion

Members of the Survey again express their deep gratitude to the numerous persons in western Pennsylvania who have assisted in the work. A very real debt is felt toward The Buhl Foundation, not only for the contribution of the funds that made the work possible, but also for the continuous assistance of the staff throughout publication.

LIST OF STRUCTURES

References to structures mentioned or illustrated in this book are listed in two columns—text and illustration citations. Structures are listed under the names of the original owners, or, in the case of public structures, by their accepted names. If the original owner's name could not be obtained the structure is not listed in this table. Key numbers over 500 indicate buildings demolished before 1932.

Structure	Key Number	Text Page	Illust. Page
ARSENALS AND FORTS			
Allegheny Arsenal	Allegheny 86	20, 23, 30, 32, 255-6	22-23, 163, 167, 256, 265, 266
Fort Bedford	Bedford 501	254	
Fort Burd	Fayette 510	254	
Fort Duquesne	Allegheny 516	254	
Fort Gaddis	Fayette 107	35	41
Fort Hand	Westmoreland 512	254	
Fort Lafayette	Allegheny 518	255	
Fort Ligonier	Westmoreland 511	254	
Fort McIntosh	Beaver 503	255	
Fort Necessity	Fayette 64	31-2	
Fort Pitt	Allegheny 41	25, 31, 254-5	162, 262, 263
Fort Presque Isle	Erie 501	32, 254	
Fort Venango	Venango 502	254	
BANKS			
Allegheny Bank of Pennsylvania	Bedford 29	267	95
Bank of Pittsburgh	Allegheny 527	267	
Merchants and Manufacturers	Allegheny 528	267	
Pgh. Branch of the Bank of Penna.	Allegheny 558	267	
United States Bank of Pennsylvania	Erie 3	20, 25, 31, 267	271
BRIDGES AND TUNNELS			
Allegheny River Bridge, Pittsburgh	Allegheny 582a	176	
Bell's Mill Bridge	Westmoreland 51	21, 176	191
Conemaugh River Bridge, Blairsville	Indiana 501	176	
Dunlap's Creek Bridge, Brownsville	Fayette 103	176	
Great Crossings Bridge, Somerfield	Somerset 24	176	188, 189
Juniata Crossings Bridge	Bedford 42	32, 176	192
Juniata River Bridge, Everett	Bedford 82		192
Monongahela River Bridge, Pittsburgh	Allegheny 501	176	
Monongahela River Bridge, Brownsville	Fayette 504	176	
Portage Railway Skew Arch	Blair 6	32, 175	161, 190
Portage Railway Tunnel	Cambria 14	175	191
"S" Bridge, near Washington	Washington 14	32	
Sixth Street Bridge, Pittsburgh	Allegheny 582b	175	
Ten Mile Creek Bridge, Waynesburg	Greene 29		191
CHURCHES			
"Beehive Church," in Greensburg	Westmoreland 509	216	
Brush Creek Salems, near Adamsburg	Westmoreland 5	21, 216	170, 237-41
Congregational in Riceville	Crawford 24	217	242-44
Covenanter, near Adamsville	Crawford 39	217	224
Fairfield Presbyterian	Westmoreland 510	215	
First Episcopal in Pittsburgh	Allegheny 507a	29	
First Presbyterian in Pittsburgh	Allegheny 508b	28	
Free Baptist in Pleasantville	Venango 38	217	246
Harrold	Westmoreland 506b	21, 216	
Independent (Unit.) Congregational in Meadville	Crawford 16	21, 31, 217, 267	234-36
Irvine Presbyterian	Warren 12	145, 216	160, 231-33
Long Run Presbyterian	Westmoreland 508a	27	
Mennonite, near Harmony	Butler 37	216	159, 245
"Old Round Church" (Epis.) in Pittsburgh	Allegheny 507a	216	
Pleasant Grove Presbyterian, near Stahlstown	Westmoreland 38	216	224, 247
Poke Run Presbyterian	Westmoreland 504	215	
Presbyterian in Bedford	Bedford 16	31	
Presbyterian in Coudersport	Potter 3	217	246
Presbyterian, near West Newton	Westmoreland 50		247
Quaker, near Perryopolis	Fayette 7	216	224
St. Luke's at Woodville	Allegheny 27	216	247
St. Patrick's Sugar Creek, near Millerstown	Armstrong 14	31, 215	246
St. Paul's in Pittsburgh	Allegheny 504a & b	216	
St. Peter's Episcopal in Pittsburgh	Allegheny 42	31	
St. Peter's in Brownsville	Fayette 1	31, 216	161, 226-30
St. Thomas'	Washington 504	215	
Salem Presbyterian	Westmoreland 502	215	
Second Trinity Episcopal in Pittsburgh	Allegheny 507b	21	
Tent Presbyterian, near Uniontown	Fayette 58	215-6	224
Union Log, near Schellsburg	Bedford 15	31, 215	225
COURTHOUSES			
Allegheny County (Second)	Allegheny 520b	20, 29, 252, 253	
Armstrong County	Armstrong 4	252-3	260
Bedford County	Bedford 49	252	260
Butler County	Butler 502	252-3	
Clarion County	Clarion 501	252-3	

Structure	Key Number	Text Page	Illust. Page

COURTHOUSES (Continued)

Structure	Key Number	Text Page	Illust. Page
Clearfield County	Clearfield 501	252-3	
Elk County	Elk 501	252-3	
Fayette County	Fayette 99	21, 252-3	261
Greene County	Greene 3	21, 252-3	257-259
Lawrence County	Lawrence 10	29, 252-3	
McKean County	McKean 501	252-3	
Somerset County	Somerset 503b	252-3	
Venango County	Venango 504b	252-3	
Washington County	Washington 505	21, 252-3	261
Westmoreland County	Westmoreland 524	252-3	

FORTS—SEE ARSENALS

FURNACES

Structure	Key Number	Text Page	Illust. Page
Bruin, Furnace near	Butler 7		279
Laurel	Westmoreland 521	28	
Mt. Vernon	Fayette 34	270	278
Ross Mountain	Westmoreland 106		279
Valley	Westmoreland 80	270	279
Wharton	Fayette 33		278, 279

HARMONY SOCIETY

Structure	Key Number	Text Page	Illust. Page
In Harmony	Butler 29, 30, 35, 47, 49	145, 193	195-199
In Economy	Beaver 35, 36, 38-42	21, 23, 28, 44, 45, 193, 194	24, 158, 200-213

HOUSES AND ACCESSORY BUILDINGS

Structure	Key Number	Text Page	Illust. Page
Anderson, Dr. John	Bedford 29	24, 31, 43, 45, 267	94-96
Baird, Thomas	Washington 67	145	170, 171
Baker	Washington 20		146
Baker, Elias	Blair 1	7, 25, 31, 108-110, 145, 270	135
Barclay, Hugh	Bedford 17	45	93
Beazell, Matthew	Westmoreland 108		147
Bigham, Thomas J.	Allegheny 176		166
Black, Jacob	Fayette 532	19	88
Black, Samuel	Washington 507	44, 268	272
Bradford, David	Washington 5	31	
Brewer, Charles	Allegheny 10	24	171
Chambers	Washington 98	44, 145	92, 160
Crumrine, Daniel	Washington 102	144	147
Church, Samuel	Allegheny 7	31, 108, 109, 267	125
Cook, Col. Edward	Fayette 71	43, 144, 267	48, 49, 148
Croghan, George	Allegheny 549	34	
Croghan, William	Allegheny 31	7, 20, 25, 28, 108, 110, 145	126-131
Cunningham, John	Fayette 97	29, 45, 108	168, 171
Cunningham, David	Washington 43	145	123
Daily, John	Westmoreland 70	43, 45, 144, 145, 267-8	73-77, 171
Danaker, Charles	Bedford 56		150
Davis	Westmoreland 92	27	151
Dickson, John	Erie 59	144	143, 152
Dinsmore	Allegheny 157	44, 145	47
Dorsey, Joseph	Washington 88	43, 44, 45, 144, 145	52-56, 171
Espy, Colonel	Bedford 14	31, 44	97
Fahnestock, Benj. A.	Allegheny 14	31	
Ferry	Allegheny 149		154
Frazier, John	Allegheny 553	34	
Frew, John	Allegheny 17	27, 44, 46, 145	50, 51
Gallatin, Albert	Fayette 3	19, 27, 31, 45, 145, 267	168, 169
Gantz, John	Washington 100		161, 162
Gordon, John B.	Greene 1	108, 110, 145	114-118, 160, 170
Guthrie, William	Westmoreland 73		167
Harper, Samuel	Greene 24	28, 282	46, 149, 172
Harris, Jacob	Fayette 93	44	72
Hartley	Bedford 69		146
Hayden, Ben	Fayette 66		149
Hegarty, John	Washington 91		49
Hendryx (Hendrix), Dr. H. E.	Crawford 28	108, 109	140, 141
Hereline, John	Bedford 80		40
Hileman	Blair 12		93, 150
Hill, Richard	Fayette 92	44	73
Hoskinson	Erie 55		154
Irvin, Guy C.	Warren 27	30, 109	136-139
Ives, Timothy	Potter 1	21-22, 108, 109, 110	142
Jackson, Hugh	Allegheny 97	44	47
Johnston, Alex.	Westmoreland 28	43, 44, 46, 173	84-87
Judson, Amos	Erie 15	43, 45, 267	102, 103
Kaddoo, James	Allegheny 116	144	157
Krichbaum, Jacob	Bedford 77		39
LeMoyne, Dr. J. J.	Washington 6	30, 31, 268	111-113, 166
Lightner, Isaac	Allegheny 129	108, 109, 110, 144	120-122
Linn	Washington 71	109-10	119
Lowry, Lazarus	Blair 11		149
Ludwick, Samuel	Westmoreland 60	44, 144, 145	49, 156, 158
Lyon, William	Bedford 48	109, 110	132-134, 159
McConnell, Alex.	Washington 111	44	46
McGill, Patrick	Crawford 46		39
McLaughlin	Beaver 30		152
Manchester, Isaac	Washington 36	7, 20, 25, 30, 31, 43, 44, 45, 46, 144, 145	78-83, 158, 163
Mann, Robert	Mercer 8	109, 110	142
Meason, Isaac	Fayette 2	7, 19, 25, 32, 43, 44, 45, 46, 144, 270	60-67, 162
Meason, Isaac, Jr.	Fayette	19	
Metz, Christopher	Blair 17		153
Miller, James	Allegheny 2	44, 46	72, 161
Moore	Blair 21	44	97
Morgan, George	Allegheny 541	34	
Morrow, Henry	Allegheny 92		39
Mulvanen, Patrick	Beaver 11	109, 110	119
Neal, Robert	Allegheny 170	34, 145	37, 38
Neville, John	Allegheny 563	34	
Neville, Presley	Allegheny 24	7, 43, 45, 46, 145	57-59, 167
Newmeyer, Peter	Fayette 89		146
Noble, Joseph	Bedford 63		93
Overholt, Abraham	Westmoreland 62	31	151
Passavant, Phillippe Louis	Butler 38	144, 193	155
Patterson, William	Washington 74	44, 145	167
Patterson, James	Allegheny 111		72
Playford, Robert W.	Fayette 84	109	124
Quail, William M.	Washington 9	45	88
Reed, Charles M.	Erie 54	31, 109	143
Rhodes, A. S.	Allegheny 138		41
Risher, Daniel	Allegheny 139		148, 162
Roberts, John	Washington 29	43, 44, 46, 144, 267	68-71
Ross, James	Allegheny 34	43, 46	73
Royer, Daniel	Blair 18	43, 44, 45, 46, 144-5, 270	98-101, 158, 160
Russell, James	Bedford 33	45	97
Saeger, Edward	Crawford 47	110, 144	143, 156
Sayer, Ephraim	Greene 36		149
Shields, David	Allegheny 53	27, 30, 267	151
Shoenberger, John H.	Allegheny 13	24, 31, 108, 109, 110, 145	125, 172
Sill, John	Bedford 81	144	157
Smith, Hiram	Washington 85		92
Snoeberger, David	Bedford 62		147
Stauffer	Butler 40		153
Stewart, James	Westmoreland 99	145	156, 157
Stewart, John	Westmoreland 2	45	89-91
Stoner	Westmoreland 94		148
Thaw, William	Allegheny 574	23, 28	
Washabaugh	Bedford 78	144	152, 157
Waugaman, Peter	Westmoreland 23		88

Structure	Key Number	Text Page	Illust. Page
HOUSES AND ACCESSORY BUILDINGS—Continued			
Way, Nicholas	Allegheny 51	108, 109, 110	119
Wetmore, Lansing	Warren 65	145	160
White, Dr. James	Crawford 37	43, 45	104-107
Wilkins, Judge	Allegheny 583	7, 22, 24, 108, 109, 110	123
Williams, John	Allegheny 79		161
Willoughby, Daniel	Allegheny 37		38
Wray, Joseph	Beaver 20	24, 28, 145	159, 160, 163, 166, 170
Wright, Joshua	Washington 62	45	88

INNS—SEE TAVERNS

MILLS

Beeson's	Fayette 527	269	
Chambers'	Washington 97	269	275
Hay's	Somerset 12	269	276, 277
Milligan's	Westmoreland 45	269	274
Naugle's	Bedford 19	269	161, 277
Roxbury, Mill at	Somerset 30	269	
Washington's	Fayette 6	32, 269	274
Way's	Bedford 12	269	275
White's	Beaver 17	269	275

OFFICES

Barclay	Bedford 31	268	272
Burke's Building	Allegheny 3	20, 24, 268	273
Cessna House, Office adjoining	Bedford 74	268	273
Lyon House	Bedford 48	268	133
Reed Mansion, Office adjoining	Erie 54	268	273

SCHOOLS

Bentley Hall, Allegheny College	Crawford 1	21, 215	218-221
Cherry Tree	Venango 30	214	222
Concord	Westmoreland 100	214	223
Edgeworth Female Seminary	Allegheny 530	215	
Hays (James) Farm, School on	Butler 505	214	
Jefferson Academy and College	Washington 57	29, 214	
McMillan's (Dr. J.)	Washington 28	214	41, 223
New Geneva	Fayette 47	214	222
Pgh. Academy	Allegheny 533	214	
Ruter Hall, Allegheny College	Crawford 15		154
Washington Academy and College	Washington 8	214, 252	222
Waterford Academy	Erie 14	215	223
Western Theological Seminary	Allegheny 531	214	
Western University of Pennsylvania	Allegheny 532	214	

STORES

Black, Samuel	Washington 507	268	272
Drake	Crawford 44	268	272
Florence, Store at	Washington 72	268	151, 172, 272

Structure	Key Number	Text Page	Illust. Page
TAVERNS, HOTELS, INNS			
Bedford, Inn at	Bedford 503	12	
Bedford Springs	Bedford 52	174	
Black Horse Tavern	Washington 512	174	
Brashear Tavern	Fayette 76		153
Coates Tavern	Allegheny 26	174	
Compass Inn	Westmoreland 27	173	184
Crockford Tavern	Bedford 52	175	
Defibaugh Tavern	Bedford 1	144, 174	156, 184
Drake Store and Hotel	Crawford 44	268	272
Eagle Hotel	Erie 13	173, 174	150, 162, 177-79
Ewing's Tavern	Fayette 36	173	
Frankfort Hotel	Beaver 1	175	
Frankfort Springs	Beaver 508	175	
Halfway House	Westmoreland 84	35, 173	42
Hill Tavern	Washington 55	174	185
Johnson Tavern	Mercer 24	173	182
Ling Tavern	Blair 20		184
Leet, Major Daniel	Allegheny 137	173, 174	180, 181
Lemon Inn	Cambria 12	173, 174	150, 183
Malden Tavern	Washington 82	173, 174	163, 185
Marie's Tavern	Allegheny 538	30, 174	
Monongahela House	Allegheny 539	174	
Morris Tavern	Fayette 68		162
Moxley Tavern	Fayette 533	173	184
Nixon Tavern	Fayette 69	34, 173	36, 37
Raftsman's Tavern	Allegheny 540	174	
Rising Sun Tavern	Allegheny 543	174	
Searight's Tavern	Fayette 45		185
Semple's Tavern	Allegheny 541	34, 174	
Smith Tavern	Bedford 65	173	
Somerfield, Tavern in	Somerset 25	21	
Way Tavern	Allegheny 153	173	183
Weaverling Tavern	Bedford 67	173	183
White Swan Bar	Fayttee 528	174	185

TOLLHOUSES

On National Pike	Somerset 22	32, 176	187
On National Pike	Fayette 35	32, 176	186, 187
On National Pike	Washington 12	176	

TOMBSTONES

Bedford Monument (Dr. Nathaniel)	Allegheny 181		249
Cross Creek Cemetery	Washington 93		247, 248, 250
Donegal, From a cemetery at	Westmoreland 109	217	248
Fels Church Cemetery	Westmoreland 107		250
Hill Church Cemetery	Washington 2	217	251
Mercer, Cenotaph in Cemetery at	Mercer 25	217	249
Peter's Creek, Stone found on	Allegheny 171	217	249
Salem Church Cemetery	Westmoreland 26	217	248, 251
Sewickley Church Cemetery	Westmoreland 50	217	250
Union Church Cemetery	Bedford 15	217	250, 251

A List of Buildings Built before 1860 in the 27 Counties
of Western Pennsylvania, Taken from
THE HISTORIC AMERICAN BUILDINGS SURVEY
Library of Congress, Washington, D.C.
from the Catalogs of March 1, 1941, and 1958

KEY TO ABBREVIATIONS

S: Sheets of drawings
P: Photographs

L18: Late 18th cent.
E19: Early 19th cent.
M19: Mid 19th cent.

BR: Brick
ST: Stone
STU: Stucco
L: Log
W: Wood

Numerals at extreme right show number of stories.

ALLEGHENY COUNTY

11S—	3P	Brewer House, 1131 Western Ave., Pittsburgh	E19	BR-2
7S—	3P	Union Church, Presqueisle St., Pittsburgh	E19	STU on L
2S		Brick Courses, Triangle Area, Pittsburgh	M19	BR
4S—	1P	Coltart House, 3431 Forbes Ave., Pittsburgh	M19	BR-2
14S—	10P	Croghan House, Stanton Hts., Pittsburgh	E19	BR & ST-2
1S—	2P	Dr. Bedford Monument, Trinity Ch., Pittsburgh	E19	ST
3S—	1P	Fahnestock House, 408 Penn Ave., Pittsburgh	E19	BR-3
2S—	1P	Mitchell House, 524 Third Ave., Pittsburgh	M19	BR-2½
2S—	3P	Neal Cabin, Schenley Park, Pittsburgh	L18	L-1
6S—	1P	St. Peters P.E. Church, Forbes Ave., Pittsburgh	M19	ST
6S—	1P	Schoenberger House, 425 Penn Ave., Pittsburgh	M19	STU on BR-2½
8S—	3P	Miller House, South Park	E19	ST-2
3S—	4P	Rhodes Springhouse, near Dravosburg	M19	ST-1
3S—	2P	Armory, U.S. Allegheny Arsenal, Lawrenceville	E19	ST-2
4S—	6P	Barracks	U.S. Arsenal	E19	BR-2
2S—	1P	Boiler House	U.S. Arsenal	E19	BR-1
	1P	Carriage House	U.S. Arsenal	M19	BR-2
1S—	4P	Entrance Gates	U.S. Arsenal	E19	ST
2S		Group Plan & Plaques	U.S. Arsenal		
2S—	2P	Guardhouse	U.S. Arsenal	M19	STU on BR-2
2S—	2P	Machine Shop	U.S. Arsenal	E19	BR-2
7S—	3P	Non-com. Officers' Quarters	U.S. Arsenal	E19	BR-2
4S—	5P	Officers' Quarters	U.S. Arsenal	E19	BR-2
8S—	4P	Commandant's Quarters	U.S. Arsenal	E19	BR & ST-2
4S—	2P	Storehouse No. 2	U.S. Arsenal	M19	BR-2

BUTLER COUNTY

24S—	10P	Stauffer-Bame House, near Harmony	M19	ST-2

CRAWFORD COUNTY

	1P	Ridgeway House, Hydetown	E19	W-2
	3P	Charles Ridgeway House, Hydetown	E19	W-2
	1P	Bentley Hall, Allegheny Coll., Meadville	E19	BR-3
	1P	Baldwin-Reynolds House, Meadville	M19	BR-2½
	1P	Independence Congregational Church, Meadville	E19	BR
	1P	Summer House, Route 98, near Meadville	E19	W-2
	1P	Flint House, New Richmond vicinity	E19	W-1
	1P	Colonel Drake House, Titusville	M19	W-2
	2P	Stevens House, Titusville	M19	W-1
	1P	Kelly House, Titusville	M19	W-2
	1P	McPheeter House, Woodcock	M19	BR-2
	1P	Methodist Church, Woodcock	M19	BR
4S—	2P	Congregational Church, Riceville	M19	W
11S—	3P	Hendryx House, Route 77, Riceville	M19	W-1
	2P	Water Grist Mill, Oil Creek, Riceville	M19	W-3
3S—	3P	Westgate-Bruner House, Route 77, Riceville	M19	W-1
	1P	Saeger House, Saegertown	M19	W-2

ERIE COUNTY

	1P	First Constitutional Pres. Church, Edinboro	M19	W
	2P	Hencke House, Edinboro	M19	W-2
7S—	3P	Hutchinson House, 155 E. Main St., Girard	E19	BR-2
2S—	4P	Blair Cabin, Blair Rd., 3½ mi SE Girard	E19	L-1
1S—	2P	Thompson House, Blair Rd., near Girard	E19	W-1
	1P	Davidson House, Harborcreek	M19	W-2
	1P	Dodge House, Harborcreek	M19	BR-2
	1P	Backus House, Moorheadville	M19	W-2
11S—	7P	Moorhead House, Moorheadville	E19	BR-2
3S—	4P	First Baptist Church, Railroad St., Northeast	M19	W
	1P	Octagon Barn, Northeast	M19	BR-1
	1P	Silliman-Phillips House, Northeast	E19	BR-2
9S—	6P	Stevenson Hse., Lake Road, N. Springfield	E19	W-2
8S—	5P	Sterrett Cabin, Conneaut Rd., Sterrettania	E19	L-2
	1P	Summit Stone School, Summit	E19	ST-1
	1P	Rockwell House, Union City	M19	W-2
	1P	Brotherton House, Waterford	M19	W-2
1S—	2P	Covered Bridge, LeBoeuf Creek, Waterford	L19	W
	1P	Doctor's Office, Waterford	M19	W-1
	1P	Eagle Hotel, Waterford	E19	ST-2½
	1P	Judson House, Waterford	E19	W-2
	1P	St. Peter's Episcopal Church, Waterford	E19	BR
8S—	3P	Waterford Academy, Waterford	E19	ST-2
	1P	Chaffee House, Wattsburg	M19	W-1
	1P	Howard Double House, Wattsburg	M19	W-2
	1P	Hughes House, 136 E. Third St., Erie	M19	L-2
2S—	3P	Land Lighthouse, Front St., Erie	M19	ST
13S—	5P	Old Customs House, 415 State St., Erie	M19	ST-2
13S—	11P	Perry Memorial (Old Tavern), Erie	E19	W-3
	17P	Reed House, Sixth & Peach Sts., Erie	M19	STU on BR-2
	1P	Whitman House, Ninth & Peach Sts., Erie	M19	W-2
6S—	1P	Woodruff (Cashier's) House, 417 State St., Erie	M19	STU on BR-3
	1P	Strong House, Perry Highway, Erie	M19	W-2

FAYETTE COUNTY

	1P	Mount Washington Tavern, Uniontown	E19	BR-2½
7S—	7P	Nixon Tavern, Fairchance Rd., Fairchance	E19	L-2
5S—	6P	Hayden House, Hopwood	E19	ST-1
9S—	3P	Colonel Cook House, Fayette City	L18	ST-2

MERCER COUNTY

	1P	Johnson House, 5 mi. S. of Mercer	E19	ST-2
	2P	Bell House, Mercer	M19	W-2
	3P	Dr. Beriah Magoffin Hse., 116 Venango St., Mercer	E19	W-2
	1P	Garrett Cenotaph, Cemetery, Mercer	E19	ST
	2P	Magoffin House, 119 South Pitt St., Mercer	E19	W-2
	1P	Old Stone Jail, Mercer	E19	ST-2
	1P	Robinson House, Mercer	E19	ST-2
	4P	Scriven's House, Sheakleyville	M19	W-2

5S—	2P Scriven's Store, Sheakleyville	M19	W-2
	3P Goodwin House, 36 Mercer St., Greenville	E19	W-2
	4P Stewart House, Greenville	M19	W-2

McKEAN COUNTY

	5P Coleman House, Port Allegany	M19	W-2
	5P Shattuck Lodge, Betula	E19	W-1
	1P Chrisman House, Eldred	M19	W-2
5S—	1P Chevalier House, near Ceres	M19	W-1
6S—	7P Backus House, Smethport	E19	W-2
7S—	3P Medbury Place, 604 Main St., Smethport	M19	W-1½
	4P Lamphier House, West Eldred	M19	W-2
6S—	1P Marsh House, Route 46, 1 mile from Crosby	M19	ST-1

POTTER COUNTY

13S—	4P Ives House, Coudersport	M19	W-2
	3P Lillibridge House, Coudersport	M19	W-2
	1P Presbyterian Church, Coudersport	M19	W
	1P Wiedrich House, Roulette	M19	W-2

SOMERSET COUNTY

	4P W. L. Shaulis House, Rockwood	E19	W-2½

VENANGO COUNTY

	1P Ridgeway House, Franklin	E19	L-2
4S—	2P Free Methodist Church, Pleasantville	M19	W

2S—	5P Quinn House, Pleasantville	M19	W-1
5S—	4P Presbyterian Church, Cherry Tree	M19	W
	1P School, Cherry Tree	M19	W-2

WARREN COUNTY

	1P House by the Pines, Irvine Estate, Irvine	M19	ST-2
14S—	1P Irvine House, Irvine Estate, Irvine	M19	ST-2
7S—	2P Miller's House, Irvine Estate, Irvine	M19	ST
9S—	1P Tenant House, Irvine Estate, Irvine	M19	ST
7S—	5P Irvine Presbyterian Church, Irvine	M19	ST
	1P Old Hotel, Pittsfield	M19	W-2
	1P Acock House, Pittsfield	M19	W-2
	1P Water Mill, Garland		
	1P Old Hotel (Ryan House), Tidioute	M19	W-3
	1P Church, Pittsfield	M19	W
	1P Rhodes House, Pittsfield	M19	W-2
	1P Terry House, Pittsfield	M19	W-2

WASHINGTON COUNTY

7S—	3P Administration Bldg., W & J College, Washington	L18	BR-2
	1P Malden Inn, West Brownsville	E19	ST-2½

WESTMORELAND COUNTY

2S—	2P Bell's Mill Covered Bridge, near West Newton	M19	W
9S—	2P Milligan Water Mill, Milligantown	E19	W

GENERAL INDEX

The General Index does not contain references to *structures* dealt with in text and illustration, nor does it contain references to the original *owners* of these structures. For all text and illustration references to buildings and original owners, see the List of Structures.

—A—

Accessory buildings and details.........................144-45
Adam brothers..15
Adams, James Truslow, Quotation from....................13
Alden, The Rev. Timothy.............................21, 215
Alterations.....................................31, 46, 144
Amateur architects.....................................21-23
American Builder's Companion, The.......................18
American handbooks.......................................18
American Institute of Architects.......................280
American Pioneer, Woodcut from........................26
Antiquities of Athens, The.........................15, 18
Architects..20-23, 43
Army fortifications...................................254-56
Arsenals and forts............11, 20-23, 31-32, 254-56

—B—

Background of early architecture.....................11-14
Banks...20-21, 267
Barns..144
Barr (early architect).................................21
Barr, John...19
Beaver and Lake Erie Canal....................14, 175, 176
Bedford...........................14, 29, 31, 175, 252, 268
Bedford Springs.....................................174-75
Benjamin, Asher....................................18, 108
Benjamin, Asher, Quotations from.................18, 20, 21
Biddle, Owen...18
"Blackburned headers"................................27-28
Blockhouses.........................12, 31, 254-55
Blythe, David G....................................21, 253
Boat-building..13
Boucher, John N., Quotations from.....27, 29-30, 215, 254, 268, 270
Brick..25, 26
Brick and stone construction........................27-28
Brick buildings.....................................25, 26, 27, 28
Bridges..21, 32, 175-76
Brown, Thomas..29
Brownsville.......................................14, 29, 31
Brunot, Dr. Felix......................................30
Brunot, Felix (engineer)..............................176
Brunot's Island.......................................30
Bryan, John.......................................21, 253
Bryan, Samuel.....................................21, 253
Buck, Solon J., Quotation from........................254
Buhl Foundation.....................7, 9, 280, 281, 283
Builders, Early..................19-30, 43, 108
Builder's Guide.......................................18
Builders' handbooks.............................17-18, 23
Builder's Jewel, The.................................18
Building costs:
    Arsenals and forts.........................255, 256
    Bridges...175
    Canals..175, 176
    Cemeteries..193
    Courthouses...............................29, 252-53
    Figures (statues)................................253
    Houses..22, 28-29
    Schools.......................................29, 214
Building laws..29
Building materials...................................24-26
Building sites......................................12, 30
Buildings, Preservation of..........................31-32
Buildings without traditional style....................17

—C—

Cabins...See Log buildings
Calahan, S. J..21
Campbell, Colonel John.................................29
Canals......................................13-14, 175-76
Canon, John..29, 214
Care of buildings......................................31
Carnegie Library of Pittsburgh—Pennsylvania Room........33, 280, 283
Carpenters.....................................See Builders, Early

Carving..21
Ceilings...24
Celoron...217
Cellars..28
Cenotaphs...217
Center-hall...110
Chandeliers......................25, 28, 110, 217
Charcoal iron industry.................................25
Chesapeake and Ohio Canal..............................14
Chimneys..27, 35, 45
Chinking...35
Chislett, John...............20, 30, 43, 253, 267, 268
Churches..19, 215-17
Cities, Growth of......................................14
"Clapboard shingles"...................................27
Classic Revival...................................15, 16, 17
Coal...14
Colonial style...17
Coltart and Dilworth..............................21, 253
Commerce and industry.............12-13, 14, 25, 194
Commercial and industrial architecture.............267-69
Committee for the Preservation of Historic Monuments....280
Common bond..27
Contractors..21
Contracts...19, 21-22, 253
Cooking fireplaces.....................................45
Copper...25
Corinthian order.......................................17
Cornices..28, 46
Costs......................................See Building costs
Courthouses.................20, 21, 29, 252-53
Covered bridges....................................32, 176
Craftsman and his materials, The....................24-25
Craftsman-architects................................19-20
Craftsman-builders..................................19-20
Craftsmen......................................See Builders, Early
Craig, Isaac...25
Cramer, Zadok..18
Crawford, Valentine, Quotation from..................269
"Cross-Cut Canal"......................................14
Cullum, Gen. G. W.................................21, 217
Cuming, Fortescue, Quotation from......................30
Cunningham, John.......................................29
Cupolas...253

—D—

"Daub and wattle"......................................27
Daughters of the American Revolution.........31, 32, 255
Dewhurst, Richard......................................21
"Diamonds"...29
Doddridge, Quotations from........................12, 254
Domestic architecture..............................108-10
Door knockers..24
Doors and doorways.............109, 144, 193, 267
Doric order..17, 20
Dormers..45
Drafting...23
Drawings..23, 282-83

—E—

Early architecture, Background of...................11-14
Eassieman, James.......................................21
Economy.............7, 20, 28, 30, 43, 193-194
"Egg" stoves...28
Eichbaum, William......................................28
Engineers..21
English architecture...................................15
"English basement".....................................110
English handbooks......................................18
English heritage...................................15, 16
Erie...14, 29
Evans (early architect)................................21
Evolution of house plan.............................44-45

—F—

Fearon, Henry B., Quotations from............................27, 28
Federal Government, Work of...............................7, 280
Federal style.............................See Classic Revival
Files, Survey...33, 283
Fire fronts...24
Fireplaces..45, 145
First architects, The...20-21
Flemish bond..27, 28
Floors...27
Flour mills...29-30, 268-69
Fortifications...21, 253-56
Forts..................................See Arsenals and forts
Frame buildings........................15, 17, 25-26, 27
Frankfort Springs..175
Franklin...29, 254
Freeport..25
French Creek Canal..176
Furnaces............................14, 25, 28, 269-70

—G—

Gallatin, Albert.....................................25, 214, 267
Gardening.......................See Landscaping and gardening
Gas..14
Georgian style.....................................15-16, 17
Germans.............................11, 13, 20, 43, 193
Gibbs, James..18
Girard Locks..176
Glass..25
Gordon, Harry..21
Gothic style...................................15, 17, 216
Governmental architecture................................252-53
Graham, Hugh..19, 43
Grant's Hill...30, 175-76
Greek heritage..15, 17
Greek Revival style........16-17, 18, 44, 45, 108-110, 216-17, 252, 267
Greensburg......................................14, 216, 252
"Gridiron plan"...29
Grist mills...See Flour mills

—H—

Halls...110
Hand work...26
Handbooks..17-18, 23, 108
Hanna, Robert...252
Hannastown..252
Hannen and Fairman...21
Harmony......................................7, 20, 28, 193
Harmony Society........7, 20, 23, 28, 30, 32, 193-94
Heating and lighting..28
Highways..See Roads
Hines (stone carver)...21
Hinges..27
Historic American Buildings Survey..........................280
Historic Monuments Committee................................280
Historical organizations, Homes of...........................31
Historical Society of Western Pennsylvania..................283
History of Butler County, Quotation from...................214
Hollidaysburg...14
Hopkins, The Rev. John H...........................21, 216
Hopwood...22, 29
Horizontal logs..12, 27
Horticulture...................See Landscaping and gardening

—I—

Imported styles...16
Indians...11, 12
Institutional architecture..............................214-17
Industry..........................See Commerce and industry
Ionic order..17
Irish..11, 13, 43
Iron...14, 21, 25, 270
Irvine, Dr. William A..216
Italian heritage..15

—J—

Jefferson, Thomas........................16, 20, 21, 255
Johnston, William G., Quotation from........................28
Jones, Inigo...18

—K—

Kelly, William.....................................20-21, 267
Kenny, James, Quotation from................................254
Kerr, Joseph W..21
Kerrins (early architect)......................................21
Killikelly, Sarah H., Quotation from..........................28
Kimball, Quotation from......................................16
Kinkead, Beck & Evans...21

—L—

Lafever, Minard...18
Landscape designers...................................19, 20, 30
Landscaping and gardening............................17, 30
Langley, Batty and Thomas....................................18
Lath..27
Latrobe, Benjamin Henry........20, 21, 23, 43, 255
Laws, Building..29
Lead..25
Le Chevalier de Cambray.....................................255
Le Mercier...21, 254
Lighting...28
Limestone...25, 145
Local characteristics..44
Log buildings
  11, 12, 17, 19, 24, 25, 26-27, 28, 32, 35, 144, 214, 215, 252, 253, 254
Log cabins...See Log buildings
Long, The Rev. Rea..21
Lothrop, S...21, 175
Lumber...24, 26, 27

—M—

McCain, Daniel..21
McGowen, John..20
Mahanna, Bradley.......................................21, 253
Mahoningtown...14
Major, Howard, Quotation from.......................16, 23
Mantels...24, 145, 282
Marble...25, 267
Maryland, Influence of..................................16, 43
Masonry..12, 17, 35
Materials...24-26
Materials, Distribution of, by period and district...........25-26
Measured drawings.......................................282-83
Meeting houses...See Churches
Military architecture.....................................253-56
Millard, James P...21, 253
Miller, Annie Moorhead (Clark), Quotation from............255
Mills...29-30, 268-69
Mills, Robert...20, 21
Modernizing, Effect of.......................31, 46, 282
Moldings...16, 17, 26
Monongahela River.......................................13, 254
Mortar..See Plaster
Moser (early architect)..21

—N—

Nails..27
National Pike.....................21, 32, 173, 174, 176
Natural resources..14
Nelson, Charles..43
Nemacolin Trail...11
New England colonies...................................15-16
New Geneva...25, 267
New Haven..19
New York state, Influence of...........................16, 17
Northern Turnpike.......................................32, 175
Northwestern Pennsylvania................12, 16, 26, 45
Nottman, John..21

—O—

Offices..268
O'Hara, James..25
Ohio River..12, 13
Oil..14
Old Redstone...215
Origin and development of styles......................15-18
Origins, Diversity of...16
Ornamental crafts..21
Ornamentation, Exterior..............................45, 110

—P—

Palladio..15, 18
Paneling...145
Partitions...27
Pegs..27
Pennsylvania Canal......................14, 21, 175-76
Permanent records of Survey..........................33, 283
"Pike towns"...29
Pikes...See Roads
Pins, Wooden..27
Pioneer period (1750-1795)............................11-12, 17
Pittsburgh Architectural Club...............................280
Pittsburgh Club...24
Pittsburgh Gazette, Quotation from...........................19
Planning.................................See Town planning
Plaster............................12, 17, 24, 25, 27, 45
Plaster decoration......................24, 110, 145
Porches.............................45, 109-110, 144-45, 173

Porticos.........................22, 108, 109, 253, 267
Post-Colonial house, Characteristics of................45-46
Post-Colonial period (1785-1830)...............16, 17, 43-46
Potomac Company....................................14
Practice of Architecture................................20
Preservation of buildings...................31-32, 46, 282
Preservation of Historic Monuments, Committee for........280
Primitive architecture..............................11-12
Pugin..15, 18
Pulpits.......................................215, 216
"Puncheons"..27

—Q—

Quarries....................................See Stone

—R—

Railroads..14
Rapp, Frederick..................19-20, 23, 43, 193
Rapp, George...............................20, 193
Raystown Path......................................11
Records of Survey, Permanent...................33, 283
Renaissance.......................................15
Revett, Nicholas................................15, 18
Rivers...13, 14
Roads.........................11, 12, 13-14, 175, 176
Roads, Influence of, upon building....................14
Roberts, Solomon W...............................175
Roberts, W. Milnor................................175
Roebling, John A................................175-76
Roman influence..................See Italian heritage
Romanticism.......................................15
Roofs...........................25, 27, 45, 144
Roosevelt, Theodore, Quotations from.............11, 26
Rupp, Israel, Quotation from......................255

—S—

Sandstone....................20, 24-25, 145
Schenley, Major...................................110
Schools.......................................29, 214-215
Schuyler, Montgomery, Quotation from................267
Scotch......................................11, 13, 43
Scotch-Irish.......................................11
Searight, Thomas B., Quotation from........13, 22, 174
Settlers, Early.................................11-12
Sharon..14
Shingles..27
Signature stones...............................25, 145
Signs, Tavern..................................173-74
Sites..12, 17, 30
Slate...25
Smith, Rev. Joseph................................214
Smokehouses......................................144
Somerfield..21
Southwestern Pennsylvania...................12, 13, 16
Spires.......................................See Cupolas
Springhouses.....................................144
Stairs and stairways...............24, 27, 45, 145
Statues, Wooden..................................253
Steam navigation..................................13
Stewart, James....................................43
Stock designs...................................23-24
Stockades......................................12, 254
Stone...............25, 28 (See also Limestone and Sandstone)
Stone buildings................12, 17, 25, 26, 28
Stone carvers.....................................21
Stone walls and textures..........................145
Stores...267-68
Strickland, William................................20
Stuart, James...................................15, 18
Stucco...21, 24
Styles, Imported...................................16
Styles, Origin and development of.................15-18
"Summer" beam.....................................27
Survey, The Western Pennsylvania Architectural:
    Field work of.................................281
    Files of......................................33
    Funds for....................................280

Permanent records of.........................33, 283
Personnel of...............................3, 280-281
Procedure of.....................................281
Publicity of.....................................281
Work of....................7, 9, 32, 280-283
Suspension bridges............................175, 176

—T—

Taverns......................21, 30, 173-74
Temple-front designs.............................109
Textures...145
Timber.......................................See Lumber
Tollhouses.......................................176
Tombstones.......................................217
Tools...26
Town planning..............................29-30, 194
Towns......................................See towns by name
Traditional forms.................................43
Trails.......................................See Roads
Transportation.........See Canals, Railroads, Rivers, Roads
Transportation, Architecture of.................173-176
Transportation, Effect of, upon architecture.........13
Travel..............See Canals, Railroads, Rivers, Roads
Tunnels.......................................175-76
Turnpikes....................................See Roads

—U—

Uniontown.....................................14, 19, 269

—V—

Van Horn, Mordecai..............................20, 110
Villages, Development of...........................12
Virginia, Influence of...........................16, 43
Vitruvius...18

—W—

Wagon travel.......................................13
Wainscoting.......................................45
Wall paper..45
Walls, Stone.....................................145
Wansey, Henry, Quotation from.....................28
Warren..29
Washhouses.......................................144
Washington, George............................14, 269
Washington (town).................................14
Waterford.......................29, 254, 267
Watering places................................174-75
Waterways..........................See Canals, Rivers
Waynesburg.......................................176
Weatherboarding....................................35
Welch, Sylvester.................................175
Wellford, Robert...............................24, 145
Welsh...13
West Alexander....................................29
Western Pennsylvania, Geographic definition of........280
Western Pennsylvania Architectural Survey.........See Survey
Western Pennsylvania Historical Survey.............281
William Penn Highway...........................32, 175
Wilson, Adam................19, 30, 43, 175
Windows.........24, 25, 27, 44, 45, 109, 110, 145
Wood in design and construction....................27
Wooden houses....................See Frame buildings
Woods, George.....................................29
Woods.......................................See Lumber
Woodwell, Joseph..............................21, 194
Wren, Sir Christopher..............................18

—Y—

Young Carpenter's Assistant, The....................18
Youth's Instructor and Workman's Remembrancer........18

—Z—

Zeigler, Abraham.................................193
Zeigler, Elias....................................193
Zelienople.......................................193

BIBLIOGRAPHY

Because of the lack of previous architectural investigation into the early history of western Pennsylvania, the text of this book was based largely upon observations made and data accumulated in the field. However, in the study of the social and economic backgrounds and the relationship of this local architecture to the national architecture, much valuable material was gleaned from library research involving some two hundred books, as well as numerous pamphlets, periodicals and newspapers. In a number of these works, ideas were stated with such force and color that the author felt this book would be enriched by making direct quotations in the text where applicable. The books from which such quotations were made are listed below, and the kindness of publishers, authors, and copyright holders in granting permission to quote from publications covered by copyright is gratefully acknowledged by the author and the sponsors of this volume.

ADAMS, JAMES TRUSLOW. *The Epic of America*. Boston; Little, Brown, and Company, 1933.

ASHER, BENJAMIN. *A Reprint of* [five of his works on architecture, originally published 1805-1833]. Plates and text selected and edited by Aymar Embury II, Architect. New York; Architectural Book Publishing Company, 1917.

BOUCHER, JOHN N. *The Old and New Westmoreland*. New York; The American Historical Society, Inc., 1918. 4 vols.

BROWN, R. C. and Company, Pub. *History of Butler County, Pennsylvania*. [Harrisburg] 1895.

BUCK, SOLON J. "The Planting of Civilization in Western Pennsylvania." Manuscript copy, courtesy of the Western Pennsylvania Historical Survey.

CUMING, FORTESCUE. *Sketches of a Tour to the Western Country*. Pittsburgh; Cramer, Spear & Eichbaum, 1810.

DODDRIDGE, JOSEPH. *Notes on the Settlement and Indian Wars of the Western Parts of Virginia and Pennsylvania from 1763 to 1783, inclusive, together with a Review of the State of Society and Manners of the First Settlers of the Western Country*. Wellsburg, (West) Virginia; the author, privately printed, 1824.

FEARON, HENRY BRADSHAW. *Sketches of America: A Narrative of a Journey of Five Thousand Miles through the Eastern and Western States of America*. Second edition. London; Printed for Longman, Hurst, Rees, Orme, and Brown, 1818.

JOHNSTON, WILLIAM G. *Life and Reminiscences from Birth to Manhood*. Pittsburgh; [New York printed, The Knickerbocker Press] 1901.

KENNY, JAMES. "Journal, 1761-1763," in *The Pennsylvania Magazine of History and Biography*, 37:1-47, 152-201 (1913).

KILLIKELLY, SARAH H. *The History of Pittsburgh, Its Rise and Progress*. Pittsburgh; B. C. & Gordon Montgomery Company, 1906.

KIMBALL, SIDNEY FISKE. *Domestic Architecture of the American Colonies and of the Early Republic*. New York; Charles Scribner's Sons, 1927.

MAJOR, HOWARD. *The Domestic Architecture of the Early American Republic: The Greek Revival*. Philadelphia; J. B. Lippincott Company, 1926.

MILLER, ANNIE MOORHEAD (CLARK). *Chronicles of Families, Houses, and Estates of Pittsburgh and its Environs*. Pittsburgh, 1927.

ROOSEVELT, THEODORE. *The Winning of the West*. New York; G. P. Putnam's Sons, 1889-1896. 4 vols. Volume 1, Chapter 5, "The Backwoodsmen of the Alleghenies, 1769-1774."

RUPP, ISRAEL DANIEL. *Early History of Western Pennsylvania, and of the West, and of Western Expeditions and Campaigns, from 1754 to 1833*. Pittsburgh; Daniel W. Kauffman; Harrisburg; W. O. Hickok, 1846.

SCHUYLER, MONTGOMERY. "The Old Greek Revival," in *American Architect*, 98:121-126, 128, 201-204, 206-208 (1910).

SEARIGHT, THOMAS B. *The Old Pike: A History of the National Road, with Incidents, Accidents, and Anecdotes thereon*. Uniontown, Pa.; the author, 1894.

WANSEY, HENRY. *An Excursion to the United States of North America in the Summer of 1794*. Second edition. Salisbury; printed and sold by J. Easton, 1798.

BIBLIOGRAPHY FOR THE 1995 EDITION

By Dell Upton and Zeynep Kezer

A selection of works building on and extending the legacy of *The Early Architecture of Western Pennsylvania.*

A photographic survey of Westmoreland county architecture, phase I. Greensburg, Pa.: Westmoreland County Museum of Art, 1979.

Arndt, Karl J. R. "A Tour of America's Most Successful Utopia: Harmonie, Pennsylvania, 1803–1815." *Pennsylvania Folklife* 32 (1983): 139–40.

Aurand, Martin. *Pittsburgh Architecture: A Guide to Research.* Pittsburgh: Carnegie Mellon University Architecture Archives, Carnegie Mellon University Libraries, 1991.

Bennett, Lola. *The Company Towns of the Rockhill Iron and Coal Company: Robertsdale and Woodvale, Pennsylvania.* Washington, D.C.: Historic American Buildings Survey/Historic American Engineering Record, 1990.

Carlisle, Ronald C. "Notes on the Architecture of Fort McIntosh and the Construction of a Blockhouse on the Beaver River in 1788." *Western Pennsylvania Historical Magazine* 62 (1979): 39–59.

Cowin, Verna L. *Pittsburgh Archaeological Resources and National Register Survey.* Pittsburgh: Carnegie Museum of Natural History, Pennsylvania Historical and Museum Commission, Pittsburgh Department of City Planning, 1985.

Cubbison, Shirley E. "The One-room Schools of the Slippery Rock Area." Ed. Andrew Shick. *Western Pennsylvania Historical Magazine* 69 (1986): 197–220.

Demarest, David, and Eugene Levy. "Remnants of an Industrial Landscape." *Pittsburgh History* 72 (1989): 128–39.

————. "A Relict Industrial Landscape: Pittsburgh's Coke Region." *Landscape* 29, no. 2 (1986): 29–36.

————. "Touring the Coke Region." *Pittsburgh History* 74 (1991): 100–13.

Elbow, Gary S. "What Happens to the Company Town When the Company Leaves? The Changing Landscapes of Pittsburgh Area Company Towns." *Places* 3, no. 2 (1976): 19–25.

Elkin, C. W. W. "Covered Bridges." *Western Pennsylvania Historical Magazine* 42 (1959): 45–54.

Ferree, Vera Burtner. "The Burtner Homestead: a Landmark to Remember." *Western Pennsylvania Historical Magazine* 52 (1969): 161–69.

Fiero, Kathleen W. *The Lemon House, Allegheny Portage Railroad National Historic Site, Pennsylvania: Historic Structure Report, Archaeological Data Section.* Washington, D.C.: U.S. Department of the Interior, National Park Service, 1984.

Fitzsimmons, Gray. *Blair County and Cambria County, Pennsylvania An Inventory of Historic Engineering and Industrial Sites.* Washington, D.C.: Historic American Buildings Survey/Historic American Engineering Record, 1990.

Glass, Joseph W. *The Pennsylvania Culture Region: A View from the Barn.* Ann Arbor: UMI Research Press, 1986.

Guidebook to Historic Places in Western Pennsylvania. Western Pennsylvania Historical Survey. Pittsburgh: University of Pittsburgh Press, 1938.

Hanna, Susan E. "The Farmhouse Styles of Lawrence County." *Pennsylvania Heritage* 4 (1978): 10–12.

Harman, J. Paul. "Stone-stack Smelting Furnaces in Westmoreland County." *Pennsylvania Magazine of History and Biography* 19 (1952): 185–93.

Harper, Eugene R. "Town Development in Early Western Pennsylvania." *Western Pennsylvania Historical Magazine* 71 (1988): 3–26.

Harpster, John W. "Eighteenth-Century Inns and Taverns of Western Pennsylvania." *Western Pennsylvania Historical Magazine* 71 (1936): 5–16.

Harrington, J. C. "Fort Necessity—Scene of George Washington's First Battle." *Journal of the Society of Architectural Historians* 13, no. 2 (1954): 25–27.

————. "The Metamorphosis of Fort Necessity." *Western Pennsylvania Historical Magazines* 37 (1954–55): 181–88.

————. "The Puzzle of Washington's Fort Necessity." *Archaeology* 29 (1976): 178–85.

Heald, Sarah. *Fayette County, Pennsylvania: An Inventory of Historic Engineering and Industrial Sites.* Washington, D.C.: Historic American Buildings Survey/Historic American Engineering Record, 1990.

Jucha, Robert J. "The Anatomy of a Streetcar Suburb: A Developmental History of Shadyside, 1852–1916." *Western Pennsylvania Historical Magazine* 62 (1979): 301–20.

Kidney, Walter C. *Landmark Architecture: Pittsburgh and Allegheny County.* Pittsburgh: Pittsburgh History and Landmarks Foundation, 1985.

Kurti, Laszlo. "Hungarian Settlement and Building in Pennsylvania and Hungary: A Brief Comparison." *Pioneer America* 12 (1980): 34–53.

Lewis, Pierce F. "Small Towns in Pennsylvania." *Annals of the Association of American Geographers* 62 (1962): 323–51.

Michael, Ronald L. "Cut Nail Manufacture: Southwestern Pennsylvania." *APT Bulletin* 6 (1974): 99–108.

————. "Wagon Taverns as Seen through Local Source Material." *Pennsylvania Folklife* 23 no. 2 (1973): 31–39.

Michael, Ronald L., and Ronald C. Carlisle. "A Log Settler's Fort/Home." *Pennsylvania Folklife* 23, no. 3 (1973): 29–46.

Michael, Ronald L., and Ronald C. Carlisle. "The Peter Colley Tavern, 1801–1854." *Pennsylvania Folklife* 23, no. 1 (Autumn 1973): 31–46.

Miller, E. Willard, comp. *Pennsylvania, Architecture and Culture: A Bibliography.* Monticello, Ill.: Vance Bibliographies, 1985.

Mulrooney, Margaret M. *A Legacy of Coal: The Coal Company Towns of Southwestern Pennsylvania.* Washington, D.C.: Historic American Buildings Survey/Historic American Engineering Record, 1989.

Page, Oliver Ormsby. "Sketch of the 'Old Round Church' 1805–1825, The Original Edifice of Trinity Church, Pittsburgh." *Pennsylvania Magazine of History and Biography* 19 (1895): 351–58.

Pillsbury, Richard. "Patterns in the Folk and Vernacular House

Forms of the Pennsylvania Culture Region." *Pioneer America* 9 (1977): 12–31.

Pitzer, D. E. "Harmonist Heritage of Three Towns." *Historic Preservation* 29 (October 1977): 5–10.

Rayburn, Ella Sue and Sally Small. *Johnstown Flood National Memorial: Elias J. Unger House.* Ed. Harlan D. Unrau. Denver: U.S. Department of Interior, National Park Service, 1986.

Soltow, Lee. "Housing Characteristics on the Pennsylvania Frontier: Mifflin County Dwelling Values in 1798." *Pennsylvania History* 46 (1980): 57–70.

Stotz, Charles Morse. *Outposts of the War for Empire. The French and English in Western Pennsylvania: Their Armies, Their Forts, Their People, 1749–1764.* Pittsburgh: University of Pittsburgh Press for the Historical Society of Western Pennsylvania, 1985.

———. "Threshold of the Golden Kingdom: The Village of Economy and Its Restoration." *Winterthur Portfolio* 7 (1973): 133–70.

Swauger, James L. "Archaeological Salvage at the Site of Forts Pitt and Duquesne, Pittsburgh, Pennsylvania: 1940 through 1965." In *The Scope of Historical Archaeology: Essays in Honor of John L. Cotter.* Ed. David G. Orr and Daniel G. Crozier, 53–62. Occasional Publication of the Department of Anthropology, Temple University. Philadelphia: Laboratory of Anthropology, Temple University, 1984.

Tilberg, Frederick. "Washington's Stockade at Fort Necessity." *Pennsylvania History* 20 (1953): 240–57.

Toker, Franklin. *Pittsburgh: An Urban Portrait.* University Park: Pennsylvania State University Press, 1986.

———. *The Roots of Architecture in Pittsburgh and Allegheny County: A Guide to Research Resources.* Pittsburgh: Historical Society of Western Pennsylvania, 1979.

Tyler, John. "Juniata Crossings: Frontier Outpost." *Pioneer America* 2, no. 2 (1970): 4–10.

Van Trump, James D. *Landmark Architecture of Allegheny County, Pennsylvania.* Pittsburgh: Pittsburgh History and Landmarks Foundation, 1967.

———. *Life and Architecture in Pittsburgh.* Pittsburgh: Pittsburgh History and Landmarks Foundation, 1983.

———. *Majesty of the Law: The Courthouses of Allegheny County.* Pittsburgh: Pittsburgh History and Landmarks Foundation, 1988.

Wallace Kim E. *Railroad City: Four Historic Neighborhoods on Altoona, Pennsylvania.* Washington: Historic American Buildings Survey/Historic American Engineering Record, 1990.

Wallace, Kim E., ed. *The Character of a Steel Mill City: Four Historic Neighborhoods of Johnstown, Pennsylvania.* Washington, D.C.: Historic American Buildings Survey/Historic American Engineering Record, 1989.

Zelinsky, Wilbur. "The Pennsylvania Town: An Overdue Geographic Account." *Geographic Review* 67 (1977): 127–47.

Ziegler, Arthur P. *Birmingham, Pittsburgh's Southside: An Area with a Past That Has a Future.* Pittsburgh: Pittsburgh History and Landmarks Foundation, 1968.